Consulting
Psychology

Consulting Psychology

Selected Articles by
Harry Levinson

Edited by
Arthur M. Freedman and
Kenneth H. Bradt

American Psychological Association
Washington, DC

Published by
American Psychological Association
750 First Street, NE
Washington, DC 20002
www.apa.org

To order
APA Order Department
P.O. Box 92984
Washington, DC 20090-2984
Tel: (800) 374-2721; Direct: (202) 336-5510
Fax: (202) 336-5502; TDD/TTY: (202) 336-6123
Online: www.apa.org/books/
E-mail: order@apa.org

In the U.K., Europe, Africa, and the Middle East, copies may be ordered from
American Psychological Association
3 Henrietta Street
Covent Garden, London
WC2E 8LU England

Typeset in Goudy by Stephen McDougal, Mechanicsville, MD

Printer: Maple-Vail Books, York, PA
Cover Designer: Naylor Design, Washington, DC
Technical/Production Editor: Devon Bourexis

The opinions and statements published are the responsibility of the authors, and such opinions and statements do not necessarily represent the policies of the American Psychological Association.

Levinson, Harry.
    Consulting psychology : selected articles / by Harry Levinson ; edited by Arthur M. Freedman and Kenneth H. Bradt. — 1st ed.
        p. cm.
    Includes bibliographical references.
    ISBN-13: 978-1-4338-0376-5
    ISBN-10: 1-4338-0376-3
    1. Psychology, Industrial. I. Freedman, Arthur M., 1937- II. Bradt, Kenneth H. III. Title.

    HF5548.8.L36964 2009
    658.001'9—dc22   2008013061

British Library Cataloguing-in-Publication Data
A CIP record is available from the British Library.

Printed in the United States of America
First Edition

CONTENTS

PREFACE

ARTHUR M. FREEDMAN AND KENNETH H. BRADT

Harry Levinson's long, distinguished career is noteworthy for his unique contributions as a psychologist to society. There are essentially three groups who have benefited either directly, from his writings, lectures, seminars, consulting, or mentoring, or indirectly, from his support of professional organizations.

The first and largest of the three may be the thousands of managers, executives, and leaders of all kinds of organizations throughout the world who have studied with him at the Harvard Business School, attended the Levinson Leadership Seminars, consulted with him, heard him speak, and read his articles in the *Harvard Business Review* and other publications.

Second are the many psychologists whose first or second career focus has been either primarily or secondarily on consulting psychology. These are folks who have profited from his thinking through his seminars and talks at professional meetings; personal mentoring; numerous books, especially the seminal *Organizational Diagnosis* (Levinson, 1972); and articles addressed specifically to fellow psychologists, many of which appeared in the *Journal of Consulting Psychology*.

Third, we should acknowledge his effect on the science and profession of psychology in general, manifest in his support of the organizations that sponsor their advancement. Within the American Psychological Association (APA), he has been active in the divisions that reflect his interests in clinical, organizational, psychoanalytic, and consulting psychology, focusing on the need for research evidence for the principles of practice and an understanding of the theoretical underpinnings of practice in these areas. Accordingly, he initiated the Harry and Miriam Levinson Award through the American Psychological Foundation, granted annually to a psychologist whose work has contributed substantially to this end. In addition to these contributions to the work of APA, he has supported other organizations with similar aims (e.g., the Society of Psychologists in Management).

This book originated with Dr. Levinson's desire to assemble a selection of his numerous articles in a single volume, reflecting his thinking on a variety of issues of concern to consulting psychologists. When he invited us to serve as editors, the first thing that struck us as we reviewed them was the timelessness of his articles. Some were written many years ago but are as relevant to our readers' concerns today as when they first appeared. We came to realize that our hardest task would be selecting from the bevy of articles published in numerous journals those that were most appropriate for inclusion.

The *Harvard Business Review* had just published in book form a selection of the many articles he had authored for that journal, but that hardly made a dent in the reservoir. Although our intent here was to select articles of particular interest to consulting psychologists—as opposed to managers and leaders in organizations—the fact is that Dr. Levinson's language and messages to both groups were often equally appropriate. Choosing was often almost a matter of flipping a coin; it seemed to us that each article had a valuable message. We had a real dilemma deciding which articles to exclude.

Fortunately, our editors at APA came to the rescue. We are especially indebted to Susan Reynolds, who shepherded us through this process with patience and aplomb.

As to the organization of the book, Dr. Levinson's original suggestion was to group the articles into four parts—Theory/Diagnosis, Consultation, Stress, and Leadership—with introductory comments by the editors for each part. Had he been less adept at presenting narratives with internal consistency and interconnecting themes, this would have been a good idea, but in this case an editorial rationale for each part seemed redundant. However, we would like to make one comment about Harry Levinson as theoretician.

If organizational consulting psychologists were surveyed as to their theoretical orientation, a wide variety of responses would follow, with a majority acknowledging that "eclectic" would best describe theirs. Harry Levinson is one of a very small number who would answer unequivocally "psychoanalytic." In an era when the general public and many psychologists view neo-Freudian ideas with great skepticism, Dr. Levinson proceeded to explain such concepts as the id–ego–superego personality model and the primacy of the pursuit of one's ego-ideal as a key to motivation in ways that made sense to a skeptical audience. He attributes his ability to help executives as a consultant to his grounding in a theoretical base—a fact that inspired him to encourage and reward others for advancing psychoanalytic theory in support of consultation interventions.

Finally, we should note the appropriateness of, and our appreciation for, APA's decision to be the publisher of this book. When Dr. Levinson first invited us to serve as editors, both of us first thought that APA would be the ideal publisher and that the primary sponsor should be Division 13 (Society of Consulting Psychology). Dr. Ann O'Roark volunteered to serve as the enthusiastic and tireless champion for our project and carried our proposal to the leaders of the division, who strongly endorsed our proposal, seeing this volume as aligned with the society's vision. We recommend this book to all who are or would become consulting psychologists. We hope you will find it to be both helpful and inspirational.

REFERENCE

Levinson, H. (with Spohn, A. G., & Molinari, J.). (1972). *Organizational diagnosis.* Cambridge, MA: Harvard University Press.

PROLOGUE

HARRY LEVINSON

My career focus no doubt arose from my earliest life experiences. My parents were impecunious immigrants, my father from Poland and my mother from Belarus, fleeing the anti-Semitic persecution in that part of the world. In 1911, my father, a tailor, settled in Port Jervis, New York, rather than work in the sweatshops of New York City. Unfortunately, he settled in a railroad town, where few men had suits custom made.

He married my mother by arrangement, 3 weeks after she got off the boat. I was born 9 months later, followed 18 months later by my sister, Mildred, and 6 years later by my brother, Samuel. Life was not easy for poor uneducated Jewish parents in a heavily Catholic community.

Fortunately, several of my teachers became supportive models. As a 10-year-old, for reasons I shall never understand, I wrote "PhD" after my name in an old notebook. When it was time to think about college, I had to deal with two problems: (a) I had no money, and (b) although I was admitted to a New York State teachers college, in those days anti-Semitism was so strong that I could not expect to get a teaching job in New York State. In desperation, after I graduated from high school in 1939, I took a job in a factory that made braid for upholstered furniture. That year my high school hired a guidance counselor, Leona Johnson, who had come from Kansas. When I sought her advice she suggested that I go to Kansas, where the tuition was low, most students worked, and there would be no discrimination. I chose Emporia State Teachers College because I had heard of William Allen White, then a famous editor and novelist. I found Emporia to be a welcoming experience. I continued to hone my writing skills and got deeply involved in campus politics.

After graduation in 1943, military service intervened. When I returned to Emporia, married to Roberta Freiman, to work on my master's degree, the Veterans Administration (VA) announced its clinical psychology training program in VA hospitals. One such center was a PhD program, in which I was accepted, operated jointly by the University of Kansas, the Menninger Foundation, and the VA at the VA hospital in Topeka. That experience opened a new, broad vista for me. Almost overnight the VA hospital, managed by Dr. Karl A. Menninger, had become the world's largest psychiatric and psychological training program. In addition to the stimulation of the highly respected Menninger staff, there was a wide variety of visiting lecturers from the United States and abroad.

As part of our training experience, the psychological interns had a 2-week rotation to the Topeka State Hospital. I was appalled by the conditions I saw there. Subsequently, for a class assignment I wrote a paper composed of abstractions from all the annual reports of the Topeka State Hospital from its founding in 1868. The instructor sent the paper to Dr. Menninger, who wrote across it in big letters, "Should be published and widely distributed," resulting in a scandal at that hospital that led to the paper's integration into the already developed Menninger training programs.

A significant contributor to the newspaper exposés that preceded the state hospital revolution was my close friend John P. McCormelly. He was simultaneously a state representative and a reporter for the *Emporia Gazette*. Through him I met many members of the legislature and the press.

The state hospital reform was moving too slowly, after the legislature responded with increased appropriations, and that worried Dr. Menninger. Although I still had not completed my psychological internship in the VA hospital, Dr. Menninger had me appointed to the Topeka State Hospital staff. I immediately developed a public relations program. Stories about long-term patients appeared in newspapers, some in other parts of the world. I brought legislators to the hospital and had the volunteers invite their wives to see the inadequate conditions. I also helped develop a statewide levy to support the hospitals. At the same time, I was writing my PhD dissertation.

After my successful 3.5-year stint in that role, Dr. William C. Menninger, wishing to fulfill an aspiration that he had developed during his military service as chief of U.S. Army psychiatry in World War II, asked me to join the Menninger Foundation staff to develop a program to help keep well people functioning well. I concluded that if any such program were to reach large numbers of people, it would have to be carried out in organizations where people worked. That meant involving business and industry. I undertook a 50,000-mile trip around the country to learn what was being done for mental health in industry. I found to my dismay that little was happening in even the largest corporations—and still less was being written about it. With a grant from the Rockefeller Brothers Fund, I created the Division of Industrial Mental Health at the Menninger Foundation and developed a series of seminars for executives on psychoanalytic theory applied to management and another series for industrial physicians. I also began to consult with companies.

However, I still did not know much about management, and there were not many large companies in Topeka in which to learn. With the help of a psychiatrist, Dr. Kenneth J. Munden, and a sociologist, Charlton R. Price (later Drs. Charles M. Solley and Harold J. Mandl joined our team), I undertook an anthropological–sociological–psychological study of the Kansas Power and Light Company. Riding the company's trucks across two thirds of the state, we interviewed 856 company employees during a 2-year period. That was an important step because almost all of the literature of management in industry consists of short studies of limited scope. After that immersion, I had a comprehensive sense of what went on in a large business.

Concurrently, I found it necessary to teach myself by writing books and articles. Doing so required me to translate what I knew clinically into language that executives and managers could understand.

My earliest orientation to organizations had to do with advocating socalled *emotional first-aid stations*. I contended that when employing organizations provided such services for their employees, stress would be considerably relieved and well-being enhanced. After the Kansas Power and Light study (see *Men, Management, and Mental Health*; Levinson, 1962), I concluded that although emotional first-aid stations (later called *employee assistance programs*) are important, it is more important to understand that when organizations are managed well, namely for their own perpetuation, employees benefit. To do so, leaders have to mobilize and effectively use all their human resources. When organizations are managed expediently, that is, for short-term advantage, it is not good for employees because they are then exploited. This conclusion led me to the conception that the fundamental purpose of employing organizations is to perpetuate themselves. To do that they have to create a fountain of youth, that is, an adaptive and evolutionary process that enables employees in the organization to become increasingly competent on their own behalf and on behalf of the organization. Thus, the organization is essentially a learning institution that strengthens its employees. By more effective adaptation an organization itself is better able to survive, as are the people who work in it.

I responded to Dr. Douglas MacGregor's invitation to spend the 1961–1962 academic year with his group at the Massachusetts Institute of Technology. The management of organizations now became my focus: I was continuing to struggle with the problem of assessing organizations. When I returned to Topeka, I began writing intensely. It was a self-teaching tool for me. In *Emotional Health in the World of Work* (Levinson, 1964), I advocated emotional first-aid stations. I followed with *Executive Stress* (Levinson, 1970), with the intention of helping managers understand the human problems they face and how better to cope with them.

However, I was still struggling with the problem of developing a diagnostic method for studying whole organizations. I discovered the answer in front of me: Dr. Karl Menninger's (1962) *A Manual for Psychiatric Case Study*, a clinical diagnostic outline. Dr. Karl's book, in turn, was an adaptation and extension of an open system biological model advanced by Ludwig von Bertalanffy's (1950) "An Outline of General Systems Theory" that Dr. Karl had applied to the diagnosis of individuals. Dr. Karl's book was the basis for my pioneering volume, *Organizational Diagnosis* (Levinson, 1972), in which I elaborated on a comprehensive method for studying organizations and seeking to understand them as they cope with their environments. I extended that model to the study and analysis of organizations to emphasize the need to understand organizations and their problems before attempting to help them. The diagnostic emphasis was a uniquely clinical contribution because so much of what had been done in organizational development was essentially ad hoc application of established techniques without adequate diagnosis.

Continuing my self-teaching, I began to write a series of articles (17 total) in the *Harvard Business Review*. These resulted in my being invited to Harvard in 1968 as the Thomas Henry Carroll-Ford Foundation Distinguished Visiting Professor. I brought with me the manuscripts for *The Exceptional Executive* (Levinson, 1968) and *Organizational Diagnosis* (Levinson, 1972). My concept of the evolving and adaptive organization was reflected in *The Exceptional Executive*, in which I integrated all of the then contemporary theories of management psychology under a psychoanalytic umbrella.

In 1968 I started The Levinson Institute to continue the seminars and consultations that I had originated in Topeka.

All my work up to this point led to teaching a novel Harvard graduate seminar on organizational diagnosis. I divided the students into five-person teams and immersed each one in an organization for an academic year to develop diagnostic consultation skills. Concomitantly, I learned that a high level of understanding appeals specifically to senior executives, who know complexity firsthand and appreciate the fact that complex problems require a sophisticated grasp rather than simplistic remedies.

My next book was *The Great Jackass Fallacy* (Levinson, 1973), an effort to demonstrate the application of psychoanalytic theory to a wide range of organization problems. In the *Fallacy*, I emphasized the need to have a solid theoretical base, rather than to throw clichés and techniques at problems. In the face of the rise and fall of job enrichment; job enlargement; T-groups; quality circles; encounter groups; and a wide range of games, gimmicks, and part theories, this basic underlying orientation continues to serve an important conceptual base and has been strengthened by time because its conceptual framework has not been made obsolete.

At the end of my stint at the Harvard Business School in 1972, I moved over to the Massachusetts Mental Health Center at the Harvard Medical School and worked with Dr. Miles Shore. I remained affiliated there for the rest of my professional career.

I refined the model I had used in *The Exceptional Executive* (Levinson, 1968) in *Executive: The Guide to Responsive Management* (Levinson, 1981). Meanwhile, I developed *Psychological Man* (Levinson, 1976), intended for 1st-year MBA students and others at that level and complemented by the *Casebook for* Psychological Man (Levinson, 1982a) and the *Casebook for* Psychological Man: *Instructor's Guide* (Levinson, 1982b). Those books were to enhance the teaching of psychoanalytic theory.

CEO: Corporate Leadership in Action (Levinson & Rosenthal, 1984) (1984) documented the leadership behavior of six top-level business executives. The interviews provided a base of information for me, as well as professional colleagues and executives. The book reinforced my authoritative role with respect to leadership.

Ready, Fire, Aim (Levinson, 1986) was intended to help managers think before they acted. *Career Mastery* (Levinson, 1992) guided career planning. *Organizational Assessment: A Step-by-Step Guide to Effective Consulting* (Levinson, 2002) is a step-by-step guide to effective consulting. Finally, *Harry Levinson on the Psychology of Leadership* (Levinson, 2006) is a compilation of 10 of my articles from the *Harvard Business Review*.

The tightly and systematically organized week-long executive seminars I conducted in the Boston area demonstrated the logic of psychoanalytic theory translated into applications. The seminars also established a frame of reference that enabled participants to understand their psychological assumptions and to form a base for critically evaluating the assumptions that various authors made. These seminars were complemented annually by a range of others: on stratified systems theory, with Eliott Jaques; on performance appraisal; and on the executive couple. I also conducted independent sessions on the management of change, on stress, and on leadership.

Four issues have dominated my effort to apply psychoanalytic theory to management. These are emotional health, leadership, organizational diagnosis, and psychological concerns that frustrate managers and executives. The first three are represented in my 17 books and the last in a range of articles. Integrated in this volume are 18 of those articles along with an introduction, "Quelling the Quills." Some are elaborations of my responses to queries that occurred in the course of consultation; some arose during presentations at professional meetings; some were stimulated by contemporary issues and problems that suggested contributions to professional journals. Taken together, the articles represent the body of my life's work in management consultation, academic teaching, executive education, and problem analysis.

I evolved my career focus from my original work at the Menninger Foundation, with the expectation of developing and applying psychoanalytic theory to managerial practice and organizational structure. It was my intention to develop a more sophisticated understanding of the psychology of leadership and organizational processes that simultaneously would inform and enrich the activities of management and leadership and, by so doing, also contribute to the mental health of the people who worked in organizations.

Thus, I created a certain kind of scientific base with respect to human behavior in organizations. It has an established theoretical position—firmly rooted in psychoanalytic theory and clinical experience—that is not likely to be outmoded by future scientific findings, although I have no doubt it will necessarily be modified and elaborated on through additional experience, thinking, and research. I hope that bulwark will survive in the face of repeated waves of popular sloganized problem-solving efforts. I hope, also, that its intellectual comprehensiveness, its professional sophistication, and its firm grounding in human experience will enable it to endure. It should not only educate managers, and particularly leaders, but also continue to inform, out of psychological and managerial experience, an understanding of psychoanalytic theory and its application to managerial problems. I hope that professional and managerial readers will then be able to translate what they learn into helping with managerial, organizational, and leadership issues.

ACKNOWLEDGMENTS

I am indebted to the following individuals:

My wife, Miriam Levinson, whose organizing and productive efforts are reflected in each page of this book. Without her this undertaking would never have happened. Because of my impaired vision, she was my eyes and my handwriting tool.

Cindy Lewis, whose technical competence taught her mother how to resolve computer problems in the production of this book.

Ann O'Roark, who perceived the need to put my articles in book form, persuaded colleagues and editors to support that effort, and consistently led a frontal assault on the political problems that had to be resolved. She has been my champion for many years.

Debra Robinson, past president of the American Psychological Association's Division 13 (Society of Consulting Psychology), who also supported this endeavor.

Charlton R. Price; Kenneth J. Munden, MD; Harold J. Mandl, PhD; and Charles M. Solley, PhD, my former colleagues.

Harriet Klebanoff, for her suggestions for "Counseling With Top Management" (Levinson, 1991).

Miles Shore, MD; Charles E. Magraw, MD; Ernest Ticho, PhD; Gertrude Ticho, MD; Philip Holzman, PhD; and Paul J. Albanese, PhD, for their suggestions and comments for "Freud as an Entrepreneur: Implications for Contemporary Psychoanalytic Institutes" (Levinson, 1990).

Marilyn Farinato, my long-time former secretary, who typed the original versions of many of the articles in this book.

Arthur M. Freedman, PhD, and Kenneth H. Bradt, PhD, for ushering this book into publication.

The reference personnel at the Palm Beach County Library.

Ken Frankel, Bruce Barron, and Larry Mellow at Florida Atlantic University Library.

Finally, I wish to extend my appreciation to the copyright holders of the articles reprinted in this volume for granting their permission to use the materials. In particular, I wish to thank John Bukovinsky, Scott Harvey, Sally A. Iacovelli, Jennifer Jones, Kathy Kuehl, Harry LeGates, Jay Lorsch, Anna Mancini, Chuck Mitchell, and Sheik Safdar for their kind assistance.

REFERENCES

Bertalanffy, L. V. (1950). An outline of general systems theory. *British Journal for the Philosophy of Science, 1,* 134–163.

Levinson, H. (1962). *Men, management, and mental health* (with H. J. Mandl, C. M. Solley, K. J. Munden, & C. R. Price). Cambridge, MA: Harvard University Press.

Levinson, H. (1964). *Emotional health in the world of work.* New York: Harper & Row.

Levinson, H. (1968). *The exceptional executive.* Cambridge, MA: Harvard University Press.

Levinson, H. (1970). *Executive stress.* New York: Harper & Row.

Levinson, H. (with Spohn, A. G., & Molinari, J.). (1972). *Organizational diagnosis.* Cambridge, MA: Harvard University Press.

Levinson, H. (1973). *The great jackass fallacy.* Cambridge, MA: Harvard University Press, The Division of Research, Graduate School of Business Administration.

Levinson, H. (1976). *Psychological man.* Cambridge, MA: The Levinson Institute.

Levinson, H. (1981). *Executive: The guide to responsive management.* Cambridge, MA: Harvard University Press.

Levinson, H. (1982a). *Casebook for Psychological Man.* Cambridge, MA: The Levinson Institute.

Levinson, H. (1982b). *Casebook for Psychological Man: Instructor's guide.* Cambridge, MA: The Levinson Institute.

Levinson, H. (1986). *Ready, fire, aim: Avoiding management by impulse.* Cambridge, MA: The Levinson Institute.

Levinson, H. (1990). Freud as an entrepreneur: Implications for contemporary psychoanalytic institutes. In L. Lapierre (Ed.), *Clinical approaches to the study of managerial and organizational dynamics* (pp. 227–250). Montreal, Canada: Ecole des Hautes Etudes Commerciales.

Levinson, H. (1991). Counseling with top management. *Consulting Psychology Bulletin, 43,* 10–15.

Levinson, H. (1992). *Career mastery.* San Francisco: Berrett-Koehler.

Levinson, H. (2002). *Organizational assessment: A step-by-step guide to effective consulting*. Washington, DC: American Psychological Association.

Levinson, H. (2006). *Harry Levinson on the psychology of leadership*. Boston: Harvard Business School Press.

Levinson, H., & Rosenthal, S. (1984). *CEO: Corporate leadership in action*. New York: Basic Books.

Menninger, K. (1962). *A manual for psychiatric case study* (The Menninger Clinic Monograph Series No. 8). New York: Grune & Stratton.

Consulting
Psychology

INTRODUCTION: QUELLING THE QUILLS

HARRY LEVINSON

Porcupines ordinarily are quiet, gentle animals. They have no reputation as predators. Unless someone is desperately hungry, no one hunts them as food. When porcupines are threatened, their quills rise as they prepare to defend themselves. Enemy animals soon learn not to impale themselves on those live needles. Animals who have yet to learn, such as braying hunting dogs, yelp in pain as they retreat from their brash attack.

People are much like porcupines. Most go quietly about their daily survival efforts and nurture their families as best they can. When people are threatened, something happens akin to the aroused porcupines: Their defenses automatically rise. As porcupines sometimes do, people may withdraw, sort of curling up psychologically. Their ready irritability, the psychological equivalent of the porcupine's erect quills, permeates their attitude, threatening to bruise anyone who comes near. Or, feeling backed into a corner, they may attack verbally, sometimes even physically.

Some people try to hide, sometimes behind stronger people; sometimes by isolating themselves in psychological cocoons through immersion in their work or hobbies; sometimes by preoccupying themselves by flitting, like butterflies, from pleasure to pleasure; sometimes by drowning their rage—at themselves for their sense of helplessness—in alcohol or drugs. Some are always

3

on the attack, constantly manipulating others to escape their own sense of inadequacy by demonstrating their superiority. Some are always on guard, anticipating threats from all sides. Some conscientiously demand reliability of themselves, convinced that they, too, share the burden for our collective welfare. To varying degrees, at one time or another, all of us behave in these self-protective ways.

In our day-to-day efforts to control our lives, we have three choices:

1. We can pursue our preferred paths in what we hope will be a merry experience, enjoying what we can and fending off, in whatever ways we know how, the threats as they occur.
2. We can take our behavior and that of others for granted, saying to ourselves in a state of naive optimism that denies the possibility of doing anything about it, "That's the way people are" or "It takes all kinds" or, as one factory worker told me, "That's the way I am. I ain't gonna change for nobody."
3. We can try to understand what goes on in people's heads, including our own, and learn how we might use that understanding to ease the strains, ours as well as theirs.

The last option is what this book is about.

The contemporary world for parents, teachers, police officers, managers, bus drivers, airline pilots, nurses, funeral directors—indeed almost everyone—is flooded with prescriptions for how to be happy though stressed. These range from seeking divine intercession, often combinations of myth and wishful thinking, to the recommendations of psychologists who extrapolate to human behavior the probable effects of rewards and punishments learned by running rats through mazes. Newspaper advice columns and television counselors cast their wisdom to the uninformed masses on giant rolls of ink-imprinted paper and vast invisible waves of whirling air. Many of their suggestions are helpful. Some recommendations indeed do work, especially if people believe that they will. The placebo effect in medicine, the power of suggestion in hypnosis, and the dramatic miraculous healing in some religious ceremonies are oft-cited examples.

Fortunately, if not offered by charlatans, such public advice, for the most part, is cheap. As befits most advice scattered like seed, much of it is disregarded. Perhaps it is just as well. Otherwise, unless they could read about the pain others experience, how would people put their own in context? Better yet, how could they know they were better off than those who took the trouble to write of their anguish?

CHARACTEROLOGICAL VERSUS REACTIVE BEHAVIOR

Although people are indeed in some way like porcupines, strange as that juxtaposition of analogies may seem, they also, unlike porcupines, protect themselves with psychological balloons. The psychological balloons we inflate are our own images of ourselves: the ways we want to think of ourselves and how we want others to think of us. Unless we are acting in movies or on the stage, we use the same images repetitively. We establish different images of ourselves that become our stock in self-presentation. We hold out different balloons, we present different images of ourselves to different audiences at different times. The manager who pictures himself as a tough but fair boss may be viewed by his or her subordinates as a tyrant; at home he or she may be a beloved parent. The quiet librarian may be a dominating mother, bristling with hostility toward her husband and children. The jovial social friend, noted for picking up bar tabs, may well be the equally jovial swindler who fleeces strangers. The public woman who cannot do enough in her charity work for others or the overconscientious man who pursues his job assiduously may do so to the neglect of their families. We are indeed multifaceted—players in multiple roles. Sometimes those roles are so widely staged that those who know us predominantly in one role often cannot believe what they hear about us in another. Police are quite familiar with that phenomenon. Most of us are astonished when we read about it in the newspapers.

Yet, if there were no consistency to how we behave, we would have no identity. Without a core of consistent behavior established early on, we would not be recognizable to ourselves or to others, even if physically we remained much the same. If you meet a former high school chum that you have not seen for many years, even though he has become more rotund and now sports a heavy beard, you are soon likely to say, "He is just like he always was." And he, of course, will recognize you, even though he has been a missionary in Tibet for some years.

Characterological Behaviors

We speak of that consistency of behavior—that continuity of ourselves by which we recognize ourselves and are recognized by others—as *characterological*. Unless we experience some fundamental severe trauma that deeply shakes us up, for example, being isolated and abused in a prison camp over a long period of time, that behavior is unlikely to be stamped out. Only some aspects of characterological behavior are likely to be changed by long-term psychotherapeutic treatment, but in only some people by particularly skilled therapists.

Detectives look beyond the many distracting images that a criminal may use to obliterate his trail for aspects of characterological behavior. During World War II, Germans uncovered an otherwise well-Germanized American spy because he picked up his fork with his left hand, as Americans do, rather than with his right hand, as Europeans do.

Reactive Behavior

Contrasted with characterological behavior, and more often illustrated by our different psychological balloons, is *reactive* behavior. Reactive behavior typically is precipitated by external events or by a person's imagination of an external event. We become angry if, while driving, someone almost runs into us. We can become almost equally angry when later we think about what could have happened to us and even physically express our anger when we tell someone else about the event. Anger in a dream may make us grind our teeth. When the terrorists destroyed the twin towers of the World Trade Center and crashed into the Pentagon, many people all over the world, themselves untouched, were angry. And the terrorists themselves were said to be motivated by visions of future glories in heaven.

It is critically important to differentiate between characterological and reactive behavior, both our own and that of others. Too often we expect to be able to change characterological behavior by some simple gimmick or psychological trick. Too often, when our best efforts to change ourselves or others fail, having beat our heads against a psychological wall in frustrated futility, we then feel guilty for not having shattered it. To angrily attack oneself (which is what guilt is) is to act stupidly because one is psychologically ignorant. If you do not read any further in this book or learn anything else from reading it, learn to avoid that stupidity.

Naturally, the next question is, "How do I, not a clinical psychologist, tell the difference?" The answer in almost all cases is fairly simple. (I say "almost all" because no answer fits all problems, and omnipotence is not one of my competences, even if my wife brings me up short with the humbling reminder that occasionally I seem to think so.) When a person who reports to you behaves in a way that is unacceptable in that role and you tell him or her that as specifically and as soon as you can after the behavior occurs, you expect him or her to take advantage of the feedback and change the behavior. If that does not happen, you may wonder why. Not being his therapist, there isn't much point in asking because probably you will get an answer that more likely is an excuse than an explanation. So you repeat your comment once again. (If the subordinate is a union member, you may have to write your comment. I believe a subordinate always must be given a written comment and a copy be placed in his or her personnel folder or there is no record of the feedback, a problem that may later come back to haunt you. Besides, when something is written it carries greater weight.)

If there is no change after you tell the subordinate for a third time, you can assume that the behavior is characterological. Of course, you could be wrong. Under different circumstances he or she might behave differently, but if the behavior is the same in other roles, then you can be sure it is characterological. Unless you have unusual, even magical, competence, you are unlikely to be able to get the person to change.

Sometimes outrageous behavior in one role may be an asset in another. A highly skilled manipulator who makes a persuasive first impression may be just the person to make an initial presentation of a marketing program but will soon get into trouble when the client learns he or she is untrustworthy. Reactive behavior may change in another environment or in a different role. If you find your subordinate's behavior was different in another context, then it would be important to learn what in the current situation is different from the previous one. A good salesperson may not necessarily become a good sales manager if in moving into that role he or she loses a primary source of gratification: his or her joking relationship with customers. A good division manager may become a poor executive vice president if he or she does not have the conceptual capacity to think more abstractly than he or she did previously.

You may help that person change by changing his or her role, providing training or coaching that will help remedy a deficiency, or by helping him or her find a role in which that behavior is an asset. An argumentative attorney with a chip on his or her shoulder may well do better at litigation than on a corporate staff. The military changes aspects of reactive behavior by prescribing the required behavior, training people in performing it, and then controlling it.

As for yourself, if you have had repetitive feedback that you would do better to change some aspect of your behavior, or if failure to change threatens your possible promotion, or you cannot hold a position, or if your spouse is talking of leaving you, then it is time to consult a competent psychotherapist. There are lots of psychologists, psychiatrists, social workers, marriage counselors, sex counselors, and myriad executive coaches. Choosing among them is not easy. Given my own training and experience, for characterological problems, I am biased in favor of therapists who are psychoanalysts or who have been trained in a psychoanalytically oriented doctoral program or who have had psychoanalytic training after they have completed other professional training. I am in favor of therapists who have had wide experience that includes work in hospitals with patients with complex illnesses, rather than short-term internships. Of course, having taught others for much of my professional life, I naturally prefer therapists who are involved in continuing professional training.

Of course, therapists with other orientations have demonstrated their usefulness, and some are very good, especially with short-term efforts to resolve reactive behavior. Unfortunately, from my point of view, too many contemporary psychiatrists have been heavily trained in pharmacology at the expense of psychotherapy; too many social workers, marriage counselors, and other specialized therapists have only limited clinical training; and too many executive coaches, even some who are psychologists, have no competence to deal with characterological problems, which necessarily require great skill and lengthy effort. There are no shortcuts.

THE PARANOID–DEPRESSIVE AXIS

The late British psychoanalyst Melanie Klein called our attention to the early rage of infants. Not yet able to process information in any other way, she theorized, infants respond to the frustration of being deprived of their fundamental source of survival, their mother's breast, with fantasies of rage when that breast is not immediately available to them when they want to nurse. That is, their fantasies become *paranoid*. In their primitive rage, they want to do away with the frustrating object. Unable to differentiate wishing something from doing it, as is the case for small children in a stage of magical thinking, infants fear that if their fantasies could indeed destroy the nurturing object, they would lose it entirely. To keep their paranoid rage from destroying their source of nurture, they turn their rage on themselves. Rage turned inwardly, an attack on the self, is depression.

One may argue with Klein's theory, as many have, but her theory alerts us to a fundamental feature of human behavior: When threatened we become hyperalert, even paranoid. When adults divorce, even though they are now mature people who are able to think rationally, frequently they quibble over trivia out of the fear that the other will take something from them that will deprive them. This is not to minimize legitimate differences over important issues, such as responsibility for children and mutual property, but it is to point out that almost simultaneously one partner has the feeling that the other is taking something that he or she should not have. If their differences are not repeatedly irritated, much like continually scratching a mosquito bite, they may ultimately calm down, even become better friends than when they were married.

In short, the articles in this volume outline some psychological fundamentals to guide organizational understanding and behavior. These fundamentals have stood the test of time and experience during my professional career. I hope they will work equally well for the reader.

I
THEORY/DIAGNOSIS

1

PSYCHOANALYTIC THEORY IN ORGANIZATIONAL BEHAVIOR

HARRY LEVINSON

Organizational behavior encompasses the behavior of individuals, groups, and larger entities as they are interrelated in the functioning of organizations. It includes, too, the characteristic pattern of organizational actions over time, which is a reflection of the organization's knowledge, values, and goals; the kinds of people, the tactical system, and the control methods it employs; as well as the sociopolitical and economic context in which those actions occur.

People interested in organizational behavior are typically guided by one of four orientations. First, practicing managers have always dealt with organizational behavior by ad hoc, trial-and-error manipulation, or change of one or another variable. Following a more refined method, some observers describe the formation of norms, group practices, ethnic differences, and similar features and their relationship to productivity, power, and environmental circumstances. The classical Hawthorne studies exemplify this sort of descriptive sociology. A third, and perhaps the most widely practiced, orienta-

From the *Handbook of Organizational Behavior* (Vol. 2, pp. 51–56), edited by J. W. Lorsch, 1987, Englewood Cliffs, NJ: Prentice-Hall. Copyright 1987 by Jay W. Lorsch. Reprinted with permission.

tion is the empirical-correlation: certain variables are defined and statistical measures representing them are then correlated with other measures of dependent variables and classes of behavioral outcome. Finally, there are those who believe that interpersonal, group, and organizational behavior can best be understood on the basis of a comprehensive conception of the individual person—in short, personality theory. The assumption behind this last point of view is that because all behavior is that of persons, one cannot have an adequate macro theory that purports to deal with behavior unless one has an adequate micro theory.

If this assumption is valid, the motivation of individuals is crucial. It is individuals who are selected, assigned, inspired, appraised, compensated, and guided. It is among individuals that interpersonal conflicts occur and are resolved, differences are mediated, and tensions are ameliorated. Even when attempting to understand the differentiation and integration of a group, one of the important variables is its personality orientation (Lawrence and Lorsch 1967). And certainly if one is to deal with stress, an increasingly widely recognized organizational phenomenon, then one has to understand what precipitates stress for individuals (Levinson 1981a).

An understanding of individuals is crucial to the understanding of groups, although this interconnection is not always recognized in the group literature. Individuals in groups are still individuals, and though a group may demonstrate phenomena beyond those of individual persons, nevertheless that behavior is the result of the behavior of individual members of the group. What occurs in groups is not a negation of individual behavior but an addition to it, or an epiphenomenon, a product of individual behavior taken collectively. Much of the fundamental theory of groups and group functioning is drawn from individual psychology (Bion 1959; Rice 1969; Bales 1970). Fundamental processes as described by these writers relate to recapitulations of filial and power struggles, as well as defensive, affiliative, and security maneuvers.

An understanding of the individual is crucial to understanding his or her relationship to the organization, whether it be a school, church, hospital, government agency, or business. Both individually and collectively, people unconsciously bring to organizations attitudes and expectations that are akin to those they developed toward their parents as reflected in the conception of the psychological contract (Levinson et al. 1962). Individuals unconsciously and symbolically treat organizations as recapitulations of the family structure in a given culture, and organizations in turn treat their members as if the individual were in some way bound to the group by familial ties (Levinson 1981b). Indeed, organizations encourage such affiliation, as contrasted with hiring individual contractors on a day rate. There is much talk of the organizational family; much effort to obtain commitment to organizational purpose, norms, goals, and achievement; much effort to create identification with organization leadership and its success; and indeed much gratification and pride on the part of individual employees in both the product or service and the organization's reputation and achievement.

There is indeed such a phenomenon as organizational personality. Organizations are created by dominating entrepreneurs who select people who serve their psychological needs and purposes. Those people in turn select others who "fit." As a result, organizations develop certain characteristic ways of behaving and relating both to their environments and to those who are within their fold. That there are model behaviors characteristic of organizations is evident to anyone who works with them. A group of managers from IBM is likely to behave significantly differently from a group of managers from Exxon or Sears, Roebuck. In terms of structure and tasks, organizations differ widely enough that they require different kinds of managers.

Organizations are concerned with understanding and meeting the needs of individuals as they seek to gratify those needs in their work. Needs may be conceptualized in many different ways, ranging from the simple classifications of Herzberg (1976), Maslow (1954), and McClelland (1975) to the much more elaborate conceptualizations of personality theorists.

Much of the managerial literature, particularly that having to do with leadership, is concerned with the manner in which managers and executives behave. There is widespread effort to develop effective managers and executives, and a large literature has developed on managerial styles and their effects on productivity, cohesion, morale, job satisfaction, stress, and the competitive position of the organization.

Individual behavior is also a key consideration in industrial and labor relations, where major goals include maintaining a sense of equity (Locke 1968), avoiding conflict and strikes, and understanding and coping with the defense mechanisms of people who are engaged in adversary relationships. A large part of the concern with organizational climate and morale has to do with determining which aspects of the work situation most affect people's feelings about themselves and their organization.

All of the policies and practices of any organization are intended to have a behavioral outcome. A building is designed so as to encourage people to behave in certain ways. An accounting method is intended to control people's behavior and to provide them with certain kinds of information, which in turn presumably will lead them to behave in certain ways. The manner in which an organization is financed will determine whether there are certain calendar points of intensified effort to meet financial obligations or whether people can behave in other ways because of different types of obligations to those who hold organizational debt.

All of these organizational phenomena imply the need to have a comprehensive understanding of the complexity of the individual.

Medial Psychology

One possibility is to assume that the observed behavior of the individual is determined by external forces. This sort of medial psychology (Eissler 1965) would include everything from assumptions about astrology to contemporary versions of conditioning and role theory. A key assumption is that the individual is responsive to external manipulations. In organizational behavior, this would mean rewards and punishments.

Research using a medial psychology as a base, referred to above as the correlation of measurable variables, has been the dominant mode of industrial and organizational psychology. Its major drawback is that the categories of data so manipulated have been at such a gross level that the variances within groups are larger than the variances between groups. Since the beginning of this kind of study, correlations have been small and limited. In addition, it is difficult to account for individual differences with such a frame of reference. It is even more difficult to integrate the large number of wide-ranging studies into a systematic mode of application.

Normative Theories

The second set of assumptions has to do with what might be called *normative theories*. These are generalizations that apply to all populations. The work of Maslow, Herzberg, and McClelland falls into this category. Researchers following the same methods tend to get the same results. Others do not. Furthermore, it is difficult to predict individual behavior from normative conceptions: conceptualizations that fit everybody in general tend not to fit anyone in particular.

Usually, the broad, normative conception requires translation into a measurable variable—for example, from the concept of self-actualization to the inferred attribute of autonomy. The effort to extrapolate from a normative conception runs afoul of criterion problems and construct validity. Is autonomy the same as self-actualization, or even a good index of it? And what about the fact that, despite what they may say, not all people think autonomy is desirable? If self-actualization means fulfilling one's potential, then how do we deal with the fact that there are no adequate measures of potential? One cannot therefore define self-actualization by a device that has face validity or obviously represents that variable.

System Theories

System theories represent a third kind of outlook. The previous two sets of assumptions are part theories because they deal with only a part of the person. All other empirical theories that presume to explain the motivation of individuals are also part theories. System theories, in contrast, are interactional theories. They seek to explain the behavior of the whole person, interacting with his or her environment, over a lifetime. System theories recognize the need for the arousal of the individual, but would include stimuli from within the person, as well as those outside the person. Moreover, between stimulus and response they would posit some mode through which the individual apperceives the stimulus, and, by doing so, gives it idiosyncratic meaning. Thus the person does not respond to the stimulus itself, but rather to his or her own interpretation of the stimulus. A system theory assumes, therefore, that the individual not only interacts with the environment, but also gives it meaning and takes initiative with respect to it. Individuals, as self-motivating actors, adopt certain postures toward their environments and simultaneously enact the dominant themes of their own personalities, for which environments become media.

A system theory that assumes the initiative of the individual must be integrated with the rest of psychology. It requires an understanding of the levels of consciousness or awareness, of developmental psychology, and of the data of physiological and experimental psychology. It seeks to understand the whole person as the device for giving meaning and acting on that meaning. It therefore requires a comprehensive theory of personality.

The most comprehensive system theory of personality is psychoanalytic theory. Like any scientific theory, it has its strengths and limits, its holes and inconsistencies, and its supporters and detractors. Though many assert it is not amenable to empirical tests, it is supported by a large body of experimental evidence (Silverman 1976).

PSYCHOANALYTIC THEORY

Psychoanalytic theory originated with Sigmund Freud in Vienna in the 1890s. Freud was heavily influenced by Darwin, by his work with Charcot in Paris on hypnosis, and by his background in philosophy. As a neuroanatomist, he was knowledgeable about the development of the nervous system. He studied the cells of the nervous system and made original contributions to the understanding of the effects of cocaine. He was necessarily familiar with the anabolic and catabolic processes—the continuous growth and destruction that goes on in all cells and therefore in all agglomerations of cells. Physiologically, life is a matter of simultaneous growth and destruction. This perception led him to what is called the dual-drive theory.

Dual-Drive

In all living organisms, if continuous physiological processes of growth and destruction go on, dual-drive theory holds that they must have some effect on the way people feel, think, and act. There must be a parallel set of psychological processes—primitive, fundamental, sexual, and aggressive drives—which are assumed to be derived from and analogous to those physiological forces. As a Darwinian, Freud saw the sexual drive as necessary for species continuity and assumed that feelings of love and affection, sources of the constructive forces of the personality, are derived from it. The aggressive drive is the attacking component of the personality, which is necessary for mastering the environment in the interest of survival. The theory assumes that ideally the two drives are fused, with the sexual or constructive forces dominant, and channeled into everyday problem-solving activities. These include reproduction, pursuit of a career, acquisition of skills, rearing children, and, in general, the adaptive efforts of the individual. When, for various reasons, the drives do not work together, then there are difficulties. People may become inordinately self-centered or self-preoccupied, as contrasted with investing themselves in other people. The aggressive drive, untampered by the sexual drive, might be expressed in naked aggression, as in attack on other people. A surgeon cuts to save lives, a butcher cuts to sustain life, but a hoodlum waving a knife on the street threatens life. A major task of the personality is to manage these sexual and aggressive drives.

Indeed, many of the problems of living together are related to that management. Most of our laws govern the expression of sex and aggression. Most mores, folkways, and taboos deal with the same issues. The development of conscience is significantly related to the internal management of the expression of these drives.

These drives are assumed to be basic feelings, which in turn give rise to thoughts, and thence actions. Psychoanalytic theory always infers backward, from behavior to thoughts to feelings. To understand any given behavior, one poses the questions "What must a person have thought to act that way?" and behind that, "What must a person have felt to have thought that?" Psychoanalytic theory therefore gives a great deal of attention to feelings and thought processes, particularly those of which the person is not aware.

The theory assumes that the drives are the energy system of the personality. Both drives constantly press for expression. They operate without our awareness, just as we are unaware of the functioning of our lives. Psychoanalytic theory divides the personality into three components: id, superego, and ego. The id encompasses the unconscious aspects of personality functioning— those memories, feelings, and thoughts of which we are not aware and cannot spontaneously nor voluntarily become aware. The superego encompasses internalized values, controls, and rules of behavior—that which we ordinarily refer to as conscience. It also includes a person's idealized expectations of himself at his future best, designated as the ego ideal.

The ego ideal is an only partly conscious target toward which each of us strives. There is always a gap between the ego ideal and the self-image, the picture of oneself in the present. This gap makes for a constant internal tension as a person strives to move his or her self-image closer to the ego ideal. When a person feels he or she is approaching the ego ideal, or at least moving toward it, then there is a sense of gratification. With closer approximation there is elation. When a person feels he or she is not moving toward the ego ideal or is moving away from it, the resulting anger with self becomes depression. Depression, or anger with self, is the core of stress. Thus, the individual's greatest asset, his wish to like himself, which results in his effort to push his self-image closer to his ego ideal and therefore is the most powerful of all motivating forces, is simultaneously his greatest source of vulnerability. The higher the level of aspiration, the greater the sense of drivenness and the sense of stress. Simultaneously, stress is necessarily increased by any forces that lower the self-image or make the ego ideal unapproachably lofty. Unless either of these two conditions is present, there is no stress.

The third aspect of the personality is the ego. This concept includes the input, processing, and output aspects of the personality: the gathering of data by the five senses; the processing of those data in the form of concepts, memories, judgments, combined with previous feelings and thoughts; and the actions based on that processing. Feelings and thoughts give meaning to the information obtained. People react not to information alone, but to the meaning that they attribute to that information. Psychoanalysis, therefore, is significantly a psychology of meaning.

A major task of the ego is to channel the drives, governed by the requirements of the superego, into adaptive and problem-solving activities. Those activities that become repetitive for the person—characteristic ways of maintaining an equilibrium among the id, superego, and ego, and of the whole personality vis-à-vis the outside world—become the dominant features of personality and are described as characterological.

Topographic

Psychoanalytic theory also conceptualizes levels of awareness or consciousness. It notes that there are aspects of ourselves of which we are not aware and cannot spontaneously become aware. These are referred to as unconscious. There are other aspects of the personality of which we can spontaneously become aware, as in remembering, recall, or in dreaming. These are referred to as preconscious. In addition then, of course, there is a conscious part of the personality: those activities of which we are aware. These three levels of awareness taken together are referred to as the topographic aspect of personality.

Developmental

Neurological development influences personality. As the brain grows, thought processes and feelings will change with the increasing capacity to think more conceptually and rationally. Dominant feelings will vary at different stages in neurological development, as evidenced by the interactions of children with others around them, especially parents or other caring figures. Given different kinds of thoughts and feelings at different points in time, children will experience the world around them, and particularly the parental figures, in different, sometimes significantly distorted, ways. Their patterns of relating to authority figures based on these early feelings will tend to become repetitive and to be apparent in their relationships with significant others. Developmental theory also conceptualizes phases in adult development and the particular adaptive efforts that characterize each phase.

Adaptive

Psychoanalytic theory also conceptualizes modes of psychological adaptation, which have to do with the formation of the personality and with maintaining its equilibrium. For example, personality is significantly formed out of the child's drive-motivated, conceptually formed feelings and thoughts leading to interaction with caring adult figures. The child, at first, emulates those figures or identifies with them. When those identifications become integrated within and are therefore a continuous component of the child, this is referred to as introjection. Another kind of adaptation is the characteristic manner of handling the sexual and aggressive drives in the form of work and play. Repression refers to the automatic process of making aspects of experience unconscious so that presumably they will be less disturbing. People also use mechanisms such as rationalization, idealization, reaction formation, and projection to cope with thoughts and feelings that might otherwise be stressful for them. To rationalize is to make up reasons for one's wish to act in certain ways. To idealize is to put a halo around others. Reaction formation refers to doing the opposite of what one feels (for example, a highly dependent person might deny those feelings by becoming counterdependent). Projection is the mechanism through which we attribute to others our own negative feelings that we are unwilling to recognize and accept.

These six aspects of personality taken together constitute a system within which all aspects of personality can be conceptualized. The system also provides a mode for conceptualizing their interactions. Psychoanalytic theory can encompass almost all of the part theories that have attempted to explain various aspects of behavior; the reverse is not true.

CONTRIBUTIONS OF THE THEORY

The most significant contribution of psychoanalytic theory has been its elaboration of unconscious thought processes. There is a realm of feeling and thinking that is not readily examined either by the individual in whom those processes occur or by ordinary modes of inquiry. Over the last century, however, work has shown that this realm of thinking and feeling is governed by its own laws, and its regularities are understandable. That they are complex and difficult to verify is a given. But that should not deter us from trying to understand what goes on in people's heads any more than the analogous methodological problems should keep us from studying distant galaxies. Psychoanalysis as a science tries to evolve hypotheses related to those unconscious processes. Psychoanalytic theory traces the impact of earliest life experiences on the developing processes of thinking and feeling, and on characteristic modes of adaptation that human beings evolve to cope with the interaction between the individual—in a given physiological, neurological, and conceptual state—and the external environment, particularly other persons who have powerful emotional significance for the dependent child. Psychoanalytic theory seeks to understand the manner in which a person evolves his character or consistent patterns of behavior that uniquely identify the individual to himself and to others. It asserts that those patterns enable the individual to maintain psychological equilibrium in the face of conflicting demands of psychological needs, pressures from the external environment, and the requirements of his or her own system of internal governance. Psychoanalysis seeks to understand how children identify with and incorporate the models that surround them and how that attachment process, together with the processes of infantile thinking, affects the development of conscience, aspiration, values, and internal direction.

Psychoanalysis is a conflict psychology. It views the interactive process within the individual as one in which basic needs and wishes come into conflict with the governing and controlling agencies of the personality, and in turn with the external world—a process that needs to be managed and whose results are likely to be adaptive compromise. It seeks to understand the symbolic meaning given to persons, groups, organizations, and events by individuals and groups of individuals as a product of the child's earliest thought processes and relationships. It views the adult world and its activities not only in terms of their conscious manifest content, but also as a stage or social platform upon which the individual plays out unresolved unconscious conflicts from the past as he or she seeks to resolve them or obtain closure on the needs or demands represented by those conflicts. Psychoanalysis is simultaneously a treatment method, a theory of personality, and a method of research. It is with psychoanalysis as a theory of personality that I am concerned here.

DIFFERENTIATING THE THEORY

How does psychoanalysis differ from other modes of conceptualizing human motivation?

Cognitive Psychology

A dominant area of contemporary psychology, cognitive psychology has to do with how one knows. Considerable research has been done on how people acquire information, how they remember it, how they organize it conceptually, how they make judgments, and what one or another perception may mean to the perceiver. However, cognitive psychology has little to say about how the perceiver *gives meaning* to his perceptions or how he determines which perceptions will be remembered and which will become unconscious. Cognitive psychology refers to goals and values, and even evolves modes of sampling those goals and values, but it rarely deals with the *origins* of those goals and values or their possible symbolic meaning.

For example, a widely quoted discussion of leadership is that of Vroom (1973). His thesis is essentially that people will seek paths to goals that are significant for them, and that career paths—paths to leadership and leadership styles—can be ascertained by questioning individuals. Clearly, people do perceive manifest goals, but those manifest goals may well be in the service of unconscious goals that cannot be uncovered by questionnaire. Indeed, as has been demonstrated, when people attain certain goals, they often find themselves unsatisfying. When that occurs, obviously there have been hidden agenda. The psychoanalytic conception of ego ideal would include the unconscious aspirations as well as those that are manifest, given greater depth and body to the concept of personal goal.

Something of the same sort might be said about the work of Deci (1971) on intrinsic motivation. Responses to questionnaires may enable us to identify needs, wishes, aspirations, and hopes but will do little to help us understand the motivations underlying those responses.

Social Psychology

Social psychology focuses on group processes, the establishment and development of norms, people's wishes to be accepted into groups, group decision making, and social learning. Much contemporary work in social psychology has been devoted to participative management. Studies on quality circles and other adaptations of group decision making generally cannot explain why norms arise and why such activities fail (when they do). Barring successful trial and error, failures cannot be remedied without an adequate theory to help understand why they occur. Frequently it is because groups cannot maintain cohesion and effectiveness without leaders. Nor can group decision making be a continuously successful mode of practice in all organizations simply for reasons of time. There is a history of failure of participative management in certain cultures. And organizations with group ownership, such as plywood factories in the U.S. Northwest, have often had difficulty retaining managers. Much of social psychology is a fraternal psychology, preoccupied with peer interaction, whereas psychoanalytic psychology would put greater emphasis on understanding the meaning of the leader to the followers and the capacity of the followers to identify with that leader and thereby to establish ties to each other (Freud 1959).

Survey research is another popular area of psychology. It follows the same process of asking questions and summarizing the manifest answers. These are reported as if the manifest content in and of itself were singularly important. Sometimes, as in repetitive comparisons, it is. However, there is no way to understand the degree to which people answer in certain ways about certain problems when they are actually concerned about something else. Nor, without a theory of unconscious motivation, is there any way of reading between the lines of such responses symbolic meanings of significance to the individual or group.

Behavioristic Psychology

Behavioristic orientations place a heavy emphasis on rewarding people for appropriate responses. Experience in industry indicates, however, that while the use of behavior modification incentives in plant operations may achieve initial success, it usually fails in the end. Apparently the rewards lose their significance and people no longer respond to them. Furthermore, a reward–punishment orientation of this kind assumes that somebody is manipulating the rewards, and people soon learn to manipulate back—a phenomenon I have called "The Great Jackass Fallacy" (Levinson 1973). Behavioristic orientations, applied to organizations, do not differentiate among conditions or individuals in significant ways and run the risk of quickly becoming rote. One incentive method is to ask people to set their own goals or objectives. After they have attained them, they are asked to set increasingly incremental goals. That kind of goal setting may have incentive relevance for limited periods of time. After a while it loses its motivating power, particularly when the goals themselves become superordinate goals requiring greater intensity of effort than the people are either willing or able to put out.

The principle of reinforcement is both old and fundamental. Yet it is a limited conception. What is reinforcing to one person may not be so to another. Today's reinforcement may not be effective tomorrow. And reinforcement will always occur in some kind of context. The significance of an organizational reward includes the person doing the rewarding and the conditions under which the reward is attained. Those issues of meaning are almost untouched in behavioristic theory.

PSYCHOANALYTIC CONTRIBUTIONS

What does psychoanalysis have to contribute to organizational behavior?

Selection

Psychoanalytic understanding is the basis for much of what goes on in contemporary managerial and leadership selection. An important contribution in recent years has been the work of assessment centers (Bray 1982). This method of selecting managers was developed from the early efforts of the Office of Strategic Services in World War II. The selection processes of that agency, in turn, were based on the work of Henry Murray in the Harvard Psychological Clinic (Murray 1938), significantly based on psychoanalytic theory. Murray evolved the Thematic Apperception Test, in which people made up stories about a series of pictures. These stories were scored according to how they reflected the twenty-six needs that Murray formulated from theory. The work of McClelland (1975), using three of the needs Murray formulated, thus also derives basically from psychoanalytic theory. Because these methods have been divorced from their conceptual foundations and narrowed to measurable dimensions, their predictive ability is limited. Nevertheless, they demonstrate the power of psychoanalytic theory to serve as a base from which researchers of orientations begin. Neither Bray nor McClelland is psychoanalytically oriented, but are closer to a medial psychology, and since their work is limited in its scope, it may be said to be based on part theories.

The fundamental issues that differentiate leadership from management are exemplified in the work of Zaleznik (1975) and Maccoby (1976), and in my own work (Levinson 1981b). A crucial aspect of the differentiation has to do with the symbolic role, as well as the creative role, of the person in the leadership position. Psychoanalytic conceptions underlie the more dynamic aspects of the leadership role, namely the psychological meaning of the leader to the followers, the manner in which identification is evolved, and the significance of identification to maintaining organization cohesion, direction, and momentum.

To aid in the selection of chief executives, I have outlined the characteristics of successful leaders (Levinson 1980). These are basically drawn from psychoanalytic theory. Two diagnostic questions are derived from the dual-drive aspect of the theory: "How does this person handle aggression, the mastery component of the personality?" and "How does this person handle affection, the need for closeness or love and being loved?" It is also important to ask how a prospective CEO (chief executive officer) handles dependency, a fundamental developmental issue with which all human beings must struggle from birth to death. And finally, from the self-governing aspect of the personality, the superego, one must consider its purposive direction: "What is the nature of this person's ego ideal?" These questions serve as the basis for a comprehensive description of the candidate's characteristic behavior in multiple arenas.

For example, one may attack a marketplace vigorously, as in a marketing campaign, but be less straightforward in interpersonal contacts and perhaps even inhibited in relation to one's own children. The management of aggression is then a configuration and needs to be understood as such. And so it is with the other dimensions. When these configurations are combined into an overall pattern of behavior, then one has a sense of the multifaceted behavior of the individual.

Similarly, a job role might be described in terms of the requirements for handling aggression, affection, and dependency, and the gratification provided if the job is done well. One might then construct a behavioral job description whose complex configuration could provide a basis for fitting candidate to role. Such a system would represent a significant advance over cruder current methods.

Psychoanalytic theory also helps us understand the consistency of behavior and, therefore, the kinds of assignments to which a person may be best adapted. It underscores the problems of assigning new roles to people who must operate with their enduring patterns of individual behavior. It calls attention to the significance of stages of adult development for occupational roles and activities, and the stresses of transition.

Because of its richness, psychoanalytic theory makes it possible to take a more comprehensive approach to career guidance and career planning. The life cycle serves as the basis for thinking about not only the stages through which a person may live and the dominant psychological tasks of each stage, but also the preferred mode of behavior in each stage. By asking themselves the questions outlined in the previous section and by putting the answers together with the life-stage conception, individuals are better able to assess themselves and their own changing needs. For example, at later stages managers may become less individually competitive, more interested in developing their subordinates, more willing to seek the cooperation of colleagues and to temper the expectations of themselves they held earlier in their careers.

Managing Change

Change represents a significant problem in organizations. To manage change successfully requires an understanding of object attachments, a fundamental contribution of psychoanalytic theory. Attachment and separation have received a great deal of attention in recent years from such people as Mahler (1968) and Jacobson (1971) in the United States and a range of theorists in Great Britain (Bowlby 1969, 1973, 1980; Winnicott 1958; Klein 1957). The process through which children become attached to adults and other objects and the significance of the loss of those attachments is fundamental to understanding the meaning of change as loss. Properly understood, change can be managed in a way that allows mourning to take place, thereby facilitating adaptation to new objects.

Performance Appraisal

A key element in the transmission of organization culture is performance appraisal. Most performance-appraisal systems do not function adequately, as reflected in the rapidity with which those systems are changed. Dissatisfied with the system's output, management repeatedly tries to deal with its frustration by changing the forms. The major cause of failure in performance appraisal is the absence of raw data, specifically examples of behavior. I have suggested a critical-incident method of noting exceptional behavior, both positive and negative, when it occurs and providing immediate feedback (Levinson 1976). Managers are often reluctant to do this, however, because of their underlying unconscious guilt, which equates giving negative feedback with destroying the individual. The feelings of guilt are derived from unconscious fantasies, which are part of the primitive thought processes of the small child. Not understanding these feelings, people may formulate elaborate devices to try to cope with the resulting evasive behavior. These repeatedly fail. Understanding that, one can create methods for relieving the guilt, which will free performance appraisal of the psychological drag that presently makes it an exercise in futility.

Creativity

Much of the work on creativity, because it deals largely with unconscious thought processes, is enriched by psychoanalytic thinking. Picasso was heavily influenced by Freud, and a large part of the contemporary literary scene is significantly shaped by psychoanalytic thinking. With the development of psychohistory, we are learning more about the manner in which the intrapsychic conflicts of individuals are translated into their particular kinds of creativity and even leadership of religious movements and nations. Efforts to increase creativity among work groups by the use of such devices as brainstorming and synectics are based on the understanding of the need to evade one's own self-judgment and conscious control in order to allow unconscious thought processes to arise to preconscious levels and thereby to contribute to organizational innovation.

Structure and Compensation

With respect to the structure of the organizations and modes of compensation, the work of Jaques (1976) is an example of the manner in which one can go from underlying assumptions of unconscious motivation to a psychologically logical organization structure with a conceptual differentiation between levels, and a compensation system that parallels that structure (all capable of empirical test). Jaques's conception of the time span of responsibility provides a stable and uniform basis of measure which is empirically verifiable (Jaques 1982). Almost all other theories of organization structure and compensation are ad hoc empirical efforts that do not systematically relate one to the other. Jaques's major simple theory is to advance.

Organizational Diagnosis

Just as a physician must identify the disease before prescribing the treatment, organizational diagnosis provides a sound basis for action (Levinson 1972). This conception takes as its model the psychoanalytic conception of evolution from birth, and the multiple influences on that evolution that in turn manifest themselves in contemporary behavior. It is a framework for taking into account organizational history; organizational crises; organizational adaptive methods; organizational values; modes of transmitting, interpreting, and acting on information; modes of coping with threats to the organism; and the evaluation of the organization's mastery patterns. A comprehensive diagnostic case study becomes the basis for selecting organizational interventions and for undertaking change efforts. Without a comprehensive view, such efforts are generally made either on an ad hoc basis or in response to some part diagnosis.

Questionnaire studies are frequently part of a diagnostic effort. As indicated earlier, however, most are too limited. One of the important contributions psychoanalytic theory can make to questionnaire interpretation and studies of climate, morale and attitude, is an understanding of the needs, concerns, and wishes of individuals and groups derived from inference and interpretations that consultants may make from answers to those questions.

Stress

Contemporary concern with stress has led to the evolution of many palliative efforts. Most of those elementary recipes for dealing with the manifest behavioral results of stress are a form of self-hypnosis. Understanding stress requires an understanding of what goes on within individuals and why one situation may be challenging to one person and stressful to another (Levinson 1981). None of the contemporary explanations of stress, except psychoanalytic theory, deals adequately with this problem. Most merely assert without explanation the fact of individual differences. Such conceptions do not reveal any relationship between specific organizational variables and specific individuals or groups that would prescribe managerial actions for preventing, alleviating, or ameliorating stress.

One important source of stress is the voluntary efforts of people to make mid-career changes, to separate themselves from their historical psychological anchors, and to assume new directions and new attachments. These efforts are merely described by other theories, but are significantly illuminated by psychoanalytic theory.

Theoretical Base

Numerous part theories have been developed from psychoanalytic theory, as indicated above with respect to selection. In addition to those that undergird empirical studies, many part theories provide a basis for therapeutic and growth activities. These include Gestalt therapy, transactional analysis, and various other ways of trying to understand people and be helpful to them. The group-dynamics movement and its growth-group successor, the encounter movement, are based on earliest conceptions of psychoanalytic practice, namely the need to make conscious that which is unconscious by being able to speak about it. In encounter groups, confrontation with other group members compels the individual to overcome the barriers to communicating thoughts and feelings and brings to awareness psychological issues that presumably have inhibited his or her growth and development.

WHITHER THE THEORY?

Psychoanalytic theory is likely to become increasingly important in the field of organizational behavior. Managers and executives are becoming more sophisticated. The higher their level of abstraction and the greater the complexity they have to deal with in the form of economics, finance, marketing, control, and other aspects of management, the more sophisticated information they will demand about human behavior. They will not be satisfied with simple answers to complicated problems or with elementary practices like "group decision making," which do not adequately differentiate among people and groups or enable managers to deal with intragroup conflicts or to manage their own increasingly sensitive interactions. The more complex their interpersonal and organizational tasks, the more sophisticated a theory they will need.

A more complex theory of personality will also enable organizations to refine their selection processes, in turn permitting them to reassign personnel more rapidly and effectively to meet the changing needs of the environment.

Present performance appraisal and compensation systems are of little real use, as reflected in the proliferation of forms and the continuous effort people make to increase their status by manipulating points or weights assigned to aspects of their jobs. Moreover, contemporary performance-appraisal practices, especially for managers, cannot be defended in discrimination suits. As a result, organizations are under great pressure to develop more sophisticated performance-appraisal systems. The absence of behavioral information needed for coaching and counseling, for promotability, for selection, for translations into consistent patterns of behavior, for fitting individual to role—all indicate a need for a level of sophistication that can come only out of psychoanalytic theory or something even more refined.

If organizations are to facilitate individual development and provide career paths, there will be a greater need for counseling people and also for recognizing their limits. Organizations cannot choose wisely and people cannot evaluate themselves accurately without sophisticated criteria for making such choices.

Today we are increasingly aware of stress, of individual differences related to stress, of the importance of specific stress sources, and of the significance of psychophysiological or psychosomatic symptoms. At present, however, students of organizational behavior are engaged only in elementary discussion of these issues; we need to advance to a level more in keeping with the complexity of the phenomena under consideration.

The future will bring a need for more flexible adaptation and more rapid change; as a result, organizations will be less able to hold themselves together by compulsion or by money. The importance of leadership will become more and more apparent. Leaders must engage with their followers, and thus must understand their followers and understand the psychology of leadership. In addition, they need to understand themselves, their own leadership behavior, and the adaptation of that behavior to specific kinds of organizations, to specific times when certain kinds of leadership styles are appropriate, and to many specific kinds of followers with whom they are engaged.

Economic theorists have great difficulty predicting the direction of the economy and response to various kinds of economic adjustments. Their failures raise questions about the underlying assumptions economics makes about human behavior. These questions will demand more and more specific psychological answers, and because such answers hinge on human motivation, there will be a greater demand for answers that include unconscious considerations. We can expect more psychoanalytic research in this direction.

What are the limitations of psychoanalytic theory? Are there types of problems to which it does not apply?

Like any comprehensive deductive system, psychoanalytic theory has many limitations. Some of these have to do with concepts that are inexact and inferences that are difficult to test empirically. We are a long way from fathoming the human mind. Some of the theory's weaknesses have to do with the nature of the scientific model itself, built on the paradigm of late-19th- and early 20th century science. However, contemporary developments in sociobiology have provided considerable support for the theory (Leak and Christopher 1982).

As a theory, psychoanalysis includes both concepts and content. The concepts will endure as a frame of reference for organizing content, which may well change over time. For example, some of Freud's conclusions about the psychology of women are less valid today than they were in his era. The content of thought processes and values will vary from culture to culture. Rivalry between father and son, for example, will have a different meaning in a culture like ours, which permits that rivalry to be in the open, than in a culture in which such rivalry must be tightly controlled because authority relationships within the family are highly structured. The degree to which that rivalry is open or suppressed, in turn, will have significance for how rivalry with more powerful others is handled in an organization structure.

To many practical problems of organization, psychoanalytic theory has little relevance. It will not have much to contribute to industrial engineering or engineering psychology. While psychoanalytic thinking may give substance to variables that are then included in computer models, it probably will have little influence on the mathematics of computer modeling. When managerial compensation must be manipulated to take advantage of changing tax laws, such empirical considerations are not likely to be aided by psychoanalytic thought.

Psychoanalysis has no theory of substantive learning, and thus cannot contribute significantly to formal education and training activities in organizations. That realm of employee and management development requires a different kind of psychology.

Like evolutionary biology, much of what is considered in psychoanalytic thinking is not yet amenable to empirical testing. Probably much of it never will be. Nevertheless, psychoanalytic thinking provides a conceptual framework for integrating the vast array of empirical findings in organizational behavior. Without such a framework, indeed, the application of empirical findings to organizational problems is a haphazard business. Too often "solutions" are tacked on to problems without taking into consideration the whole context, and because there are vast gaps in the empirical work done to date, the practitioner must rely heavily on intuition. While any profession will always require the application of intuition and experience, the more scientifically based that application, the better the practitioner can state his diagnosis as hypothesis and the more logically he can derive his applications, which are always then a test of that hypothesis. Psychoanalytic theory, with its potential for systematic integration of empirical findings and its comprehensive understanding of the individual, offers an opportunity both to enrich empirical research by providing new and testable hypotheses, and to bridge the work of organizational behavior researchers and theorists and organizational consultants.

REFERENCES

Bales, R. F. 1970. *Personality and Interpersonal Behavior*. New York: Holt, Rinehart and Winston.

Bion, W. R. 1959. *Experience in Groups*. New York: Basic Books.

Bowlby, J. 1969, 1973, 1980. *Attachment and Loss*. 3 vols. (1, *Attachment*; 2, *Separation*; 3, *Loss*.) New York: Basic Books.

Bray, D. W. 1982. "The Assessment Center and the Study of Lives." *American Psychologist* 37, no. 1:180–89.

Deci, E. L. 1971. "Effects of Externally Mediated Rewards on Intrinsic Motivation." *Journal of Personality and Social Psychology* 18:105–15.

Eissler, K. R. 1965. *Medical Orthodoxy and the Future of Psychoanalysis*. New York: International Universities Press.

Freud, S. 1959. "Group Psychology and the Analysis of the Ego." In *Complete Psychological Works of Sigmund Freud*, vol. 18. London: Hogarth.

Herzberg, F. 1976. *The Managerial Choice*. Homewood, Ill.: Dow Jones-Irwin.

Jacobson, E. 1971. *Depression*. New York: International Universities Press.

Jaques, E. 1976. A *General Theory of Bureaucracy*. New York: Halsted Press.

———. 1982. *The Form of Time*. New York: Crane, Russak.

Klein, M. 1957. *Envy and Gratitude*. London: Tavistock.

Lawrence, P. R., and J. W. Lorsch. 1967. *Organization and Environment: Managing Differentiation and Integration*. Boston: Division of Research, Harvard Business School.

Leak, G. A., and S. B. Christopher. 1982. "Freudian Psychoanalysis and Sociobiology." *American Psychologist* 37, no. 3.

Levinson, H. 1972. *Organizational Diagnosis*. Cambridge, Mass.: Harvard University Press.

———. 1973. *The Great Jackass Fallacy*. Cambridge, Mass.: Harvard University Press.

———. 1976. "Appraisal of *What* Performance?" *Harvard Business Review* 54, no. 4:30–48.

———. 1980. "Criteria for Choosing Chief Executives." *Harvard Business Review* 58, no. 4:113–20.

———. 1981a. "Power, Leadership, and the Management of Stress." In *Making Organizations Humane and Productive*, ed. H. Meltzer and W. R. Nord. New York: Wiley.

———. 1981b. *Executive*. Cambridge, Mass.: Harvard University Press.

Levinson, H., C. R. Price, K. J. Munden, H. J. Mandl, and C. M. Solley. 1962. *Men, Management, and Mental Health*. Cambridge, Mass.: Harvard University Press.

Locke, E. A. 1968. "Toward a Theory of Task Motivation and Incentives." *Organizational Behavior and Human Performance* 3:157–89.

Maccoby, M. 1976. *The Gamesman*. New York: Simon & Schuster.

Mahler, M. 1968. *On Human Symbiosis and the Vicissitudes of Individuation*. New York: International Universities Press.

Maslow, A. H. 1954. *Motivation and Personality*. New York: Harper & Row.

McClelland, D. C. 1975. *Power: The Inner Experience*. New York: Irvington.

Murray, H. A. 1938. *Explorations* in *Personality*. New York: Oxford University Press.

Rice, A. K. 1969. Individual, Group and Intergroup Processes. *Human Relations* 22:562–84.

Silverman, L. H. 1976. "The Reports of My Death are Greatly Exaggerated: Psycho-analytic Theory." *American Psychologist* 31, no. 9:631–37.

Vroom, V. H., and P. W. Yetton. 1973. *Leadership and Decision-Making.* Pittsburgh, PA: University of Pittsburgh Press.

Winnicott, D. W. 1958. Transitional Objects and Transitional Phenomena. In *Collected Papers: Through Pediatrics to Psychoanalysis*, ed. D. W. Winnicott. New York: Basic Books.

———. 1975. "Objects and Transitional Phenomena." In *Collected Papers: Through Pediatrics to Psychoanalysis*, ed. D. W. Winnicott. London: Hogarth.

Zaleznik, A., and M. F. R. Kets de Vries. 1975. *Power and the Corporate Mind.* Boston: Houghton Mifflin.

2

RECIPROCATION: THE RELATIONSHIP BETWEEN MAN AND ORGANIZATION

HARRY LEVINSON

The concept of reciprocation, which focuses attention on the relationship between a man and the organization in which he works, offers the possibility of integrating a wide range of data and concepts from industrial psychology, sociology, and clinical psychology. It explains the psychological meaning of the organization to the man and vice versa, an area so far almost untouched by psychological investigation in industry. It therefore provides the basis for better psychological training problems, of job evaluation and personnel selection, and of research on role performance. It also offers the clinical psychologist the possibility of access to a wide range of data, which, heretofore without a dynamic base and unrelated to the psychology of the individual, had little relevance for him.

In keeping with the style of much of American and British psychology, industrial psychology places heavy emphasis on variables that lend themselves readily to measurement. This focus arises, in part from the fact that traditionally, industrial psychology has had to deal with large numbers of

Adapted from "Reciprocation: The Relationship Between Man and Organization" by Harry Levinson published in *Administrative Science Quarterly*, 9(4), pp. 370–390, by permission of *Administrative Science Quarterly*. © 1965 The Johnson School.

people and therefore to deal with them statistically rather than individually. The pragmatic tradition of industrial psychology gives more weight to empirical findings than to systematic theory. As a result, much has been learned about many aspects of the man at work, but, for the most part, the study of his personality has been neglected.[1]

Unconscious motivation, the twin drives of love and hate, the struggles with dependency and identity, and other important concepts of personality, get scant attention in texts on industrial psychology. Although some of these topics have been touched upon by Argyris,[2] Jennings,[3] Pederson-Krag,[4] and McMurry,[5] among others, as interrelated topics they are left to be discussed in texts on clinical psychology and personality.

There are as yet few ways to make a bridge between these intrapersonal variables and the traditional interests of industrial psychology. Psychoanalytic theory is one way, and although it has limits as a bridge, it has promising possibilities. Many people believe it to be limited to the psychology of the inner man, but it is in fact a theory of man–environment relations. As Gill[6] has noted, "The explicit theoretical accounting for the role of the organized environment is relatively recent and it is true that only relatively recently has the effort begun to encompass object relationships within psychoanalytic theory."

This paper[7] attempts to realize some of the possibilities of this bridge, suggesting that what a work organization means to a person has an important bearing on the variables that have been of major interest to industrial psychologists.

IMPORTANCE OF ORGANIZATIONAL AFFILIATION

Social Change and Personal Loss

Increasing mobility, both social and geographical, has made it more difficult for people to establish relatively enduring friendships. Many who anticipate further moves from one area to another are reluctant to involve themselves deeply in friendships, to avoid the later pain of separation. Thus

[1]Marvin D. Dunnette and Bernard Bass, "Behavioral Scientists and Personnel Management," *Industrial Relations*, 2 (1963), 115–130.
[2]Chris Argyris, *Personality and Organization* (New York: Harpers, 1957).
[3]Eugene E. Jennings, The *Executive: Autocrat, Bureaucrat, Democrat* (New York: Harpers, 1962).
[4]Geraldine Pederson-Krag, *Personality Factors in Work and Employment* (New York: Funk and Wagnalls, 1955).
[5]Robert N. McMurry, "The Executive Neurosis," *Harvard Business Review*, 30 (1952), 33–47.
[6]Merton Gill, "The Present State of Psychoanalytic Theory," *Journal of Abnormal and Social Psychology*, 58 (1959), 1–8.
[7]Invited address, Division of Industrial and Business Psychology, American Psychological Association, September 3, 1963. I am indebted to Charlton R. Price, Kenneth J. Munden, M.D., Harold J. Mandl, Ph.D., and Charles M. Solley, Ph.D., my colleagues in the study from which this paper is derived; to Martin Mayman, Ph.D., John A. Turner, M.D., and Joseph Satten, M.D., for critical reading of various versions of the manuscript; and to Mrs. Helen Friend for invaluable editorial help.

they lose some of the impetus for consistent ties with others, and therefore opportunities to give and receive affection.

The extended family unit is less likely to be found living in the same geographical area where family members can turn readily to each other for social activities and mutual aid. Family elders in many cases are too far away from their grandchildren to become models for identification and sources of psychological support. This means both fewer sources of support and less sense of family continuity. People who seek professional help when under stress frequently indicate this lack of support with "I have nobody to turn to."

Social services, voluntary health agencies, hospitals, nursing homes have become progressively more institutionalized. These and similar organized efforts have taken the place of the more personal services and charitable acts characteristic of a previous era, "more personal" meaning that people believed there was more affection and concern in the noninstitutional services. The change therefore represents a perceived loss of certain sources of love— "Nobody really cares."

Even in work some sources of gratification are being lost. Rapid technical changes have altered the composition of work groups and work tasks. Occupational and status achievements are somewhat tenuous when skills can readily be made obsolete or when their social value can depreciate rapidly, as a result of technical changes and new industrial developments.[8] Many of the services formerly performed by small entrepreneurs are now carried out by larger units of production and marketing. Movement from a small business to a larger enterprise usually means some loss of personal freedom. For those who were part of a work group, these changes contribute to the loss of a sense of group purpose about work and of group solidarity.

Replacement of Losses

Affiliation with an organization in which a person works seems to have become a major device for coping with the problems resulting from these economic, social, and psychological changes. Organizations have recognized and fostered the desire of employees to seek financial security in the organization by means of long service. Seniority advantages in union contracts, vested rights in pension funds, and promotion within a given organization rather than upward movement from one business to another have encouraged long-term affiliation with one organization. Indeed, often a man enters a work organization before he marries and remains in it long after his grandchildren are grown.

Instead of a geographical orienting point, many now have an organizational orienting point. They identify themselves with an organization—

---

[8]Donald N. Michael, *Cybernation: The Silent Conquest* (Santa Barbara, Calif.: Center for the Study of Democratic Institutions, 1962).

whether a company, church, university, or government department. In a man's movement from one neighborhood or community to another, the work organization is his thread of continuity and may well become a psychological anchor point for him.

Frequently his social friendships arise from his work associations. Old Navy men have long had a ready bond for friendship, and two strangers who work for IBM are already likely to have much in common. In the course of some research on mental health in utilities companies, it was found that a number of men who had moved from one electric generating station to another in the same company would frequently drive long distances on their days off to visit their old work buddies. They did not mention visiting others in their old communities.

It is not unusual for the company, both by means of its staff services and the personal interest of an employee's associates and superiors, to come to the assistance of a person in emergency circumstances. The "kitty" for emergencies is a ubiquitous phenomenon in organizations, whether raised by contributions or profits from coin machines. Fellow workers mobilize for blood transfusions as well as money, and in some instances the organization continues a man's salary beyond sick leave provisions until he can return to work. When a man's fellow workers mobilize to help him, this support is seen by the recipient as the personal giving by good friends because of their common interest as organizational members.

If technical change eliminates a man's job, the company will often retrain him, thereby helping him to cope with the change and assuring him of long-term job security. Recent contractual innovations in the steel industry provide for cushions against job displacement as a result of technological obsolescence. Organizations recognize some obligation to help their employees, particularly those of long service, to cope with change.

In the past a man was introduced to others by his name or by identifying him with his trade. Today he is identified not merely as John Smith, but John Smith, foreman in the Midland Utilities Company, or more simply as being "with Midland Utilities." And mostly he will identify himself the same way. Together with the movement from small businesses to large organizations, this means relatively less recognition of the individual as an individual and relatively more recognition of the individual as part of an organization. It gives added weight to the importance of the relationship between a man and his work organization for gaining social power. Within that relationship, however, the individual seeks increasing individual recognition, consideration, and responsibility,[9] and looks to support from his supervisor to obtain them.[10]

---

[9]Douglas McGregor, *The Human Side of Enterprise* (New York: McGraw-Hill, 1960); Rensis Likert, *New Patterns of Management* (New York: McGraw-Hill, 1961).

[10]Floyd Mann and Richard Hoffman, *Automation and the Worker* (New York: Holt and Dryden, 1960).

Affiliation seems to be as important to executives as it is to people on hourly wages. A far larger number of graduates of business schools go into companies than start their own businesses. A recent Bureau of the Census[11] report indicates that salaried men now outnumber self-employed professional and businessmen in the income bracket that includes the top five per cent of the earning population. Managers and salaried professionals, according to the report, account for half of these, whereas self-employed number only one-fourth. These figures are a reversal of those of 1950 and reflect the growth of corporations and the increasing number of executives in them. Moreover, executives have social and economic influence only as long as they hold positions in organizations. This is one reason many give for not wanting to retire, for to retire means, as they put it, to become a "nobody."

Reinforcement of Defenses

Organizations have important social functions to perform: they produce goods or render services; they also provide the means for people to earn a livelihood. These are fundamental functions of organizations, and it is because these functions are basic that organizations become important psychological devices as well.

Jaques[12] has observed that, in addition to serving the many economic, social, and psychological purposes already referred to, organizations reinforce individual defenses against unconscious anxiety. In this he follows Melanie Klein's[13] conception that infants respond to early frustration by experiencing the outside world as hostile and potentially harmful. She calls the two kinds of resulting anxiety paranoid and depressive.

Jaques[14] suggests that as people grow up, they are on guard against the recurrence of these anxieties and use social institutions as modes of warding them off. For example, dividing people into good and bad, commonly observed in clinical practice, is one way of handling paranoid anxiety. The "bad" impulses of people in an organization may thereupon be projected onto a "bad" figure or figures. Jaques calls attention to the way in which the first officer of a ship is commonly regarded by the crew as the source of all trouble, permitting the men to idealize the captain and identify themselves with him. There is often a similar polarity in the army between the executive officer and the commanding officer or "old man." Industrial psychologists will recognize key figures in other divisions of a company who are seen as the bad ones who cause all the problems.

---

[11]Bureau of the Census, "Self-employed Have Place at Top of Top Pay Group," *Wall Street Journal*, July 15, 1963.
[12]Elliott Jaques, "Social Systems as a Defense Against Persecutory and Depressive Anxiety," in Melanie Klein, ed., *New Directions in Psychoanalysis* (New York: Basic Books, 1955).
[13]"A Contribution to the Psychogenesis of Manic-Depressive States," *Contributions to Psychoanalysis, 1921–1945* (London: Hogarth, 1948).
[14]Jaques, *op. cit.*

Depressive anxieties can be dealt with by identifying with an organization which "does good" and by working hard at its activities, thus relieving guilt feelings. After the 1936 hurricane that devastated New England, employees of a major public utility came from many parts of the country to work long hours under dangerous conditions in unfamiliar territory to restore service. In their six weeks of intensive work there was not one accident. The work in itself was sufficiently guilt relieving that accidents did not occur.

Whether one agrees with the specifics of Jaques' hypothesis about paranoid and depressive anxiety is of little consequence for this discussion. The point is that relating personality variables to organizational problems makes it possible to interrelate morale, motivation, leadership, and most of the other concerns of industrial psychology systematically.

Transference

The question might arise, "How can you speak of man–organization relationships?" An organization is created as a legal fiction which meets certain requirements and has certain capacities, but, as Peter Drucker[15] argues, "it has no life of its own apart from people. It, the organization, cannot therefore relate to people."

One can speak of man–organization relationships, first, because phenomena with typical features of transference can be observed; second, because many employees in their relationships with other people, act as agents of the organization. Transference means unconsciously bringing past attitudes, impulses, wishes, and expectations (particularly those usually experienced toward powerful parental figures), in exaggerated form into present situations, whether in or out of the consulting room, as shown by Freud,[16] Fenichel,[17] Hendricks,[18] and Anna Freud.[19] Transference phenomena occur constantly in everyday life. It occurs with respect to organizations and institutions just as it occurs with individuals; that is, people project upon organizations human qualities and then relate to them as if the organizations did in fact have human qualities. They generalize from their feelings about people in the organization who are important to them, to the organization as a whole, as well as extrapolating from those attitudes they bring to the organization. Transference makes it possible to use a hospital as a therapeutic device simply because patients believe it to have therapeutic powers.

Selznick[20] argues that organizations quickly become invested with psychological meaning for their members. Organizations could not endure for

---

[15]*The Practice of Management* (New York: Harpers, 1954).
[16]Sigmund Freud, "The Dynamics of the Transference," in *Collected Papers*, Vol. II, (London: Hogarth, 1912).
[17]Otto Fenichel, *The Psychoanalytic Theory of the Neuroses* (New York: Norton, 1945).
[18]Ives Hendricks, *Facts and Theories of Psychoanalysis* (3rd ed.; New York: Knopf, 1958).
[19]*The Ego and the Mechanisms of Defense* (New York: International Universities, 1946).
[20]Philip Selznick, *Leadership in Administration* (New York: Row, Peterson, 1957).

very long if this did not happen. Simmel,[21] discussing the management of a psychiatric hospital, spoke of creating "a positive attachment to the institution as such . . . so that the patient may be thus secure of a firm foundation. . . ." Reider[22] reported that patients maintained ties to the psychiatric outpatient clinic rather than to the therapists who treated them. He said that "as soon as a medical institution achieves a reputation, it is a sign that an idealization and condensation of the magical power and the benevolent greatness of parental figures have been posited in the institution. . . . The phenomenon is widespread and *touches upon every type of institution which has any characteristics of benevolence* (italics mine)." Reider sees such transference as a way of dealing with reality by participating in a great organization.

Wilmer[23] speaking of transference to a medical center as a cultural dimension in healing, points out that, "One cannot understand staff–patient relationships in any institution without an appreciation of this important psychologic (*sic*), social and, particularly cultural dimension of its healing powers. Physicians, just as patients, are enmeshed in transference feelings toward the institution. . . ." He adds that the institution can stand as the symbolic parental surrogate, and the positive or negative attitudes of the person toward the institution may well be, in part at least, transference reactions.

Transference is not new in relationships with other institutions. In this country some men seek to enroll their sons in their *alma maters* (italics mine) as soon as they are born. In England there is a similar attitude toward some clubs. In both countries some men look upon the army as others would upon their college or club.

Describing the elements of an institution that contribute to transference feelings, Wilmer observes that a medical center is a great institution which occupies many large and impressive buildings and has certain institutional rites of introduction, examination, and treatment, which gratify the dependent and narcissistic needs of patients. The personality of the physician is endowed with the power of the center. The institution endures beyond and transcends the individuals who work there. The more famous the institution the greater the anonymity of the individuals representing it. "The very name of the institution is a cherished and sacred title, a powerful symbol to which much transference feeling is attached." Then Wilmer adds a critical element: "It is in *affiliation*—to take a son—that the whole phenomenon of transference to a center takes on new meaning and new members."

The modern organization has some of the benevolent characteristics Reider discusses. It is a medium for recouping psychological losses in a rap-

---

[21]Ernst Simmel, "Psychoanalytic Treatment in a Sanitarium," *International Journal of Psychoanalysis*, 10 (1929), 70–89.
[22]Norman Reider, "Transference to Institutions," *Bulletin of the Menninger Clinic*, 17 (1953), 58–63.
[23]Harry A. Wilmer, "Transference to a Medical Center," *California Medicine*, 96 (1962), 173–180.

idly changing society. Moreover, the actions of individual people in an organization are viewed by them, by the objects of the action, and by observers, as actions of the organization. For example, if a local manager of Midland Utilities cuts off someone's service for nonpayment, that action is seen as the company cutting off the service. There are many reasons why this should be so.

1. The organization is legally, morally, and financially responsible for the actions of its members as organizational agents.
2. The organization has policies which make for great similarity in behavior by agents of the organization at different times and in different geographical locations.
3. These policies are supplemented by precedents, traditions, and informal norms as guides to behavior.
4. In many instances the action by the agent is a role performance with many common characteristics throughout that organization regardless of who carries it out, for example, the personnel officer.
5. Selection processes in an organization tend to result in the clustering of people whose personality structures have much in common and who would therefore tend to act along some personality dimensions in the same general way. These factors result in what is sometimes referred to as a "corporate personality," a generalized mode of behavior on the part of employees in a given company, recognized by others both in and out of the organization, which supports continuity of characteristic relations with the organization.
6. There tends to be a consensus of perception of a given employee by others in an organization as a result of discussions among one another about their experiences with the man and their review of his actions. This is particularly true if there are systematic appraisals in the organization.
7. As a legal and group entity, the organization has power independent of that of its agents. Often it also has financial and other resources which can be used on behalf of employees. The organization's capacity for aggressive and benevolent power can be perceived by its members, particularly when it is used either against employees or to support them in emergency situations.
8. It is often difficult for an employee to know who in the organization has done what to him. People speak of an undifferentiated "they" who make decisions and take action. Vague organization policy allows fantasies to come out.
9. Those who act within the power structure can often rationalize transference feelings that they act out. The boss who com-

plains that his subordinates are too dependent may be treating them as children, using the product of his behavior as a rationale for continuing it. Another might justify his sadistic behavior with the familiar, "It hurts me more than it hurts you."

In *The Devils of Loudun*, Aldous Huxley[24] says, "Partisanship is a complex passion which permits those who indulge in it to make the best of both worlds. Because they do these things for the sake of a group which is, by definition, good and even sacred, they can admire themselves and loathe their neighbors, they can seek power and money, can enjoy the pleasures of aggression and cruelty, not merely without feeling guilty, but with the positive glow of conscious virtue. Loyalty to their group transforms these pleasant vices into acts of heroism. It was this thesis that permitted men of the church to torture a victim to death, all the while crying, 'Dicas'" (confess). Huxley adds, "When Grandier criticized the monks of Loudun, it was, we may be sure, with a sense of righteous zeal, a consciousness of doing God's work. For God, it went without saying, was on the side of the secular clergy and of Grandier's good friends, the Jesuits."

The generalized mode of behavior characteristic of organizational agents as they act on behalf of the organization, together with the demonstration of the organization's power, make it possible for transference phenomena to occur which give the organization a psychological reality in the experience of the individual members.

Transference From Organization to Employee

The very phenomena which are the necessary conditions for the existence of transference phenomena in one direction also make for transference in the other. Those who act on behalf of the institution or organization have power and use their power in the manner of parental surrogates, according to the folkways of the organization. The purpose of a mental hospital, for example, is to help patients get well. If a patient does not improve, the staff may reject him. In a typical state hospital, he is consigned to the back wards. In a more enlightened institution, the rejection takes place informally, as happened in one short-term treatment center on the west coast, which admitted only acutely ill patients and placed heavy emphasis on psychotherapy. The physicians, who were serving their residency in psychiatry, clipped informal notes to the log book for the officer of the day. Each resident was officer of the day in turn, and the officer of the day was also the admitting officer, so each had before him the notes of all the others. These unofficial notes emphati-

---

[24]*The Devils of Loudon* (New York: Harpers, 1952).

cally instructed the officer of the day not to readmit certain patients who, in their judgment, would not profit from treatment. As apprentice psychiatrists, they naturally preferred to work with those patients who would be most responsive to their efforts. Economics alone would make this a reasonable point of view. This, however, does not explain their strong feeling about those whom they were not able to help and the indirect way they chose to keep them away, even when the hospital had no formal policy of rejection.

In industry, there is a similar phenomenon. The management of a major heavy manufacturing industry, for example, believes that employees should want nothing from their jobs except their salaries. It complains that though it pays its people relatively well, they do not understand that the stockholders need a return on their money, and they keep demanding higher wages. "Look at all that we give them in fringe benefits," the management says, "Look how good we are to them. Why don't they understand our point of view and not keep demanding more money?" The parallel between this attitude and that of many parents is obvious. The industrial culture is replete with such examples.

In these illustrations of transference, those who have power in the organization perceive the individual as a member of the organizational family and react to him as such. Although an employee may be a complete stranger in the personal sense to other persons in the organization, at the very least, what the person does reflects on the organization and its members. The underlying reason for the appearance of transference phenomena from the organization to the person is the importance of the person to others in the organization, who, taken together comprise the organization as it relates to the person.

The relationship is important to the organization because the major concern of the top management of most business organizations is not today's profitability, though that is important, but the long-term survival of the organization. With larger capital investments that must be amortized over longer periods of time and with an emphasis on organizational growth and creative innovation as a means of surviving in a competitive economy, corporate managements encourage personnel to remain in the company. Their permanence will presumably make for greater loyalty, productivity, and willingness to assume increasing responsibility, and their psychological investment will make for greater creativity. Legal decisions relating to workmen's compensation and labor relations, pressures from labor unions, and concern about the company's public image, all tend to foster company interest in the individual, transcending the interest of any given management group. There is, in addition, a growing sense of social responsibility on the part of business executives, partly because today's business leaders have higher levels of education than their predecessors, and partly because the corporation recognizes that it cannot afford to be irresponsible. Taken together, these forces make the man–organization relationship highly important to the organization.

In brief, the man–organization relationship is important to the person because it meets certain needs; in addition, he uses the organization to replace certain psychological losses, to reinforce his psychological defenses, and to serve as a major object of transference. The relationship is important to people who comprise the organization because of reverse transference phenomena toward organizational members, and because of the need for the organization to survive.

Relation of Unions to the Man–Organization Relationship

Just as in the family, however, the relationship is not a simple two-party one. It is not without good psychological reason that one speaks of paternalism in industry and that some companies are referred to by their employees as "Mother (name of company)," and that companies called "Mother" by their employees are benign and kindly and have either no union or a relatively nonmilitant union. In fact, some of the kindliness of the organization is an effort to head off unionization. This tells something about one psychological meaning of the union, namely its mothering function, which Purcell's[25] dual-loyalty studies have pointed up. Purcell notes that employees expect the union to protect them and obtain security provisions for them; whereas they look to management to run the business, and feel loyalty to management for doing so.

When the union plays its mothering function well, it enhances the employees' relationship to the organization. A good example is the way in which the Scanlon Plan,[26] conceived by a union leader, involved employees in the survival efforts of a company and saved the company from failure. This plan, incidentally, is the basis for the present Kaiser Steel pact. When, the union does not serve this function well, however, it either inadequately replaces the organization or deprives the worker of significant psychological ties to his work.

Some of the major industrial unions are examples of the first problem. They are highly militant, define the company as an exploitive enemy, and, with unwitting co-operation from a too-aggressive management, encourage the worker to identify with them. Unions whose members are hired from their hiring halls deprive their members of psychological ties to their work. Without a consistent relationship to any single producing organization, most of these men work primarily for immediate monetary return and do not have much interest in their work. They are among those much criticized for featherbedding, for failing to use their skills to produce high-quality work, and for their seemingly exhorbitant wage demands.

---

[25]Theodore Purcell, *The Worker Speaks His Mind on Company and Union* (Cambridge, Mass.: Harvard University, 1953).
[26]Fred G. Lesieur, *The Scanlon Plan* (New York: John Wiley, 1958).

But even under the best of circumstances, the union cannot provide the worker with the gratification that ideally he could and should be getting from his work,[27] because the union does not manage productive processes. This discussion is not to be construed as an argument against unions. Rather, it illuminates some of the psychological meaning of the union and the ways in which union–management relations can affect man–organization relationships.

THE CONCEPT OF RECIPROCATION

Examination of some of the psychological meanings of the man–organization relationship should make it possible to refine the concept so as to contribute to the development of research and to begin to integrate intrapersonal concepts with those of industrial psychology.

The concepts of identification, transference, and psychological defense, which are drawn from the literature of clinical psychology and psychiatry, were evolved to organize experiences going on psychologically within the person. They therefore have limitations when extended beyond their original limits. Identification and transference account for only one side of a dual relationship, for only part of a process, referring to one person or group at a time, not to interaction. Identification already has a variety of meanings. Not only did Freud[28] use the concept in many different ways but others, such as Becker and Carper,[29] Bronfenbrenner,[30] and Sanford,[31] have added connotations. What is needed then, is a concept which encompasses a continuous two-way process, which can incorporate and accommodate other concepts, and which is not colored by previous connotations.

In a study of mental health in industry,[32] it was apparent that transference phenomena and people's efforts to fulfill various psychological needs in their relationship with a company arose out of efforts, by both parties, to fulfill expectations (only part of which were conscious). This process of fulfilling mutual expectations and satisfying mutual needs in the relationship between a man and his work organization was conceptualized as a process of *reciprocation*. Viewed another way, it is the process of carrying out a psychological contract[33] between person and organization. It is a complementary

---

[27]Frederick Herzberg, Bernard Mausner, and Barbara Snyderman, *The Motivation to Work* (New York: John Wiley, 1959).

[28]Sigmund Freud, *Group Psychology and the Analysis of the Ego* (London: International Psychoanalytic Press, 1922).

[29]Howard S. Becker and James W. Carper, "The Development of Identification with an Occupation," *American Journal of Sociology*, 61 (1956), 289–298.

[30]Urie Bronfenbrenner, "Freudian Theories of Identification and their Derivatives," *Child Development*, 31 (1960), 15–40.

[31]Nevitt Sanford, "The Dynamics of Identification," *Psychological Review*, 62 (1955), 106–118.

[32]Harry Levinson, Charlton R. Price, Kenneth J. Munden, Harold J. Mandl, arid Charles M. Solley, *Men, Management, and Mental Health* (Cambridge, Mass.: Harvard University, 1962).

[33]Karl Menninger, *Theory of Psychoanalytic Technique* (New York: Basic Books, 1958).

process in which the person and the organization seem to become a part of each other. The person feels that he is part of the corporation or institution, and, at the same time, that he is a symbol standing for the whole organization. That is, he sees himself and is seen by others who are not fellow employees as the company personified. The public image of the organization is displaced onto the person and vice versa.

For example, a middle-management man in a medium-sized company, perhaps unknowingly speaking for all middle-management men, said, "After all, in this locale I *am* the company. Anything I say reflects back on the company." Another man at the same level in the same company observed, "You can't divorce your position from yourself. Various social groups catalogue you." He then enumerated the community activities and specific jobs within these activities, which he had been asked to assume because he was a manager in his particular company. A foreman in the same organization had a similar experience, as do many line employees. "In your neighborhood, you are the company. The neighbors think if you weren't the right sort of a fellow, you wouldn't be with them. Most people think our salaries are above average, so you have to keep your place looking half-way decent and your kids in shoes."

If reciprocation is a continuous process of fulfilling mutual expectations, of carrying out a psychological contract, and thereby, of enhancing the man–organization relationship, how can it contribute to integrating many of the heretofore disparate areas of industrial psychology?

FUNCTIONS OF RECIPROCATION

Reciprocation facilitates the maintenance of psychological equilibrium (defense), psychological growth, and the mastery of a part of one's world.

Defense

It is relatively easy to see defensive phenomena and how the organization may support the individual under stress. It is not so easy to see how the individual supports the organization under similar circumstances. An example would be the spontaneous mobilization of employees to help a public utility company keep its franchise in a community, though the employees would have no difficulty obtaining other jobs if the company lost its franchise.

Better understanding of defensive needs and the ways in which they shape the meaning of work and the work organization for the individual could be the basis for further development of aptitude, interest, and value inventories. In turn, also, a comprehensive theoretical basis for aptitude and interest studies would make it possible to relate them to studies of motivation and morale, making possible a better understanding of morale and defining it with greater precision. This conceivably could help us avoid such inadequate studies of morale as those reported by Brayfield and Crockett.[34]

Growth

Reciprocation fosters psychological growth in several ways. When the organization is functioning well, and the person feels an integral part of it, he is identifying with his superiors. This means that he is making some of their skills, experiences, points of view, and knowledge a part of himself. By making multiple identifications and reorganizing them in keeping with his own personality structure, a person grows more skilled and occupationally mature.[35]

When there is reciprocation, a man receives guidance from his superiors. If one interviews executives about their work, most will spontaneously mention some older person in an organization who took a special interest in him and "was like a father to me." Rarely do first-level workers spontaneously make the same comment, suggesting that the guidance of an experienced superior can make a difference in career progress.

Reciprocation opens up opportunities; for where the relationship between a man and organization is a good one, he is far more likely to move to greater responsibility than if reciprocation is not being fulfilled. Drucker[36] cites the different degrees of progress made by comparable young management trainees in two different parts of the Sears organization where the psychological contract was fulfilled differently.

The organization also contributes to the growth of the person by the demands it makes upon him which stimulate him to new learning. Technical changes, new problems to surmount, and the changing functions of the organization all stimulate the person to grow.

The growth of the person contributes to the character of the organization. A man may identify himself with his superiors, but he also brings something of his own personality to the organization. As he grows more experienced, others will identify themselves with him. He leaves something of himself in the organization and thereby contributes to its growth.

The organization is stimulated to growth by the collective demands of its employees, which may force it to greater efficiency, as in the coal industry; by the determination of its employees to take on new challenges as in the Scanlon Plan;[37] and by the behavior of its employees as they seek to use the organization for their own psychological needs. The contemporary trend to-

---

[34]Arthur H. Brayfield and Walter H. Crockett, "Employee Attitudes and Employee Performance," *Psychological Bulletin*, 52 (1955), 396–424.
[35]Joseph Adelson, "The Teacher as a Model," *American Scholar*, 30 (1961), 383–406.
[36]Drucker, *op. cit.*
[37]Lesieur, *op. cit.*

ward more flexible and innovative management, stems in part from the increasing rejection of autocratic leadership by employees.

These facets of the occupational growth of the individual are important considerations for management development, for supervisory training, for leadership selection, and for evaluation and appraisal. Too little attention has been given to the psychological values of the teaching functions in industrial leadership. Reciprocation makes it an imperative function of the executive. Management development activities cannot therefore be simply relegated to the training department.[38] With a *psychological* conception of the man–organization relationship, a psychologist's contributions are significant; with only an economic conception, they can have only a marginal purpose.

Mastery

Besides the psychological task of maintaining the equilibrium of ego–id–superego forces in their interaction with the environment, a person has the task of mastering enough of his world that he can survive in it. His job is a major way of attaining and maintaining that mastery. Work that serves all of these purposes might be looked upon as creative adaptation.

When channels for constructive mastery of the organization are inadequate, efforts may be directed toward indirect controls. For example, one company supplied its men with new shovels of a type they did not like. These inadvertently were left in the field, run over by trucks, or disposed of in other ways. After that the men were consulted on the tools they wanted. Another group of men, dissatisfied with their manager's failure to obtain better physical facilities for their equipment repair shop, managed to collect enough surplus paint and other items to refurbish their shop to the chagrin and embarrassment of higher management. Every company knows the problem of subtle empire building, and the *fait accompli* which commits the organization to actions never intended by official policy formulations. That people in organizations resist change and avoid responsibility by means of passive resistance is widely recognized.

Considerable attention has been given to mastery of the job with various forms of psychological engineering studies, achievement and performance measures, and appraisal practices. Herzberg and his colleagues[39] in particular have shown how important it is to the employee to master his work. But with reciprocation, an important part of mastering the job is to master a part of the organization.

---

[38]Harry Levinson, "A Psychologist Looks at Executive Development," *Harvard Business Review*, 40 (1962), 69–75.
[39]Herzberg, *et al., op. cit.*

That the organization tries to make itself the master of the man is a problem that has been the focus of much recent research. The company requires that task demands be fulfilled, that some people accept the direction of other people. It also controls the ways in which people may behave on the job by how it allocates financial and production resources. It may even require certain off-job behaviors. The men who spoke of how they were expected to behave at home because they were employees of the company were not told they had to behave that way, yet they felt obligated to do so. Employees are not usually told they must believe in the free enterprise system, or that they must give to the United Fund, but there are powerful informal forces in the organization which influence them to do both.

While some people deplore the fact that the organization to some extent shapes the man, in reciprocation it is inevitable and not always undesirable; for the shaping can contribute to his growth. Moreover, the man is not merely a Pygmalion in the hands of an industrial behemoth; reciprocally he makes demands, too. If the organization does not meet his needs he can leave it. No department wants to be known for having high turnover or absenteeism. Work groups establish informal production norms and frequently control work processes and thereby production schedules, profitability, and other factors that presumably are under the control of management, as Whyte[40] and Mechanic[41] have shown. The ultimate direct-control technique of the employee is the strike. In some instances, the employee clearly exploits the organization and in effect forces it to adopt certain formal courses in its own defense. In other instances, as in the Scanlon Plan[42] companies, employees have a more direct influence on shaping organizational processes and products.

SUMMARY

In reciprocation, each partner shapes the other to some extent. When one speaks of the alienation of the employee from his work in industry, one usually means that the employee does not feel he is making an impact on the organization.[43] Conversely, if the organization feels it has little possibility of shaping the employee, that it is pretty much at his mercy, then organization leadership takes a hostile view of him, as is so common in the construction industry.

---

[40]William F. Whyte, *Money and Motivation* (New York: Harpers, 1955).
[41]David Mechanic, "The Power to Resist Change Among Low-Ranking Personnel," *Personnel Administration*, 26 (1963), 5–11.
[42]Lesieur, *op. cit.*
[43]Leonard I. Pearlin, "Alienation from Work: A Study of Nursing Personnel," *American Sociological Review*, 27 (1962), 314–326.

This mutual shaping of each party by the other is examined in detail from a sociological point of view by Bakke.[44] Taking role theory as his point of departure, he comes to similar conclusions. He describes the interaction of man and organization as the "fusion process." Other role theory formulations account for specific job behaviors as the result of the person's place in the formal structure of the organization. Such formulations, when they also allow for psycho-dynamics and the effect of the person on the role, as in the work of W. E. Henry[45] and Daniel Levinson,[46] can be integrated into the concept of reciprocation.

If reciprocation facilitates the operation of psychological defenses, growth, and mastery in the individual, and if it contributes to similar processes in the organization, then it should have a significant relationship to the mental health of the employee and to the effective functioning of the organization. When the process is operating well, the employee obtains psychological support and stimulation to psychological growth from the organization. He has a contributing responsible role in the company and a continuing opportunity for personal development. The company has his cohesive support and his creative investment in the organization's tasks, therefore it gains the potential for both growth and survival. When reciprocation between the two is inadequate, both man and organization suffer.

---

[44]E. Wight Bakke, *The Fusion Process* (New Haven, Conn.: Labor and Management Center, Yale University, 1953).

[45]*Executive Personality and Job Success* (Personnel Series, No. 120; New York: American Management Association, 1948).

[46]"Role, Personality and Social Structure in the Organizational Setting," *Journal of Abnormal and Social Psychology*, 58 (1959), 170–180.

3

ANGER, GUILT AND
EXECUTIVE ACTION

HARRY LEVINSON

Why, after 15 years in his company, is Ed Stearns looking for a new job? The search for the answer to that question leads us to a little explored aspect of managerial practice—management by guilt.

Ed Stearns was in the new products division of a food products manufacturer. He was generally acknowledged in the company to be brilliant but lazy. He could develop information about a new market or a new field in short order, but he seemed unable to follow through to the point of action.

In the last year and a half, Stearns had produced no innovations in product or market. As a result, he was not given a salary increase. Stearns protested angrily, saying that he had rendered valuable service. Although he had been complimented by superiors many times during his employment, he said, he had never been adequately paid. He attributed the company's failure to recognize him to the jealousy of his supervisors and political undercurrents in the company.

When his superior investigated Stearns's work record, he discovered that all of Stearns's past supervisors reaffirmed the present judgment that he

From *Think*, 30(2), 10–14. Copyright 1964 by International Business Machines Corporation. Reprinted with permission.

was highly intelligent but never completed a job. Many said he should have been discharged shortly after he was hired. No supervisor wanted him back. When all this was reported to Stearns, he was forced to resign.

Why did Stearns's supervisors not tell him truthfully about his performance? The answer lies in their failure to recognize and understand human feelings, particularly the meaning of their own feelings.

Management philosophies, by and large, attempt to evade feelings. Ever since the pre–World War I days of industrial engineering, many people have sought to make management a highly rationalized process devoid of the influence of feelings. We therefore have such conceptions as management by task force, management by system, management by goals, management by control and management by coordination. As a matter of fact, however, most decisions about people are not made in such rational terms. Often they are made, as with Ed Stearns, irrationally because each supervisor must maintain his psychological equilibrium.

Specifically, much of the irrational in management practices arises because of people's efforts to cope with their own anger and to avoid the anger of others. Executives go to great lengths to avoid conflict because of their discomfort with feelings of anger. But the very fact that they have angry feelings, when they so often think they should not have such feelings, or that it is wrong to feel angry, leaves them feeling guilty for their anger. With these two feelings to contend with, executives frequently make decisions in such a way that they can deny their anger to themselves and appease their consciences. In short, we can speak of management by guilt.

THREE CONSEQUENCES

Frequently, there is a repetitive sequence of events in management by guilt: disappointment in the subordinate; failure to confront him realistically about his job behavior; procrastination in reaching a decision about him; cover-up compliments to ease the guilt of managerial anger; transfer to another position; finally discharge. Equally often, management by guilt has three consequences:

- The subordinate's occupational opportunities are either impaired or destroyed in the name of kindness.
- Executives hurt each other as they transfer the subordinate from one to the other, each feeling guilty about unloading him on the other.
- The company suffers because the subordinate often draws his salary for years without producing adequately.

In the case of Ed Stearns, the story does not end with his dismissal. The manager who had to confront him was angry not only at Stearns for failing to do his job, but more importantly at his colleagues and superiors. The latter had passed the buck from year to year and thereby had allowed Stearns to build up a false picture of his performance. With each transfer they gave Stearns a "northeast promotion." They could not, of course, promote him, but they felt so guilty about their own anger toward him and their feelings that perhaps they, too, were at fault, that they compensated for their feelings with compliments and a "promotion." Not a real promotion, mind you, but an almost-promotion, a small raise and a fancier title. Stearns's superior felt he had been made the goat for everyone else's procrastination. He had to carry the responsibility—and the blame—for terminating a man of 15 years' service.

A person must see adequate reaction to his behavior if he is to govern it according to the realities he must deal with. Without adequate information about himself he is operating in the psychological dark. When he discovers that he has had inadequate or incorrect information, usually after many years, he is then justified in saying that he has been treated unfairly. He has. Every man has a right to know in unmistakable terms how he is performing in his job.

LONG-TERM EMPLOYEES

Often management by guilt arises out of misdirected concern for employees with long service. This is not to imply that long service should not be recognized and rewarded. However, failure to tell employees about their performance is a poor reward for such service.

Take this example. An accountant in his mid-50's had spent 35 years with his company, the last 15 as controller. He was energetic, loyal and noted among his superiors for running a well-disciplined department, although he rarely originated anything new. In time, as more and well-trained younger people entered the business, problems began to arise. People from other departments complained that the controller intruded into their work. He complained that the company's standards were slipping and was dissatisfied with prospective candidates for his job. He became more indiscreet in his criticism of higher management. When he was finally told straightforwardly about his own behavior, he was shocked. He demanded to know why he had not been told before. Without such information he had believed that his performance was acceptable. In effect, he had been permitted to be irresponsible. The controller was able to improve his performance when told about the effects of his behavior. He could have done so long before.

A superior at any level must supervise; he cannot neglect to do so out of his guilt feelings because the subordinate has been in the organization a long time.

An important function of the organizational structure in any business is to control impulsive behavior; ideally, it also prohibits behavior destructive to the organization. When, as in this case, the superior fails to supervise, he pulls the structural rug from under the subordinate. In the case above, this man became increasingly uncontrolled in an almost desperate bid for controls. The cost over some years: failure to train a successor; little initiative and innovation; impairment of team effort because of friction with others, plus endless hours of conference time about the problem. In this case, the man probably would have been helped considerably by discussion with him about his feelings of being displaced in the organization and by the support of his superiors in adapting to the problems of competition by newer, younger men.

A frequent problem which leads an executive to management by guilt is his anger toward someone to whom he feels obligated. He feels, therefore, quite consciously, that he has no right to be angry with the person who has been so loyal or helpful. He suppresses his disappointment and the anger that goes with it. He tries to find organizational solutions to his problems—new assignments, different tasks. These, however, never overcome his disappointment. Moreover, he continues to feel guilty for his hostility to his faithful subordinates. He cannot express his anger directly, and he does not even dare let on that he is disappointed and angry, and thus he displaces his anger unconsciously. It comes out in subtle, critical ways; for instance, he gives assignments on which the target of his anger is bound to fall.

Here is such an example: A young executive took over the management of a small organization in which he found two long-term middle management employees, Del and Mac. Both turned out to be invaluable to him, as they had been to the previous management for some years. Del particularly served the new executive in an elder statesman role. When it became apparent that the company was not moving ahead as it should, the young executive formulated plans for change, but discussions with Del showed that he neither understood the need for change, nor did he want it. Despite his limitations as a businessman, Del did well as a public representative on behalf of the organization. The executive liked Del, and, despite his disappointment with Del, kept him close in both organizational structure and personal contact. Then he discovered Mac was doing Del's thinking for him. Angrily, he created a new assignment for Del, a combination of make-work and trivial duties. In private conversations the executive started to criticize Del's family, while at the same time protesting his loyalty to Del. This relationship lasted 14 years, during which time Del had many health problems. The executive believed them to be due to tension, but he was unaware that he himself might have helped increase the tension.

No executive can make something of a subordinate other than what he is capable of being, despite whatever feelings of loyalty and obligation he has toward the subordinate.

Del was essentially a public relations man. He could have been, and was, in many ways, highly successful at that job. But the executive felt obligated to make something else of him, something he was not and could not be. When Del failed to meet these unrealistic demands, after being pushed and prodded to greater heights, the executive saw him as an obstructionist. He punished him by putting him "on the shelf" and criticizing his family. At no point in this sequence did the executive speak freely and frankly with Del about his expectations and disappointment. Neither, therefore, could deal directly with a problem which was never defined. As a result, Del lived for years with his boss's thinly veiled hostility and his feelings of failure. He paid a high psychological price, as did the executive, because the latter was guided by his guilt feelings instead of rational judgment.

TOO MUCH KINDNESS

Many people outside of managerial ranks have a picture of management as harsh, autocratic and exploitative. However, management more often is destructive to people by procrastination and overkindness in mistaken efforts to make people better.

This example is a clear demonstration: Allen's supervisors described him as limited in ability. He had a poor personality. He was unable to handle employees in his capacity as office manager. He was unwilling to suggest, adopt or agree to new ideas. His thinking was muddled and his decisions never definitive. So they transferred him as manager to a new smaller office. His new superior saw Allen as a "challenge" and spent 10 years trying to "develop" him. When he tried praise, Allen's reaction was that praise was overdue. When he became tough, Allen decided he would just have to live with his boss's intolerance. When he tried group pressure in staff meetings, Allen changed some of his forms and cut down a little on his paper work. Repeated discussions, the addition of automated equipment—these and other efforts failed. Finally, Allen was given early retirement.

When, after two or three direct discussions of a man's performance, he is unable to change his behavior to meet the requirements of his position, it is a reasonably safe assumption that the man cannot change voluntarily.

This company prided itself on its lenient attitude toward long service employees. In Allen's case, it served merely as a license to attempt to manipulate the man. The price of its lenience can only be imagined. How much rejection and hostility did Allen experience from his subordinates? With how much anger did his subordinates have to live over the years? By what stretch of the imagination could Allen possibly consider his work life successful when all he knew was failure?

The movement of a younger man into a position of authority over older men usually seems to result in conflicting feelings in both parties. The younger man's feelings usually include some sense of guilt that he has vanquished his older competitors. It is hard for him not to feel that he has taken from them an opportunity to move up—and natural for them to agree privately. His pleasure with success is often tempered by an underlying disquiet. His guilt feelings make it difficult for him to make rational decisions, for so much of his decision-making is tinged with his effort to appease the older men—without success. He seems to be chagrined, too, that nobody warned him of these feelings and the problems they produce.

One young president put it this way: "I am many years junior to the other executives in our organization who report to me. Unfortunately the fact of age differences is seldom faced and the difficulties between us are blamed on poor communications. . . . Can some method be devised that recognizes the possibility of this conflict immediately upon the appointment of a younger man to an important managerial position with older subordinates? Might it not be beneficial to have frank discussion with the parties involved about the possibility of such problems developing? Would a committee method of decision-making give some relief to me in my relationship with them?"

The guilt here is most evident in the new president's inability to take charge. He does not see that the older men will continue to fight him until they are certain that he is stronger than they. He is afraid to be stronger. Unconsciously, and therefore, unrealistically, he feels guilty because he has surpassed older men. He would rather turn to a committee, in effect abdicate leadership, in an effort to appease them and his conscience.

Unless the leader in any situation takes charge, and makes it clear that he is in charge, his subordinates are likely to continue to challenge him and to be in conflict with each other.

Probably the most painful situation involving management by guilt takes place when an executive feels that he is being forced to take action which he feels is unfair or unwarranted, such as discharging a subordinate at the request of a superior. Without an adequate basis in his own mind for taking the action, he seizes upon some minor incident which he then magnifies out of proportion. His anger becomes equally exaggerated as he reacts to his own guilt. But when the subordinate mounts his own attack, the superior finds himself even more on the defensive because he cannot cope with both the subordinate's anger and his own guilt feelings simultaneously.

Rusk was the manager of local operations of a large manufacturing company. He was in this position five months when two of the company's more prominent directors visited his location. They had no criticism of his management, but they had plenty to say about his lack of social grace. In their view, therefore, he should not be the local manager. The president, taking his cue from the directors, began to suggest to the vice president who was Rusk's superior, that the vice president should begin looking for a new manager. The pressure mounted from above, but there seemed to be no adequate managerial reason to discharge the man. The vice president kept a constant alert for an obvious managerial failure to serve as a cause for dismissal, or for an obvious demonstration of managerial success to support his contention that Rusk could manage satisfactorily. Unfortunately, Rusk provided an opening for criticism just at this time. His budget proposal was late and unusually high. When the vice president attacked him sharply, Rusk counterattacked by pointing out various ways in which higher management had violated its promises to him and had failed to support him. The vice president knew Rusk's complaints were valid. Higher management did not have confidence in him. He should have told Rusk long before, but his guilt feelings did not permit him to do so.

In such a situation, the executive who must take the action has only one simple fact to communicate to the subordinate, which is valid despite the feelings of the executive and the subordinate.

Whenever any subordinate does not have the support of his management, regardless of why he does not have it, he might just as well find another job because he can move no further in that organization.

These are only a few of the instances in which anger and guilt for anger become significant determinants of executive action. Such behavior occurs when aggressive impulses are stimulated beyond the person's capacity to deal with them more constructively, and the conscience reacts to the rising aggression.

Many times it is difficult to recognize subtle forms of one's own anger or that of others. Often one has fairly evident cues in his own behavior: a feeling of uneasiness and self-criticism after a decision about another person; feeling less comfortable with the other person than before; avoiding the other person; seeing him less, having difficulty conversing with him; criticizing him more to others repeatedly or justifying one's own actions repeatedly; giving him the dirty jobs; or bending backwards to be nice to him, as if he were something special.

As you review problem situations with this idea in mind, you might ask yourself: What were the conditions under which my own or someone else's anger and guilt might have been stimulated? If you recognize that you or someone else is angry, and that you are trying to avoid saying so, then the sooner you can put an end to the game of make-believe, the better for both parties. This does not mean open warfare or a verbal slugging match. Rather, it requires that, recognizing your anger, you control it sufficiently to sit down with the other person and state the problem, together with his feelings about it. Then you have the often difficult task of hearing the other person out.

QUESTIONS TO ASK

What was particularly threatening to the other man? What made him so afraid (often unconsciously) that he had to defend himself in this way? You cannot ask him these questions, nor could he give you adequate answers if he wanted to, but you can sense some of the feelings the subordinate might have had in the situation. Your awareness of such feelings, however vaguely he understands them, will help him gain another perspective.

If the problem has to do with job performance, it is important to reassess whether he can do what is expected of him. Too often people are expected to make drastic changes in their personalities, which is impossible. Is the superior asking too much? What kind of help will the subordinate, with his particular assets and shortcomings, need to get the job done?

In fact, does he belong in this organization? Regardless of whether he has not been able to grow, or should not have been hired in the first place, or he does not fit with the new management, or some other reason—is this really not for him? If the man really does not have a reasonable opportunity to satisfy himself and the organization, then he might be better off in another organization where he can savor success. It is a fairly common experience that many men were boosted along in their careers by being fired, an action which required them to find some more rewarding work.

This is not to be used as a rationalization for wielding the ax of discharge. Irresponsible treatment of human beings is nothing less than sadistic behavior.

A more responsible way of facing this problem is to spell out the pros and cons together and weigh the alternatives. A clear statement of fact as you see it is an important part of your subordinate's reality. You may not be completely right, but you must act on your own judgment, and that in itself is fact for the other person.

If you and the subordinate together decide the subordinate must go, or if you decide it yourself (assuming that the man is not being discharged for cause), then you can give him invaluable help in finding another job. Probably you know companies other than your own and one may well have a place where the subordinate can make a contribution. You do not have to pass him off on someone else. You have only the reasonable responsibility for reporting his abilities and the conditions under which they thrive. If you can also indicate the conditions under which the subordinate does not do well, that will command the respect of the other organization for your honesty and make it more willing to employ the subordinate.

A fundamental guideline in this, as in any other human relations situation, is the question, "What are the equities in this situation?" What is fair to the man and to the organization? Decision by equity is a high sounding phrase. It is not easy to define. It neither punishes the man nor overcompensates him. Punishment is thinly disguised anger. Overcompensation results from not too thinly disguised guilt. Either behavior leaves both parties feeling angry, for when one "bends over backwards" he leaves the other person with the feeling that he does so to make up for a wrong or that he is patronizing the other. In either case, he is managing by guilt.

4

INTUITION VS. RATIONALITY IN ORGANIZATIONAL DIAGNOSIS

HARRY LEVINSON

One of the issues that arises as people become involved in consultation is the formality of the diagnostic process they are going to use. Some organizational consultants who obtain training in individual or family therapy, where there is a heavy emphasis on intuitively sensing the feelings of the client and a corresponding rejection of what is labeled as formalism, disdain formal diagnosis and other forms of conceptualization. To engage in conceptualization, they argue, is to risk missing an important aspect of what is going on. Diagnosis, in short, is significantly whatever the consultant senses.

A number of consultants newly trained in these therapies advocate this position as if it were a new discovery. In this article I offer an opposing view. The debate about these points of view merits the careful consideration of those new to consultation because the position one takes significantly affects the style and outcome of consultation practice.

As a matter, of fact, these issues have been long debated. The argument about intuition vs. conceptualization is especially familiar to those of us who have come out of a psychoanalytic background. More than fifty years ago,

Oberndorf (1930) warned against the use of rigid criteria in diagnostic categories. The practice of psychoanalysis and psychoanalytically oriented psychotherapy involves a hovering attention to the associative processes of the client or patient. Therefore, the use of intuition, or distilled unconscious empathic wisdom, to help "diagnose" what is going on within the client is taken for granted. One always treats the patient and not the diagnosis. One always follows the patient, rather than some preordained classification or schema. Note, however, that the intuitive method applies to an established relationship with a patient or client for the purposes of understanding the client's feelings and thoughts, which in turn presumably would help free that person from irrational anxieties or from certain emotional barriers to more appropriate or more effective behavior. The therapeutic relationship is an established frame of reference, or the constant, for sensing what transpires. Outside of such a relationship, "spot" sensing may well be little more than psychologizing or attributing motives.

Nevertheless, despite this sensitivity to the uniqueness of the individual, therapists of psychoanalytic and other orientations evolve modes of grouping certain kinds of patients or clients and differentiated ways of working with them. The standard method of any given orientation requires variation depending on the defensive structure of the individual, his or her focal problems, the nature of the transference to the therapist, and the degree of motivation for therapy of the patient or client among other factors. Careful diagnostic psychological testing can assess such issues and frequently can help to avoid therapeutic failures.

Before undertaking to do analysis or therapy, one must be certain that one is not dealing with symptoms of physical problems or other kinds of impairments that have to be dealt with before the therapeutic work can be undertaken. If, for example, the person has an addiction, it may be necessary to hospitalize that person before one can work on the underlying depression, which often precipitates or accompanies the addiction. So it is with barbiturate poisoning or brain tumors, or something else that may pass for psychological stunting, inhibition, impotence, or ineffectiveness. This requires a formal diagnostic evaluation. Similarly, in an organization, one must have some understanding of the impact of organizational structure and processes on the problems at hand. How an organization is financed, who its clients or customers are, what the state is of its technical proficiency, all have an influence on its efforts to master its environment. They must therefore be assessed and weighed.

THE NEED FOR DIAGNOSIS

In any helping relationship, including organizational consultation, particularly in the complexity of a psychological relationship and for some of the reasons I have outlined above, one encounters a plethora of data. In addition to objective information and information about the nonpersonal factors mentioned above, these have to do with the feelings of both the consultant and the client, with the feelings of relevant others if there are numbers of people in the client system, and with whatever attitudes, perceptions, and psychological postures the client(s) brings from the past into the present. One can never deal with the "here and now" without also dealing with what one brings from the past—attitudes, feelings, repetitive behavior—into the "here and now." That is what is encompassed under the rubric of "transference," and what constitutes the dominant and continuous themes of anyone's personality. There is no "here and now" independent of the past even though one may not necessarily deal with the past specifically. Indeed, one never really deals with the past, only with people's attitudes and perceptions which may be significantly influenced or distorted by unremembered previous experiences. These may surface in the "here and now" or they may have no relationship to the therapy or consultation at all. One is always dealing with what feelings are being expressed directly or between the lines, and also those that are expressed toward the consultant or therapist.

For example, in my experience, when an executive client is presented with a report that has to do with his or her management, he or she almost invariably experiences that as an indictment no matter how much the client has wanted the consultant's findings. That reaction in my frame of reference is a product of the person's earliest unconscious experience of being "found out" by the parents.

Careful diagnosis integrates the rational and the intuitive. By rational I mean a formally stated method using an explicit theory of personality that is reproducible. Certainly one must always exercise sensitive intuition or one will miss critical data. It is not unusual to sense tension in a classroom or factory merely by walking into the room. Simultaneously, one also must be making order out of a wide range of other complex data.

There is no consulting relationship without diagnosis. One always has a working hypothesis however much one may be unaware of it. Furthermore, one is always making mini-diagnoses. Every time one says something in the role of consultant, one implicitly has made a mini-diagnosis. Every time one takes one action rather than another, or doesn't take such an action, one has made an intervention or exerted influence based on an implicit or explicit decision. Whether one puts those mini-diagnoses and a summary of them down on paper, or whether one keeps his or her judgments in one's head, one is diagnosing and choosing interventions based on those diagnoses.

My argument is that a rational consultation process requires specifying one's assumptions, inferences, and interpretations. It is important to be aware of what assumptions one is making about what is going on, both within oneself and in the other(s), and the reasons why (to whatever extent that is possible) one makes a particular intervention rather than another intervention. Otherwise, there is the danger that diagnoses may be based on one's projecting one's own problems onto the organization, just as happens in therapy, which is why it is helpful to have had one's own psychotherapy or analysis. The fact that one is being intuitive about diagnosis isn't by definition any better than being formally logical about it.

Diagnosis is hypothesis. If one is to go about one's work in a reasonably systematic way, then one has to make one's hypotheses clear to oneself and to test them in ways that allow one to be self-correcting. If one finds one's intuition to be wrong, then one seeks to correct oneself. If one has no system for doing that then one does so only randomly. To do anything randomly when it is possible to do it systematically is not only inefficient, but also is beyond the control of the consultant.

To undertake a formal diagnostic process is also to intervene. During the diagnostic phase, consultants are simultaneously carrying on relationships as a result of which the client system may respond by moving in one direction rather than another. Thus, even during the diagnostic phase of consultation, consultants are always having some effect. The organization, in turn, always has some effect on them. They must be sensitive to the effects of the organization on them and their effect on it. For that reason I ask my students to keep diaries recording their feelings about every contact with the organization and among themselves as a team (Levinson, 1981). They are to understand the impact of the conflicts that go on in the team. They are to try to understand the transference and counter-transference effects. In fact a part of the diagnostic outline calls for them to discuss those particular issues (Levinson, et al, 1972).

For example, an executive repetitively broke appointments with a consulting team. This demoralized the team. They could not pin him down, could not get data to understand him or his perception of his organizational problems, and could not get their work done. They were frustrated and critical of themselves and ready to reject the client. They clashed among themselves about what course of action to take, just as the people in the organization clashed. They debated repetitively the best course of action. They could see how the behavior of the executive demoralized others in the organization. After examining their feelings, they understood the flight of the executive to be a product of his fear of having to engage with others and deal with their anticipated hostility, including that of the team. They concluded they might ease his anxiety when he discovered them to be supportive. But to do that, they had to pin him down to a meeting. They trapped the executive by making an appointment and being unavailable by phone to have it broken. The executive at last expressed his anxieties about his many enemies from whom he had to escape by being a moving target They were then able to help him see his reality more clearly and to support him in taking more constructive steps to cope with it.

THE MEDICAL MODEL ARGUMENT

Frequently, those who object to a formal diagnostic model and even the word "diagnosis" itself reject what they call the medical model. In that model, like a physician, the expert defines the problem and does something he or she decides should be done to the person or organization. They prefer to speak of a "growth" model in which the client or patient makes his or her own decisions based on clarification of facts and feelings.

The issue of medical model versus growth model is a straw man in my opinion. The basic model for formal diagnosis of either individual or organization is an *open system*, equilibrium-maintaining conception derived from biology. That is the concept behind Karl Menninger's diagnostic case study model (Menninger, 1962), and of the extrapolation I have made. Certainly that model is consistent with issues of health and disease, and it is equally consistent with issues of growth and development. Indeed, a part of the model calls for assessing the strengths of either the individual or the organization, and what either can do with respect to its more effective adaptation.

Does a formal diagnostic process leading to a logical intervention mean that there is a "right" or "wrong" intervention? That depends on the criteria for success. Psychology is deterministic. It presumes that behavior does not occur by chance, and that behavior is a product of multiple forces.

Diagnosis therefore ideally leads to the optimum intervention because one intends to define as clearly as possible the constellation of forces which constitute or impinge upon the problems and then to choose the most logically promising mode of resolving or ameliorating those problems, taking into account the nature of the organization, its resources, its limits, the competence and skills of the consultant, and so on. And it is true, as is evident from many therapeutic and OD interventions, that certain interventions are "wrong" because they either make things worse for the individual or the organization, or do not help the people or organization move in the direction that they or it want to go.

Those consultants who lean heavily on intuition and sensing the problems of the organization often speak of themselves as facilitators. They disclaim expertise. It is difficult to see how one can deny the "purchase of expertise." No organization needs or wants a consultant unless it perceives or anticipates a problem. Sometimes the problem is euphemistically called a "felt need" or masked as an "interest." In my experience, there is rarely a felt need or interest unless someone has or anticipates some kind of pain. No one is likely to seek a consultant unless that person holds himself out as expert. All consultants purport to be experts of one kind or another. They offer themselves as having expert skill, and charge for that expertise. The consultant's work is the application of his or her expertise to, for, or with another. To deny that is to evade and deny one's degree of responsibility for the relationship.

THE MECHANISTIC ARGUMENT

The argument that a formal diagnostic method is mechanistic is also in my judgment, a straw man. To gather information and integrate it, to define one's hypotheses and to try to become more aware of them, as well as of one's own internal logic, is not necessarily a rote process. True, diagnosis can easily lend itself to the definition of classes and therefore to undifferentiated interventions. That kind of mechanistic thinking has no place in dealing with human beings. It is also true that one doesn't really know the diagnosis, in the sense of knowing most of the forces that have been at work, until the intervention has been completed. One doesn't know how well his or her hypotheses have worked until he or she has tested them. Outcome is the final test.

To be aware of one's own sensations, feelings, and emotional states is not less useful for diagnosis than a formal method, nor is it necessarily harmful to the diagnostic process. Indeed, to make a psychological assessment without taking them into account is like assuming that the functions of the right and left hemispheres may be considered without relationship to each other. However, taken by themselves as the basis for intervention, they may well lead to actions such as those repetitively exemplified in the psychotherapeutic literature as "wild analysis."

THE IMMERSION CONCEPT

One way to test the relative value of an intuitive versus a rational method and to establish a balance between them is by involvement in an organization. In many forms of organizational consultation, the consultant is a participant-observer. Indeed, an important way to learn about organizations is by participant-observation. It is out of such immersion experiences that one learns to become intuitive and also learns the need for organizing information and experiences. A significant part of my seminar on Organizational Diagnosis is that of immersion (Levinson, 1981). One cannot gather the data that are asked for in my book, *Organizational Diagnosis* (1972), without becoming immersed in the organization as a participant-observer. In my program, graduate students in groups of up to five are placed in an organization for an academic year. They evolve a study plan that includes interviews and observations, history, document study, and other sources of information. They are, in a sense, psychological and sociological anthropologists. They discuss their work in their own team meetings with a psychological or psychiatric consultant and weekly in class. The students make a year-long academic commitment, and a commitment of at least a day a week in the organization.

The major problem with participant-observation is exactly what I noted above: one becomes so overwhelmed with data that it is hard to know which of one's feelings to trust in which situation, and which action should precede which other action. Intuitive responses may sometimes be very effective, as certainly they are with many skilled therapists and consultants, but one can't readily teach intuition nor can one develop from it a logic of consultative relationships. Furthermore, the students must deal with their own anxieties, their own unconscious stirrings, their guilt about their voyeuristic impulses, and their sense of disquiet as they try to master the complexities of their experience. That is difficult to do without a systematic mode of acting in an organization which surfaces those issues.

✻ ✻ ✻

To do justice to discussion of the issue of the intuitive versus the rational in diagnosis, one should look at those arguments, now many decades old, in the psychotherapeutic and psychoanalytic literature. One of the problems with newcomers in any field is that they tend not to be aware of the history behind what they are thinking, writing, saying, and doing. That problem is no different for learning consultation. There is indeed a rich history to most of these issues. The world did not begin with Fritz Perls and Eric Berne.

The derivative orientations ultimately will come around to what the original psychodynamic orientation ultimately had to come around to: that feelings by themselves are not enough, that different problems require different kinds of interventions, and those interventions cannot be undertaken merely on the basis of intuition or one's own unconscious thought processes. It is only after long experience that ways of recognizing these complex differences have been evolved. One cannot pretend that they have no significant meaning.

In sum, everyone who engages a client has a diagnostic system of his or her own, whether he or she wants to admit it. Every consultant needs to know what that system is and the manner in which that system determines the data he or she selects, whether factual or feelings, or some combination, and the manner he or she goes about dealing with them. What happens inside the consultant is as important as what goes on outside the consultant. But a consultant who doesn't specify a diagnostic approach, and the logic of the intervention at least for him or herself, is simply "shooting from the hip" and, as long therapeutic experience demonstrates, often does more harm than good.

REFERENCES

Levinson, H., "Professionalization in consultation: Training issues," CONSULTA-TION, 1982, 1, (2), 38–42.

Levinson, H., Molinari, J., and Spohn, A. G., Organizational diagnosis. Cambridge: Harvard University Press, 1972.

Menninger, K. A., Mayman, M., and Pruyser, P. W., *A manual for psychiatric case study*. New York: Grune and Stratton, 1962.

Oberndorf, C. P., "The psychoanalysis of borderline cases," *New York State Journal of Medicine*, 1930, 30, 648–651.

5

ORGANIZATIONAL CHARACTER

HARRY LEVINSON

Character, referring to the consistency of individual behavior, is also a useful concept for understanding organizations. Its early origins in an organization are reflected in the people chosen successively to manage it. Its ingrained nature is reflected in the behavioral consistency of its managers. Its characteristic modes of adaptation are indicative of its enduring embeddedness in the organization. Both origins and continuity presage difficulties in consultation for organizational change, requiring both confrontation with the realities the organization faces and support to counteract the sense of helpless guilt in individuals aroused by the need to change their established modes of behavior.

On February 13, 1997, the *New York Times* carried an extended article headlined, "Patching the Cracks in the Rock." The subhead was "A Shaken Prudential Tries to Atone as It Expands Beyond Insurance" (Treaster, 1997). The article described how Prudential failed to live up to its character, the picture of it held within the organization and by customers, the financial and insurance communities, and the public at large. The newspaper report said that the corporate behavior was out of character, that the organization was

Reprinted from the *Consulting Psychology Journal: Practice and Research, 49,* 246–255. Copyright 1997 by the Educational Publishing Foundation and the Division of Consulting Psychology.

not behaving in the way that it held out to its multiple constituencies that it was trying to be.

Questions about the character of organizations have proliferated since massive downsizing became the vogue in the business world. Many articles have appeared questioning the fairness and justice of downsizing (Boroughs, 1996). Others discuss the implications of "being lean and mean" (Deutsch, 1997). Still others (Etzioni, 1993) call for efforts to restore a sense of community in an increasingly individually competitive era. Some business leaders themselves are questioning the outcome of laissez-faire capitalism (Sanger, 1997).

But can we speak of organizational character? Individuals have character, but can we say organizations have it as well? Individual Prudential salespeople, inadequately supervised, behaving in response to the corporate compensation policies, manipulated customers by "churning" their policies, meaning advising them to take out new policies that were less favorable than the older ones. The result was that customers were misled and exploited and the corporation itself, because the salespeople were acting in its behalf, was held responsible. Their behaviors, taken collectively, reflected organizational character, according to the article.

Character has been described as that body of skills that emotional intelligence represents (Goleman, 1994). Character in individuals is reflected in characterological behavior. By that I mean that consistent behavior over time by which a person recognizes himself or herself and is recognized by others. That consistency is captured in the phrase that one usually utters upon meeting an old friend one has not seen for a long time, "You haven't changed a bit." Pick up a telephone and listen to an old friend say hello, one needs only to know that person to identify by the one word who he or she is. Characterological behavior therefore refers to specific aspects of behavior that are identifiable by others and also identify us to them.

Individual character evolves out of a genetic temperamental posture and those consistent relationships with others who have power over one over an extended period of time (Kagan, 1994). Infants begin to devise means of managing their parents before they learn to talk. Those patterns of parent management become the characterological patterns for subsequent relationships to other authority figures. We all evolve characteristic modes of adapting to our environments, of managing our basic drives. We also evolve psychological defense or coping mechanisms. Just as an introverted person might be less conspicuous to his fellows and others with whom he comes in contact and be described as "shy," so organizations identify themselves in the same way. Northwestern Mutual Insurance Company, for example, advertises itself as a company that many people have never heard about.

One may speak of characterological behavior in an organization when there is ingrained consistency of behavior in a significant number of the people who work in that organization that causes employees themselves and others to identify organizations as "moribund," "manipulative," "solid," or "reputable." Often those who know many organizations will differentiate among organizations on the basis of that characterological behavior (Kets de Vries & Miller, 1984).

Individual characterological behavior has a heavy moral base or component. Organization characterological behavior occurs when organizations selectively bring together people whose values are consistent with those already established in the organization or create training and other experiences that reinforce the expected and desired behavior of representatives of the organization. Characterological behavior, whether individual or organizational, can become deeply ingrained in people and then it is extremely difficult to change, which is why many large corporations have great difficulty changing to meet the demands of competition. Efforts of organizations to change frequently involve sacrificing aspects of their character. When AT&T reorganized itself and rejected its previously passive stance as a haven for dependent employees, its senior officers repeatedly rejected allusions to the organization as it previously was by saying, "Ma Bell doesn't live here anymore." Prudential similarly is a case in point.

Other companies, seeing competition from other industries, and moving to retain their competitive edge, frequently get themselves into businesses that they know little about and fail. That happened to Prudential when it entered residential insurance and health care, lines outside of its dominant life insurance position. To change the character of an organization without undermining its established values is a long, involved process.

Much of the consultation in organization change fails when the leadership of the organization and the leadership of the consulting activity fail to recognize how deeply held the behavioral positions are in an organization and how resistant, therefore, they are to what has to be done. One can only be amused with reports from consultants who write about their change efforts in major corporations, such as AT&T, Xerox, and others, when those same corporations subsequently flounder, some even fail, inevitably raising the question, "What did the consultants do and with what sophistication?"

One can describe the origins and continuity of organizational behavior in the same terms as one uses to describe individual behavior. But first, one must differentiate temperament from character. In the case of organizations, one can conceptualize temperament as "the nature of the business" behavior, which includes all organizations that are in that industry. For example, one can think of electric power companies and regulated utilities and recognize that they cannot move as quickly as other kinds of organizations that are not regulated. That means that the people in them are less likely to be intensely competitive. For example, Theodore Vail created AT&T as a public utility and structured it hierarchically with detailed job descriptions and quantitative measures of performance (von Auw, 1983). Like all regulated utilities, AT&T could not compete for managerial talent in terms of compensation with nonregulated businesses. It could, and tacitly did, offer long-term employment. Because its customers could complain to regulatory bodies that could penalize the company, it had to choose employees who were conscientiously willing to please the customer. When storms disrupted service, linemen, for example, climbed up poles to restore service, often while the storm was still raging. And, when they came down from the poles, they were the good citizens who served as scoutmasters and solicitors for the United Fund. Managers could not be intensely competitive in an organizational culture that valued compliance to attain slow promotion. Thus, the company recruited and fostered dependent, relatively less aggressive employees. The phrase, "Ma Bell," came to characterize the company as reliable, but slow moving.

By way of contrast, when Julius Rosenwald and General Robert E. Wood structured Sears, Roebuck in 1922, they created three levels of management (Katz, 1987). The span of control was so wide that the level above the store managers could not closely supervise those managers. As a result, store managers could innovate to meet local customer needs and could take initiatives that would not have been possible if they had been more tightly controlled. The behavior of those managers required them to adapt quickly to customer needs which they determined by their interaction with those customers.

When Sears corporate management moved into its skyscraper Sears Tower in Chicago in 1972, the many floors that comprised the world's tallest building also symbolized the increased number of organizational levels that subsequently paralyzed innovation. Subsequently, new leadership and a move to the Chicago suburbs led to regaining market position and profitability. Thus, Sears' character could be said to be more aggressive and adaptive than that of AT&T. Organizational temperament can therefore be described as the characteristic behavioral posture of employees in a given industry.

Characterological behavior may be differentiated from reactive behavior. Reactive behavior is that which occurs under conditions of acute stress and is identifiable by its change at given points in time. Thus, a person who is quietly effective and regarded highly by peers and others may, under stress, become impulsively angry. Seeing such behavior, those who know the person are likely to say that he is not being himself. When that stress passes, then the person returns to his previously characteristic behavior. In companies, one can see such behavior in the form of impulsive downsizing, as contrasted with working out more adaptive mechanisms of competing. The downsizing process in AT&T and in Eastman Kodak are cases in point. These were not the characterological behaviors of those two organizations. Thus, when they downsized, employees experienced that as a violation of the psychological contract (Levinson, Price, Munden, Mandl, & Solley, 1962). Therefore, when undertaking consultation with an organization, consultants should differentiate between characterological behavior and reactive behavior. They should also recognize that they have to get at those firm roots of corporate behavior if they are to establish modifications of characterological behavior.

Conceptually, organizations, like people, have character. They have a consistent and extended way of behaving toward their customers, toward their environments, toward governments, toward their competitors. Many organizations tout their years in business as if to say by their length of service shall you know them. Indeed, both customers and employees do come to know them that way. That knowledge comes to be recognized as their reputation. Fombrun (1996; Jones, 1996) cited a number of traits that characterize companies with strong reputations: an environment that promotes trust; a willingness to empower employees; the ability to inspire pride; the capacity to generate strong earnings; maintaining stability and showing good prospects for growth; the ability to champion quality and put the customer first; and a desire to serve the community, particularly related to environmental concerns.

However, reputation by itself is not necessarily the same as character, for character undergirds reputation, because the behavior of an organization is significantly determined by the requirements of what it does and the kind of industry in which it finds itself. People in advertising, for example, do not have the same reputation for being stolid as people in the steel business, nor is the behavior of those firms the same. The steel manufacturing process is slower, continuous, and in bulk form. The industry is often described as "heavy." In advertising, the process is creative, erratic, hard to predict, and even people involved in advertising agencies change rapidly.

To return to the Prudential example, for years, Prudential held itself out to be as solid as the Rock of Gibraltar. It offered itself to the public as a business that could be trusted and became the nation's largest insurer with almost 50 million customers and nearly $180 billion in assets. There is serious question whether Prudential can regain the dominant position it held in the insurance industry and the respect in which it was held by its peers, as well as its customers and employees.

UNDERSTANDING ORGANIZATIONAL BEHAVIOR

How does one begin to understand organizational behavior, as contrasted with merely describing it? To understand organizational character, one must begin with its history, who structured it, and how the organization evolved. Organization history is never linear. Like individuals, business organizations have their ups and downs. They exist within political bodies and economic systems. They must cope with competition, technical changes, customer preferences, fashions and styles, and catastrophic "acts of God." Most are heavily dependent on other businesses as customers and suppliers of services or products, and many are also dependent on local communities for personnel, tax benefits, and protection against such casualties as fire and crime. In many cases they are affected by government regulations and controls and protected by that same government to maintain a level competitive playing field, as well as providing devices for resolving conflicts.

Consultants must understand its developmental patterns, that is, what happened to the organization in the course of its existence? What problems did it face, what did it do about them, and what were the consequences? For example, electric power companies started out as trolley car lines. They were constructed by "boomers," rough and tough laborers who went from one project to another. However, when those same companies were forced by the federal government to stay within state boundaries, they became heavily dependent on regulatory bodies for their rates and permission to operate. They also frequently had to have local franchises. As a result, they had to recruit people who were highly conscientious and who were willing to serve under adverse weather conditions and who wanted the stability of long-term employment.

When AT&T was threatened by electronic and computer competition, at a time when it was being deregulated by government fiat, it had to turn itself from being predominantly an engineering organization into one that was heavily involved in marketing (von Auw, 1983). It first employed a former IBM executive vice president as a chief marketer, but he could not survive in the more traditional AT&T climate. AT&T's various efforts subsequently to become competitive with those who are at its flanks have been not particularly successful. Although "Ma Bell doesn't live here anymore," many of the executives who were reared in the "Ma Bell" tradition still do. To outside observers, its competitive efforts, therefore, seem to have been scattershot and unfocused. To become more competitive, the company has gone outside to choose a prospective new CEO whose reputation lies heavily on having managed change in another organization.

To be an effective consultant for AT&T at this point in time, or any other company for that matter, one should know not only its historic pattern before radical change occurred, but also what efforts were made in what ways to cope with that change process and with what success (Levinson, Spohn, & Molinari, 1972). From that experience, the consultant, now called on to be helpful, would no doubt have to seek an integrative focus around which the now fragmented organization could once again cohere and help the leadership regain the trust that it has lost through these multiple rapid changes. The consultant would have to understand the heavily dependent, relatively passive managerial corps. He or she would also want to know why, despite the use of myriad consultants, AT&T seems not to have "found itself."

Having developed a sense of how the organization got to be the way it is, what particular kind of help does it now seek? That is, how does its management define its problems and its needs and to what extent is that definition realistic? How does a consultant help the organization understand what its needs are and what will have to be done to meet the contemporary demands of customers, employees, government, and the competition?

The consultant also must understand how the organization is comprised and how it operates. He or she will want to know what kind of information the organization gathers, both from inside itself and from the outside, and how it responds to that information. For example, for many years General Motors did not respond to the competitive positions of Japanese car makers. It assumed wrongly that they would not become a competitive threat. Despite all the information from its own data that reported the lost market share, General Motors persisted in ignoring that information. Once, when a Fortune reporter asked the then CEO of General Motors what was wrong, he replied that he did not know (Loomis, 1993). And he did not. When Ralph Nader criticized the company, instead of responding to the criticism by investigating his complaints and changing what was wrong, General Motors set out to discover what dirt they could find about Ralph Nader. This is commonly known as "killing the messenger."

One can see in these examples the consistency and continuity of organizational character. In the case of Prudential, that character floundered when Prudential executives had to concentrate on health care, real estate, and other matters in which they were less experienced and did not have an organizational template to follow. In addition, changing modes of compensation that undermined the company's collective moral posture resulted in the kind of behavior that led to embarrassment, shame, and government action.

The consultant can readily determine what an organization holds itself out to be in the form of its mission statement and the degree to which that statement is reflected in the behavior of its managers. A mission statement is a formulation of the organization's ego ideal, those distant goals toward which it aspires and never fully reaches, but, being what they are, determine the standards of behavior as the organization seeks to reach those goals. Thus, organizational mission statements are a form of organizational conscience, the fundamental element of which is trust. Trust refers not only to the integrity of the organization in financial terms, but more importantly to the reputation of the organization for the quality of its products or services, the degree to which it stands behind them, and the consistency of behavior within managerial ranks. Furthermore, it includes the recognition and the managerial hierarchy of individual needs that comprise the psychological contract (Levinson et al., 1962) for the organization. That contract includes how dependency within the organization is legitimately mobilized, how people customarily are to attack problems, and how they will be recognized positively by each other. In short, the psychological contract fosters cohesion and, conversely, violation of its terms, however unconscious, fosters disruption. Thus, all organizations, like all individuals, need an enemy (Volkan, 1988). The larger the number of people in an organization involved in any change effort toward a well-defined enemy or problem, the more likely they are to cohere in their attack on that enemy. The greater the identification of managers and employees in the organization with their leadership, the greater the likelihood of cohesive effort.

Probably the most important empirical evidence for the usefulness of a shared value system to the profitability of the organization is the work of Collins and Porras (1994). Comparing two sets of corporations that endured over the same period of years, they determined that those corporations that they described as creative, had profitability nine times that of their noncreative peers and 15 times that of the Standard & Poor average.

The consultant will want to know to what degree the organization perceives its environment and its competitive position accurately. And then, what does it do with that perception? It may ignore what it sees, as with the case of General Motors, or it may anticipate the competitive position of its competitors and the implications of newer discoveries and inventions. It may ignore its past and concentrate on its future or vice versa. It may assume that its core competence is in management and bring together a wide range of disparate activities that in reality simply do not respond to its ability to manage them. The present business climate in which many businesses are concentrating on what they do well and shedding those activities they do less well is illustrative.

The consultant will want to know about the tone and detail of the language in its publications, its bulletins, and its modes of communicating to those inside and those outside the organization. He or she will also want to have a sense of the emotional atmosphere in the organization, the degree to which people are fearful and dispirited, or the degree to which they are enthusiastically mutually supportive.

The consultant will want to know about the client's relationship to its multiple constituencies. How does it relate itself to government and unions? How does it treat its customers?

According to the Treaster article, Prudential was a place where managers received their bonuses whether or not they made their annual goals and where regular hours and uninterrupted weekends were regarded as an entitlement. It was a very comfortable, somewhat stuffy place where the chain of command was richly observed and where the saccharine form of corporate circumlocution known as "Pru polite" often left managers wondering what top executives were trying to say.

The company expanded beyond insurance into about a dozen separate businesses. But instead of operating under a comprehensive strategy, those businesses, as well as the five regional headquarters of the life insurance division, each addressed the world on their own terms. It was not only a matter of little central control. Each of the units had its own computer system, its own purchasing system, and its own advertising program. They did not share information about their customers so that the company could make the most of each relationship. And, all too often, one Prudential unit would be elbowing another for the same piece of business.

Thus, we hear about a company whose executives were unable to exercise appropriate control, in effect managing by abdication. One might describe the character of the company as one of obsequious passivity, at least as far as its leadership went. As in families where parents do not exercise appropriate controls, and the children follow their own impulses, at Prudential, the insurance salespeople simply followed their own selfish interests. For misleading clients, the company paid $1.5 million in fines, compensation, and legal costs. Besides, all of the businesses that Prudential thoroughly dominated only a few years ago are still losing ground to competitors. Prudential's standing with the insurance rating agencies has been slipping too.

From this example we can readily infer that the character of a company needs continuous reinforcement and controls. Its leadership must not only stand for a value system, but must be actively involved in guiding, directing, and supporting the behavior that enables the company to live up to the character it professes.

ORGANIZATIONAL DIAGNOSIS

Suppose a consultant had been called in to help Prudential recover, what would he or she do? Obviously, the consultant would find the same data as described in the newspaper story and would point out the need for more active direction and control. But apparently merely pointing that out would not help much because if the top management group could behave differently, it would.

A good consultant would have recognized the futile behavior of the top management group and its attitude and would have recommended new leadership be brought in from the outside. He or she would not have expected to be able to turn turkeys, those who characterologically were passive and dependent, into tigers, those who would attack the problems aggressively. And then he or she would have recommended that the company confront the realities of its malfeasance, malfunctioning, and declining position. However, recognizing the helplessness of the top management to deal with the problems that presumably they could not confront, the consultant would then have to describe the behavior required in their respective roles to rescue the company. The consultant's description of what had to be done would make it immediately apparent to much of the leadership that this kind of behavior was not something that they were comfortable with. As a result, they would have to give up their positions and yield the leadership to somebody who could undertake that activity.

So the first step in dealing with character problems in an organization is to confront people with the realities of the data. Ideally, if there is time and no crisis, such as the death of the leader or prospective bankruptcy, that information should be gathered by people in the company as a task force under the guidance of the consultant. People have great reluctance to accept information from somebody else and do much better both gathering and presenting that information to their own colleagues than from the staff of an external consultant.

The board went to the outside and hired an executive who could and did take charge. He consolidated the subsidiaries; 12 of the 14 executives who report directly to him are new to their jobs; of the top 150 executives, two thirds are new. About half were recruited from the outside. The others were long-time Prudential employees who passed the test of the new mission. He has cut deeply into the ranks of the company's notoriously unproductive insurance agents.

Once those data have been gathered and organized, the next task, of course, is to present the information to the CEO. Here it is important for those who gathered the information to present it. Some years ago, when I was consulting with the U.S. State Department (1970) and set up a series of task forces to gather information, the chairman of the task forces wanted me to report their findings. I declined and insisted that they do so. They knew the information firsthand, they were trusted by those whom they had questioned, and they were not regarded as being manipulated by the consultant. The information was both valid and trustworthy.

The next step is to provide an opportunity for the data to be discussed by the members of the organization. Those who are involved in the discussion will hinge on what the consulting arrangement is. In some cases, it will be only the top management group or in others selected managers; in some cases, ideally, if the company is not too large to make that functional, by everybody in the company. Ideally, out of such discussions a set of recommendations will arise, together with a timetable for their implementation. This set of recommendations will say something about expected leadership behavior, and the leader or leaders at this point may have to decide whether they are the people who can carry this set of recommendations through or whether there needs to be outside leadership. In those instances where the consultant is engaged to make a diagnosis and make the recommendations directly, he may well have to help the top management decide whether it should be in place or yield to somebody else.

Under some extreme circumstances, the consultant may have to make that kind of recommendation to a board committee. The recommendations may involve restructuring part of the organization, changing not only accountabilities, but compensation as well, and may call for considerable training and retraining of people in the company. For example, when Reginald Jones was CEO of General Electric, he called on The McKinsey Company to prepare a summary of the state of the art in electronics (Levinson & Rosenthal, 1984). The 15-volume report was then circulated to the technical staff of General Electric indicating therefore what they needed to do to shift their orientation from the electromechanical to the electronic, and training programs were offered to help them do so.

When such changes are brought about, or even recommended before they are brought about, that introduces a sense of loss, perhaps of power or prestige, technical dominance, and other issues. That loss, like any other loss, has to be mourned. The engagement of people on task forces or committees or other change efforts enables them to cope with the sense of loss because they are simultaneously engaged in detaching themselves from what is and engaged in developing mastery of the problems that they are going to have to deal with. When the consultant or team confronts the organization with their findings, when people in the organization are brought face to face with the realities that require change, opportunity for mourning must be provided for organizational members so that by discharging their rage at what has happened to them and at the sense of loss, they then are free to turn their anger into more productive avenues for solving their problems. Otherwise, the depression, the sense of loss and anger about it, becomes a drag on the adaptive efforts of the organization.

Although this outline of appropriate steps is a general one, it should apply to those cases in which there are specific problems as well. By specific problems I mean certain kinds of character patterns in organizations like hyper-aggressiveness, severe narcissism, exacerbated dependency, or even psychopathic manipulation (Levinson, 1994). In some cases, change will call for drastic reorientation of the management group. For example, in a heavy industry such as General Motors, when it becomes necessary to develop teams and for managers to coach those who report to them, if the preponderance of technically oriented managers feel incompetent to do so, that means large numbers of them will have to be trained or retrained. That is currently a problem faced by the U.S. Army as it undertakes peace-keeping responsibilities by many municipal police departments that have refocused their efforts on community policing.

A consultant must understand that there are limits to characterological change. Some people may never be able to change. In some cases, the leadership of the organization is in that kind of posture. At Prudential, the old leadership had to retire. If there is a reasonable possibility of change, the consultant usually then will have to work in a one-to-one relationship to help that particular person or those particular people to examine their own behavior and to be coached into behavioral styles that may enable them to do so more comfortably. In some cases, usually those that require more clinical sophistication and greater time commitment, those executives and managers might be referred to therapeutic help. Even if the consultant is clinically trained, he or she should not undertake therapy while simultaneously consulting on organizational problems. To do so contaminates the two functions and exacerbates transference problems, meaning unconscious attitudes toward the consultant.

The need to change behavioral styles is a particular problem in large financial organizations, high-tech organizations, and heavy industries where the preoccupation of the managers is largely to make as much money as possible or to attain technical perfection or to work at technical processes like mining or drilling for oil. A significant problem, particularly for chief executives, is whether their level of conceptual capacity is sufficient to cope with the problems they face (Jaques & Cason, 1994). That issue also may be valid further down in the organization, but judgment will have to be made about the top. Often people, aware of their limits, feeling incompetent to cope with the new behavioral demands required by their particular role, will be able to speak about their sense of inadequacy and the wish to leave that particular role. At this point, the consultant will have to help them deal with their sense of loss and their need to put themselves in another role.

In the case of individual coaching, the consultant may have to help people look at their fear of losing control if they behave differently and their fear of their inability to operate in a different manner. The consultant, as a coach, may make use of individual incidents asking the question, "How do you think the other person felt when you said or did that?" Or, "What kind of behavior followed?" By attuning a given executive to the impact of his or her own behavior and examining with him or her the cost of that behavior, and supporting the executive's self-image in the process, the consultant can help give an executive greater confidence about the changes in his or her behavior that may lead to a different climate in the organization.

Before initiating a continuing relationship with a client organization or even with a single client, it behooves the consultant to develop a prognosis for his or her activity, that is, how much can he or she reasonably expect to have happen in the organization or in the individual over what period of time. It becomes important to establish a prognosis because, failing to do so, the consultant is likely to experience a continuous sense of defeat because he or she hasn't achieved the results that, in fantasy, he or she wanted to achieve.

CONCLUSION

Organizational character refers to the more enduring characteristics of the behavior of the employees at an organization by which they are identified to others and to themselves. Character is reflected in the reputation an organization achieves and the degree to which it seeks to sustain that reputation. Usually it is a product of the value system of the founder or whoever followed the founder. McDonald's and Sears, Roebuck are two examples of organizations that were developed by successors of the founders. Character also is reflected in the ingrained behavior of people in the organization. Because it is so deeply ingrained and therefore embedded in the psychological contract of the organization, changing organizational character is never easy. It can be brought about more successfully if the consultant understands its origins, confronts the organization with the realities of its presence, and helps people in the organization both mourn their loss and acquire new competencies to enable them to attack the problems they face.

REFERENCES

Boroughs, D. L. (1996, March 20). The bottom line on ethics. *U.S. News and World Report*, pp. 61–66.

Collins, J. C., & Porras, J. I. (1994). *Built to last*. New York: Harper Business.

Deutsch, C. H. (1997, May 27). Cooling down the heated talk. *The New York Times*, p. D1.

Etzioni, A. (1993). *The spirit of community*. New York: Crown.

Fombrun, C. J. (1996). *Reputation: Realizing value from the corporate image*. Boston: Harvard Business School Press.

Goleman, D. (1994). *Emotional intelligence*. New York: Bantam.

Jaques, E., & Cason, K. (1994). *Human capability*. Arlington, VA: Cason Hall.

Jones, O. (1996). Human resources, scientists and internal reputation: The role of climate and job satisfaction. *Human Relations, 49,* 269–293.

Kagan, J. (1994). *Galen's prophesy: Temperament in human nature*. New York: Basic Books.

Katz, D. R. (1987). *The big store*. New York: Viking.

Kets de Vries, M. F. R., & Miller, D. (1984). *The neurotic organization*. San Francisco: Jossey- Bass.

Levinson, H. (1994). Why the Behemoths fell. *American Psychologist, 49,* 428–436.

Levinson, H., Price, C. R., Munden, K. J., Mandl, H. J., & Solley, C. H. (1962). *Men, management and mental health*. Cambridge, MA: Harvard University Press.

Levinson, H., & Rosenthal, S. (1984). *CEO: Corporate leadership in action*. New York: Basic Books.

Levinson, H., Spohn, A. G., & Molinari, J. (1972). *Organizational diagnosis*. Cambridge, MA: Harvard University Press.

Loomis, C. J. (1993, May 3). Dinosaurs. *Fortune,* p. 39.

Sanger, D. E. (1997, April 6). Look at who's carping most about capitalism. *The New York Times,* p. D1.

Treaster, J. B. (1997, February 13). Patching the cracks in the rock. *The New York Times,* p. D1.

U.S. Department of State. (1970). *Diplomacy in the seventies* (Department of State Publication 8551, Department and Foreign Series 143). Washington, DC: U.S. Government Printing Office.

Volkan, V. (1988). *The need to have enemies and allies*. Northvale, NJ: Jason Aronson.

von Auw, A. (1983). *Heritage and destiny*. New York: Praeger.

6

WHY THE BEHEMOTHS FELL: PSYCHOLOGICAL ROOTS OF CORPORATE FAILURE

HARRY LEVINSON

The failure of many American corporations to adapt to changed economic circumstances has become a major social concern. Many reasons have been alleged for those catastrophes. These allegations describe the ostensible reasons, but they do not explain adequately. The explanations are fundamentally psychological, significantly having to do with individual and organizational narcissism, unconscious recapitulation of family dynamics in the organization, exacerbating dependency, psychologically illogical organization structure and compensation schemes, inadequate management of change, and inability to recognize and manage cognitive complexity. To deal more effectively with such problems calls for greater psychological sophistication among boards of directors and senior executives.

Articles based on APA award addresses that appear in the *American Psychologist* are scholarly articles by distinguished contributors to the field. As such, they are given special consideration in the *American Psychologist's* editorial selection process. This article was originally presented as part of a Distinguished Professional Contributions to Knowledge award address at the 101st Annual Convention of the American Psychological Association in Toronto, Ontario, Canada, in August 1993. Reprinted from the *American Psychologist, 49,* 428–436. Copyright 1994 by the American Psychological Association.

For the past several years, major headlines in the business media have revolved around the problems that large and previously highly successful organizations have in adapting to changing economic circumstances. Media discussion of prominent executive officers and the continued speculation in the business press about the possible departure of others attribute those respective companies' inability to master their difficulties significantly to the management style of their chief executives.

There is also much discussion of stumbling giants and their difficulties with rigid corporate cultures and cumbersome hierarchies, such as that of Mercedes-Benz (C. Miller & Aeppel, 1993). As far back as 1986, the business headlines said that IBM trailed Digital Equipment Corporation in getting its computers to talk to each other (Kneale, 1986). Later, IBM top management told some employees to move, retire, or quit (Carroll, 1991). The fact of those five years is indicative of how long it took that organization to change as drastically as it had to. Indeed, that change process is not yet complete.

In the case of General Motors (GM), the inability of top management to grasp early on the importance of Japanese competition, the consumer demand for better quality, and the shift of consumer interest to safety and economy are given as "reasons" for the GM problem. IBM has been criticized for its rigid attachment to mainframe computers and for its emphasis on sales and financial matters, rather than on frontier technology. The latter criticism also was made of General Motors (Byrne et al., 1991). Perhaps that criticism is an oversimplification, but it certainly appears that IBM's problems are related significantly to the denial of its own data, just as General Motors for years denied the reality of the increasing success of its Japanese competitors.

These and similar allegations describe some of the problems those companies faced, but they do not explain why their managements were unable to sense, even from their own data, their growing competitive disadvantage in the marketplace and to conceive of the changes they therefore had to make. Critics alluded also to the reluctance of those chief executives to disrupt the corporate cultures (Loomis, 1993a). But they did not seem to understand why, in the face of extended painful losses, those executives were unable to do so. A *Fortune* reporter asked Roger Smith, chairman of General Motors from 1981 to 1990, what went wrong. He replied, "I don't know. It's a mysterious thing" (Loomis, 1993b, p. 41). The answer to such problems, according to the news stories, is to bring in new chief executives from the outside, as several of the troubled companies did (Hayes, 1993). Indeed, that may be a wise course under some circumstances, but the problems of Paul D. Kazarian, ousted as CEO of Sunbeam-Oster Company, and those of Harvey Golub, whose alleged impulsive abrasiveness has been reported to be disruptive to some at American Express Company (Lipin, 1993), suggest that that course has its own consequences. That unidimensional response, therefore, carries with it the risk that the new leader may well stumble on the same issues that became problems for his or her predecessor. Chief among these are subtle psychological assumptions of which many business leaders apparently are unaware.

Although many symptoms have been described in the business media, few underlying answers have been provided. Description is not explanation. Without adequate diagnosis, it is difficult to arrive at appropriate solutions. There is a need for greater depth of understanding of how and why such problems as these arise and for more careful thought about what to do about them.

PSYCHOLOGICAL FUNDAMENTALS

There are several psychological verities about organizations:

1. All organizations recapitulate the family structure and the behavioral practices of the culture in which they are embedded.
2. All animals and human beings differentiate themselves into in-groups and out-groups and develop what might be called an in-group narcissism, the "we–they" phenomenon.
3. All organizations, by definition, being made up of people, are living organisms. They have developmental histories and evolve adaptive patterns that deal with different levels of complexity.
4. All living organisms experience continuous change, both within themselves and in their environments. All animals and humans that have the capacity to attach themselves to others experience most change, however advantageous, also as loss. All loss has to be mourned if the resulting depressive feelings are not to retard adaptive effort.
5. All groups follow a leader. Different groups at different times in their life experience require different styles of leadership, but the founding leader's policies, practices, and organizational structure frequently endure.

How do these verities relate to what happened to the behemoths?

From the outside, without firsthand knowledge of these companies, several important psychological factors are sufficiently self-evident from public information to be considered fundamental among the causes of their inability to adapt effectively. Among them are these:

1. General Motors and IBM and most of the other prominent troubled companies have been significantly "family organizations."

2. All promoted exclusively or disproportionately from within.
3. All became significantly narcissistic.
4. There is little evidence, from a plethora of business media, articles, and books describing them, about the degree to which the failed chief executives had the conceptual capacity to cope with the increasingly complex level of information that the top management of a contemporary major corporation must comprehend.
5. That same flood of information reflects the fact that all of the chief executives were unable to take psychological factors seriously into account in viewing, understanding, and acting on their organizations' problems.

Fundamentally, that is why they stumbled.

The Organization as a Family

Historically, businesses have begun as family affairs. Most still are. Some grew to become giants. As these family businesses became large corporations whose business presumably was strictly business, their founders and leaders nevertheless recognized that their executives, managers, and employees were human beings. Therefore, psychologically they continued to emphasize their internal relationships as constituting "one big family." Sometimes paternalistic leadership went out of its way to foster the family relationship, maximizing dependency. In earlier years, IBM even went so far as to establish country clubs for its employees. Such companies also often went to considerable lengths to be helpful to members of the organization family, and some, like Kodak, to their host community as well. Concomitantly, there was a heavy emphasis on loyalty to the corporation. Historically, dominant executives, like Thomas J. Watson, Sr., and Thomas J. Watson, Jr., were viewed as benevolent patriarchal figures. In General Motors, William C. Durant and Alfred Sloan, Jr., were the patriarchal figures who handed down the general design of the organization and its tradition, as was George Eastman at Kodak.

Similar figures in all organizations are revered, their contributions are lauded, and their history in the organization is widely known. However, not one of their successors stands out in the public mind as an innovative leader. Psychologically speaking, they are dwarfed by the shadows of the "greats."

Patriarchal leaders frequently can take unilateral action, despite the doubts (and in crises, the opposition) of members of their boards, their subordinates, or their critics. Psychologically, by definition, they are the respected fathers. To foster loyalty, they generate an atmosphere of "We are the best (family)" by promoting only from within. The successors of the patriarchal leaders, however, grow up in an organization with many peers. When they become managers, they are socialized to carry out the organization's familial obligations to their subordinates and peers. They arrive into their chief executive roles not as dominant paternal figures but as the first among equals. They are psychologically more in fraternal roles.

Guilt

It is extremely difficult for fraternal chief executives to take what they perceive to be hostile action against their organizational siblings. Kay R. Whitmore, former CEO of Eastman Kodak, specifically could not do so (Cowan, 1993). Therefore, they find it difficult to make demands on or discipline those who report to them.

The conscious guilt any manager of conscience has about terminating someone else without cause is compounded by the unconscious guilt that arises from the sense that he or she is destroying the other. Guilt becomes a very powerful inhibitor, particularly when it has unconscious overtones of fratricide. As the news stories indicate, the failed executives were inhibited by the prospective bloodletting that they had to undertake, and they were reluctant to destroy the very people who grew up managerially with them. To compound the matter, many senior managers in such organizations live in geographical proximity to each other.

Moreover, fraternal chief executives have neither the power of their charismatic predecessors nor the internal support of those against whose interests they may have to act. Usually, their boards of directors were chosen by their predecessors. The board members are not "theirs." At IBM, for example, John Akers's board included three of his predecessors.

Bonding

Until very recent years, business organizations were exclusively masculine in their management and leadership. Although they are less so now, there continues to be a strong male orientation as reflected in the many military and athletic metaphors used in organizational discourse. When men particularly are engaged in combat against other men, as is the case in almost all business organizations, that intensifies bonding, the "we against them" position, and the attachment to each other. The homoerotic orientation that is so vividly evident as hockey and soccer players embrace each other is demonstrated less in the business world but nonetheless is evident. It is reinforced in various kinds of off-site meetings, ranging from Outward Bound activities to forms of hazing.

Spokespersons for the women's movement have been quick to pick up the obvious differences between men and women in both their individual and organizational behavior (Henry, 1983). The male orientation is described as penetration and thrust versus the female orientation of enveloping and surrounding. The whole psychology of management is that of aggressive attack and dominance, sexual in its imagery: "screw or be screwed," to be on top or on the bottom—helpless, dependent, and victimized. This masculine sexual orientation has not only made it difficult for women to move into higher management but also has led to masculine fears of becoming femininized, making management less aggressive and therefore less competitive. The theory is that management cannot be soft but must be hard and practical, as if to be sensitive to psychological factors was, by definition, to be vulnerable.

Self-Image

The winners in this socioeconomic combat become dominant players in society. Their leadership is sought for the boards of nonprofit organizations. It is they who are asked to make major grants and donations to charitable organizations. It is they whom leading political figures seek out for advice and support. Their competitive achievement is reflected in their publicly reported scores, akin to those of athletic teams: quarterly earnings, profit improvement, stock price, executive perks, and similar indices of outstanding success.

The importance of sustaining the self-image of success is reflected in annual reports. There, when profits are down, it is almost invariably attributed to the economic environment. When they are up, that, of course, is the product of good leadership and management. Fortunately, few American leaders who fail commit suicide, as is more frequently the case in Japan. Nevertheless, one of the products of that pursuit is the concomitant fear of failure, as verbalized by John F. Welch, CEO of General Electric Company (Tichy & Sherman, 1993).

Attachment

As we age, we also become specialized and habituated. We seem to learn more and more about less and less. We become comfortable with theories, logic, and experiences that have enabled us to become proficient. We become expert in the use of certain techniques, tools, and mechanisms. If we become truly skilled in a major facet of our self-perceptions, we become our occupational roles: "I am a cardiologist"; "I am a carpenter." Part of the esteem in which others hold us is derived from our public occupational personae. That same narrowing identification with occupational role also leads us to extreme positions, both as individuals and organizations (D. Miller, 1990). In a sense, we become stark caricatures of ourselves, behaving in a manner that might be pictured by some sharply perceptive cartoonist as the underlying remnant of who we are. Thus, Digital Equipment Corporation, originally an organization of engineering craftsmen under Kenneth Olsen, became an organization of tinkerers.

A company can be tied not only to old attachments, technology, and ways of doing business but also often may be caught up in the imagery of its history and still be fighting the battles of the past. When the chief executive of a large petroleum company with which I was consulting sought to reorganize it to adapt to multiple marketplaces, the response of his vice presidents was, "This is no way to run an oil company." They were still living in pre-OPEC days. IBM's problems are said to have arisen significantly because of top management's attachment to mainframes, as earlier it was wedded to punch cards and vacuum tubes. Of course, it is difficult to detach one's organization from its most profitable product, as was the case with GM and big cars and IBM and its mainframes. But it is a widely appreciated axiom that the peak of success is the time to be thinking of change.

The attachment to one's professional skill and orientation and to its translation into a given set of products, into an organizational value system, into identifiable products, into a certain kind of relationship with one's customers—all these attachments become psychological anchors whose pull inhibits adaptive change. A major leadership task is to free people from their attachment to their established practices and favored products and to wrench them from modes of work and organizational structures that have become an intrinsic part of themselves.

STRUCTURE

Organization structure is a derivative of the orientation of the founder. When Theodore Vail organized AT&T, he adopted an engineering model that emphasized hierarchy and control. Whether businesses were organized by product line or function or geography, they were formed into hierarchies labeled "towers" in the petroleum business and "chimneys" in the automobile business. These structures made it difficult to cooperate across such divisions of control and led to efforts to protect function and role. When Julius Rosenwald structured Sears, Roebuck, he deliberately set up only three levels of hierarchy, to maximize the flexibility of the store managers. Ultimately that was lost, as reflected in Sears Tower, the world's tallest building, where hierarchical power increased by floor level.

People become attached to a given structure because it allocates authority to them and becomes an arena within which their roles are defined and in which they function and because it is assumed that that is the way to do business. The customary mode of distributing power and authority defined organizational turfs that became arenas for the political maneuvers that accompanied them. Psychologically speaking, structure also becomes a defense against anxiety (Hirschhorn, 1988).

While much of the business world moved to smaller, more flexible units, the behemoths did not. The Gap, with its rapid ability to replace merchandise from overseas manufacturers, quickly outflanked Sears. Japanese methods of producing new cars by using teams undercut American manufacturers' assembly lines (Kantrow, 1984).

DEPENDENCE

The combination of paternalistic leadership, attachment to established structure and role, and the use of organizational structure as a defense against anxiety makes for a certain clinging, as it were. Large business organizations, as noted earlier, historically encouraged people to be dependent on them. Even though business organizations no longer can deliver on such promises, many still cling to them in an effort to meet their dependency needs.

Although all of us have dependency needs and we seek to gratify them in different kinds of relationships, when they are heavily gratified in an organization, people are less likely to buck the system or to advocate new ideas. Conformity is the first rule of survival. Efforts to exhort highly dependent people to assume competitive postures are usually exercises in futility. As the British historian Trevor-Roper once put it, "That's like asking a jellyfish to stand on its hind legs and grit its teeth."

INDICTMENT

Conscientious people, by definition, are driven by severe consciences. These are reflected in the standards that chief executives set, in the ego ideals to which those people aspire, and in their efforts, as indicated above, to avoid catastrophes on their watches. Demanding consciences reflect harsh self-criticism. Like the rest of us, business leaders seek to avoid it. Modes of avoidance include attributing blame to others, as management has done historically with respect to labor and government, denying threats that increased the sense of helplessness and inadequacy, and attenuating the potential criticism of others, both inside and outside the organization.

A special problem of any chief executive is that whenever he or she changes something that his or her predecessor established or supported, the very fact of making such a change becomes an indictment of the predecessor. It is as if to say the predecessor was wrong or the incumbent would not now have to be making certain changes. That problem becomes especially acute if predecessors continue to be on the board of directors. In the case of IBM, John F. Akers had to live with the history and actions of three previous predecessors, all of whom were on his board of directors, in addition to those of the Watsons, Sr. and Jr.

CEOs, like others, want to be held in esteem and regard by their peers. Few want to take major risks that might embarrass them among their peers.

The dissenting leader, he or she who structures the organization in ways that are atypical, therefore is in a difficult position. As a result, short of crisis, few undertake drastic innovative action, even when the need for that kind of action has been apparent for a long time. Few chief executives of major corporations have implemented some of the concepts of the Herman Miller Company (DePree, 1989), or those of W. L. Gore and Associates (Shipper & Manz, 1992), or Semco in Brazil (Semler, 1993), or CRA in Australia (Jaques & Clement, 1991). That reluctance is one of the major reasons that significant managerial innovation tends to occur in small companies first.

Furthermore, chief executives of major corporations are usually not as imaginatively creative as those of smaller organizations (Moretti, Morken, & Borkowski, 1991). Senior executives of major corporations tend to demonstrate a better balance in their breadth of managerial executive skills and excel in interpersonal skills, development of teamwork and employee potential, and leadership experience and financial responsibility. However, they do not confront the same adaptive problems as do chief executives in smaller organizations who characteristically are themselves in the front lines of their organizational progress. Chief executives of large organizations, therefore, must go to greater lengths to stimulate and ensure creativity and continuity in their organizations. Some are trying to do this by breaking down their larger organizations into relatively independent units whose chief executives must act more like entrepreneurs.

ORGANIZATIONAL NARCISSISM

The combination of collective masculine competitive striving, attachment to aggressive self-images and established corporate structures, and efforts to avoid failure and indictment reinforce organizational narcissism. Overvaluing themselves, and deluded by the self-satisfied thinking that usually follows, some CEOs develop condescending contempt for competitors and critics. Denial is the handmaiden of narcissism. When information from the outside is ignored or rejected, those on the inside can neither see nor hear what their environments are telling them. As a result, they lose their ability to compete. That kind of corporate narcissism on the part of General Motors led it to discount the Japanese automakers; in the computer industry, it led IBM to ignore the shift in emphasis from hardware to software. Executives and managers caught up in corporate narcissism cannot hear from their own people, let alone those from the outside. No wonder Roger Smith did not understand what was happening to GM. The sense in an organization that "we are the best" negates the wish to become the best. A corporation no longer needs to strive for that which has been attained.

Thomas J. Watson, Jr., spoke of analyzing customer reports exhaustively, particularly those having to do with customers who were threatening to buy somebody else's products or who were not satisfied with IBM. One can only wonder what happened to such analyses in IBM. Furthermore, if a company is limited to analyzing customer reports, then it does not hear about those who are not customers and who are unlikely to become customers because they are already someone else's customers.

IBM's stock became the dominant holding of many mutual funds, and its service put it competitively ahead of many other computer manufacturing organizations. Customers could depend on IBM. That reputation at the same time muffled the criticism that IBM products were not as good technically as some others and that IBM did not innovate as well as others.

EXECUTIVE NARCISSISM

Narcissism or self-love is essential for self-respect and self-confidence. However, when it becomes inflated or less subject to social controls, it becomes potentially destructive. The more successful one becomes, the higher one's occupational self-esteem. The higher one rises in an organization, the more self-confidence one is likely to develop about one's proficiency in one's roles. Concomitantly, the higher one rises, the less supervision one is likely to have. The combination of these factors frequently gives rise to narcissistic inflation that becomes overconfidence and a sense of entitlement. That, in turn, leads to denial of those realities that threaten the inflated self-image and to contempt for other individuals and organizations. It also leads to less tolerance for deviations from the already successful model.

The personal dominance orientation means that the powerful need not attend much to those with less power because there is less need for the powerful to regard their subordinates (Fiske, 1993). The narcissism of the chief executives often sets a similar tone for the corporation as a whole.

"I never thought that because you were the head of a business you were some kind of a damn king. I've been in a lot of people's airplanes that were fixed up like palaces inside and for what? What right does anybody have to do that?" (Levinson & Rosenthal, 1984). Watson, Jr., was wary about anything that might smack of haughtiness. He did not see how the successful organization that he had built might, in its own way, become haughty.

Another form of chief executive narcissism is the kind of behavior that assures that all significant decisions eventually will rise to the CEO's level. Often that is done by creating an organization structure that makes it difficult, if not impossible, to hold any single manager accountable. Such a structure fails to provide sufficient authority for individual managers to carry out what they must if the organization is to adapt. In the business organizations that have had the greatest difficulties, the leaders have tended to be aristocratic (Miroff, 1993), reinforcing organizational narcissism when it has become increasingly necessary for them to be more democratic. The difference between George Bush and Bill Clinton, the former adopting a posture of distance and insensitivity and the other opening himself to hearing from all sides, typifies what is happening psychologically and sociologically in the relationship between followers and their leaders in all organizations.

That top-down behavior was reflected in John F. Akers's criticizing his own sales force for not being aggressive enough (Carroll, 1991). He failed to understand that the style of behavior in an organization descends from the top and that when errant behavior arises, one has to examine how and to what extent it is a product of that top management style. Whipping people into shape is not a concept of motivation that is conducive to enthusiastic effort.

STRUCTURE AND COMPENSATION

The underlying reward–punishment philosophy, together with the psychologically inadequate structure of almost all organizations, fosters continuous political machination as people try to maximize their individual gains and vie for political position. Where there is powerful downward pressure for individual achievement, that exacerbates internal competition and political machination, often at significant personal cost to the individuals in the organization, and simultaneously makes it difficult to evolve cooperative effort among them. With the exception of the Saturn development in General Motors and the original personal computer effort in IBM, there is little in the managerial literature that holds up those prominent organizations as exemplars of group effort.

Heavy emphasis on reward–punishment psychology, although often having short-term advantages, militates over the long term against identification and cohesion, and indeed against potentially creative dissension that would foster adaptation. I have called the assumptions underlying that conception of motivation "The Great Jackass Fallacy" (Levinson, 1973).

Most organizational structure is without a psychological logic. In some organizations, there are 32 levels. Many organizations are attempting to condense these levels but without any inherent rationale for doing so. In fact, in some, there is the naive thesis that hierarchy should be abolished. There is no way of abolishing hierarchy as long as business organizations must have accountability (Jaques, 1990). Some people necessarily must have greater power and authority than others.

There is a conceptually logical theory based on the work of Elliott Jaques (1989) that allows organization structure to evolve out of the established conceptual capacities of people, ranging from the most simple and concrete modes of making judgments to the most complex. Business organizations that evolve a structure based on levels of conceptual capacity or the ability to handle complexity develop an accountability hierarchy in which each successive level of managerial responsibility is conceptually able to handle greater complexity of information than those below it. Thus, each higher level person adds value to the work of those below him or her.

MANAGING CHANGE

Because almost all change involves an experience of loss, that loss precipitates feelings of depression, and those feelings, as indicated earlier, then become an anchor that constitutes a drag on organizational innovation. The implication is that all organizations must have ways of enabling people to mourn—to detach themselves from their previous attachments to technical orientation, traditional ways of doing business, and obsolete historical encumbrances. To do that, they must enable people to confront the realities that they are up against and to systematically manage the change process.

Few organizations do that. There is no indication in the contemporary managerial literature of major organizations undertaking such efforts before downsizing, or even after having downsized, to sustain the morale and spirit of those who remain. As a consequence, once downsizing occurs, those who remain inevitably are worried about when the same will happen to them and devote a considerable amount of energy to self-defense and feelings of anxiety. It is no surprise that several reports have concluded that downsizing has not led to greater productivity, even though it may have contributed in some cases to lower costs because organizations are not paying for the people who have been terminated (Fuchsberg, 1992; Noer, 1993).

CAPACITY TO MANAGE COMPLEXITY

A major issue that is getting practically no attention in the management literature is the reality that in many cases the chief executive officer does not have the conceptual capacity to grasp the degree of complexity that he or she must now confront. In short, they simply do not know what they are really up against and what is happening to them and to their organizations, let alone knowing what to do about it. They simply cannot absorb the range of information they should and organize it from its multiple sources and focus it on the organizations' problems in a way that would both become vision and strategy. It was at the point where Eastman Kodak's CEO, Kay R. Whitmore, could not offer his directors "a concrete plan for leading the company's remaining businesses into the future" that he was fired (Cowan, 1993).

This is a particularly vulnerable point for those chief executives who have chosen their own successors, either because their boards are weak or do not want to interfere with the CEOs' choices, or because those whom they have consulted have not taken conceptual capacity into account. As a result, they have a great tendency to choose people who are guaranteed not to succeed (Levinson, 1974) and particularly to choose successors who are not as smart as they are. That means those people, unable to deal with the same level of complexity, limit themselves to problems that they can deal with that more often are of an immediate fire-fighting kind. The upshot is that they are very busy putting out fires but cannot conceive of the multiple new directions the business should take.

That problem becomes even more complicated when people who do not know the business are placed in top management roles. According to the public press, for a long time General Motors was dominated by financial types who seemed not to know as much as they should about building and marketing automobiles. IBM has been criticized for dominance by sales and financial types, with insufficient knowledge of technology. Kodak's board said a successor would have to have a broader background than financial management. That same issue has led many companies to select CEOs who presumably could take greater initiative with respect to building a product and selling it.

This is not to say that a person who has not grown up in a given business should not undertake to lead it. There are many examples of highly successful executives who have moved from one industry to another: Particular cases in point are John Sculley, who went from Pepsi-Cola to Apple Computer, and Louis V. Gerstner, Jr., who yielded his rescue effort of RJR-Nabisco to assume that task at IBM.

However, the important point here is that we know that people have different levels of conceptual capacity and proceed along various trajectories to different levels of achievement of their maximum capacity at different points in time. There is no excuse for not assessing that kind of capacity and undertaking predictions when it is likely to mature. A chief executive of a major corporation with a global view has to be able to think ahead from 20 to 50 years (Jaques & Clement, 1991). Failing that, he or she is simply not going to be able to understand what must be done, let alone do it. That seemed specifically the case at Kodak (Cowan, 1993).

Most important is the need to assess the conceptual level of people in senior and top executive roles. This is something that is rarely done, particularly because so many executives are afraid of psychological testing or even having extended psychological interviews for high-level candidates or high-level officers. Yet there is no substitute for knowing how any given person will handle what level of complexity. As the world becomes more complex and people are required to handle higher level abstractions and more data over a wider range of geography, the conceptual capacity of the individual is fundamental to his or her ability to function effectively in such a role. It is certainly the place to begin. My impression of a number of publicly quoted chief executives is that, conceptually, they are not up to the level they should be and their problems become magnified as their organizations take on new and different marketplaces.

PSYCHOLOGICAL IGNORANCE

Psychological ignorance is endemic in management circles. I was once invited by the vice president of human resources of a major corporation to address their management on executive stress. The invitation was rescinded by the chief executive who said he did not know what his human resources vice president was thinking of: He had no stress, and what's more, he did not know what stress was. To talk about it made no sense to him. It was no surprise that he had come out of a rigid military background. If you cannot let yourself be afraid, that contributes to bravery, but it does not do much for sensing what goes on around you.

Key executives who have arisen through financial or engineering backgrounds particularly often took up those paths to avoid having to become aware of their own feelings and to fend off consideration of other people's feelings. They often are very good at manipulating numbers. Indeed, IBM had an outstanding reputation for its financial achievements. Many mutual funds leaned heavily on IBM's record, as did others that invested heavily in General Motors and the other automobile companies. Those backgrounds often were necessary for making a financial or technical assault on the marketplace, but they served less well when it came to grasping complexities of human feelings among their customers and their employees. Efforts by consultants are unlikely to effect significant changes in long-term characteristic behavior of executives. That fact is widely known, but it is not seriously taken into account in selection either by boards or by many executives themselves.

Of course, none of this considers the psychological and physical problems a chief executive may have. Chief among these is depression. Discussing the future direction of his company with a chief executive, I pointed out that increasingly top management people were going to have to be involved with the outside world. They would have to be engaged with customers, politicians, and social problems. The chief executive said rather sadly, "I can't do that." He didn't. He withdrew into his office, overwhelmed and depressed. His board fired him some months later. Occasionally, executives in this position commit suicide, as did Vincent W. Foster, Jr., of Bill Clinton's entourage, often because the people around them do not recognize their depression and the significance of their behavior.

Physical impairments also can intrude into executive decision making. Such problems are well documented (Post & Robins, 1993). The problem so often is that boards do not meet often enough, do not have enough public members who can question the chief executive, do not follow the Dayton-

92   HARRY LEVINSON

Hudson Corporation's policy of appraisal of chief executive performance, and, above all, are not sensitive enough to psychological factors in executive behavior that might alert them to such problems. Usually, they will act only when the behavior is too blatant to be ignored.

TOWARD ACTION

There are a number of actions that one can take to cope with the issues I have outlined. These are some suggestions:

1. All organizations and individual executives are vulnerable to these psychological problems. It is therefore imperative for boards and top managements to consider them in their decision making. That means, among other things, that one must set up organizational structures that compel managers at all levels to communicate with each other and to get information from the outside that then can be transmitted to all parts of the organization.

   There are a number of ways of doing so. For example, people in technical areas can report on frontiers in those areas and have those reports discussed and transmitted to others who must take action based on them. Twenty years ago, when there was a reorganization of the United States Department of State, it was agreed that consuls whose reports previously had been changed successively as they went up the line would not only submit those reports, but also that they would go forward with the comments of their superiors so that the original information would not be lost or distorted en route (U.S. Department of State, 1970). In business organizations, such information can come from technical, legal, financial, or marketing groups who are alert to the frontiers of their fields and discuss such information together. They then can transmit it to appropriate levels for further consideration and action. The contemporary use of teams is a method by which this can be done face to face around specific tasks or problems.

2. One useful way of breaking into the rigidly narcissistic hierarchy is to bring people systematically into the organization from other companies at the divisional vice presidential level. If enough of them are brought in at that level, many soon will rise to higher corporate levels. They will be able to introduce other perspectives. At that level, they will also have a four-year purview, that is, they are likely to be able to look ahead four years, which will enable them to bring informa-

tion into consideration that otherwise might be too short term or too elementary to contribute to significant organizational foresight.

All of us bring to our present positions the ideas, concepts, and orientations that we had many years ago. Therefore, there is already a certain obsolescence built into contemporary executive leadership. That obsolescence is tempered somewhat when one has the doors open to new ideas from the outside. The increasing effectiveness of on-line behavior is inevitably to be required of all of us.

3. There should be the opportunity in all organizations when change occurs for confrontation with the reality that the organization is up against, together with a mourning process, so that people can detach themselves from the old and confront the realities of the new (Levinson, 1976). The process of expressing disappointment, regret, and frustration for having to give up the old and the process of coping with the sense of helplessness such change inevitably induces require mutually supportive group discussion of the realities of what would be missed and what will have to be faced. Otherwise, the depressive feelings simply will endure, although people may, in effect, grit their teeth and try to master them with sheer effort. Of course, sometimes they will succeed, but it would be far better to have disgorged the feelings of depressive rage that are widely unrecognized by senior managers that impede all organization change and all intellectual efforts to facilitate that change.

4. Executives and managers must learn to recognize and understand depression and physical illness and have the authority to do something about them. I have enumerated a method for doing so in Levinson, 1964, and there are many other sources.

5. There should be room for creatively abrasive people in organizations, encouraged and supported by top management. Thomas J. Watson, Jr., himself said, "I never hesitated to promote someone I didn't like. . . . I look for those sharp, scratchy, harsh, almost unpleasant guys who see and tell you about things as they really are. If you can get enough of them around you, and have patience enough to hear them out, there's no limit to where you can go" (Watson & Petre, 1990, p. 290). In particular, one needs somebody to keep prodding and pushing, as Jim Birkenstock, one of the key executives responsible for IBM's entry into the computer business, did for him.

One also has to have the support to carry through. It wasn't enough for Watson to turn to companions: He had the famous mathematician John von Neuman come from the Center for Advanced Study at Princeton to teach his engineers and scientists about computer technology. Reginald Jones, former CEO of General Electric, did the same thing by having McKinsey & Company prepare a 15-volume survey of the frontiers of science and technology with which he then confronted his technical groups and compelled their shift from electromechanical to electronic orientation (Levinson & Rosenthal, 1984).

However, when one is introducing and supporting abrasive people in an organization, the abrasiveness must be focused on those practices that interfere with the development of constructive and cooperative effort, effective technical advances and marketing orientation, and reasonable and effective financial modes. More often than not, such people simply wind up with harsh interpersonal differences when they are not focused on the tasks to be accomplished. When they are held to that focus, they often can make significant contributions.

Apropos of the abrasive and scratchy people, it is important for people in top management to know who are the mavericks in the organization, why they left, where they went, and what they did after they got there. Of course, some will be cast to the periphery of all organizations, but some indeed will be creatively innovative. The managerial literature is replete with stories of people who could not sell their ideas to their bosses, but who then established their own highly successful organizations.

6. High-level executives, particularly in top management, have to interact with their multiple constituencies. This, too, gets to be a problem for people with a heavy financial or engineering orientation who are less comfortable interacting, and even more difficult for those executives who do not want to hear from or about anyone else. Nevertheless, as Bill Clinton's experience has demonstrated, people want to have contact, want to know that they are heard, and develop faith and confidence in leaders who at least will hear and at least will try to act on what they hear, despite the complexity and difficulty of the problems to be dealt with.

FINALLY

To return to Thomas J. Watson, Jr., who said he never hesitated to intervene if he saw the company getting bogged down, there is no substitute for action, and therefore there have to be built-in mechanisms for attenuating the guilt of chief executives. One important way, of course, is to have that kind of continued consultation with either outside professionals or people whose judgment they trust who are close to them that will help them free themselves to act. Another way, becoming increasingly popular, is to have outside members of their boards continuously question them and their lieutenants as those boards meet more frequently among themselves and with the top managements. All of the contemporary urging to excellence, the total quality management, the "put the customer first" efforts will flounder unless the chief executive is the agent of thoughtful action, rather than paralytic guilt.

REFERENCES

Byrne, J., Diepke, D. A., Verity, J., Neff, R., Levine, J. B., & Forest, S. A. (1991, June 17). IBM. *Business Week*, p. 25.

Carroll, P. B. (1991, May 21). Akers to IBM employees: Wake up. *Wall Street Journal*, p. B1.

Cowan, A. L. (1993, August 7). Unclear future forced board's hand. *New York Times*, p. 37.

DePree, M. (1989). *Leadership is an art*. New York: Doubleday.

Fiske, S. T. (1993). Controlling other people. *American Psychologist*, 48, 621–628.

Fuchsberg, G. (1992, May 14). Quality programs show shoddy results. *Wall Street Journal*, p. B1.

Hayes, T. C. (1993, January 18). Faltering companies seek outsiders. *New York Times*, p. D1.

Henry, F. W. (1983). *The making of a woman MBA*. New York: Putnam.

Hirschhorn, L. (1988). *The workplace within*. Cambridge, MA: MIT Press.

Jaques, E. (1989). *Requisite organization*. Arlington, VA: Cason Hall.

Jaques, E. (1990, January–February). In praise of hierarchy. *Harvard Business Review*, pp. 127–133.

Jaques, E., & Clement, S. D. (1991). *Executive leadership*. Arlington, VA: Cason Hall.

Kantrow, A. M. (1984). *The constraints of tradition*. New York: Harper & Row.

Kneale, D. (1986, October 3). IBM is trailing Digital in getting computers to talk to each other. *Wall Street Journal*, p. 1.

Levinson, H. (1964). *Emotional health in the world of work*. Waltham, MA: The Levinson Institute.

Levinson, H. (1973). *The great jackass fallacy*. Boston: Harvard Graduate School of Business Press.

Levinson, H. (1974, November–December). Don't choose your own successor. *Harvard Business Review*, 53–62.

Levinson, H. (1976). *Psychological man*. Cambridge, MA: The Levinson Institute.

Levinson, H., & Rosenthal, S. (1984). *CEO: Corporate leadership in action*. New York: Basic Books.

Lipin, S. (1993, June 30). Golub solidifies hold at American Express, begins to change firm. *Wall Street Journal*, p. A1.

Loomis, C. J. (1993a, May 3). Dinosaurs. *Fortune*, p. 39.

Loomis, C. J. (1993b, May 3). Dinosaurs. *Fortune*, p. 41.

Miller, C., & Aeppel, T. (1993, January 20). BMW zooms ahead of Mercedes-Benz in world-wide sales for the first time. *Wall Street Journal*, p. B1.

Miller, D. (1990). *The Icarus paradox*. New York: Harper Business.

Miroff, B. (1993). *Icons of democracy*. New York: Basic Books.

Moretti, D. M., Morken, C. L., & Borkowski, J. M. (1991). Profile of the American CEO: Comparing INC. and Fortune executives. *Journal of Business and Psychology*, 6(2), 193–205.

Noer, D. M. (1993). *Healing the wounds*. San Francisco: Jossey-Bass.

Post, J., & Robins, R. S. (1993). *When illness strikes the leader*. New Haven, CT: Yale University Press.

Semler, R. (1993). *Maverick!* New York: Warner Books.

Shipper, F., & Manz, C. C. (1992, Winter). An alternative road to empowerment. *Organizational Dynamics*, pp. 48–61.

Tichy, N. M., & Sherman, S. S. (1993). *Control your destiny or someone else will*. New York: Doubleday/Currency.

U.S. Department of State. (1970). *Diplomacy for the 70s* (Department of Foreign Service Series 143; Department of State Publication 8537). Washington, DC: Superintendent of Documents.

Watson, T. J., & Petre, P. (1990). *Father and son*. New York: Bantam.

7

PSYCHOLOGICAL CONSULTATION TO ORGANIZATIONS: LINKING ASSESSMENT AND INTERVENTION

HARRY LEVINSON

Psychological consultation to organizations takes many forms and is based on many different assumptions about the causes and precipitants of human behavior.

VARIETIES OF ORGANIZATIONAL CONSULTATION

Historically, in industrial–organizational (I-O) psychology, organizational change was brought about through the design of work (Jaques, 1996), by evolving selection methods (Kehoe, 2000), attitude survey methods (Kraut, 1996), and various derivatives of organizational development methods (Lawler, 1986). Consultation therefore was focused on practices and procedures. It assumed essentially a reward and punishment motivational model. From the days of the Hawthorne studies (Roethlisberger & Dickson, 1939),

From *The California School of Organizational Studies Handbook of Organizational Consulting Psychology: A Comprehensive Guide to Theory, Skills, and Techniques* (pp. 415–449), edited by R. H. Lowman, 2002, San Francisco: Jossey Bass. Copyright 2002 by John Wiley & Sons. Reprinted with permission.

it also assumed that manipulations of the work environment would have significant effects on productivity and work satisfaction. Furthermore, it assumed implicitly that top management had the right to manipulate the organization and those who worked in it to attain those ends. Implicit also was a psychology of individual differences and individual comparisons.

To a lesser degree, organizational and industrial consultation involved working with managers and executives in a counseling role. Executive coaching (see, for example, Kilburg, 2000; Hall, Otazo, & Hollenbeck, 1999) recently has reached fad-level proportions. To an even lesser degree, sometimes masked by the executive coaching rubric, clinical relationships have become acceptable to practicing executives (Levinson, 1991; Kets deVries, 1984).

With the development of the group dynamics movement (Bradford, Gibb, & Benne, 1964), much psychological consultation early on took the form of sensitivity training and similar experiences, such as encounter groups, and subsequently, other forms of group process, such as team building. The underlying motivational assumptions were built around self-actualization (Maslow, 1954), group membership, and the honest and accurate expression of feelings. Thus, the implicit theory of motivation was broad and nonspecific (little mention of how one might solve specific problems of people, or apply specific leadership behavior in specific organizational settings). The major techniques advocated were catharsis and group participation in decision-making. Much of the current organizational development movement is derived from this model. Concurrently, there was frequently an assumption of an open system model of organization (Katz & Kahn, 1978), but rarely was this model considered explicitly in detail in published accounts of consultation.

In both modes, the more traditional industrial-organizational and the group dynamics–based, the role of the consultant is essentially temporary and transient. Even when the latter-day organizational development consultant becomes involved in career counseling and the management of human resources, her relationship usually is short-term and technique-oriented. The consultant's observation of group processes and facilitation of group effort tend to be bounded by the discrete meetings in which they occur (Schein, 1987). There is an underlying assumption that motivation is conscious or readily can become so, that one is dealing with learned behavior, and that people effectively can use the feedback of both personal and group psychological data garnered from the group experience to enhance subsequent personal and organizational behavior over extended periods of time (Marrow, 1972).

Many have learned about some aspects of both individual and group behavior from these experiences, and much contemporary consultation on organizational change proliferated from them. However, interest in the experiences themselves (T-groups and some of their more prominent derivatives such as encounter groups) declined. Today, even their once prominent and enthusiastic proponents no longer advocate them. They fell into disuse because the behavioral changes largely were temporary. Also, confidence in the methods decreased as evidence of their ineffectiveness increased (Truax & Carkhuff, 1967). The proponents or trainers, usually without clinical training, failed to take into account the fact that much behavior, particularly that which is troublesome to oneself or others, is characterological (Levinson, 1976a). That is, the behavior is consistent and enduring. Usually, its origins are beyond the awareness of the individual. It is therefore not amenable to enduring, significant change by short-term feedback methods. Another reason why managements backed off and prominent practitioners gave up the methods was the incidence of psychological casualties, denied by the clinically untrained trainers, but familiar to corporate medical departments and the outside clinical consultants who treated them. There are no statistics on the incidence of casualties, but I heard much about them in seminars I was then conducting for physicians employed by organizations.

Few methods for assessing organizational behavior are comprehensive. There is a wide range of such methods, largely focused on part-problems such as organizational development, organizational design, organizational training and staffing, organizational culture, and rewards (Howard, 1994). Some consultants lean heavily on survey techniques, some on role analysis, some on interviews, some on evaluating organizational structure. Few combine their analyses of these part-problems or processes, undertaken with circumscribed methods, into a more comprehensive understanding of an organization that encompasses its history, statistics, characteristic mode of behavior, methods of discovering and solving problems, its crises, adaptive patterns, leadership, ethnographic composition, communications patterns, financial features, competitive posture, relations to its competitors, community, and government, and the variations in its relationships with the consultant, let alone the consultant's involvements with various components of the organization, and his feedback. Even fewer clearly identify their assumptions about motivation, personality, and environment. Therefore, most consultants have difficulty being scientific, for example, establishing fact, making and identifying inferences from fact, and drawing interpretations from those facts and inferences. Their methodological limitations also constrain their interventions. Few consultants discuss a flexible range of intervention methods that they can draw on. Too often, organizational consultation consists of techniques in search of a problem.

Systems Models

My own consultation model (Levinson, 2002) takes more seriously the concept of the organization as an open system, drawn from biology (Von Bertalanffy, 1950; Fuqua & Newman, 2002). Such a living system seeks to sustain an equilibrium among the multiple forces, inner and outer, acting upon it, and simultaneously pursues a developmental course toward adaptive effectiveness, mastering its environment and maintaining its stability. In this model, adapted and extrapolated from the psychiatric case study method (Menninger, 1962), an organization has a history, characteristic modes of operating, enduring values, recallable crises, and folklore, modes of gathering, processing, and acting on information, leadership, and relative degrees of flexibility. In short, there is an organizational personality. Using this model, and assuming an underlying psychoanalytic theory of motivation, a consultant is responsible for understanding the organization as a whole, in its context, and against its history. This knowledge becomes a base for evaluating the organization's capacity to approach its collective aspirations and its competence for relieving its internal strains, for helping the organization as a whole perceive accurately its self-image against its ideal expectation of itself, and to evolve steps toward more effectively pursuing its adaptation.

To those ends, the consultant must be in a continuing relationship with the organization, as an outside source of knowledge about the organization, about which it is not readily aware (for example, most employees in most organizations know little about their organization's history, let alone its implications for current behavior), and a point of stability for an organization in turbulence (change always implies turbulence). The consultant must have evolved diagnostic and prognostic hypotheses and a mode for working with the organization that simultaneously will respect its integrity and help it move toward a higher adaptive plane. In this chapter, I propose to illustrate some critical intervention issues that usually followed upon that kind of assessment process, or a frame of mind that assumed that process, and the logic that led to the particular consultation activity in each situation. The several illustrative cases exemplify a range of diagnostic and prognostic conclusions from the assessments and subsequent consulting behavior that followed from the psychological logic that was developed. I also note some more important lessons I learned from each.

The Consultant's Responsibilities

Using this method, the consultant assumes responsibility for gathering, integrating, and assessing information about the organization, sometimes with the help of its internal resources and participants, and defining an intervention based on his assessment and prognosis. Some might feel that this is a physician–patient model in which the know-it-all physician therapeutizes the passive patient. But the reality is that all change agents operate this way, no matter how much they deny it. Each brings his or her own training, prejudices, ignorance, perceptions, methods, and skills. Each does things in, with, and to an organization, based on some (usually tacit) assumptions about himself, about the organization, and about motivation.

With this method, I make my assumptions as explicit as I can, although these illustrative cases are too short to do so in detail here. I make the assessment and prognosis based on clinical psychological training, a classic psychoanalytic theory of motivation (Levinson, 1987), and a biological model of the organization following Von Bertalanffy (1950). That model assumes that the organization is a living organism that evolves a pattern of growth, development, and adaptation, methods for competitive survival, modes of maintaining its equilibrium in the context of social and economic changes, and, to the extent that it coheres, does so around a set of values. Necessarily, it requires processes that have to do with creating or providing products or services, making them known, communicating both internally and with its contextual worlds, and getting, controlling, and expending money. I assume that the organization not only has strengths, but also that there are limits to how and how well it can change. After all, organizations necessarily are heavily influenced by the nature of their leadership, as well as by financial, technical, educational, political, and sociological forces. In consultation practice, this means the consultant undertakes different kinds of interventions under different circumstances, with a specific logic for choosing those interventions that also allow for the consultant's self-correction.

CASE STUDY: STUCK IN PSYCHOLOGICAL MUD

Here is a classic case, a frequent model for many consultations. Often, consultants are called upon to help with a crisis situation. Too frequently for his professional comfort, he quickly discovers that there is no time for a comprehensive assessment, that he must act to relieve the crisis, and only later follow up with more thorough consideration of broader issues to be dealt with. To complicate matters, when he discovers that the organization for years not only has been in a constricted, rigid managerial pattern, but also controlled from behind the scenes by a dominant board member, he is soon walking on delicate psychological eggs as he tries to help the organization awaken to its realities and adapt to them. He also discovers that if there is frequent organizational change in a long-term consulting relationship, particularly in a large organization, it is wise to train and supervise the internal human resources staff to anticipate, assess, and carry out most of those changes.

The case in point was a large profitable single-industry company that was faced with a predictable, radically changing competitive and governmental environment. Its largely technical employee group and their managers had been over-controlled tightly for years by a succession of authoritarian chief executives. Their resulting dependency was reflected in their reluctance to act unless the action was prescribed by policies or directed by their superiors. They were not noted for bold innovations or imaginative ideas. The company's ethos was one of don't make waves, obedient middle-class conformity, and stable employment. There was strong new leadership in the form of a young executive, promoted from within but shadowed by his predecessor, now chairman, who had appointed him. The new leader not only had the capacity to conceptualize the business environment, but also the ways in which the organization would have to change to master it. Not long before his appointment, and perhaps in anticipation of it, he had been enrolled in a university advanced management program. He was willing to take risks and to encourage others to do so. His vision of where he wanted the organization to go was clear and firm. He could articulate a direction.

The enduring core values of the company, as reflected in the comparisons with other companies in the same industry that the employees made in interviews, had to do with integrity and how change was managed. Both stemmed from the religious orientation of the founder. For example, when changes were made, people rarely were fired. Managing change was left to the CEO, and had largely to do with finding and developing the company's natural resources. It was fundamentally a conservative organization that respected its leadership, but one in which most people did not have information beyond their narrow managerial and technical roles within the half-dozen major tracks (called silos) through which the company pursued its business, and in which, once assigned to one, they remained. Each was headed by a vice president who dominated his track. They had little flexibility to act on their own.

Results of Consulting Interviews

Getting no innovative movement from his vice presidents after a year of effort, at the insistence of the in-house psychologist, the frustrated CEO asked for consultation. My interviews with the several vice presidents who headed the six tracks and staff functions led me to hypothesize that they were in a depressed rage because of the changes that the new CEO was urging. Historically, and because of their characteristic over-controlled personalities, they were unable to disagree with him, let alone speak up publicly. It was difficult for some to see the competitive handwriting on the environmental wall, and for others to see that the business could be operated differently than it had been for years, and indeed would have to be.

The acute depressive rage that paralyzed the vice presidents was quickly apparent to me in the initial interviews. They were tightly controlled in their curt, deliberate, angry answers to my unwelcomed questions, and had little to say spontaneously about their respective roles. Some became red in the face and responded irritably as I pressed them for information about their work. They said little about the president's proposed innovations. They were not about to express their feelings, especially their anger, and certainly not to a psychologist.

I thought that, to loosen that angry constriction and to begin to open up the organizational system so that consultation could proceed further, rapid action was called for before a comprehensive assessment could be completed. The organization, having been stalled for a year, could not continue to be frozen in its tracks. These circumstances (here necessarily highly condensed) led to the choice of the method of dealing with the depression that allowed the top management group to mourn its past in a way congenial to its characteristic mode of behaving, to face contemporary realities, and to organize around its leadership. The method also had to undo the rigidity of the tracks, open the avenues for the next level of managers to act, and facilitate their identification with their new leader. Whatever other steps had to be taken would follow subsequent in-depth assessment.

Off-Site Consultation

The top eighty people in the company met off-site for three days under the guidance of another consultant colleague and myself. In the first step, we asked the CEO to start the meeting by tracing the directions from which the organization had come, its current status, and what he anticipated to be its current challenges. We recommended that he deliberately not offer his own recommendations or directions about what changes should be undertaken, as we might ask a CEO to do in other situations. We wanted to encourage contributions from the participants. After his presentation, discussion followed in ten-person small groups, whose participants were drawn from all of the major tracks. Their interaction enabled the participants to anticipate and mourn collectively the losses that might follow any change. It also enabled them to become more closely acquainted with each other, encouraged them to support each other in raising questions about the presentation, and permitted them to discuss their doubts and concerns about what they had heard. They then comprised a plenary session in which feedback and questions from the small groups to the CEO became a new model for interaction with authority.

In my experience, in most such meetings where trust of the leadership has not yet been established, managers usually feel they are being manipulated. In this case, our concern was that they might feel they were being persuaded of the CEO's perception of the industry's future. Therefore, as we recommended, the second step was a presentation by a respected futurist, an economist knowledgeable about the industry but unrelated to the company. His predictions necessarily complemented those of the CEO, because the data about the industry and the economy on which both based their judgments were public, even though most of the participants were not as knowledgeable about them. Discussion in the same small groups, and subsequent questions of the futurist in the plenary session, served to counteract whatever suspicion there might have been about the CEO's picture of the future of the industry and the business. In the third step, the participants were asked to specify the major problems they thought the company faced, and who should do what about them. They did so in the same small groups and reported back to the CEO in the plenary session. The CEO indicated which problems he could and would do something about, which would require greater thought or policy reformulation, and which would require action by the board.

In the fourth step, the participants were reassigned to small groups composed of executives and managers in the same tracks and departments. They were asked to decide what they were going to do about what they had learned in the meeting on the following Monday morning when they were back on the job. Each group reported subsequently in plenary session. I then summarized what had gone on psychologically, followed by a summary by the CEO of his understanding of the meeting.

We then took the same steps within the respective tracks, including those managers who had been at the top management meeting and the next levels of managers, but not first-line supervisors. It was a mistake not to include them because our assumption that the managers would follow up with their subordinates turned out to be invalid.

The enthusiasm of the managers for the new way of doing business was both remarkable and contagious. Their identification with their new leader and their subsequent interaction with him stimulated their cooperation with each other and undermined the rigidity of the depressed, unyielding vice presidents.

Supporting the Leader

Using this method also requires that the consultant support the leader. I had to help him understand and accept the turbulence that would take place in the small groups, and the hostile questions or criticisms that would arise when those groups reported in plenary sessions. Although I knew those pointed words would be mild, CEOs in that position inevitably feel them to be harsh. I had to help him experience their long-suppressed anger and formulate his responses in ways that would encourage the participants to redirect their anger into problem-solving efforts. The CEO had to encourage initiative and counteract the heavy dependency of the organization on authority. Later, I would have to help him think through what to do and how to do it with those now-obsolete senior executives who could not change. This phase called for careful management of separating those who had to be separated, so as not to demoralize the organization further and exacerbate the guilt of either those who had to terminate them or their erstwhile subordinates (Tomasko, 1987; Noer, 1993). This method also required supporting the successor executives and managers who took their places, who were new in their roles. They were caught up in their feelings both about usurping these positions and displacing their symbolic fathers (Brockner, Gibb, & Benne, 1985). We had to teach those new executives, some of whom never had been executives or managers before, how to support lower-level people amidst turbulence and change by making their rounds among them, being in touch with them, entertaining their fears and disappointments, and demonstrating care and concern. Simultaneously, we had to teach them to take firm action with some subordinates, often former colleagues and peers, who tested them.

We also had to further the support and development of the internal human resources function so that both training programs and organizational development activities could be undertaken to strengthen the organization's inner-capacity for change. I had to abstain carefully from being involved in the selection of people who were moved into new roles, lest I be seen as the power behind the organizational leadership. I had to limit my contribution in that area to helping define criteria for roles and teaching managers to write behavioral job descriptions (Levinson, 1976b). These enabled them to make their own choices with greater assurance. To have become involved in selection in this case would have violated the implied contract that placed me at the side of the whole top management group in its efforts to accomplish its changes. I had not contracted with them to contribute judgments about individuals.

In this organization, there were strong financial resources with which to cope with the inevitable economic ups and downs, and the organizational turbulence during the change process that affects effectiveness and profitability. There was solid technical competence, and people, generally speaking, had relatively high educational levels. The organizational culture (Schein, 1992; Trice & Beyer, 1984; Deal & Kennedy, 1982; Geertz, 1973), while somewhat varied among the respective tracks, was essentially cohesive and internally consistent. There was no history of previous failure or organizational crisis. Over its century-long history, the organization had adapted well. The odds were that it could continue to do so if it pursued change proactively, although one could predict that, like most organizational change in large organizations, it would take a five- to ten-year period during which the major changes would come about.

Changes in the Company Over Time

Actually, the organization went through six major changes over a ten-year period, three of which were precipitated by major changes in the industry. The change processes we introduced were internalized by the human resources personnel who carried out the subsequent changes. The consulting relationship continued for several more years in monthly meetings in support of the top management group, which itself had undergone three significant changes. The initial client CEO, who failed to take seriously my warning about his rivalry with his predecessor, the dominant figure on his board, was summarily fired. The consultation ended when the company spun off most of its major tracks, and contracted its size and function to only one of them.

One important lesson in this consultation was the need to take charge and act in what, in a sense, was an emergency situation, before I could do the usual comprehensive assessment. I had to take my initial clinical impressions seriously and trust myself to be guided by them. I could do that only with the trust of the CEO, who was unable to understand and therefore break out of the bind he was in, and the in-house psychologist, whom he trusted and at whose instance he had invited me to help. Despite his trust, he could not think psychologically enough to grasp my cautions about his relationship with his predecessor until it was too late.

In sum, crisis intervention might have to precede a formal assessment, but assessment can then unfold. Implementation might require developing mechanisms for greater managerial involvement, handling terminations, guilt relief, selection and training of new personnel, and support for the CEO.

CASE STUDY, U.S. STATE DEPARTMENT: SWAMPED IN A POLITICAL FISH BOWL

A formal consultation process carried on by the consultant, as in the previous case, is preferred. But some consultations are too large to be dealt with by a single consultant or even a large team of consultants. With a necessarily large team, some consultations can be too expensive, which is why many large organizations such as Sears, Roebuck, and IBM use attitude surveys (Kraut, 1996) regularly. Furthermore, without the continuous stability of top management over extended periods of time, issues of who is to implement any consultant's recommendations become bureaucratic fodder. All too often, organizations resist recommendations and reforms by ignoring them. This is especially the case with large governmental organizations. Confronted exactly by that kind of a problem after a relatively cursory assessment did not mean that I, the consultant, declined the opportunity. Instead, I made use of the organization's department heads themselves to pinpoint their issues, and to agree on and make public their recommendations. I learned, incidentally, that using members of an organization's own personnel to make their own assessment was instrumental in getting information, and crucial to the acceptance of those findings by the organization.

Organizational History

The U.S. Department of State had a long history of chronic attack, often purely political, and low self-confidence as an organization. From time to time there was even political talk of doing away with it altogether. It was

ridiculed by successive presidents and a wide range of congressmen and sena-
tors. There was little experience in the organization of getting at and solving
management problems, nor did people in the organization feel they had any
right to do so. The professional staff had been subjected to a variety of consultants, including an aborted sensitivity training program for senior officers.
State was, and continues to be, a large, unwieldy, bureaucratic organization
in which the major figures were rotated through the system. Some secretaries
of state, notably John Foster Dulles and Henry Kissinger, operated as Lone
Rangers, ignoring the rest of their organization; some were outmaneuvered
by other advisors politically closer to the President; none seemed to hold
effective management as a primary goal despite the repetitive criticism. Other
agencies were created independent of State that carried out specific international programs, sometimes in conflict with it. The historic tradition of dominance by Ivy League graduates had long since given way to a more democratic ethos that led to recruiting prospective Foreign Service Officers from
many other universities. But nothing seemed to affect the rigid barriers between managerial levels, or the manner in which the system undermined its
own people. For example, at the time of the consultation, in a consulate,
whose staff presumably was immediately the closest to the host country's
people, staff observations and recommendations were subject to change by
every immediate superior through whom they passed. By the time they reached
whatever authority needed that information, there was no knowing how valid
it was.

Since the top management leaders were political appointees, there was
no extended continuity of leadership and no guarantee that there would be
any long-term relationship between any consultant and the organization.
Usually, in an organizational consultation, the relationship of the consultant
with the top management is crucial. The Department of State operated in a
context of multiple international political forces, many in conflict with each
other, and often those appointees who were responsible for diplomacy in a
given country knew little of that country's culture, traditions, or political
currents. State had an extensive internal education program for its professional staff, the Foreign Service Institute, which included such topics and
language training, and also sent selected officers to various university programs. However, the policy of rotation, required to broaden officers' experiences, and the fact that no one could know the languages of all of the countries to which he or she might be assigned, limited the immersion of many in
different foreign locales, and made many dependent on local translators. There
was also the issue of physical danger. Some rarely left their diplomatic com-
pounds, particularly in unstable nations, for fear they might be attacked.

However, the new political leadership at the time of the consultation
was strong, felt secure in its role, and, mindful of the criticism, wished to
bring about change. The late Elliott Richardson, then undersecretary of state,
invited me to consult.

From my previous experience with them, I knew that the officers in the Foreign Service, the elite component of State, were highly educated, had considerable professional competence, and were strongly identified with their role and function. They had a long history and what they regarded to be a noble tradition. They had already organized the Foreign Service Officers Association to make their wishes and feelings felt in the system. Thus, there was some capacity to act in a politically unstable setting that could not provide continuing sanction for consultant-guided action. However, to my mind, given the multiple problems I referred to, prognosis at best was dubious, no matter what the intervention. I could imagine the officers shuddering at the thought of yet another set of recommendations by outsiders that would likely be ignored or shelved as were previous critiques, as they themselves later documented (U.S. Department of State, 1970).

There was an opportunity to act, but by whom and how? True, there was a formal authority structure, but how long would those political appointees remain in place? And if they did, who would be willing to take the necessary action steps? What actions would be most beneficial to the system?

In my judgment, those that would be most effective would cut across bureaucratic barriers to illuminate common concerns, give sanction to initiative, legitimize lower-level initiative to bring about change, and quickly produce visible results as a product of initiative. Ideally, people should discover that they could indeed have an effect, and acquire a degree of competence for doing so. That, in turn, meant that a large number of people had to be involved in cross-level activities that would resolve problems that, though in some cases not major, nevertheless constituted psychological thorns in the organizational body.

That set of factors led to my recommendation that a number of internal task forces gather the data and make the recommendations that followed. I would guide and consult with them. In our first meeting, the officers who were invited to become the heads of the projected task forces questioned the possible usefulness of the project and the sincerity of higher management wishing it on them. When they learned that I, who had respected academic credentials and occasionally had taught in the Foreign Service Institute, was to be involved with them, they accepted the seriousness of the assignment. The deputy undersecretary of state for administration, William B. Macomber, Jr., appointed thirteen task forces, each designed to deal with a topic the project heads had nominated. Two hundred fifty Foreign Service Officers and others participated over a five-month period in what they described as a massive modernization plan. The diverse range of participants, and the range of topics, precluded *group think* (Janis, 1972), or agreement based on pressure to cohere at the expense of individual opinions. The topics they addressed were: career management and assignment policies; performance appraisal and promotion policies; personnel requirements and resources; personnel training; personnel requisites; recruitment and employment; stimulation of creativity; the role of the country director; openness in the foreign affairs community; reorganization of the Foreign Service Institute; the roles and functions of diplomatic missions; a management evaluation system; and management tools.

The Modernization Effort

"This modernization effort," they later wrote (U.S. Department of State, 1970, p. 1), "is an unusual one. It does not follow the traditional procedures for reforming a large bureaucracy. It is not based on the creation of a new outside study commission, nor does it involve a program developed and imposed in detail by top management. On the contrary, at the request of that management, this reform program has been developed not from the top or from the outside, but from *within*. It is the work of 13 task forces made up of outstanding career professionals from within the Department of State and Foreign Service augmented by distinguished career personnel from other agencies in the American foreign affairs community."

I remained at a distance from the activity, meeting only three times with the project heads: first, to give them official sanction and let them know that there was indeed serious intention from the top managerial level of the department; second, to help them formulate how the task forces should go about gathering information; and third, to insist that they report to the first three levels of the executive hierarchy, to overcome some of the barriers to implementation of their recommendations. There were two reasons for insisting that they themselves report their findings to higher management: they were reluctant for structural and historic reasons to confront their superiors and they wanted me to do so; and there would be no "not invented here" resistances. "Not invented here" refers to organizational members' frequent rejection of external consultants' recommendations because the consultants are assumed to impose solutions that are not derived from experience in the organization.

They subsequently published their findings and more than 500 recommendations in a 600-page volume (U.S. Department of State, 1970). They distributed updates of the action plans, called Management Reform Bulletins, to those who had participated, on how the recommendations were being carried out.

Two earlier meetings with the undersecretary of state and the deputy undersecretary for administration and the three meetings with the task force leaders constituted the entire intervention.

Thus, this consultation was short-term, highly focused, and with limited goals in a turbulent setting. It established precedent and left open an avenue for further consultation when, and if, such might be appropriate and necessary. The task forces had done a commendable job, so I recommended that the heads of the task forces be constituted as an advisory council to pursue continued innovation. However, the deputy undersecretary for administration was reluctant to do so for fear that such an advisory council might become another power center in a setting that already had too many fiefdoms. Two years later, an internal study disclosed that a significant portion of the task force recommendations had been carried out.

Consultation does not always mean that the consultant assess and recommend, or even have a continuing relationship with top management. He or she might well do better, especially in large, complex organizations, to guide the internal managerial personnel to do so. They then acquire a skill for looking at their own organization, and are more likely to implement their own recommendations.

CASE STUDY: SURVIVING DEMORALIZATION

In the previous case, I maintained a distant relationship to the client system. In this case, I was called on to pick up the pieces. Although a consultant might have neither a relationship with the top management of an organization nor even the usual leverage to help it change, there still might be ways to strengthen it and those who work in it so that both can become more adaptive. This kind of intervention calls for greater imagination and initiative on the part of the consultant, as well as simultaneously helping the client group avoid political problems as they strengthen themselves and the organization. The important lesson for me in this case was that the client's situation was not as hopeless as it seemed at first, and that I had to be more active in helping the client staff arrive at their solutions than was the case in either of the two previous cases.

A large state agency had a narrow functional responsibility. It ran the state's lottery, which meant that it publicly chose the winning numbers each week on television, validated the winning numbers, notified the winners, distributed the winnings, and forwarded books of coupons to retail operations that sold them. It was staffed at the top with political appointees, each of whom was seeking to maximize his political potential, and none of whom had any significant interest in or competence with the activities of the agency. Those activities were managed largely by a civil service cadre who had limited technical competence, and who saw the agency as a device to increase their social and economic status. However, since they could not get direction, guidance, authority, resolution of conflict, or political protection from their superiors, they were demoralized and constantly bickering among themselves. Their management was terrible and they knew it. Apart from the state's mandated administrative processes, their executives initiated few innovations. Performance was appraised by checklist with only limited interaction between the appraiser and appraisee. Almost all employees were rated acceptable. There was no history of organizational success, achievement, or proficiency. There was no tradition, no enduring reputation, or commitment to any kind of professional values, except minimal service to the public. In short, the agency was pasted together by a civil service structure to carry on its nonprestigious, little-valued activity.

A change in top management resulted in greater support for the human resources function, but no significant interest on the part of top management itself to become involved in the managerial functions and activities of the agency. The civil service cadre were like abandoned orphans, left to fend for themselves in a complex political world in which they were vulnerable to possible predatory attacks in the legislature and political maneuvering by their superiors in which they could become potential victims, both as an organization and as individuals.

Issues in the Organization's Demoralization

The director of human resources asked for the consultation to combat the demoralization, and that agency became the client. The director thought he had sanction to act, but since his superiors were uninterested, he could expect no support from them. Of course, they would not want any activity that would attract public attention or make political waves. There were no consistent efforts to resolve conflicts or to increase the efficiency or effectiveness of the agency. The human resources staff itself was a hopeless, demoralized, disappointed group of people who saw themselves going nowhere.

There was no place to go but up, but to what and how? The civil service people could not move far in the hierarchy; the top-level managers were all political appointees. The only opportunity for upward mobility available to them, I discerned, was to increase their own capacities and skills in their management roles so they could ultimately move out of this agency into other civil service roles or into private management. They could improve the present system and themselves out of enlightened self-interest. Therefore, my task as the consultant, after making this assessment, was to become the ally of the human resources function, which, in turn, became allied with the middle management toward their own self-enhancement.

The function of the human resources department became primarily to build into the system that kind of managerial training and development that would enable people to improve their competences and skills, even to acquire academic or professional credentials, and to prepare themselves as individuals for personal advancement. This meant that they had to learn to solve managerial problems together, to evolve better working modes, to improve their own leadership skills, and to use the agency as a laboratory for increasing their managerial effectiveness. Doing so would enable them to organize around common problems, and to develop cohesion that was mutually profitable to themselves and to the organization. As long as they left top management alone and did not cause those officials any difficulties, that management was not very concerned about what they did and how they did it. It could only profit from the increased effective management below them. The prognosis for such an activity was good.

Here, once again, my consulting role was minimal: assessment and subsequent support of the human resources function. After the assessment and my recommendations, my task was to help that staff define their realities and the avenues for steering among them to do an effective job in the absence of strong leadership. The consultation left the human resources staff in a position to choose the appropriate training and development activities that would be most relevant to the people involved, who could not by themselves see the wider range of managerial functions to which they might aspire. Theirs was now the task of helping their constituents to take advantage of their own wish to improve, by defining the skills they needed in their present roles, as well as those they would have to have to move on or up. In some ways, I served in loco parentis, giving sanction, permission, encouragement, and some direction to the human resources staff that otherwise experienced itself as being alone and rudderless.

There are times, as I learned in this case, where the consultant has to become like a benign father, giving more direct advice and counsel to people who need information, guidance, and direction. He also has to become politically attuned in such poorly governed situations, lest his advice stir up higher-level hostility from superiors who want only not to be disturbed. The issues are the same whether in state government, as in this case, or in a business, church, school, or hospital, where management is fuzzy and leadership only nominal.

CASE STUDY: THE PASSIVE PRESIDENT

In the preceding case, the consultant had to help the demoralized management group find their way in an ambiguous political situation; in other situations, the consultant becomes an agent of long-term stability for the chief executive officer and the senior management. Assessment in this case disclosed that I was dealing with a highly dependent chief executive who also was subject to the whims of a quarrelsome top management trio that was incompetent to lead. My sense of the situation was that the chief executive had a character problem that called for long-term support and protection. The CEO's problems, I hypothesized, were not going to be dealt with by such techniques as team building alone, nor would the constricted personality characteristics of the technical staff (Roe, 1956) lend themselves to easy give and take. I had to be prepared for the challenges and hostilities, as well as the unrealistic expectations, of an extended relationship.

This manufacturing company of highly technical equipment, a division of a larger corporation, was being torn apart by the seventh president in five years. No sooner were the presidents appointed than they were in the midst of conflicting top management directions and quickly resigned. The new chief, almost immediately after his appointment, had come into conflict with its scientific and technical executives, who were the sources of the organization's innovative ability. They were becoming increasingly demoralized and threatening to resign because of his authoritarian manner. Indeed, some had resigned. The financial vice president of the parent company earlier had been in a seminar with me. Because there was a telephone strike at the time the consultation was requested, the financial vice president, many miles distant from my office, wired the request for immediate consultation.

Consulting in the Crisis

In this crisis, my task was to gain immediate information about that group, which I did by interviewing each of the sixteen people in the division's senior management. I then summarized those interviews in a meeting with them and their new chief executive, so that they could check on the validity of my findings and so he had accurate and honest information about how they felt. They were pleased that I accurately had tapped the nature of their feelings and concerns. Because of the urgency of the situation, I did not then interview the corporate top management to whom the division reported. As it soon became evident, the top management trio was itself dysfunctional, which then required me to protect the divisional management from the trio's potentially disruptive intrusion.

The interviews disclosed a cohesive group of scientific and technical people with a previous record of group accomplishment in new technology. They wanted to continue to work with each other. They did not want to be mechanized with traditional management formulae. They were not going to be boxed in or ordered about.

When these data were then reported, the task of the group was to determine what they wanted to do about their feelings and how they wanted to go about doing it. I led a series of half-day meetings, during which they thrashed out some of their concerns about the way they were being managed, the freedom they felt they had to have, and their lack of trust in their chief executive. That executive also took part in these meetings, to respond and be tested by their questions when appropriate.

After each meeting, I met privately with the division chief executive, my client, to review what was going on and what kinds of steps needed to be taken to bolster the effort he was making, and to assure his subordinates of his open interest, concern, and support. He moved from his authoritarian position to a more passive one, which provoked significant concern because he would not interact effectively with his people. It took a great deal of my effort to get him to interact, because he was afraid that he would produce the same kind of reaction that he had stimulated in the first place.

Results of Diagnosis

My diagnostic hypothesis was that his initial authoritarian over-control was a reaction formation against his underlying passivity. To compensate for his sense of inadequacy and helplessness, he went to the opposite extreme in his behavior. He would demonstrate that he was a strong leader. However, when threatened, he again became passive. He needed my support to take a more active stance. That became my near-term focus. Other consultants with different psychological orientations might formulate other diagnostic hypotheses. Whatever one's orientation, a diagnostic formulation is critical for a systematic intervention plan and process.

Although cohesion between the leader and the followers increased, there was still a significant gap. As they began to accommodate to each other, they also tried to slough over significant differences. It was clear to me that the denial mechanisms were setting in as these generally more passive technical people (Roe, 1956) and their fundamentally passive leader worked out a way not to come to grips with each other. I could see that this accommodation would result in their once again pulling away from each other and barely touching psychologically as they passed each other.

At this point, I chose to risk their anger by pointing out these avoidances and becoming the common enemy. I felt I could do this because I had a strong enough relationship with both the group and the chief executive that they could take that abrasion on my part. I knew also that, given the kinds of people they were, they would be unlikely to become overtly hostile; the leader had the capacity to absorb the hostility of the group if and when it occurred, and to deflect it into problem solving, particularly with my encouragement and support.

There were strong financial, technical, and educational resources, and a reasonably consistent organizational character. The organization's expensive new products were highly regarded in the marketplace, and the organization had good prospects for becoming profitable. Despite their intrusions, after my resistance, the parent organization trio left it largely autonomous. These factors, together with the strong motivation of the top management group, augured well for the prognosis. Though the organization's history had been a turbulent one, marked by initial success, followed by five years of relatively poor productivity through the series of presidents, it was beginning to experience positive change. They rallied to my provocation, and the interaction became more intense as they worked out some of their problems. The organization began to grow rapidly and ultimately divided itself into two, requiring a new generation of team-building activity to create two separate interactive teams.

However, at this point, the president decided that, in addition to my own work in the company, now three years into the relationship, he also wanted to use a more traditional organizational development consultant who would make lists of issues and paste them on walls or easels, and who also would provide certain kinds of academic social psychological input. He told me that he had been impressed by a young female consultant whose presentation he had seen at an industry meeting. He was quite fearful, however, that if he were to retain her, I would leave him. He was also fearful, hinting that if he did not do so, he would no longer be in charge of himself, but rather be a puppet for me. I inferred that his intention arose from his concern that he might become too dependent on me. I accepted these feelings and the president proceeded with his new program. That activity continued sporadically for about a year and then petered out as its superficiality became apparent to him.

Ultimately, the president became fatally ill and had to retire from his role. Serious conflict at the corporate top management level contributed to the deterioration of the parent organization and therefore of its subsidiaries. The corporate top management yielded to a new, more effective CEO, who promptly closed the unprofitable subsidiary and ended the consultation.

Problems in the Consultation

There were three additional problems in this consultation. The first was that the married president was carrying on a sexual liaison with his reluctant secretary. I referred her for professional help that enabled her to break off that exploitation. The second problem was the corporate top management trio. Two of the three had been constantly in rivalrous conflict with each other for years. Each had a stake in the corporation, and therefore would not leave, nor could either buy out the other. I recommended to the two that they each get personal psychological help. Instead, they retained a clinically untrained trainer who urged them and their spouses into confrontational behavior that only exacerbated their conflict. When they tried to get the subsidiary president to accept him into the subsidiary, I objected. Fearful that I might abandon the now blossoming subsidiary, they backed off. The third problem was their intrusive attempts to interfere with the management of the subsidiary. I had to rebuff them early on because obviously the president at that time could not.

Among the important things I learned in this case was the need to protect the client. A consultant often might not be able to fend off higher management, and no doubt many consultants do not see that as part of their function. The rationale for doing so stems from clinical experience: one has to act in many different ways for many different clients. In this situation it was possible, partly because of my reputation and partly because they did not want the subsidiary to collapse. In addition to assessment, in the course of managing the consulting relationship, one must bring to bear whatever clinical skill one has.

This case illustrates the varying facets of extended consultation, ranging from crisis response, to supporting a passive CEO, to resolving conflict, to evolving a cohesive team, to protecting both the client organization and its leader from intrusive machinations by higher management, to clinical referrals. It points to the need for having an armamentarium of intervention skills and the competence to manage long-term consulting relationships.

CASE STUDY: NO WAY

In the preceding cases, I undertook consultation, but sometimes one must not. An issue that arises infrequently in the consultation literature is when not to take on a client. An important aspect of a consultant's decision to do so or not hinges not only on the client's degree of readiness for help but also on his willingness to be helped. A client or client system often has great pain, but is unwilling or unable to do something about it. Sometimes a consultant spends weeks of work assessing a situation only to have the client fail to settle into a course of action. Making the judgment not to enter into consultation is a crucial part of the assessment. This case is illustrative.

A medium-sized service organization had some 300 technical and professional people, with a supporting staff of about twice that number. The chief executive had been exposed to various kinds of organizational development activities and wanted more for his organization. New to his role, he hoped to build a lively and participative organization. All of his key professional staff who would go were sent off to various kinds of group experiences. However, when they came back, nothing much happened in their day-to-day application of what they supposedly had learned.

The organization had a fifty-year history of eminence in its field. Its staff had strong identification with it and its services. Many were preeminent in their disciplines. Many also were professionally and socially close to each other. However, they had long been dominated by a charismatic chief who made certain that no successor would arise from the professional group by reorganizing the structure when it seemed that someone among the group had developed a significant following. He maneuvered his board, most of whom were old friends, into choosing his successor. The staff had no part in choosing their new chief executive, nor did they respect the competence of the person chosen.

The new chief executive engaged a series of consultants, including some from abroad, but he seemed unable to make effective use of any of them. They waited around for him to decide how to use them, and then, bored with waiting, they left. The organization lost many of its key staff, who departed in three successive waves at two-year intervals. Only those remained who had no options to go elsewhere or felt it was too late to do so. Sizing up the situation in the initial meeting, I decided that there was nothing to consult about because there was no client. If the chief executive could not act, and if others in the organization could not do so without being perceived as rebels, then I, the consultant, perforce would be viewed as a fomenter of rebellion. There was little possibility of change. Ultimately, the organization hemorrhaged and desperately sought to be acquired by another, an effort that failed because the chief executive did not want to give up his organization's autonomy. Now diminished in size, reputation, and function, it remains a money-losing shadow of its former self, barely surviving until its financial reserves run out.

Learning to say "Thanks, but no thanks" has to become a fundamental technique for a consultant. Despite the urgent wish to consult, and sometimes the pressure to sustain one's income, it is the better part of wisdom not to allow oneself to be exploited uselessly. In this case, I could have been paid well for not doing very much, but time is too precious to waste in such an exercise in futility. If one has time to spare, better to use it to develop new clients or catch up on professional reading.

PUBLIC SCHOOL CASE STUDY: NO LONGER A FIT

Most organizational consultations range from helping individuals with career problems to resolving intraorganizational differences, managing change, and helping to formulate new directions. Sometimes, more unusually, the consultant is called upon to assess fundamental elements of a community. For most organizational consultants, this is a long way from their industrial-organizational or clinical paths. Such a task particularly calls for systematic assessment. In this case, it calls specifically for both clinical and sociological understanding.

The superintendent of a public school system in a suburban community sought consultation because he could not understand why his community several times had rejected a bond issue to build a new high school, despite its commitment to a high level of secondary education. He wanted to know how decisions were made in his community. Although he had lived there for some years, that process eluded him.

An assessment disclosed that he had been chosen by one school board to be, in effect, an errand boy for that board, which insisted on making its own decisions. However, another board subsequently was elected, and the new board wanted him to assume more active leadership. Given his established characteristic mode of behavior that had made him the appropriate choice for the previous board, he could not do so. It was quite clear that this rather unaggressive man, who needed to be able to please others, could not engage in that kind of take-charge leadership activity that his situation now demanded.

The subunits of his school system had become empires of their own. He was unwilling and unable to confront and challenge the respective principals and the power structures in the community that supported them. The princi-pals had no reason to allow themselves to be organized into a cohesive sys-tem, because each had his or her own domain that he or she viewed as need-ing to be protected. The financial resources and political structure of the community allowed them to operate independently, because the citizens of each neighborhood were mobilized behind their respective schools. The com-munity had a history of quiet, middle-class, Caucasian personal and social over-control, and of making no waves. When assessment disclosed the ag-gressive but diplomatic leadership activities that now had to be carried out, the superintendent was so dismayed that he refused to allow the results of the assessment to be presented to his school staff and board, as he had agreed. Instead, he delayed the feedback for six months. By that time, although some of the findings were relatively obsolete, the fundamentals had not changed. He no longer fit the role. He chose to resign.

The situational definition of the kinds of leadership behavior required (Hersey & Blanchard, 1977), based on a comprehensive assessment of that community, clarified the leadership role with such vividness that it was ap-parent to the client that the redefined role was not his cup of tea. When I emphasized the situational requirements, it allowed the leader to juxtapose himself against those requirements without loss of face. His unrelieved dis-comfort in that situation made it impossible for him to continue to deny the reality of the assessment that had been offered to him. He chose his own prescription. Prognosis was poor for any intervention while he was in that role.

What was most important here, I learned, was the need for a very care-ful description of the behavior required in each of what now were two differ-ent roles, together with an evaluation of the community context. Once hav-ing done that, the next important step was to help him understand that he was not guilty of doing anything wrong, but that his occupational world had changed around him. Confronting a now well-defined reality, without being criticized by the findings, he could choose other options with his head held high.

CASE STUDY: MANAGEMENT ON THE RUN

In a preceding case, the crucial problem was with the CEO who did not grasp the radical change in his work environment. Here is a situation in which the consultation is frustrated by the personality of the CEO.

There are times when undertaking a consultation is a calculated risk. Without yet having assessed an organization, a consultant might have vague impressions from general knowledge in the community or from having heard of specific incidents about an organization. He or she also might know of an organization's relationship to a larger entity that could influence its practices, or of its heritage that becomes a form of control of the people who operate it. Such organizations often are managed by executives who are not formally trained in management and therefore do not know how they should manage. That is especially true of organizations that are operated by religious denominations. With the best of intentions, one might want to help, but discover too late that he is in a psychological morass, as in this case.

High nursing turnover was the bane of a nun administrator of a rehabilitation hospital. In addition, there was open conflict between the administrator and the medical director. That conflict precipitated the request for consultation by the director of human resources with the grudging consent of the administrator, with the expectation that the consultation would ameliorate the conflict between the two authorities.

Results of Interviews

My student consulting team interviewed all five of the top management group, nine department heads, a sample of twenty-one ward aides on the three shifts, and a sample of support workers (such as janitors, electricians, and dietary personnel), and reviewed the hospital's various statistics and history. They observed six administrative meetings, and visited the wards where patients were largely aged persons who primarily needed nursing care. Given the debilitated state of most of the chronic patients, they did not interview patients. Diagnostic assessment (Levinson, 2002), primarily the interviews, disclosed inadequately trained people in supervisory roles, inadequate support for those in positions of power, show-and-tell meetings of administrative heads, and the administrator's intolerance of leadership initiative other than her own.

The history of the hospital, according to most of the interviewees, was one of passive acquiescence to that kind of administration that substituted rigid smiles for leadership action, and smoothing, denial behavior in the face of repetitive conflict just below the surface. From early on, it was apparent that the prognosis was guarded because the character of the hospital reflected the character of its administrator, who had been in her role eighteen years and reported to the head of her order many miles away in Nebraska.

The likely conclusions of the assessment were becoming more apparent with each passing day. Efforts by the student team to remain in continuing liaison with the director during the course of the assessment were of little avail. Ordinarily, I prefer to meet at least weekly during a consultation with the chief executive of the client organization, to apprise her in a general way without violating confidences about where the consulting team is in its work, and of the general themes that are arising so that she can be prepared for the conclusions when later they are presented formally. That practice was not to be in this case. She would avoid meetings, make only brief and passing contacts in the halls, and continue to operate in a passive-aggressive way, acting in a clandestine manner behind the scenes. Even the priest-chaplain complained about this style of communication. She would manage to attack people, without their knowing clearly how they had been attacked and with no direct opportunity to respond. With that style of leadership, predictably the consequence was that, in the end, when the report and its recommendations were presented to her, she listened politely and then declined the usual post-feedback discussion with the chief executive that I recommend and the subsequent report to the staff.

Given the kind of organization, it soon was clear that the opportunity for significant organizational and personal change was going to be limited. She would and did flee any kind of involvement with me and members of the consulting team that would have required looking seriously at problems and taking forthright action. She fled from her subordinates in the same way. They had no support. Problems remained unaddressed. However, there needed to be a long enough test of various efforts in order to establish a supportive relationship to make certain that no technical and therapeutic stones were unturned to try to help solve these problems. Systematic assessment frequently serves that purpose.

The most important lesson I learned was not to undertake a consultation without prior discussion with and making a judgment about the authoritative executive. If I will not be comfortable working with that executive and she cannot make use of what I have to offer, there is little point in continuing.

CASE STUDY: LEARNING TO SAY NO

In contrast to taking a calculated risk, as in the preceding case, there are times when it becomes apparent in the initial interview with the executive who is seeking consultation, that there is no point to undertaking consultation at all. This might be the case when that person does not have the authority to engage a consultant, as is often the case when a pained member of a family business wants to impose consultation on his uninterested authoritarian boss. It also might be the case when some members of a top management group in conflict see no need for consultative help, or, as in the present case, simply want to be rid of the business and each other.

A management consultant who had been trying to rescue a family company of three brothers, one of whom was a seriously ill alcoholic, recommended I consult with the three. He hoped that the highly respected chain of quality shoe stores, founded by their grandfather and long headquartered in the community, was still a good business that might be perpetuated.

My interviews with the three disclosed no way in which they could come together. Each had erected a decades-long wall of anger against the others. None had sufficient leverage to bring the other two into significant discussion. One, more desperate to preserve the business than the others, had assented to organizational assessment; the other two were uninterested. They had engaged the management consultant to help them prepare to sell their business. Their only compromise was to sell the company so they could go their respective ways.

Sometimes, given this kind of history and problem, it is the task of the consultant to indicate that nothing further can be done. None of the parties has the wish or other motivation to save themselves as a group (in this case a family), or the organization as an organization. Sometimes this might be the case because the leader does not know what to do. Even though the words of the assessment are clear and the recommendations are specific, and even with the collaborative help of the consultant, the leadership task is beyond the leader's capacities, competences, and skills. While intellectually he might be capable of understanding whatever might be recommended, psychologically he is inadequate to do so. This often happens with executives who have been number two persons to very powerful leaders, who then have passed their mantle on to long-serving loyal lieutenants (Levinson, 1974). Sometimes those to whom the business has been bequeathed have no interest in running it, especially if they are members of the third or fourth family generation. Sometimes the uniqueness of the founder's insights, technical knowledge, or innovative perception cannot be replicated by those who follow.

Sometimes the chief executive has deteriorated physically or mentally to the point where, although propped up by his staff, he cannot seriously engage in consultation. On one occasion, a chief executive, who had sent several of his executives to my leadership seminars, wanted to follow up with consultation. However, another consultant was already conducting a time-and-motion study in his plant. I demurred, saying that having two different consultants at the same time in the same factory would confuse the employees, and therefore we should wait until the other consultant was finished. An executive accustomed to having his own way, he angrily rejected my position, and my prospective consultation as well.

Whatever the case, the prospective consultant must learn quickly to make the judgment that he cannot undertake the consultation, and, if at all possible, inform the prospective client why. Sometimes he can explain his reasons, but often discretion dictates the statement that the consultant cannot be helpful with this problem.

Saying no might be a problem if one has an established reputation for successful consultation. Prospective clients then have high expectations, particularly if they feel that this consultant is their last resort. Nevertheless, the consultant cannot be motivated by guilt. His major task then might be to help the client manage his disappointment (Zaleznik, 1967).

CASE STUDY: COMMUNITY MENTAL HEALTH CENTER

The contemporary scene of radically changing demands on organizations raises a different kind of disappointment that requires consultation. Assessment is fundamental to helping the organization create and develop a momentum if it has become somewhat confused about what it is supposed to do. This set of circumstances arises when its economic or philosophical ground is no longer as solid as it once was. What do you do if you have been making buggy whips profitably and you see that people are buying fewer buggies and more autos? Or what do you do if your organization of highly skilled professionals is now being asked to render new services for which its staff, well-trained for present functions, feels unprepared, perhaps even unwilling, to undertake? What happens to the morale of a proud staff if its prized, hard-earned skills become less valued? In such events, a consultant has a multiple task: not only to help the organization recognize and confront its new reality, but also to help its members mourn the loss of their cherished functions and adapt themselves to new demands. This case is illustrative.

A community mental health center with fifty-seven professionals on its staff and a fifty-year history had a new director who followed a much-beloved charismatic predecessor. The center was in crisis because other community agencies (the police department, the school system, the courts), increasingly sophisticated about psychological aspects of their work, were demanding more varied services. They were not satisfied with the consulting and psychotherapeutic services they were getting. Other public and private community service groups whose work overlapped with that of the center were arising. Budget pressures were mounting and relationships with HMOs were rocky. Some key people had moved on.

In the face of this turbulence, the new director chose to take active control. But that was largely of the budget. There was little quality control of services and little movement toward redefining the center's goals and priorities. There was no overall planning. The center was essentially a fragmented assembly of autonomous subunits. Communication among them was poor despite a large number of meetings. The director had little contact with most of the staff, and never discussed reports from the subunits or attended their meetings. None of their respective heads came to see him informally. There was a lack of overall direction, leadership, and strategy.

The staff had high standards. It wanted to perform well and did so clinically. As individual professionals, they always had. However, they talked around issues and jargonized them rather than solving problems. Their mood was one of harassed but controlled professional concern. Both they and the leader were pained by their situation. They could not seem to attack their internal problems despite the great deal of energy expended on them. The staff had little confidence in their new leader, especially after their sense of loss of his predecessor. They shared the perception that the director required direct control. The frustrated director, not knowing which way to turn first, asked for consultation.

Given the shared pain, and the motivation of both the director and the staff as reflected in the assessment interviews, the prognosis was good, but it would take a long time to implement significant change. My goals as the consultant, after assessment, had to include presentation of reality to the organization, that is, that the community wanted more than the individual and group treatment in which the staff prided itself. The goals also had to include mechanisms for change. There was a need to repair the current functioning of the organization before attempting to modify its basic activities. There also was a need to mobilize the staff behind its leader, and to establish his and their confidence in me.

To present the assessment findings, as is my practice, I met with the director alone, then with the director and department heads, and then with the rest of the staff, followed by a presentation to the board. I made explicit the staff's dedication to its historic professional aspirations, together with its limits in meeting the present community's contemporary demands. My summary pointed to the need to develop upgraded programs that were specifically focused on the community's stated requests, and for expanding the staff's aspirations. I also recommended further differentiating and decentralizing the task groups of the organization, and then integrating them more cohesively for better cooperation. I recommended internal task forces to clarify roles, purposes, and goals of the center, specifically stating what the center could and could not do, and how much it would do in each area. This work was to become the basis for a realistic strategy for the center to respond to the new demands being made on it. I asked the director to concentrate his energies primarily on managing the center, and all of the department heads to do the same in their units. That required that they be trained in management and leadership. Recognizing that clinical supervision alone was no longer enough, and being as conscientious as they were, the opportunity to improve their leadership and management skills attracted their interest.

There was a solid history and tradition here, pain from both inside the organization and complaints from the outside, as well as the wish to meet and sustain higher standards while retaining professional vitality and reputation. These comprised sufficient motivation on the part of highly intelligent people to be able to bring them together. Given an accurate perception of both their internal and external realities from a trusted consultant, they could understand what they had to do. However, had I stopped with assessment and recommendations, they would have felt helpless about how to go about implementing the recommendations. I doubt if there would have been sufficient momentum to move ahead. I learned that confronted by a sense of helplessness, I also had to push. Apparently this consultation worked very well, as reflected in the response of the center's director and staff. Some of the staff, later having moved to other agencies and now in charge of them, asked for similar consultation.

CASE STUDY: PHARMACEUTICAL RESEARCH AND DEVELOPMENT GROUP

How to use power wisely was the essence of the preceding case. In this one, the question for the consultant is what does he do in the absence of appropriate managerial power. All organizations are power structures. Leadership is the exercise of power that enables a group of people to work together toward a common purpose. Too frequently, power is not exercised well, as was too often evident in the preceding cases. Sometimes it is dissipated in conflict, sometimes in manipulation that leads those in the organization to distrust their leadership, and sometimes in over-control that undermines spontaneity and initiative. Worse still, in some kinds of organizations, those in authoritative roles who presumably are to exercise power eschew even the appropriate exercise of that power. When that happens, turmoil follows and demoralization ensues. What can a consultant do when assessment makes it clear that appropriate authority cannot act to resolve the turmoil? Here is one way.

In a large pharmaceutical company's research and development division of five major research areas, an interdisciplinary team was organized to pursue innovation possibilities in a prospective new field. The members of the team were assigned by their respective area chiefs. Four of them were male Caucasian physicians. The fifth was a small, Asian woman. She had both an M.D. and Ph.D., was highly knowledgeable about research design, and more highly specialized on the topic than her colleagues. She had been nominated by her area chief and appointed by the vice president of research to head the project when its previous director retired. She soon found herself embroiled in unpleasant conflict with the four men, who resented a chief who was a small, Asian woman, and because of three aspects of her person: size, gender, and quiet demeanor; she did not have a particularly authoritative manner. When she called a meeting, one or more failed to attend. They complained that she was not a good manager. They resisted her leadership efforts. When she turned to her area chief, conflict-avoidant as many scientists are, he counseled her to appease them. In desperation, she appealed to the director of human resources for the division.

Concern About the Leader

The director of human resources interviewed the four men and concluded that they did not want to be led by this small, Asian woman. It was as if to accept her leadership reflected on their masculinity. The director had neither the authority nor the power to resolve the conflict. The project head turned to the corporate vice president of human resources for help. That officer interviewed the five parties and attempted to ameliorate the conflict. When her conciliatory efforts failed, she asked for consultation.

I interviewed all of the participants. Two of the hostile men thought they should have been chosen to head the project. One of them had the support of his empire-building chief, who wanted the project for his own area. That chief was a prominent scientist who was locked into his role by his research reputation, and therefore refractory to higher management control. The other area heads did not want to tangle with him either. Another of the four engaged in oppositional behavior that bordered on the unethical. When the vice president of research had appointed the project head, he had instructed her to recruit scientists to expand the project that likely would have great promise. The project was supported in part by government and foundation funds whose grantors valued and expected high-level science. She set about doing so and invited the four to interview the candidates, all of whom necessarily were better qualified for this research than they. Predictably, they rejected all of the applicants.

As I assessed the organization, I concluded that the vice president of research, himself preoccupied with larger scientific and political issues, had little wish to become involved in interpersonal conflict several levels below him, especially if it involved differences among area heads. The area head to whom the project head reported was weak, as manifested by his lack of support for the project head and his advice to appease the men. Internal efforts to alleviate the problem had not been successful, and one area head indirectly was fostering the conflict for his own purposes. "Neither the director of human resources nor the vice president of human resources had power over the team members or their area chiefs. There was no person who could support the project head. She was left to flutter in the political breeze. She did not want to quit, nor did the vice president of human resources want to lose a project head, reputable in her specialty, respected by and well-funded by grantors. She was competent as a manager, a good scientist, and demonstrated enthusiastic imagination for the project. Besides, if she quit, her leaving would contradict the company's oft stated stance of promoting women and minorities. In addition, the company could be vulnerable to a lawsuit for discrimination.

Although I indicated earlier that it was unwise to undertake consultation if the consultant could not have a continuing relationship with an authoritative executive, there was no such person in this situation. The vice president of human resources was desperate for a solution, as was the project head. I determined that if the power vacuum somehow could be filled and someone could exercise authority, the problem might be resolved. Since those who logically should have exercised their power were not doing so, and there were no other internal mechanisms for dealing with the issue, either I had to withdraw or initiate another mechanism for exercising power. I decided on the latter. I recommended that the division create an advisory committee to the project, comprised of prominent women scientists from outside the company. The director of research, glad not to have to be involved in the problem, agreed. The vice president of human resources, in consultation with the project head, recruited such a panel. The panel members interviewed the five participants, coming to the same conclusions I had reached. When they confronted the four men with their findings, the four, who also were involved in other roles in their respective areas, withdrew further into those roles, contributing only nominally to the project. The advisory committee interviewed and helped select the scientific candidates that the project head had recruited. By supporting the project head, they removed a psychological thorn in the body of the organization. The project head was promoted several times as her project became more successful and autonomous.

The Consultant's Concerns

Psychological organizational consultants usually are preoccupied with three major concerns. The first is getting people to talk to each other. That might be to resolve conflict, develop cohesion and mutual support, evolve new directions, or mourn losses, and similar issues. Much of that is done with group processes, ranging from activities that precipitate and then resolve conflicts within a group, to those that encourage people to share losses, to challenging outdoor group projects like Outward Bound. Some of that is done by survey methods.

The second concern tends to be with helping organizations counteract authoritarian power, to cope with ineffective leadership, and to help organizations select and develop their personnel. These activities can take the form of collective feedback, as in upward appraisal or 360-degree feedback, or sometimes group encounters. They might also include job analysis, psychological testing, career counseling, and executive coaching, as well as training and development programs.

The third concern is helping organizations cope with or compensate for incompetence or ineffectiveness. This can take the form of organizational assessment, using some of the techniques referred to above. However, to be thorough, such an assessment, as I have reiterated frequently above, should be systematic and comprehensive. It should establish fact, develop inferences from fact, and make use of a theory of motivation to give body to those inferences.

There is one other issue that psychological organizational consultants characteristically avoid: the exercise of power. Characteristically, they fear and decry power as if the existence of power is bad. That doesn't make it disappear. Psychologists view as their major task helping people increase their flexibility to make their own choices and develop their own directions. Much of the time, psychologists should not, cannot, and do not make choices for their clients, although some, however inadvertently and perhaps even unconsciously, urge their clients in one direction or another.

There are times when a client cannot act intelligently on its own behalf, whether this arises because of being too upset, too incapacitated, or frozen into some kind of position from which he cannot break free, as was the situation of the project head in this case. When I presented this case to a group of colleagues, their recommendations almost exclusively were to have the respective participants talk further to each other, or talk more with the higher authorities, although much of that had been done before to no avail. What my colleagues did not see, indeed did not want to see, was the need for the consultant to fill the power vacuum. They, as with most psychologists and most of the scientist–executives in this case, were reluctant to exercise power, and did not see themselves as creators of power. Inevitably, to be successful as organizational consultants, sooner or later, as this case illustrates, they must.

CASE STUDY: A SIGNIFICANT DIFFERENCE[1]

A significant difference between the mode of consultation illustrated here and that which ordinarily is carried on under the rubric of OD (organizational development) is exemplified by a case developed by David Nadler, Webster Hull, Tom Scanlon, and Bill Englehoff and called the Medteck Corporation. The case begins as follows:

> "We have a basic problem of performance here in the Technical Division." John Torrence (30) Senior Vice President of the Medteck Corporation and director of the company's Technical Division (R&D) was talking with several members of a consulting team that he had brought in to help with the problems in the Division.
>
> "We have a bad case of technical constipation; this Division has not brought out a successful new product in two years. If we don't do something about this problem soon, the whole company is going to be in big trouble."
>
> The Medteck Corporation was founded in 1939 by Paul Torrence, the father of the present chairman and CEO, Arthur Torrence, and the grandfather of the present Senior Vice President for Research and Development, John Torrence. Paul Torrence died in 1968.

[1] I am indebted to David Nadler for permission to use this case.

The consultation took place in 1972. The issue that it raises continues to be valid. I presented this case to several groups of organizational development consultants and asked them what they would do. Their immediate recommendation was to define the problems, list them on a board or easel, conduct team building, and similar kinds of activities. The problems to be dealt with, they assumed, would arise from the group. Also, they presumed, so would corrective actions. However, from the point of view of comprehensive personality theory (Levinson, 1987), I believe the problem was clearly evident in the first two paragraphs, and corrective action could be much simpler and more direct.

According to my assessment (Levinson, 2002), the client is the thirty-year-old grandson of the entrepreneur. He is likely to be under great pressure to prove himself for two developmental reasons, apart from any other considerations: first, as the grandson in a family business, because of what we have known for a long time about intrafamily conflicts in family businesses (Levinson, 1971); second, because at that point in his chronological time, he is in the intimacy stage of psychological development (Erikson, 1963). In that stage, he would likely be concerned with establishing his own track record. His probable sense of urgency for both of these reasons is likely to be exacerbated by the economic realities of the marketplace and the structural interdependencies of the organization; for example, if there are no new products, there is nothing to manufacture or sell.

Furthermore, he himself offers us the metaphor of technical constipation. Unconsciously, he himself senses the problem. The psychoanalytic frame of reference (Levinson, 1976a) enables us to understand that he is talking about a derivative of the anal period of child development. His metaphor refers to stubborn children being toilet trained who won't give. The technicians are holding on; they won't get out new products. We might understand, as a hypothesis, this is their response to the pressure being exerted by the new young boss, operating under the configuration of forces our theory has enabled us to derive. Therefore, rather than get involved in elaborate meetings, problem definitions, teambuilding efforts, and similar typical OD activities, it would be much simpler and more direct to work with the young executive himself. Helping him to understand his present psychological position is likely to reduce his anxieties and concerns to manageable proportions, and thereby diminish his pressure on the technicians that results, however unconsciously, in their stubborn withholding. More importantly, he would not be subject to his subordinates' likely confrontation and attack that might well exacerbate his guilt and paralyze his initiative.

Without a comprehensive theory of personality that includes an understanding of unconscious motivation, stages of development, and characteristic occupational behavior, a consultant could beat all around the organizational bush with a wide range of techniques, none of which really would get to the core of the problem.

CONCLUSIONS

These examples illustrate a range of activities that an organizational consultant can undertake, indeed in some instances must undertake, when he or she bases their activities on a comprehensive theory of personality and a comprehensive assessment procedure, both of which lead logically and systematically to the methods of intervention that the consultant chooses. Such interventions are based on their assessment of the historical momentum of the organization, its limits and resources, its adaptive capacity, the quality of its leadership, and its freedom psychologically, sociologically, and economically to act in its own self-interest.

This series of cases highlights some more frequent typical organizational consulting problems, and how they were managed. Some called for greater initiative on the part of the consultant than one ordinarily finds in the consulting literature. When there was an emergency situation, for example, when an organization was frozen into a rigid managerial posture, I undertook more active charge of the steps toward easing the crisis without undermining the organization's stability. In another situation, I kept my distance from the client system, and, as a benign parental figure, guided the client personnel in doing their own assessment, and making and implementing their recommendations. In still another situation, I not only had to coach the dependent client executive to greater flexibility and autonomy, but also had to protect him and his organization from potential threats from top-level executives and predatory consultants. Despite the impulse to help, on occasion I had to be firm in my refusal to undertake a consultation. When, unwittingly, I was so unfortunate as to have become enmeshed, I learned to evaluate my client executive before undertaking a consultation. At times, after assessment and recommendations, I found that I had to give the client organization a big push to get it started in the right direction. Sometimes assessing an organizational problem meant assessing a host community, and when the focal problem involved the unrecognized shift of a role for a significant authoritative person, I had to help that person find his way out of his occupational dilemma. Group processes and other psychological devices won't solve power vacuums; sometimes I, not fearing power, had to initiate an organizational device to exercise power when those in positions of power would not or could not do so. Finally, difficult managerial problems sometimes do not need elaborate group processes. It was enough in one case to help the executive client understand his stage of psychological development and his place in his family constellation.

Not all consultations are likely to be successful (Mirvis & Berg, 1977). Some are calculated risks. In some, the odds are against success, but entering such situations with a carefully considered prognosis enables the consultant to avoid becoming demoralized when the consultation turns out negatively, as, from time to time, inevitably it does. Such a consultation posture makes for maximum flexibility of operation, specificity of assessment hypotheses, and self-correction.

REFERENCES

Bradford, L. P., Gibb, J. R., & Benne, K. D. (Eds.). (1964). *T-Group theory and laboratory method: Innovation and re-education.* New York: Wiley.

Brockner, J., Davy, J., & Carter, C. (1985). Layoffs, self-esteem, and survivor guilt: Motivational, affective and attitudinal consequences. *Organizational Behavior and Human Decision Processes, 36,* 229–244.

Deal, T. E., & Kennedy, A. A. (1982). *Corporate cultures: The rites and rituals of corporate life.* Reading, MA: Addison-Wesley.

Erikson, E. H. (1963). *Childhood and society* (2nd ed.). New York: Norton.

Fuqua, D. R. & Newman, J. L. (2002). The role of systems theory in consulting psychology. In R. L. Lowman (Ed.), *Handbook of organizational consulting psychology* (pp. 76–105). San Francisco: Jossey-Bass.

Geertz, C. (1973). *The interpretation of culture.* New York: Basic Books.

Hall, D. T., Otazo, K. L., & Hollenbeck, G. P. (1999). Behind closed doors: What really happens in executive coaching. *Organizational Dynamics, 27,* 39–53.

Hersey, P., & Blanchard, K. H. (1977). *Management of organizational behavior: Utilizing human resources.* Englewood Cliffs, NJ: Prentice Hall.

Howard, A. (Ed.). (1994). *Diagnosis for organizational change.* New York: Guilford Press.

Janis, I. L. (1972). *Victims of group think.* Boston: Houghton Mifflin.

Jaques, E. (1996). *Requisite organization: A total system for effective managerial organization and managerial leadership for the 21st century* (2nd ed.). Falls Church, VA: Cason Hall.

Katz, D., & Kahn, R. L. (1978). *The social psychology of organizations.* (2nd ed.). New York: Wiley.

Kehoe, J. F. (Ed.). (2000). *Managing selection in changing organizations.* San Francisco: Jossey-Bass.

Kets deVries, M.F.R. (Ed.). (1984). *The irrational executive: Psychoanalytic explorations in management.* Madison, CT: International Universities Press.

Kilburg, R. R. (2000). *Executive coaching: Developing managerial wisdom in a world of chaos.* Washington, DC: American Psychological Association.

Kraut, A. I. (Ed.). (1996). *Organizational surveys: Tools for assessment and change.* San Francisco: Jossey-Bass.

Lawler, E. E., III. (1986). *High involvement management: Participative strategies for improving organizational performance.* San Francisco: Jossey-Bass.

Levinson, H. (1971, March–April). Conflicts that plague family businesses. *Harvard Business Review, 45*(2), 90–98.

Levinson, H. (1974, November–December). Don't choose your own successor, *Harvard Business Review, 52*(6), 53–62.

Levinson, H. (1976a). *Psychological man*. Boston: Levinson Institute.

Levinson, H. (1976b, July–August). Appraisal of what performance? *Harvard Business Review, 54*(4), 30–46.

Levinson, H. (1987). Psychoanalytic theory in organizational behavior. In J. W. Lorsch (Ed.), *Handbook of organizational behavior*. Englewood Cliffs, NJ: Prentice Hall.

Levinson, H. (1991). Consulting with top management. *Consulting Psychology Bulletin, 43*(1), 10–15.

Levinson, H. (2002). *Organizational assessment: A step-by-step guide to effective consulting*. Washington, DC: American Psychological Association.

Marrow, A. J. (1972). *The failure of success*. New York: AMACOM.

Maslow, A. H. (1954). *Motivation and personality*. New York: HarperCollins.

Menninger, K. A. (1962). *A manual for psychiatric case study* (2nd ed.). Philadelphia: Grune & Stratton.

Mirvis, P. H., & Berg, D. N. (1977). *Failures in organizational development and change: Cases and essays for learning*. New York: Wiley.

Noer, D. M. (1993). *Healing the wounds: Overcoming the trauma of layoffs and revitalizing downsized organizations*. San Francisco: Jossey-Bass.

Roe, A. (1956). *The psychology of occupations*. New York: Wiley.

Roethlisberger, F. J., & Dickson, W. J. (1939). *Management and the worker*. Cambridge, MA: Harvard University Press.

Schein, E. H. (1987). *Process consultation: Vol. 1. Its role in organizational development*. Reading, MA: Addison-Wesley.

Schein, E. H. (1992). *Organizational culture and leadership: A dynamic view* (2nd ed.). San Francisco: Jossey-Bass.

Tomasko, R. L. (1987). *Downsizing: Reshaping the organization for the future*. New York: AMACOM.

Trice, H. M., & Beyer, J. M. (1984). Studying organizational cultures through rites and ceremonials. *Academy of Management Review, 49*(4), 653–669.

Truax, C. R, & Carkhuff, R. R. (1967). *Toward effective counseling and psychotherapy*. Hawthorne, NY: Aldine de Gruyter.

U.S. Department of State. (1970). *Diplomacy in the 70's*. (Department of State Publication 8551, Department and Foreign Service Series 143). Washington, DC: U.S. Government Printing Office.

Von Bertalanffy, L. (1950). An outline of general systems theory. *British Journal of Philosophical Science, 1*, 134–163.

Zaleznik, A. (1967, November–December). Management of disappointment. *Harvard Business Review, 45*, 59–70.

II

CONSULTATION

8

ASSESSING ORGANIZATIONS

HARRY LEVINSON

Organizations come in a wide variety of shapes, sizes, functions, activities, resources, and intentions. Each, however new and young, quickly establishes a culture, a set of symbols, traditions, customary practices, values, and even local language (in-words and jargon). Some of these are drawn from the industry, service, or tradition of which they are a part; some from the policies, practices, and values of its founder; some from national character; some from the specialties of people employed in their work. In this chapter, I offer my own method of assessing organizations, developed out of more than fifty years of consulting experience, and nearly forty years of teaching graduate seminars on the topic, much of which involved student teams working with organizations.

CONTEXT FOR ASSESSING ORGANIZATIONS

There are no organizations without people; therefore, an organization can be considered to be a living organism. As an organization ages, like all

From *The California School of Organizational Studies Handbook of Organizational Consulting Psychology: A Comprehensive Guide to Theory, Skills, and Techniques* (pp. 315–343), edited by R. H. Lowman, 2002, San Francisco: Jossey-Bass. Copyright 2002 by John Wiley & Sons. Reprinted with permission.

living organisms, it evolves through a series of recognizable stages (Adizes, 1988; Greiner, 1998), each, as with the developmental sequence of human beings (Erikson, 1963; Levinson, Darrow, Klein, Levinson, & McKee, 1978), with its own dominant issues and theme. It soon develops a character (Levinson, 1997), that set of values that leads to established attitudes, and, in turn, to customary repetitive behaviors. These differentiate one organization from another in the same industry, business, or service. As its components mature, they, too, begin to differentiate themselves, as do children in a family. The subcultures of marketing differ from those of finance. Sometimes, in large organizations, those components vary so widely that their incumbents have difficulty communicating with those in other units.

A classic example is the Roman Catholic Church, a venerable, worldwide institution. Although the individual churches practice the same liturgy, and a parishioner entering any of them would find the service familiar, the social and emotional atmosphere of the churches, even the languages of ordinary discourse, vary widely.

Those consistencies of behavior, organized around the core organizational character, become what one might call an organizational personality. They make for a certain identifiability, that stable sameness that enables those within the organization to recognize they are part of it, and those outside to recognize what the organization is and what it does. A parishioner can always know what practices to expect in a Roman Catholic Church or an orthodox Jewish synagogue or a Muslim mosque. A customer knows what to expect to buy in a Wal-Mart store or what to expect to eat in a Kentucky Fried Chicken restaurant. The differences that then arise in the dispersed components of a large organization, just as the differences that begin to arise very early on among siblings, make for a certain uniqueness within that identifiability.

Consultants to organizations, and consulting techniques and methods, come in as many varieties as the organizations they serve. Most focus on a specific functional area (for example, marketing), or a specific process (for example, tax accounting), or an organization-wide task (for example, design of organizational structure). Each focus tends to be narrow, problem-centered, and governed by equally narrow diagnostic and intervention techniques. For example, financial consultants who specialize in assessing the market for a potential stock issue are unlikely to consider the personality of the director of manufacturing, however important that person is to the profitability of the company, which, in turn, is crucial to the sale price of the stock.

The recommendations that follow such analyses are necessarily equally narrow, a product of the specialty of the consultant's method. Such recommendations rarely take into account the potential unintended consequences or implications beyond the purview of the consultant. For example, a marketing consultant recommended to a major international company that it use the same colors on its packages and the same slogans in its advertising all over the world. The consultant did not take into account the fact that various colors have different meanings in different cultures, as do slogans, idioms, and advertising phrases (Axtell, 1993). Only when the product failed in several countries did the company discover its costly error.

Precipitating Events for Consultation

Typically, a board of directors, a chief executive, or some intermediate manager, decides the organization or one of its components has a problem. Depending on the executive's own judgment, he will attribute the problem to a cause he suspects. He will then request consultation either by going directly to a consultant or inviting bids for a consultation project. If the company official goes directly to a consultant, that executive is likely to fall back on previous experiences. For example, a major financial organization from time to time senses rumbles of discontent among its employees. Each time the vice president of human resources hears echoes of that disquiet, he calls on the same consulting firm to distribute a questionnaire among the disaffected work group, followed by some limited corrective effort. Some businesses routinely survey their employees at regular intervals to keep abreast of morale (Kraut, 1996). Some will call on experts they have heard at professional meetings, or whose promotional brochures interest them. Some, preoccupied with a problem, might save published articles, procrastinating about that problem for years, before they call the expert featured. Some seek recommendations from peers. Some do not seek consultation until their organizational problems become crises.

Types of Consultants

Much of the consultation on psychological issues is done by industrial–organizational (I-O) psychologists, some by social psychologists, some by counseling and clinical psychologists, and much by many who are not psychologists. I-O psychologists are involved significantly in macro-organizational problems such as organizational design, organizational climate, selection by objective tests and assessment centers, compensation, performance appraisal methods, job analyses, and similar topics that lend themselves to categories, systems, and measurement (Kraut & Korman, 1999). The second type of consultant works largely with group processes on such issues as conflict resolution, team building, participative management, stress management, and organizational culture (Waclawski & Church, 2002). The third type focuses more heavily on individuals, emphasizing executive selection, career development, coaching, and leadership (Silzer, 2002).

Depending on their skills and training, there is considerable overlap in consultation activities among these types. At one end of the continuum of psychological consultants, the training and emphasis in the first group is heavily concentrated on the scientific (by which they mean measurement), empirical, atheoretical, and rational. At the other end of the continuum is clinical psychology, with its heavy dependence on theory, particularly its attention to the dynamics of personality development, emotions, conceptualization of motivation of which a person or group is unaware, and its effort to understand the sequence, however irrational, that proceeds from feelings to thoughts to behavior. Those who are highly trained in one area are less likely to be equally skilled in another. However, they are all governed by the same code of ethics (Lowman, 1998), by which they are constrained from undertaking consultation in areas for which they are not trained. But, like professionals in other wide-ranging disciplines, too often they are not well enough aware of what they do not know. Equally often, they might not be able to accept the usefulness of another point of view. Between not knowing and not accepting, many do not adequately define the boundaries of their competence.

Often, those who call upon psychologists for consultation cannot differentiate among the specialists. Those who most frequently are the contact persons, namely the directors or vice presidents of human resources, often are no more knowledgeable in this respect than other executives. Therefore, the prospective consultant must herself delimit the nature of the organizational problem and her competence to help resolve it. Unfortunately, too often, some with a limited range of skills are ready to apply them to every problem. That tendency recalls the old saw that if one gives a child a hammer, everything gets hammered.

There is nothing necessarily wrong with being empirical and dealing directly with problems of which an individual is aware. All of us are likely to take an aspirin for a headache or put fuel in the automobile gas tank when the dial reports the fuel to be low. Similarly, employees in an organization can be angry because they feel underpaid, and become enthusiastic when their pay is raised. But if the headache arises repetitively when a person becomes enraged, aspirin will be of little relief, and if the gas is low because of a leak in the tank, putting more in will be of only temporary help. So it is in organizations: when employees feel infantilized, their pent-up feelings can result in poor morale. When surveyed, they might attribute their malaise to poor communication with their higher managements. Without an understanding of the phenomenon of displacement, that is, unwittingly transferring the feelings stimulated by one situation to another, efforts to improve communications might be equally inadequate to raise morale.

The implication, of course, is that when a problem is more than transient or casual, before trying to fix it, the consultant should understand what caused it and why it persists. Primitive peoples might have tried to avert epidemics by propitiating their gods, but doing that is unlikely to relieve the endemic AIDS problem among them.

Cause-Finding in Assessment

The issue of cause, or *why*, raises the question of what constitutes adequate diagnosis or cause-finding. This chapter describes my particular method for doing so, but there are many possible answers to that question. Here is a list of some:

Who is doing the finding-out?

What is the consultant's specialty?

What is the consultant's competence or reputation in that specialty? (Remember that half of any graduating class is in the bottom 50 percent of that class.)

How narrow or comprehensive is the consultant's focus?

To what degree does the consultant understand what motivates individuals and groups, that is, the why of behavior?

How does the consultant take that understanding into account?

How long will it take to discover the causes, because all behavior has multiple causes?

How much will it cost?

What is the trade-off between the time and cost on the one hand, and tolerating the pain and discomfort on the other?

Who feels the pain most acutely?

Who doesn't want to be bothered?

How long has this pain been going on?

What was done about it before?

Why now?

Who now can do what about it?

Who will be helped by finding the causes?

Who will be hurt?

What are the odds on bringing about useful change?

What might be the unintended consequences?

TOOLS FOR ASSESSMENT

Most psychological efforts to diagnose or assess organizational problems are focused on *part-problems* or processes (Howard, 1994). By part-problems, I mean subjects or topics that are circumscribed, sometimes by a model of an organization, sometimes by a problem. Using models enables consultants to gather and organize their information about an organization into subjects or categories. Among the more prominent models are those of Burke (1994), Hornstein and Tichy (1973), Nadler and Tushman (1988), and Weisbord (1978). However necessary to organize what otherwise would be an overwhelming plethora of data, diagnosis by categories risks boxing in or limiting what the consultant sees, and therefore what she does about it.

By processes, I mean such issues among others, for example, as training (Odiorne & Rummler, 1988), selection (Bray & Byham, 1991), performance appraisal (Milkovich & Wigdor, 1991), building and managing teams (Lawler, 1992), and managing change. In my view, concentrating on processes too often does not take adequately into account the history, structure, and culture of the organization in which the processes take place.

Different types of consultants use many of the same methods: interviews, questionnaires, compilation of organizational statistics, analysis of organizational culture, evaluation of goals, and, in addition, specialized skills in which they are expert. Few take into account the historical evolution of an organization, the impact of its past on the present, its level of energy, the meaning of the problem to the organization members, its adaptive pattern, or the typical repetitive behavioral characteristics it develops. Failure to do so means that often the consultant has an inadequate grasp of the complexity of the problem and limited logic for undertaking specific processes for change.

My preferred assessment or diagnostic procedure goes beyond and ideally integrates both the part-problems and processes (Levinson, 2002a). It is based on Von Bertalanffy's biological conception of a living organism as an open system (1950), and adapted from Menninger's psychiatric case study method (1962). My psychological orientation is psychoanalytic and my basic professional training is clinical. Four years of training in a psychiatric hospital led to a heavy emphasis on diagnosis and the therapeutic use of the hospital environment as a treatment method. This background, taking into account the family background and psychological development of the individual, leads me to consider the impact of the founder on the organization, the concept of organizational evolution, stages in growth, and interactions both with and on the organization's environment, as well as the influence of the environment on the organization, interaction among its components, and adaptive efforts toward internal integration and mastery of the environment for survival. I assume that all organizations, even nonprofits, necessarily compete for resources and acceptance. One way or another, they seek a return on their investment, whether money or energy. The fundamental thrust of an organization is to perpetuate itself.

PRELIMINARY STAGES OF CONSULTATION

Organizational consultation often begins with a generic proposal from a consultant who offers her services to address a specific area or problem. The proposal may be *cold*. In a cold proposal, the consultant identifies frequent problems in organizations and offers his services, either in a self-initiated visit to a prospective client or by a brochure, to ameliorate or remedy them. The generic proposal might be a response to interest from or a request by an official in an organization. In either case, acceptance of the generic proposal usually leads to an interview by the consultant with one or more persons representing the organization.

In the initial interview, usually the organization's representatives state the problem or issue that needs professional attention, seek to learn about the consultant's training, experience, and previous consultations, and how this problem is proposed to be addressed, and arrive at an estimate of time and cost of the proposed effort. Rarely, the initial interview is a ruse to get the consultant to provide an answer to a problem without formally engaging him to do so.

The consultant concurrently makes a preliminary private assessment of the nature and complexity of the problem, the authority of those who are interviewing him to retain him for a prospective engagement, or who they represent, the likelihood of success in consulting with this problem in this organization at this time, and the competence and resources of the organization to undertake the necessary change.

The consultant should ask why he or she is being considered and learn what other consultants have worked with the organization, on which problems, and with what success. The consultant should also find out what the organization expects from the consultation, and what, if any, constraints there will be on areas, functions, or people to be interviewed, surveyed, or observed. It is also important to learn what makes the consultation important to be undertaken at this particular time, how the information will be fed back to the organization, and how confidentiality will be maintained. The consultant also will need to learn the key figure in the organization to whom he or she will be accountable, and the person or persons to be worked with directly to accomplish the project.

If the preliminary mutual exploration satisfies both parties, the consultant might then submit a preliminary exploratory proposal to sample the problem described which might be a symptom of a more complex issue. The preliminary exploration usually means interviewing several people at different levels in the organization, but sometimes only those at a given level if the problem is attributed to that level. That exploration might lead the consultant to redefine the problem with the management.

For example, the top management of a financial company attributed the seeming lack of interest of the clerical staff and their unrelieved repetition of errors to the management's unwillingness to accept a union. Preliminary interviews with six clericals disclosed that the clerical staff was demotivated by management's repeated threat over several years to downsize the function. They did not know whether they would continue to have a job in the immediate, let alone the more distant future.

In another example, the superintendent of a school system sought consultation to relieve the high absentee rate among teachers, which he attributed to inadequate salaries that he could not change. Interviews with eight teachers in four elementary schools disclosed that the superintendent practically never visited the classrooms or talked with individual teachers. His motto seemed to be that if they did not make problems for him, he wouldn't bother them. As a result, they felt abandoned.

After the exploration, the consultant might submit a formal proposal describing what is proposed to be done, over what period of time, and at what cost (see Appendix B of Levinson, 2002b, for proposal examples). When that proposal is accepted, preferably in writing, it becomes a formal contract for the consultation. If the consultation continues in phases, and the organization is required to bind its obligations, as, for example, government organizations usually are, the contract might have to be renegotiated at the beginning of each phase. However, I have been engaged in a number of long-term consultations without renegotiation.

THE ASSESSMENT PROCESS

Following the preliminary stages, the consultant enters the organization. I have summarized the steps in my method and described them in detail elsewhere (Levinson, 1993, 2002a, respectively). In those works, I organize the process into four steps, the first three for gathering data, and the fourth for the inferences drawn from the data. These are:

1. Genetic data (identification and description of the organization, its history, and the reasons for the consultation)
2. Structural data (the formal organization, plant and equipment, finances, personnel demographics and policies, general policies and practices, and time cycles)
3. Process data (information and communications transmission)
4. Interpretative data (how the organization perceives itself and its environment, its basic knowledge and how it makes use of that knowledge, the emotional atmosphere of the organization and its capacity to act, and attitudes about and relationships with multiple stakeholders, things and ideas, the consultant, power, and itself)

The facts and inferences are then integrated into an analysis (depending heavily on the psychological orientation of the consultant), and then into a summary and conclusions.

The Consultant as a Diagnostic Instrument

The consultant herself is the most important instrument in her work. Therefore, I recommend that the consultant keep a diary of her contacts, activities, impressions, and feelings about the process throughout her consultation. Such a diary is imperative if the consultant is to understand the ups and downs of her relationships in the organization, the resistances and hostilities she encounters, and the efforts of various organizational members to use her for their own organizational purposes.

For example, a consultant observing a machine shop in a steel fabricating company wrote in her diary, "This is the cleanest machine shop I have ever seen. Although the milling machines necessarily create lots of scrap metal, the machine operators repeatedly sweep the floors around their machines. They invited me to don safety glasses and to take an initial cut at a piece of steel. They explained what they were doing even though to do so required that they take time from their work. When the bell rang for the lunch break, they gathered in small cliques around the radios to listen to Paul Harvey, a conservative commentator. They invited me to take my lunch with them."

After feeding back the consultation report to the head of a private school, the leader of the consulting team wrote in her diary, "He constantly interrupted me as I was reading him the report, repeatedly making minor corrections and raising questions about the methods and findings although I had kept him apprised all along in a general way about what we were learning. His continued querulous attitude irritated me and finally I told him that he was quibbling at the expense of learning about the school's problems."

Transference

It is especially important for the consultant to understand *transference*, or the unwitting transfer of attitudes toward the consultant from an interviewee's past relationships to power figures (Racker, 1968). Some might regard the consultant suspiciously, others as omnipotent, still others contemptuously. The consultant also must try to understand her own varied feelings about and attitudes toward those organizational members with whom she comes into contact. These feelings are called *countertransference* (Racker, 1968). The consultant might not be aware of her feelings as they occur, but maintaining a diary enables her to review her own behavior and infer those previously unrecognized feelings and attitudes that might have intruded into her work.

For example, the team head above who complained about the querulous client, in a subsequent discussion with me about why she vented her anger at him, came to understand that she overreacted because she identified him with her father, who had corrected her repetitively about trivial aspects of her behavior.

In other situations, a consultant needs to learn why she becomes irritated with a client manager who she thinks is trying to control her, or why she bristles when a director of human resources proposes to fall back on 360-degree feedback whenever a morale problem arises, and similar irritating or frustrating experiences. Sometimes she needs to understand why she prefers some people in an organization over others, and why, perhaps, she gives greater weight to their opinions.

Subjectivity in Organizational Assessment

Another reason for maintaining a diary is because all organizational assessment is necessarily subjective. No matter how many instruments a consultant uses and how much statistical data he amasses and reports, inevitably he has had to choose what aspects of the organization to examine, which to pass over or ignore, and how he interprets what he has found. In his final report, he does not merely quote statistics. He explains or gives meaning to his data. It follows that an assessment conclusion necessarily is hypothesis. This, the consultant ultimately reports, is what was done and found (facts); this is what was learned (inferences); this is how the consultant understands them (interpretations); and this is what is recommended (methods to bring about change).

Most consultants, of whatever theoretical orientation, are likely to agree on the facts. They might differ in what they infer from the facts. They certainly will differ in their interpretation of their inferences depending on their specific theoretical orientations, which is why each needs to have a firm theory to guide the work and to keep inferences separate from interpretations. A consultant's recommendations likely will follow preferred methods and the espoused or implicit theory. When reporting back to the organization, the consultant's findings and interpretations are subject to the critical analysis of the organizational members. They might or might not follow the recommendations, or might offer or seek other solutions to their problems. The consultant also might recommend other consultants to deal with problems not within the consultant's area of expertise.

Organizational assessment involves viewing the information gathered from several different vantage points. This is necessary because, given the subjective nature of the process, the overlap of perspectives that become repetitive confirmations assures the assessor (and the organization) of the validity of the findings. The diary is an additional device for checking on oneself, perhaps reinterpreting what one is learning, and reviewing various options for change as the consultant becomes more familiar with the organization's potential for change. It is also a device for maintaining one's professional humility.

146   HARRY LEVINSON

There are two other important reasons for maintaining a diary. When something goes awry, when the information gathering is not going as well as it should, the consultant can review the basic organized facts, recheck the inferences derived from them, and review the interpretations. Since all assessment is hypothesis, and all tentative hypotheses (the hunches or temporary understandings) the consultant makes along the way must be checked out, only by being able to review both the data and logic can the consultant maintain a scientific, self-correcting posture.

When a consulting team was returning by car to its home base from its work in the branch office of a public utility company, one of the team members complained about the behavior of the team leader in the regional office they had just visited. He wrote in his diary, "The team leader pressed the local manager to designate his best and his worst crews. The elderly local manager, close to retirement and preoccupied with a sick wife, seemed unable to do so. The team leader abruptly took over, told the manager which of us would ride the gas crew trucks, which the electrical line crew trucks, and which would interview in the office. The manager had no say in the matter. I thought that was an impatient and discourteous way to manage the situation and said so in the car."

The Detail of Organizational Assessment

As I view it, fully elaborated, organizational assessment is highly detailed. It cannot be comprehensive and be otherwise. Such detailed attention often dismays the prospective consultant and leads him to avoidance, in favor of more simple assessment methods, or none at all (Schein, 1999). But complexity does not become simplicity solely by denying it or choosing to ignore it. As a matter of fact, such an outline is extremely helpful to the consultant, especially the beginner, because it tells the consultant what kinds of information to gather, and, in addition, how to order that information so that it leads to logical inferences and conclusions regardless of one's theoretical orientation. Thus, the detailed outline provides both structure and guidance and enables him to continue organizing and integrating his work as it progresses. If the consultant elects not to use it fully, at least he knows what he has chosen to leave out. Furthermore, with experience, the consultant need not always undertake a comprehensive, detailed assessment, as the range of cases in another chapter in this volume illustrates (Levinson, 2002b). A client once asked me how I arrived at a diagnostic conclusion after only five minutes of conversation with him. My reply was, "Five minutes—and forty years of experience before that."

The Importance of History in Organizational Assessment

My conception of organizational assessment makes much of history. Apart from my clinical orientation that gives important consideration to a person's history, there is good reason for tracing an organization's history. One important reason is that it establishes both the pace of growth and the basic focus of the organization. It is not without good reason that many businesses and other organizations are shedding components that were acquired when it was assumed that expansion (to become a conglomerate if the organization was a business) was wise. There is much contemporary management effort to get back to basics, and to recognize and reassert the fundamental core of the organization. But in consultation, the importance of history largely has been ignored.

Much has been written about more traditional organizational development (OD) consultation and the problems inherent in ignoring history (Coglan, 1997). But even in the early days of OD consultation, few took seriously Greiner's admonition (1967, p. 2) that ". . . future researchers and change agents need to give greater weight to historical determinants of change with special emphasis being attached to the developing relationship between an organization and its environment. It is within this historical and developmental context . . . that we may be able to explain better why a 'planned' change program may succeed in one organization and not in another." Even before there was an OD movement, Meltzer (1944, p. 166) observed that ". . . segmented studies of such problems as illumination, fatigue and monotony do not get at the heart of the realities in industry. The realization of the significance of human attitudes and the development of techniques for human understanding has more to contribute. . . . What are the realities of problems of management in industry? Can they be realistically and comprehensively understood without a fairly thorough study of personality organization as they emerge in life situations in industry?"

Not only was history largely ignored in OD consultation, but it continues to be. In the most recent volume of varied OD methods (Waclawski & Church, 2002), there is no reference to history in the index, and none of the chapters discusses organizational history. With rare exceptions (Argyris, 1958), subsequent writings on OD tended not to address problems the consultant encountered in long-term relationships with an organization, and particularly with its key figures. Nor did those writings identify the kinds of feelings the consultant had when she gathered information for assessment and intervention when that effort was extended and comprehensive.

All organizations fundamentally are interactions of people. This implies that, despite nearly 100 years of effort to make management scientific (Taylor, 1911), that is, reduce as much analysis of management practices to numbers as possible, the basic currency of all organizations is people's feelings. No matter how logical or rational organizational decisions presumably are meant to be, almost all decisions ultimately are judgments, and, like all human behavior, judgments necessarily are based on feelings and thoughts.

De Geus (1997) points out that the average life of companies is 12.5 years. He concludes that, "Companies die because their managers focus on the economic activity of producing goods and services, and they forget that their organizations' true nature is that of a community of humans. The legal establishment, business educators, and the financial community all join them in this mistake" (p. 3). Other institutions that are not driven primarily by economic issues do not have the same mortality rate, he adds.

The Role of Power in Organizations

All organizations are power hierarchies and necessarily must be so. Every organization is headed by a board of directors or an owner. That individual (or they) establish(es) the direction of the organization and is responsible for decisions about the organization. She or they often delegate(s) subsidiary decision-making to executives, and they, in turn, delegate authority to others who are accountable to them. She or they employ(s) people with various levels of authority and control to carry out the policies and practices of the organization. Employees at each level are accountable to or report to a person at the next higher level for the effectiveness of their work. Sometimes people report to more than one person, each of whom has some degree of control over the reporting person. It is crucially important for the consultant to understand where power lies in an organization and how it is distributed, both manifestly and covertly, and not to be prejudiced against its appropriate exercise. Some people in some organizations at some time should indeed be fired, sometimes for their own benefit. True, power often is abused in organizations (Hornstein, 1996), and all too often over-control inhibits innovation and adaptive effort. But attempts to abolish power or to make business organizations more democratic by having employees choose their own leaders (which is not the same as inviting employee participation in some aspects of decision-making), as was the case in some communist political systems, can only lead to organizational chaos. The most conspicuous examples in nonprofit organizations are the elections of abbots in monasteries. There, the effort to balance the interests of all factions results in the compromise choice of the candidate least offensive to any faction, and therefore most nearly acceptable to all of the monks. If that leader is not a skilled manipulator, and most monks are not, that choice leads to organizational paralysis and often to subsequent splits.

All organizations are attack devices. That's one of the reasons so many writers about leadership and organizations offer military and athletic models or metaphors. On the military side, these range from Attila the Hun (Roberts, 1991) through contemporary generals. The athletic model is exemplified by descriptions of highly successful coaches like the University of North Carolina's championship basketball coach Dean Smith (Chadwick, 1999). Schools attack ignorance, churches inveigh against sins, charitable organizations seek to alleviate poverty or strife, healthcare organizations fight illness and death. All living organisms seek to master their environments for their survival and to perpetuate their species. For the organizational consultant, it is important to learn what the organization attacks, how well that attack fits with its purpose, and how effectively it does so.

Identification With the Organization

All organizations foster identification of their members with the organization. Some go to great lengths, often paternalistically, to further the feeling of being one big family. That identification is necessary if people are to assume initiative, and to act responsively and authoritatively on behalf of the organization's values, standards, and practices. However, when organizational members become overly identified with their employer, they risk becoming narcissistically preoccupied: for example, "We are not only the best, but also, competitors deserve only our condescension." Such an orientation exacerbates dependency and inhibits innovative adaptation in the organization (Schwartz, 1990; Levinson, 1994).

Ideally, power in an organization is organized and implemented in a five-step process, usually beginning with the *ego ideal* of the founder. An ego ideal is one's wishful fantasy about himself at his ideal best (Freud, 1961). However vague that mental picture of oneself, one is always implicitly and unwittingly striving toward it. When transformed into organizational leadership, that personal ideal aspiration becomes an organizational ideal. To the extent to which members of the organization are organized in its pursuit, the organizational ideal becomes their dominant sense of purpose. It addresses the question, "Why are we doing this?" Purpose is then translated into vision: "What is the nature of the field in which we are pursuing our ideal?" Vision, in turn, is narrowed to mission. For example, a company whose founder failed to be accepted to medical school pursued his ego ideal as one who cured illnesses by forming a business that manufactured drugs, his vision. Since he could not manufacture drugs for all illnesses, he then had to choose from among many illnesses those toward which he would direct his efforts: his mission. The mission then had to be refined into goals, or long-term steps toward purpose, and goals, in turn, into objectives, or short-term steps.

Unfortunately, most organizations are not organized as logically as I have outlined in the preceding paragraph. In fact, few are based on solid psychological logic (Jaques, 1996). Many heads of business organizations, especially if they are not the founders and they come from outside the organization, are not clear about the first two issues, purpose and vision. With the usual limited, mechanistic psychological training offered in schools of management, or none at all, they tend to jump into mission and objectives without giving adequate consideration to the more fundamental psychological issues. As a result, they do not build their organizations to last (Collins and Porras, 1994; Collins, 2001). In addition to failing that knowledge, they are intensely preoccupied with reaching quarterly profit goals or other short-term targets to achieve their bonuses and to please the financial community or their boards (Stevenson & Cruikshank, 1998). Their circumscribed focus leads to high leadership turnover about which the business press repetitively complains. Further, when managerial difficulties then arise, they tend to flee repetitively into managerial fads (Levinson, 1985; Shapiro, 1995).

Next Steps in the Assessment

After the initial mutual exploration and the acceptance of a formal proposal, the consultant speaks at length with the chief executive, or whichever executive is responsible for the unit about which the consultation is proposed. If the accountable executive or manager is not involved, she is unlikely to support the consultation and might even sabotage it. In effect, to enter an organization without her assent is to intrude into her management prerogatives. The consultant should discuss with that person how he plans to assess the organization and how he proposes to go about doing it. This discussion might even be in the nature of a mutual diagnosis. If not already the case, the responsible executive must get to know the consultant and be assured that he or she will continue to be in charge of what is happening in the organization. The consultant must be careful not to undermine the authority of the responsible executive. That executive might help the consultant avoid some problems and even steer the consultant around potential blocks. For example, in my first study in the Kansas Power and Light Company (Levinson, Price, Munden, Mandl, & Solley, 1962), the chief executive recommended that I, not one of my colleagues, interview the union leader only after my team had been accepted in the field. That proved to be a fruitful recommendation.

The responsible executive also might be the best contact for arranging interviews with board members and community influentials. The responsible executive or the person in charge of the human resources function will have to help lay out the plan of the consultation to the extent that the consultant must take into account geographical distribution of functions and locations, as well as the range of work roles that must be sampled. The responsible executive usually is the person who must interface with the organization's many environments and stakeholders (those who have something at stake in their relationship to the organization). She or he also might describe most comprehensively what issues and problems the organization faces, and what its particular achievements have been. Unless there are strong reasons why the consultation report is to be limited to the responsible executive, permission for it to be presented subsequently to all employees can be given at this time. The consultant will inform them of that agreement in his initial presentation to them. The discussion with the responsible executive also will provide the consultant with a perspective on the organization's history and its dominant competitive edge or core competence, for example, what it tries to do better than competing organizations. It also sets the stage for a regularly scheduled conference between the two when the consultant keeps the responsible executive informed about where he is in the organization, and, without violating confidences, tells her or him in a general way what he is doing, for example, interviewing, observing, or examining financial reports. As the consultation progresses, without identifying individuals or groups, the consultant should report general themes arising in the interviews and informal discussions with employees or groups that are likely to appear in the final report. By doing so, the consultant alerts the client executive to what later might be reported so that there are no significant surprises for her or him in the final report.

In my preferred approach, the consultant then prepares a letter to be signed by the chief executive (or approves one that she has written) that is sent to all employees describing the reasons for the approaching consultation and what the consultant will do. That letter should assure the recipients that their privacy will be respected and confidentiality will be maintained both in interviews and observations of their work. Following the distribution of that letter of introduction (see Appendix B of Levinson, 2002a, for examples of all suggested written communications), the consultant then presents an oral statement to the top management group (however that is defined) of what is proposed to be done, emphasizing confidentiality and the agreement about feedback. The consultant follows with similar presentations to successive lower levels in the organization, following the organization's formal accountability structure, allowing for questions and discussion.

The Company Tour

The consultant should then tour the physical location(s) of the organization where feasible, and describe in his diary the circumstances of the various work environments and their impact on those who work in them. Some organizations are in one location, some are scattered throughout the same community, and some are dispersed nationally and even worldwide. The September 11, 2001 collapse of the World Trade Center towers illustrated the distribution of several companies in New York and their subsequent dispersal into temporary quarters both within the city and outside of it. Some organizations (for example, Boeing, General Electric, American Red Cross) might have a headquarters in one community and manufacturing or service facilities in several others. Some American companies (for example, Nike, Lucent) have their products manufactured overseas by contractors. Even some Japanese companies are contracting their manufacturing to Chinese firms. Some companies have distant contractors (in India, China, and Ireland) that tally data, or call centers that respond to inquiries. Some universities have branches in foreign countries, as do many religious organizations. Some major medical centers, such as the Cleveland Clinic, have developed local centers to serve populations distant from their headquarters.

Interviews

The consultant then will develop a sample of employees to interview and a schedule for interviewing. I prefer to interview all of top management, a 10 percent sample of middle management, and a 5 percent sample of line employees. (It will be helpful early on to interview a long-time employee who is familiar with the evolution of the organization and who can identify the informal power brokers.) Those classifications might be arbitrary, but the consultant should assure both himself and the client organization that he has interviewed a representative sample. I generally include all single-person specialists (for example, a hospital pathologist). I allow at least two hours for senior level employees. Some people might have to be interviewed several times. The most unusual interview in my experience continued for eleven hours. Usually, line-level employees are less verbal than managers and executives, so an hour often suffices. I prefer to dictate summaries of my interview notes in the ten-minute break after each interview, because tape-recorded interviews require four hours of transcription for each hour of interview. If one waits until the end of a working day to dictate from notes, the notes might be cold by then, and much information as well as observations of interviewee behavior will be lost.

A questionnaire that follows the interview outline (both are illustrated in Appendix A of Levinson, 2002a) is then distributed to all employees. Unless the client organization is small or heavily individualized, such as a modest-sized law firm in which everyone is interviewed, the questionnaire provides information beyond that from the interviewees. As with the individual interviewees, the respondents are assured of confidentiality. If, being unfamiliar with the consultant, some respondents doubt his integrity, the consultant can suggest that they call anyone they know in other organizations with which he has worked.

The consultant must be aware of the different capacities for abstract thinking among interviewees, as well as the different languages they speak. Although the managers of an Argentinian client spoke English, for them it was a second language. Therefore they asked for an interpreter to be present during the interviews so that they could be sure they both understood the questions and responded accurately in English. In a Boston hospital, the questionnaire had to be translated into Spanish for the kitchen staff. Similar adaptations must be made for the varied ethnic personnel both in the United States and abroad.

In the process of understanding the organization's history, the consultant should give particular attention to the stages in the organization's growth and how it has coped with crises. For example, for many years, public utilities were protected from competition. That fostered long-term employment and heavy dependence on the employer. When those companies were deregulated and had to become more competitive, that change became a crisis for many managers and executives who were less able to compete. In turn, the organizations were less able to compete and experienced a high turnover in their managerial ranks. Some companies are still recovering from that drastic change in organizational personality. Some dignified, mainline Protestant churches are being outflanked by more fundamentalist churches that foster emotional expression. Medical practice has become more strictly controlled by HMOs at the cost of more personal relationships that formerly characterized most physicians' practices. Elementary schools are being pressed to test pupils at certain grade intervals, leading teachers to complain about having to teach to the tests.

It will be important to know how the organization is financed. The consultant unfamiliar with interpreting balance sheets might find it advantageous to ask an accountant to help him understand its implications.

When there have been changes in its products or services, and especially when the organization has confronted technological changes both in its internal processes and among its work with clients, parishioners, students, patients, or customers, the consultant might also want to ask for guidance by someone technologically knowledgeable. Though technological change has been a boon for many organizations (Trist & Murray, 1997), even nonprofits, many employees do not have the conceptual capacity to learn the now-required skills. In some cases, recent employees who are computer-knowledgeable have been asked to teach older, higher-level executives (who do not have ten-year-olds at home) how to use their computers. But in a few years, there will be no computer illiterate executives.

The Organization's Leadership

No organizational issue is more important than leadership. Several dimensions merit examination. The most significant is the personality of the leader and the fit between the leader's characteristic behavior and that now required by the organization's contemporary environment (Silzer, 2002). For example, it is not a new finding that, characteristically, most entrepreneurs have difficulty becoming managers. The freewheeling entrepreneur often finds it difficult to shift from doing as his impulse moves him to the more rigid, impersonal control of people and processes, from selling a product that he invented to a limited audience to catering to a mass market. The manager of a small operation with close relationships among colleagues might find it difficult to enforce impersonally policies and practices that necessarily must transcend friendships. This is a particularly difficult problem in family businesses (Levinson, 1971; Kets deVries, 1996). People in positions of power over others must meet their dependency needs, because followers necessarily depend on leaders, while simultaneously keeping those relationships free of personal ties and obligation (Zaleznik, 1989).

Choice of the Leader

In addition to the fit of the personality of the leader to the behavioral requirements of the leadership role, another fundamental issue is how the leader is chosen (Vancil, 1987). Some boards of directors are wise enough to analyze the behavior to be required of a prospective leader and then choose one who fits their projections. Most are not (Levinson, 1980). Some large organizations like General Electric, Citicorp (Levinson & Rosenthal, 1984), and the Roman Catholic Church, keep careful track of promising executive candidates, and rotate them through assignments to test them. Some wise organizations have their board members meet regularly with a diverse number of promising candidates for upward mobility to get to know them personally. Unfortunately, most chief executives are not so wisely chosen, and some are carefully chosen for the wrong reasons. Furthermore, often chief executives endorse favorite candidates for nepotistic or dynastic reasons without an adequate appreciation of what the successor will have to do differently than they did. In any event, the choice of a new leader always involves significant, sometimes drastic, adaptive problems, not only for the new CEO, but also for the followers (and for the consultants who are working in the organization).

There are certain dangers in the selection of executives. The most common in my experience is the promotion of previously successful executives into roles that are conceptually beyond them; they cannot think at the required level of abstraction (Jaques, 1996). Many chief executives, let alone lower-level executives and managers, are in roles that exceed their conceptual capacity. A second major problem is narcissism. All of us necessarily must like ourselves well enough to have self-confidence. But some people like themselves too much and inflate that self-confidence unnecessarily to compensate for their tacit sense of inadequacy. They are particularly attracted to executive roles in which their grandiosity sometimes can be destructive to the organization (Kets deVries, 1989; Maccoby, 2000). Similarly, a third major problem is paranoia. A certain level of suspicion of others' intentions and motives is necessary to survive in competitive executive ranks (Grove, 1996). Too much suspicion, the worry that there are threats behind everyone else's actions, becomes paranoia. A fourth problem is that of dependency. Often an executive succeeds because he is dependent on a stronger leader. The apparent success might mask a dependency that becomes apparent when the dependent executive is promoted to succeed an erstwhile predecessor and proves to be unable to act independently.

Leadership Dangers

There are two tragic dangers among those executives who build highly successful organizations. The first, more frequent, is that sometimes those who succeed too well are seduced into excesses that lead to their demise

(Miller, 1990). That allegation was made of Ken Lay when Enron collapsed (McLean, 2001). The second, fortunately comparatively rare, concerns executives who lead their organizations into destruction only after the organization has attained a high level of success so that their failure will be spectacular. Some argue that American business organizations are their own worst enemy and are destructive to the country (Weaver, 1988).

If the progenitors of these styles of leadership behavior remain in position long enough, their personal styles lead to similar, characteristic subordinate behavior, or efforts to escape or evade the leader's influence. This can affect entire organizations (Kets deVries & Miller, 1984). Employees frequently complain about the contradictions and confusion in their organizations. Given so many different people in authority, with differing perceptions of reality, differing points of view about appropriate actions, and differing conceptual levels, that reaction should not be surprising.

Just as some people should not be parents, some (perhaps most) should not be managers and executives. Sometimes managerial pathology can be turned to an advantage. Many manipulators become spectacular sales executives. Some narcissists have channeled their grandiosity into building expansive organizations, even though they cannot sustain mechanisms of perpetuation in them (Maccoby, 2000). To be unduly suspicious can undermine trust in others, but many with a paranoid bent might be good at uncovering and guarding against financial trickery. The more dependent person might be a good mentor. Indeed, given the wide range of behaviors, society survives because people find ways to turn even those behaviors that are pathological to their occupational advantage. Organizations should, and often can, do the same.

Leadership Succession Plans

Once, during his inauguration, I asked a newly elected college president who his successor was. One of his board members who overheard the question protested that this was no time to ask that question. The president understood the significance of my question and reassured his board member that it was appropriate. The importance of this story is that all organizations should have succession plans. No one can predict when an emergency will require a successor. Without such a plan, turmoil necessarily ensues. Too many chief executives, uneasy about contemplating their departure or denying their mortality, do not institute a plan. The usual accompaniment of that neglect is the absence of a management development program that insures the organization that all of its leaders are being prepared for upward mobility. Such a program is psychological money in the management bank. The consultant should give careful attention to this element of organizational perpetuation, especially if he has to help the chief executive release his constricting grip on the organization (see the example in Chapter 3 of Levinson, 2002a).

Structure

Most organizational structures presumably define accountability, designating who reports to whom, and indicating indirect accountability by dotted lines on the organizational chart. Few have structures based on psychological logic. The best such logic that defines and categorizes management activities and relates them both to the requirements of the organization and the levels of conceptual ability that should differentiate them is that of Elliott Jaques (1996).

Cognitive Processes of Leaders

Jaques defines all work as the exercise of discretion, judgment, and decision-making (cognitive processes), within limits, in carrying out tasks, driven by values, and bringing skilled knowledge into play in a given role. He describes cognitive processes as those mental processes used to take in information, play with it, pick it over, analyze it, put it together, reorganize it, judge and reason with it, draw conclusions, make plans, arrive at decisions, and take action.

Jaques (1996) posits eight levels of conceptual ability or cognitive power among humans, each defined by how far ahead an individual can think and plan. Fundamentally, this capacity is a given; people are born with it. Those who have the basic capacity, if given the right kind of stimulation, training, and experience, will mature in their cognitive power along predictable lines according to their age. Just as we do physically, we grow cognitively at different rates in specific discontinuous steps.

Those same eight levels, given their universality, become the basis for organizational structure and compensation. Jaques (1996) contends that no organization, however large, should have more than eight levels. Roles should be defined according to the cognitive level required to fulfill their tasks. People should be placed in roles who have the cognitive power to carry out the requirements of those roles. Jaques measures cognitive power in terms of an individual's time horizon (the maximum time span at which an individual is capable of working at any given point in his life, or the person's working capacity).

Although often the case, Jaques contends that no person should report to anyone who is not at a higher conceptual level than he. When a manager reports to another who is at a lower conceptual level, his superior cannot supervise him adequately or add value to his work. This condition is widespread in organizations, which contributes to their ineffectiveness. Also, if the manager to whom one is accountable is more than one conceptual level above him, the conceptual distance between them is so great that the superior can only be bored by the kinds of problems the subordinate brings to him. This means that ideally organizations are structured according to a management accountability hierarchy (Jaques, 1996).

The conceptual level required of an organizational leader will vary with the size of the organization and the complexity of its work. A large multinational corporation will require a chief executive at Stratum VIII (Jaques, 1996), who must be able to anticipate problems fifty years ahead and plan options for dealing with them. That person must project political trends, economic cycles, cultural changes, and shifting market needs, among other forces. To build a nuclear power generating plant requires the capacity to think ahead fourteen years, because that is how long such a project takes from conception to completion. An organization that undertakes to build such plants in various countries requires a chief executive to deal with multiple issues several times more complex. By way of contrast, a secretary, social worker, or teacher must be able to think ahead one year, even though many decisions require far less time, and would be in Jaques' Stratum II. These levels are grouped into three domains: system leadership, organizational leadership, and direct leadership.

Intelligence capacity (IQ) measures usually include tests of vocabulary, memory, attention, logic, and other capacities that are organized as intelligence. Conceptual capacity, as Jaques uses the term, goes beyond IQ. It is the *ability* to grasp and explain matters at different levels of abstraction. The capacity to deal with abstractions not only varies among people, but also with their age, experience, and training. The time line of that growth can be plotted, which is a significant contribution to selection, career development, and assignment. It can be assessed by tracing how far ahead people planned in their previous roles, and now, in their present roles.

Jaques (1996) has delineated the kinds of thought processes, reflected in how people speak and write, which mark their conceptual capacity. These are declarative, cumulative, serial processing, and parallel. Declarative entails putting forth one reason at a time. Cumulative brings together a number of ideas, none of which is sufficient to make the case. Serial is exemplified by a chain of linked reasons, each leading to the next. Parallel addresses the examination of a number of possible positions, each reached serially.

Most charts of organizational structure simply separate roles into line and staff. That makes for inadequate separation of functions and activities, and does not delineate those that are more directly focused on the thrust of an organization and others that support them. Jaques (1996) separates the major functions that constitute that thrust: developing or improving products or services; producing the goods or services; procuring the materials or components needed for doing so; delivering the goods or services; client/customer relations; marketing, in the sense of analysis of needs of the client population, and promotions to encourage the clients or customers to seek the products or services; and new business development. All other roles and functions, however important, are ancillary. Failure to understand this differentiation led one major automobile company to choose a financial executive as CEO, whose failure to understand the importance of styling led to its near demise.

With respect to staff functions like human resources, legal, safety, and accounting, Jaques differentiates their functions into prescribing, auditing, coordinating, monitoring, serving, advising, and collateralizing, and charts how each relates to the others and to operational managers.

The Organization's Communication System and Methods

If the human skeleton is the analogue for organizational structure, its communication system is analogous to the human nervous system. That mechanism is responsible for perceiving a wide range of data, both from within the organization and the outside. It must process those data, distribute them to their appropriate receptors, and devise the mechanisms for putting them to use.

Communication has three aspects: input, processing, and output. Input refers to what information an organization seeks from outside itself and where it gets that information. Some organizations are heavily involved in trade and professional organizations. Some send their staff to academic training programs; others have significant internal educational programs. Some conduct customer surveys, focus groups, and other customer follow-up activities. Some carefully review their cash register tapes. Those that are publicly held give careful attention to financial news. In short, all organizations are swamped with a plethora of information. Necessarily, they must be selective about what they review and absorb. Some information stops with the chief executive; some goes to those whose specialties require it. Most of it is unshared; much of it is unused.

Two important kinds of information come from inside the organization: that which the organization creates by research or generates by creative innovation; and the feelings and attitudes of employees, and the statistics of their work. Some organizations routinely sample employee feelings and attitudes, some do so in crises, and most not at all.

Processing refers to what happens to the information: who gets it and what is done with it. Most organizations rely heavily on the printed word: annual reports, bulletins, manuals, books of policies and procedures, and organizational newspapers and magazines. Some have turned to television and e-mail. Most communications intended to inform employees do not really inform. For example, if a strike is threatening, one might read about the discontent in a community newspaper, but rarely will one find that unease reflected or addressed in a corporate publication. Therefore, most organizational publications, having been spun to present the organization in the best possible light, are not regarded as adequate sources of information about the organization. For financial information about publicly held companies, investors turn not to annual reports, but to the completed public 10K forms submitted to the Securities and Exchange Commission. These usually are available from the corporations themselves. The consultant also should do so.

In addition to financial information, the consultant must learn how the organization gets information about how its employees feel, and what it does about its findings. Of particular importance is how people within the organization communicate with each other, a critical issue not only for efficiency, but also for cooperation and mutual support.

With respect to output, three important aspects of communication should be reviewed by the consultant. How does this organization want the outside world to view it, what does it do to further that wish, and with what success? What does the organization do about the gap between how it is viewed by the outside world and how it wants that world to view it? All organizations go to great lengths, some more aggressively and expensively than others, to impress those audiences in the external world that are important to them. All seek customers, patients, adherents, clients, students, donors, and public approval. In short, all to varying degrees engage in public relations.

The Psychological Contract

All people who work in organizations develop implicit psychological contracts with those organizations, and the organizations with them. The psychological contract is not a social contract, a conscious agreement about wages, hours, and working conditions, even if unwritten. It is an evolving, unconscious set of expectations that the individual and the organization have of each other (Levinson et al., 1962). Employees expect the organization to understand their dependency needs, their need to express affection and aggression appropriately in their work roles, and to help them manage change. For its part, the organization expects people to do their work responsibly, to represent the organization well, and to be loyal to its norms and standards. When these mutual expectations are met we can speak of reciprocation; when they are not, even though they are implicit and might be poorly understood on both sides, there is a contractual violation that then leads to symptoms of discontent.

Communication Problems

In my experience, most organizations do a poor job of communicating for several reasons: first, as indicated earlier, because they rely too much on the printed word; second, because they do not adequately train their managers in communication techniques; and third, because top management does not interact sufficiently with employees.

Unfortunately, most people do not read much, even about what concerns them. (I find that even consultants don't read much.) When employees do read, too often, they understand only poorly what they read. Wise chief executives create opportunities to hear what their employees have to say, and learn to listen. Some have cross-level meetings with employee groups. Some make it a point to lunch with their employees in the employees' cafeteria. Some create relaxed social occasions where management and employees mix more freely, thus opening communication doors. Some make it a point to visit various locations, particularly to better understand their employees' work and working conditions. The best example I know is what happened to a miner, working deep in a coal mine, who asked his new, helmeted neighbor who he was. The miner was startled to discover that his new companion was the CEO. The miners in that company subsequently knew they had a friend in executive ranks who knew their work problems first-hand, a conviction reemphasized when another time that CEO took his teenaged son into the mine with him, and also worked to upgrade the safety of the mines and the quality of their communities.

Speaking to employees is not a comfortable task for CEOs. The late Thomas J. Watson, Jr., then head of IBM, and Reginald H. Jones, then head of General Electric, spoke of how painful it was for them to learn to do so (Levinson & Rosenthal, 1984). When I told another CEO that the contemporary business environment now required that he interact with his subordinates, he said simply, "I can't do that." He hid in his office until he was fired.

Chief executives, and often others, must be a presence, especially when there are tragedies. Former New York mayor Rudolph Giuliani demonstrated the importance of being there in the tragic World Trade Center towers collapse (Alter, 2001). Like it or not, they must meet the dependency needs of their people. Willing or not, they are identification figures for their organizations.

CONCLUSION OF THE ASSESSMENT

Feedback of the Results of the Assessment

In my experience, three steps are helpful in the feedback process. The first is to prepare a summary of the assessment that can be read in an hour or less to successive audiences in the order in which the consultant presented his initial announcement, followed by an opportunity for questions and discussion. That summary should describe what the consultant did, what was found, what was inferred from the findings, how the consultant understands those inferences, and what remedial action is recommended. Depending on the size of the organization, the number of levels, and the respective cognitive levels of the listeners, different forms of the report might have to be prepared. In some cases, the report might have to be translated and subsequently read by someone who knows a particular language.

As a second step, before presenting the feedback to successive levels, I recommend that two feedback sessions with the chief executive be arranged.

I hold these to be an inviolate requirement. I require one meeting the last two hours of the day, during which I read the report to her and ask her how it sounds to those who will hear it, and what factual errors might have to be corrected. The second must take place the first two hours of the next morning. The reason for making it a requirement is simple: no matter how much the chief executive has wanted the assessment, nor how well the consultant has prepared her for the issues that are to be reported, the report inevitably, at least partly, will be seen as an indictment. When the CEO takes that report home to review it further, anger and paranoid feelings will arise. Unless the consultant meets with the CEO immediately the next morning, those feelings will not be dissipated and the consultant might well lose the client. In one instance, I had to hold five supportive feedback sessions with a CEO to clarify several such psychological bruises, the upshot of which was the recognition that his kindly but over-controlling paternalism was neither appreciated nor desired by his employees. He recognized that he no longer fit the contemporary CEO role and resigned.

The third step is to do the actual feedback by reading the report to the successive groups of employees, answering questions and inviting discussion. They should be told what remedial actions or follow-up steps are likely to be taken, these already having been approved by the CEO. Ordinarily, I do not distribute copies of the report to the assembled employees even if the chief executive wants me to do so. The CEO must be made aware of the possible exploitation of the report by whoever wants to cause harm to the CEO or the organization. There is one exception: when I do feedback with the top management level, I distribute numbered copies of the report to facilitate their critical examination, and collect the copies at the end of the session. The reason for doing so is that this group, as with the CEO, is likely to feel most injured, and requires more time to vent their anger, debate the consultant, and question the findings.

Termination of the Consulting Relationship

All relationships must end. It is best that they end on a warm note. If further consultation is not to follow the assessment, the consultant should take the time formally to say goodbye to those he has interviewed and observed, and to thank them for taking time from their work and for helping him. The consultant should give them permission to call him at a later date, and to speak to anyone from other organizations who might want to ask them about the assessment experience or for a referral for personal help. Unless the consultation has been undertaken for previously agreed on research purposes, if the consultant wishes to publish something about what was learned, the permission of the organization should be obtained. What is written should be carefully disguised so that neither the organization nor anyone in it is recognizable.

SUMMARY AND CONCLUSIONS

Most organizations are complex. Most organizational problems are even more so. To understand that complexity, a consultant must recognize that consultation is a process and the consultant is an actor in that process. To carry out the role effectively, in most cases, the consultant must recognize the emotional nature of the relationship with members of the consultee organization. The consultant's impact on the organization, whether real or imagined, inevitably evokes many varied feelings. That relationship also stirs up aspects of his own feelings. While interviewing, using questionnaires, observing, or examining data, the consultant must keep a record of his own feelings about his contacts and experiences in the organization. In the last analysis, organizational assessment is a subjective experience. To sustain his own integrity, the consultant must have a device for keeping himself as honest as he can.

Although much organizational consultation is short term and narrowly focused on specific problems, to understand an organization, one must have a sense of its history, its adaptive methods, its relative degree of success, and particularly how it maintains its internal cohesion while focusing its efforts on its aggressive attack on its competitive problems. A detailed outline of what is to be analyzed in what steps, as described in this chapter, will be especially helpful.

REFERENCES

Adizes, I. (1988). *Corporate life cycles.* Englewood Cliffs, NJ: Prentice Hall.

Alter, J. (2001, September 24). Grit, guts and Rudi Giuliani, *Newsweek,* 32.

Argyria, C. (1958). Creating effective research relationships in organizations. *Human Organization,* 17, 34–40.

Axtell, R. E. (Ed.). (1993). *Do's and taboos around the world.* (3rd ed.). Janesville, WI: Parker Pen.

Bray, D. W., & Byham, W. C. (1991). Assessment centers and their derivatives. *Journal of Continuing Higher Education,* 39, 8–11.

Burke, W. W. (1994). *Organizational development: A process of learning and changing.* Reading, MA: Addison-Wesley.

Chadwick, D. E. (1999). *The 12 leadership principles of Dean Smith.* New York: Total.

Coglan, D. (Ed.). (1997). Grandmasters of organizational development. *Organizational Development Journal,* 15, 2–90.

Collins, J. C. (2001). *Good to great.* New York: Harper Business.

Collins, J. C., & Porras, J. I. (1994). *Built to last: Successful habits of visionary companies.* New York: HarperCollins.

De Geus, A. (1997). *The living company*. Boston: Harvard Business School Press.

Erikson, E. H. (1963). *Childhood and society* (2nd ed.). New York: Norton.

Freud, S. (1961). Group psychology and the analysis of the ego. *The standard edition of the complete psychological works of Sigmund Freud* (Vol. 18, p. 131). London: Hogarth Press.

Greiner, L. E. (1967). Antecedents of planned organizational change. *Journal of Applied Behavioral Change, 3*, 51–85.

Greiner, L. E. (1998). Evolution and revolution as organizations grow. *Harvard Business Review, 5*, 55–68.

Grove, A. S. (1996). *Only the paranoid survive: How to exploit the crisis points that challenge every company and career*. New York: Doubleday.

Hornstein, H. A. (1996). *Brutal bosses and their prey*. New York: Riverhead Books.

Hornstein, H. A., & Tichy, N. M. (1973). *Organization diagnosis and improvement strategies*. New York: Behavioral Science Associates.

Howard, A. (Ed.). (1994). *Diagnosis for organizational change*. New York: Guilford Press.

Jaques, E. (1996). *Requisite organization: A total system for effective managerial organization and managerial leadership for the 21st century*. (2nd ed.). Falls Church, VA: Cason Hall.

Kets deVries, M.F.R. (1996). *Family business: Human dilemmas in the family firm*. London: International Thomson Business Press.

Kets deVries, M.F.R. (1989). *Prisoners of leadership*. New York: Wiley.

Kets deVries, M.F.R., & Miller, D. (1984). *The neurotic organization*. San Francisco: Jossey-Bass.

Kraut, A. I. (Ed.). (1996). *Organizational surveys: Tools for assessment and change*. San Francisco: Jossey-Bass.

Kraut, A. I., & Korman, A. K. (Eds.). (1999). *Evolving practices in human resource management: Responses to a changing world of work*. San Francisco: Jossey-Bass.

Lawler, E. E., III. (1992). *The ultimate advantage: Creating the high involvement organization*. San Francisco: Jossey-Bass.

Levinson, D. J., Darrow, C. M., Klein, E. B., Levinson, M. H., & McKee, B. (1978). *Seasons of a man's life*. New York: Ballantine.

Levinson, H. (1971). Conflicts that plague family businesses. *Harvard Business Review, 45*(2), 90–98.

Levinson, H. (1980). Criteria for choosing chief executives. *Harvard Business Review, 58*, 113–120.

Levinson, H. (1985). Fate, fads, and the fickle fingers thereof. *Consulting Psychology Bulletin, 37*, 3–11.

Levinson, H. (1993). The practitioner as diagnostic instrument. In A. Howard (Ed.), *Diagnosis for organizational change*. New York: Guilford Press.

Levinson, H. (1997). Organizational character. *Consulting Psychology Journal: Practice and Research, 49*(4), 246–255.

Levinson, H. (2002a). *Organizational assessment: A step-by-step guide to effective consulting*. Washington, DC: American Psychological Association.

Levinson, H. (2002b). Psychological consultation to organizations: Linking assessment and intervention. In R. L. Lowman (Ed.), *Handbook of organizational consulting psychology* (pp. 415–449). San Francisco: Jossey-Bass.

Levinson, H., Price, C. R., Munden, K. J., Mandl, H. J., & Solley, C. M. (1962). *Men, management and mental health*. Cambridge, MA: Harvard University Press.

Levinson, H., & Rosenthal, S. (1984). *CEO: Corporate leadership in action*. New York: Basic Books.

Lowman, R. L. (Ed.). (1998). *The ethical practice of psychology in organizations*. Washington, DC: American Psychological Association.

Maccoby, M. (2000). Narcissistic leaders: The incredible pros; the inevitable cons. *Harvard Business Review, 78*, 68–78.

McLean, B. (2001, December 24). Why Enron went bust. *Fortune*, 58–68.

Meltzer, H. (1944). Approach of the clinical psychologist to management relationships. *Journal of Consulting Psychology, 8*, 165–174.

Menninger, K. A. (1962). *A manual for psychiatric case study*. (2nd ed.). Philadelphia: Grune & Stratton.

Milkovich, G. T., & Wigdor, A. K. (Eds.). (1991). *Pay for performance: Evaluating performance appraisal and merit pay*. Washington, DC: National Academy Press.

Miller, D. (1990). *The Icarus paradox*. New York: HarperCollins.

Nadler, D. A., & Tushman, M. L. (1988). A model for diagnosing organizational behavior. In M. L. Tushman & W. L. Moore (Eds.), (2nd ed.) (pp. 148–163). Cambridge, MA: Ballinger.

Odiorne, G. S., & Rummler, G. A. (1988). *Training and development: A guide for professionals*. Chicago: Commerce Clearing House.

Racker, H. (1968). *Transference and countertransference*. Madison, CT: International Universities Press.

Roberts, W. (1991). *Leadership secrets of Attila the Hun*. New York: Warner Books.

Schein, E. H. (1985). *Corporate cultures and leadership*. San Francisco: Jossey-Bass.

Schein, E. H. (1999). *Process consultation revisited: Building the helping relationship*. Reading, MA: Addison-Wesley.

Schwartz, H. S. (1990). *Narcissistic process in corporate decay: The theory of the organizational ideal*. New York: New York University Press.

Shapiro, E. C. (1995). *Fad surfing in the boardroom*. Reading, MA: Addison-Wesley.

Silzer, R. (2002). Selecting leaders at the top: Exploring the complexities of executive fit. In R. Silzer (Ed.), *The 21st century executive*. San Francisco: Jossey-Bass.

Stevenson, H. H., & Cruikshank, J. L. (1998). *Do lunch or be lunch*. Boston: Harvard Business School Press.

Taylor, F. W. (1911). *The principles of scientific management*. New York: HarperCollins.

Trice, H. M., & Beyer, J. M. (1984). Studying organizational cultures through rites and ceremonials. *Academy of Management Review, 49*, 653–669.

Trist, E. L., & Murray, H. (Eds.) (1997). *The social engagement of social science: A Tavistock anthology*. Philadelphia: University of Pennsylvania Press.

Vancil, R. F. (1987). *Passing the baton: Managing the process of CEO selection*. Boston: Harvard Business School Press.

Von Bertalanffy, L. (1950). An outline of general systems theory. *British Journal of Philosophical Science, 1,* 134–163.

Waclawski, J., & Church, A. H. (Eds.). (2002). *Organizational development: A data-driven approach to organizational change*. San Francisco: Jossey-Bass.

Weaver, P. H. (1988). *The suicidal corporation: How big business fails America*. New York: Simon & Schuster.

Weisbord, M. R. (1978). *Organizational diagnosis: A workbook of theory and practice*. Reading, MA: Addison-Wesley.

Zaleznik, A. (1989). *The managerial mystique*. New York: HarperCollins.

9

EXECUTIVE COACHING

HARRY LEVINSON

The key issues for consultants who are also coaching others have to do with broad managerial experience. I think it is impossible to coach someone about role behavior unless one has a comprehensive understanding of organizations and can be recognized by the person being coached as being authoritative with respect to the psychological and coaching process and also authoritative in his or her knowledge of the business world. Age is an advantage in many cases, for from time to time my clients will refer to me as a "wise old man."

To be an effective coach of high-level business and government executives, one must have a broad understanding of the business and government worlds, which requires that he or she be widely read and contemporarily knowledgeable. In one situation, I had to be able to demonstrate that I knew something about the world of high-level organization finance, although I am not knowledgeable about finance itself. In another situation, I had to demonstrate that I was familiar with the insurance business and its problems. In still another, I had to demonstrate that I knew something about textiles and their manufacture, and in yet another, that I knew something about the currency exchange problems of Argentina.

Reprinted from the *Consulting Psychology Journal: Practice and Research*, 48, 115–123. Copyright 1996 by the American Psychological Association and the Society of Consulting Psychology.

In addition to being knowledgeable about the business world, one also must be knowledgeable about the political world and its implications for the organization with which one is working (if the coaching is within an organization). For example, what is the important effect of the Food and Drug Administration (FDA) and breast implant litigation on the behavior of executives in pharmaceutical companies? What is the effect of the lobbying of those companies on FDA executives?

A knowledge of psychological dynamics is particularly important when trying to understand the manager–subordinate relationships in the context of adult development. An understanding of adult development is especially helpful when there are issues of prospective retirement and postretirement planning. The choice of a successor is fraught with conscious and unconscious conflicts and, once that person is in place, with the predictable ambivalence both parties experience.

In the course of executive coaching, it is particularly important to avoid becoming psychotherapeutic because executive coaching does not allow time for developing a therapeutic alliance, dealing with the transference problem, and dealing with the ambivalence engendered when the client becomes dependent on the coach. The word *coach* must he taken seriously, and the relationship must be one of peers, although the client is necessarily dependent on the coach for advice, guidance, insights, and even for real information. The executive is in his or her geographic location and is experiencing coaching as a form of support, rather than a device for changing himself or herself, although ideally, when necessary, some aspects of the client's dysfunctional behavior will be changed.

METHOD

A clinical psychologist by training, I have been involved in consultation on leadership, management, and organization problems for 40 years. My basic conceptual orientation is psychoanalytic, broadly encompassing the major psychoanalytic orientations with a heavy emphasis on psychological and organizational diagnosis, while appreciating the organization as an open system. Psychoanalytic theory values understanding oneself as much as possible, with an emphasis on the interdependent integrity of one's relationships to others and one's ability to use his or her capacities and resources fully in mastering his or her environment, particularly for obtaining gratification in work. When coaching executives, usually the basic task is to help the client free himself or herself from ungratifying, unsatisfying, or conflict-laden work or to help him or her plan for a new or different occupational role.

To be a successful executive (Levinson, 1980), one must be able to take charge of his or her authoritative role comfortably, to manage the inevitable ambivalence of subordinates and the rivalry of peers and superiors, and to avoid being caught up in the regressive behavior of the work group he or she leads (Kernberg, 1978, 1979). Executives must not sacrifice their authority for the need to please. Often executives must manage the troublesome behavior of customers, clients, and their own superiors or board members. They must be able to accept their own limitations and make use of the specialized contributions of others, as well as the support of their colleagues and followers. They must be able to plan ahead for periods appropriate to their role (Jaques & Cason, 1994).

With respect to individual coaching, my heavy emphasis is on interviewing and counseling with a focus on reality problems, using little interpretation or effort to deal overtly with the transference. Transference problems are those unconsciously motivated attitudes on the part of the client toward the coach that may threaten the coaching relationship. For example, if, in the course of examining the client's rocky relationship with his or her peers, the client interprets the coach as a punitive policeman, the coach cannot help the client to understand the sources of his or her projection, as would happen in psychoanalysis. Instead, the coach would confine himself or herself to clarifying his or her role and differentiating that role from the client's definition of power figures in the client's other relationships.

Although the focus of the coaching relationship is on present behavior, the coach may usefully call attention to repetitive problems that the client has not recognized (e.g., discomfort with bosses while seeking their approval). Recognizing such an issue may help the client choose a new role in which his or her prospective manager preferably is paternalistic rather than tightly controlling. Unless clients spontaneously make the comparison, or repetitively raise those experiences, usually there is little need to interpret their early relationship to their parents to illuminate their present problems.

Executive coaching usually involves coping with focal problems, mostly of maladroit executive behavior that must become more adaptive. On occasion, the negative behavior is reflected in difficulties in supervision, on other occasions in problems with peers or superiors. Sometimes coaching consists of helping a given executive to conceptualize his or her role, to prepare for retirement, or to assess new possibilities in other organizations or even upward mobility in the present one. Sometimes it involves providing counseling on family problems, even recommending psychotherapeutic resources, and sometimes it involves helping the person resolve career dilemmas.

If the coaching task is to assess a given subordinate or even the executive's own role behavior, I use a simple derivative of psychoanalytic theory as a method for analyzing problems, namely, I ask the person in question how he or she typically handles affection (the need to love and be loved), aggression (the attacking or mastery component of the personality), and dependency (the need to work interdependently with others). I also ask what is the nature of his or her ego ideal (the picture of the self at his or her future best).

For example, a client tells me she is an intense, driven securities analyst whose supervisors complain about her abrasiveness with her colleagues and about her perfectionistic practice of "going it alone." In my theoretical frame of reference, I infer that her aggression is focused not only on task accomplishment, but also on "taking it out of her own hide." Such behavior is a product of an inordinately high ego ideal. The focus of my coaching must be on tempering the angry self-demands that spill over into her relationships with other people. There is little point in trying to help her relate better to others without dealing with the source of the drivenness. If coaching proves to be insufficient to counteract the unconscious pressure she experiences, then I would recommend intensive psychotherapy.

If the task has to do with fitting a person to a role, the same questions can be asked of the role, namely, what are the behaviors required in the terms just stated? Finally, I want to help the person assess for his or her candidate or for himself or herself how far ahead the role requires the person to plan and what degree of complexity he or she must be able to master (Jaques & Cason, 1994).

I ask the counselee to give me specific examples of his or her behavior in the wide range of executive practices he or she has experienced. I ask in particular what has provided him or her with special gratification, peak experiences, or highly gratifying achievements (Czikszentmihaly, 1990). My concern is less with the specifics of achievements and more with the continuities of behavior; in short, what did he or she actually do and how? I am particularly interested in elucidating the continuities of behavior, especially if the counselee has not recognized them because the achievements themselves have obscured his or her awareness of the actual behavior. I am also interested in the client's disappointments, failures, and mode of recovery from them. I want to know when the client was not challenged in his or her roles, and also when he or she was in over his or her head. It is helpful to know when clients stumbled and how they understand their error. Of course, it is important to know how they dealt with authority figures, peers, and subordinates.

I have in mind, sometimes typed on 5-inch × 8-inch cards to be certain I have covered all of the topics, the criteria for selecting chief executives (Levinson, 1980). Others may find different sets of similar characteristics useful (e.g., Tobias, 1990). I draw from our discussion the specific data of the counselee's work history, but, more important, I infer from these words, or lyrics, the underlying melody or emotional pattern of his or her life experiences and their likely import for where he or she would like to go in his or her career trajectory and what problems he or she must solve or master to do so.

Of course, I am interested in how clients see themselves and their conscious rationale for the trajectory of their career. But I am more interested in those underlying forces of which they are less aware or even unaware that are reflected in the continuities of their behavior. These represent the compelling thrust of their adaptation and will continue to be the momentum of their vocational pursuits no matter what the specific roles they pursue.

The starting point for establishing continuities of behavior is the clients' recall of their earliest experience of pleasing their mother (or substitute). For example, the earliest such experience I can recall is learning a simple four-line part for a kindergarten play. My mother, an uneducated immigrant who knew no English, was very proud that I was going to school. As I rehearsed my part, she learned the words with me. One of my major activities, and one that I would have pursued no matter what profession I would have undertaken, is teaching and lecturing. Behaviorally, there is little difference between the earliest event I can recollect and what has been a consistently dominant aspect of my life activity since.

When I meet clients for the first time, I ask them to tell me about themselves in any way they think would help me understand them and the issues they want to deal with or problems they must surmount. Much of the time they start with where they are occupationally, which enables me to ask about their work history and then their family background, including their relationship with their parents and parental figures. I ask them to explain their educational and career choices and their varied job experiences and relationships.

For example, a CEO asked me to coach his recently employed COO who had not, it seemed, gained the acceptance of the other top executives. The COO began by telling me about his most recent managerial success, rescuing a branch of a major financial institution. Then, as we traced his work experience backward, it became clear that his lower-class parents had demanded good academic grades and that he "found himself" in graduate school after mediocre high school and undergraduate performance.

My working hypothesis was that pressure and demands from higher authority would be likely to result in passive resistance and reluctant conformity; turned loose to exercise his abilities, the COO would shine. He had demonstrated that he could take charge of a failing organization of strangers and make it profitable. His ego ideal demanded specific managerial achievements. But what was also clear was that the CEO had not differentiated the accountability of his various subordinates, nor had he prepared them for the new authority figure he was interjecting between himself and them, thus fostering resistance to their new boss. He also had not spelled out his expectations for the new COO, nor had he delineated the division of their functions.

The CEO had said that he had not yet decided how their roles should be differentiated and that he had chosen the COO on the basis of his success in rescuing his previous organization, which, like the present firm, consisted of individual professionals who operated relatively independently. To lead, I inferred, the COO would have to earn the regard of the subordinates in a relatively unstructured situation without them having clear accountability to him. He would have to take charge without seeming to do so. He would have to ingratiate himself not only to gain acceptance, but also to gain identification with himself as a leader. He could not assert control in a situation without defined accountability. Fortunately, the CEO had asked him to be sure that one of the failing operations did not indeed fail. This constituted his authority to take charge. His rescue both of the subordinate responsible for the operation and of the operation itself demonstrated to all the subordinates both his strength and his right to be their chief.

From a psychoanalytic point of view, appropriate and effective role behavior require the incumbent of a role to take charge of that role, to recognize and accept his or her accountability to the values and methods of the organization and to those to whom he or she reports. A manager or executive is also accountable to his or her own conscience (of which the ego ideal is a component), for the executive must live with himself or herself. Therefore, the executive should not violate his or her own standards even if he or she must leave the role.

Psychoanalytic thinking values openness and integrity of relationships. The consultant who uses a psychoanalytic frame of reference must help clients understand the potential destructiveness of the actions they contemplate to themselves, to the people who work with them, and to the organization. The consultant should help clients think psychologically. He or she should also help clients recognize their strengths, talents, and achievements with pride and without apology. Furthermore, the consultant should help clients recognize decisions motivated by unconscious guilt, unconscious rivalry, and other irrational behaviors that would likely invoke negative behavior in others. The consultant would wisely help clients to understand the psychology of their stage of adult development and both the problems and advantages of characteristic behavior in that life stage.

The consultant may help clients understand and come to terms with that behavior that causes difficulty for them and may teach them how to respond or how to act more wisely according to that understanding. The psychoanalytically oriented consultant would be likely to recognize symptoms of psychological distress or disturbance and to refer to appropriate clinicians. Fundamentally, psychoanalytically oriented consultants help their clients attain greater psychological freedom to make their own choices and assume responsibility for their own behavior. Unlike psychoanalytic practice, however, coaching consultants may offer suggestions, information, and guidance consistent with their understanding of the psychology of the client in his or her organizational context.

CASE STUDY

The client is a 60-year-old chief executive of a large company that makes animal feeds. He is a New England Brahmin whose family has long been involved in this business, and he himself is a product of an elite secondary school and an Ivy League university. The company's headquarters are in New England and the plants are scattered in the South and the Midwest. Following his graduation from college, the client worked for 2 years in a Wall Street financial firm before going to the Far East, where he worked in a liaison position between an American financial institution and a Japanese bank. In the course of that experience, he learned to speak Japanese and developed an effective manner of negotiating with the Japanese. He was able to build good working relationships because not only could he be congenial, but also he could await the opportune moment to close an agreement.

Although his family had been in the feed business for many years, the company had become publicly owned and was professionally managed. However, that management could not keep up with the changing demographics of the animal feed industry. As beef, pork, and chicken producers became increasingly larger, and as issues of the infusion of antibiotics and vitamins into feeds and genetic modification of the animals (e.g., to get leaner pigs) became more pressing and competition became keener, the incumbent CEO became overwhelmed. The family still retained a significant share of the company's stock (20%) and asked the client to return to manage the corporation. He did so, and in a few years increased the company's volume from $600 million to $890 million. Now he was a respected chief executive officer who was on the boards of three other major corporations. He also served on government advisory boards having to do with his business and with business in general. He did not play a significant part in the company's political efforts, except for occasionally working with the lobbyist his industry maintained in Washington, DC. His wife, who also had come from a Brahmin family and who had a similar educational background, was heavily involved in nonprofit and charitable organizations. She was prominent in local high society.

The organization faced three major problems. The first was a continuing argument about the use of antibiotics and other chemicals in animal foodstuffs in the context of a broader argument about the role of the FDA. The company was under constant pressure from environmentalists on the one hand and from producers on the other.

The second problem was whether the business should acquire another business as part of a growth strategy, allow another company to acquire it, or remain independent. There was a possibility of extending the company's reach to other animal-raising countries like Argentina and Australia. However, to do so would mean extensive travel for the CEO and more complex financial and currency arrangements, as well as the problem of political instability in South America.

A third problem, which was internal, revolved around two executive vice presidents. Each was responsible for a major part of the business, although their responsibilities were not equal in the sense of number of people managed or the volume and profitability of their respective units.

The elder of the two executives was a thoughtful PhD in animal husbandry whose conceptualization and advice had been instrumental in reorganizing the focus of the company when the CEO had started as a new chief. A conservative, well-mannered gentleman, he operated his part of the organization profitably and quietly. He was widely liked in his organization and by the board. He thought broadly about animal husbandry and the direction the company should take. The younger executive had moved up in the company by demonstrating that he could manage plants that had labor conflicts, settle those conflicts, and reduce the number of employees. A more aggressive take-charge person, he was less sensitive than his peer and somewhat more hard-nosed, which made him a more bottom-line-oriented manager and perhaps better suited to coping with the ups and downs of increased competition and conflicts with government regulators. He did not think as conceptually as his peer.

The CEO had to think about his own prospective retirement and succession. He did not want to choose one or the other of his lieutenants for fear that the one who was not chosen would leave. He also recognized that the two of them working together with him did a better job than either of them could do alone. He wanted to sustain the triumvirate as long as he could, but he knew that sooner or later he would have to choose. He agonized over that problem.

The initial contact was made by the CEO on the board of another company with whom I had been consulting. The client knew I had for some years been consulting with the chief executive of that company. His primary question had to do with his prospective retirement and succession. Although he would retire in 5 years, he might, he thought, do so even sooner. The question, then, was what kinds of options were open to him and what would he do after he retired? A secondary question involved succession and his struggle about having to decide between the two executive vice presidents, while at the same time sustaining their momentum, cooperation, and morale. Although he also had to think about the possibility of acquiring another company or being acquired, that did not seem to trouble him particularly. Those issues, it seemed, would be decided on a purely financial basis. He was not strongly attached to the family tradition of a stint in public service. The first two issues had to be addressed, and that occurred during our biweekly consultations over a period of 7 months.

The client can be described as having obsessive (in the clinical sense) personality features. Like most such executives, he was conventional in his conformity to social and business norms. He was orderly, logical, and precise: He provided stable and consistent direction to the organization. Yet he could also enjoy the social activities he and his top managers shared during their meetings in vacation resorts. He had high personal standards and had similar expectations of his staff, but he was not a prude. He attended his mainstream Protestant church regularly and served on its governing boards.

While I was at company headquarters, I also met with the two executive vice presidents, the senior vice president of human resources, and another executive who was the nominal chairman of the board to assess how things were going in the company. They knew I was concerned with their effectiveness as a team. The vice president of human resources gave me added background on the respective executive vice presidents and their relative strengths. In addition, I lectured to the larger top management group on the management of stress and change because the company had gone through successive changes and would be undergoing more.

With respect to the CEO's prospective retirement and what might come after, particularly if he were interested in a government position, I pointed out that he would have to establish himself as an authority in the field of government in which he wanted to work. That meant he would have to write for publications that provide information to those who made government appointment selections. Such articles would have to be published in professional journals related to the field of animal feeds and having to do with the economies of the industry and sometimes with the relationship of the industry to the government. I suggested also that he have public relations specialists in his company interview him to draft prospective papers for him, including one for the *Harvard Business Review* and another for *Foreign Affairs*.

I also pointed out the need to establish and sustain political contacts with appropriate people in Washington and urged that he make use of the industry lobbyist to establish such contacts for him. We talked about how he would feel about retiring and also about how he would feel about having to cope with all the rivalries, conflicts, and pressures of working in the government. He was not one to have such experiences threaten his equanimity, nor was he narcissistically preoccupied. His ego ideal included, but did not compel him to take, a government role to sustain that family heritage. He seemed to look forward to the challenge.

I suggested repeatedly that at every opportunity he address his two lieutenants with the fact that they did better collectively than they did separately and that their respective and collective track records indicated how well they were working together. He reported how he did so in their successive meetings. He was operating with them as if they were collectively an office of the chief executive.

I further suggested that he defer making a choice between the two executives until the need to choose became imperative. Part of the problem in making a choice had to do with the fact that the wife of one of them apparently presented herself as a rather helpless person when the three couples were together and therefore was not viewed positively by the other two wives. If that executive were to become CEO, then his wife psychologically would be a drag on the social network of the organization. Her helpless posture did not sit well with the CEO's Brahmin wife, whose forays in society and volunteer services were quite the opposite of that behavior. Neither she nor her husband acknowledged that she needed help. Therefore, I did not suggest psychotherapy.

The CEO was widely read and both culturally and managerially sophisticated. That proficiency enabled us to discuss business issues in their social and political context. We also talked about the importance of being able to conceptualize on the one hand and make relatively hard-nosed leadership decisions on the other. The implication was that the more thoughtful, older executive vice president probably should be the first choice as a successor. Presumably, he could formulate wide-ranging strategy and set the organizational frame of reference, which the younger one subsequently could implement. There was some risk that the younger executive vice president would not wait for that opportunity, but logically, that was the optimal way to go. When the time came to make the decision, I suggested that the CEO might do well to prepare them so that they would understand the logic behind his decision. Simultaneously, he needed to keep emphasizing their effectiveness as a team.

I experienced some uneasiness when the CEO asked me for a referral for his son, a college student who was having some academic difficulties. He obliquely referred to his wish that the therapist be one with whom upper class people like himself and his wife would be comfortable. I detected a note of anti-Semitism between the lines of that inquiry, but did not explore the transference elements of his request. Fortunately, I was able to refer him to a therapist whose background, education, and social position were quite acceptable.

The coaching sessions with the CEO went well. He made good use of my suggestions. He reviewed the ghost-drafted pieces with me and began to establish his political ties to Washington. He frequently met with the two executive vice presidents and constantly reiterated their success as a team. We talked about the probable acquisition of his company, which would enlarge it considerably. But suddenly, when I arrived one day, he told me that the prospective acquiree company, in turn, had made a bid for his company. He quickly accepted that bid, which netted him a personal gain of some $20 million, and retired. The acquiring company, unaware of my logic of conceptual development in the organization followed by operational development, and probably uninterested as well, pushed aside the older, conceptualizing executive vice president, who went on to head another company, and named the younger, operational one chief executive.

The CEO followed through with a major government position that he held for about 3 years. When the political winds shifted and he was no longer a Washington appointee, he concentrated his efforts on several corporate boards on which he served and joined another group of executives in a venture capital firm.

I do not know how the client would evaluate the coaching sessions, except to note that he had referred other executives to talk with me who were interested in business issues similar to those we had discussed. Neither of the two vice presidents, now CEOs in their own right, asked for further consultation. In all fairness, both were doing quite well in their executive roles and saw no need to do so.

CONCLUSION

All the parties involved seemed to have realized significant personal goals. I was satisfied that the CEO had consistently carried out my advice in maintaining the integrity of his team and that he carefully chose his postretirement career with excellent preparation that cleared the way for his appointment. I do not think the character of any of the people involved changed that much, nor did their respective rivalries. Nevertheless, while they were together, they were able to work congenially and cooperatively, and when the time came, they were able to go their independent ways appropriately. As a consultant, the most important thing I learned was the need to be widely informed about management issues and about what was going on politically as well as economically. Although my psychoanalytic orientation helped me understand how best to coach this client, it was equally important in enabling me to manage the professional distance between us. As a result, although I was in no way a social peer of my client, he nevertheless respected my knowledge, perspective, and professional advice. I was certainly more conscious of being a coach than was the case in most other consultations with senior corporate executives.

REFERENCES

Czikszentmihaly, M. (1990). *Flow: The psychology of optimal experience*. New York: Harper.

Jaques, E., & Cason, K. (1994). *Human capability*. Falls Church, VA: Cason Hall.

Kernberg, O. F. (1978). Leadership and organizational functioning: Organizational regression. *International Journal of Group Psychotherapy, 28*, 3–25.

Kernberg, O. F. (1979). Regression in organizational leadership. *Psychiatry, 42*, 24–39.

Levinson, H. (1980). Criteria for choosing chief executives. *Harvard Business Review, 58*(4), 113–120.

Tobias, L. (1990). *Psychological consultation to management*. New York: Brunner/Mazel.

10

CONSULTING WITH FAMILY BUSINESSES: WHAT TO LOOK FOR, WHAT TO LOOK OUT FOR

HARRY LEVINSON

It's safe to say that no two family businesses are alike. Yet the consultant called to intervene when problems strike such firms should be aware of the broad categories into which these firms fall. (He or she should of course be aware of much more as well—but first things first.)

KINDS OF FAMILY ORGANIZATIONS

There are three kinds of family organizations: family traditional, family conflictful, and entrepreneurial. Let's take a look at each in turn; first let's examine family traditional organizations.

Family Traditional

These companies are long established, usually over several generations and, in business terms, are going along quite well. They usually have a good

Reprinted from *Organizational Dynamics*, *12*(1), Harry Levinson, "Consulting With Family Businesses: What to Look For, What to Look Out For," pp. 71–80, 1983, with permission from Elsevier.

reputation for customer service or product quality. They have a planned continuity in the sense that it is taken for granted by both parents and offspring that the sons (and now, sometimes, daughters) will follow the fathers. They anticipate continuing to be in the same business. Customarily they are not caught up in pressure for rapid expansion, but rather anticipate slow and steady growth, usually as a product of their reputation. Growth is from within.

These are essentially quiet organizations. People don't say much about them or hear much about them. They tend to be heavily paternalistic in their orientation. The problems that arise from time to time are likely to be intergenerational and handled with refined self-control. There may be professional managers between given fathers and sons if the age gap between them is too large; often, a major problem has to do with the fate and future of those managers. In many cases, the chief executive had to wait many years for his own role before his father retired.

Family members usually have significant influence in their local communities because most such organizations tend to be in relatively small communities. For estate reasons many of these organizations have disappeared into larger acquirers.

Consultation with such organizations may frequently involve dealing with suppressed generational differences, particularly an effort of the young to initiate change in managerial practice. Issues of succession usually are quite clear, with younger sons assuming in turn the roles in which they are preceded by older sons. At times other family members are brought in, usually sons-in-law, and they take their respective places in the organization, though ordinarily not as successors to top management.

The consultation process in such organizations is usually a sporadic one. That is, people will call upon the consultant to help them cope with specific problems, often of selection or of dealing with loyal employees about whom major decisions now have to be made or dealing with individual clinical-type problems or sometimes conflicts between two major employees. Rarely are group process activities entertained because of the turbulence they stir up, unless one of the sons, having succeeded his father, becomes enamored of something in which he has participated. Referral for professional help for family members through the consultant is also rare. They usually take care of such problems on their own.

Family Conflictful

The second kind of family organization follows from the first. Family cohesion is maintained and there is an effort to sustain a certain kind of tradition, but major conflicts arise, usually out of differences of opinion about the direction in which the business ought to go and sometimes over power. Faced with potential product obsolescence or with declining markets, the older and more established family members want to intensify their efforts to continue to do more of the same. Others, seeing certain handwriting on the wall, are unable to sustain their interest in or commitment to that course of action and want to pursue another. A split in the family usually follows along these two lines. That split is exacerbated if the family business is headed by one or more brothers who are also split along those lines and each in turn is supporting his own dominant son. Yet a consultation with such organizations usually fails because the split is so wide and each position is based on different sets of rigidly held assumptions. More often than not, the outcome of that kind of conflict is the sale of the organization.

Entrepreneurial

The third kind of family organization, the one that features the most difficulty, is that in which the entrepreneur who started it continues his leadership or is followed by one or more sons whose leadership efforts are going less well. In such situations, family feuds are precipitated, family conflicts are engendered and maintained, and family bitterness is endemic. After the founding father has left the scene, problems in such organizations are compounded by the growing number of children, grandchildren, and even great-grandchildren who continue to enter the business or, alternatively, who ultimately want their inheritance in cash.

Entrepreneurial family businesses are the most difficult of all to deal with, whether as an employee, a family member, or an outside consultant. The two major psychological reasons lie in the unique psychodynamics of the entrepreneurial founder and in the fact that historical family rivalries, which under other circumstances would ordinarily be dissipated in work roles removed from the family, are perpetuated in the family business.

The family business that grows beyond the Mom and Pop grocery store does so because of the entrepreneur's drive. That drive arises out of a characteristic interpersonal configuration—specifically the rivalry between father and son, which is most acute in the period from three to six years of age of the child, and which Freud referred to as the Oedipus complex. Ideally, that rivalry is resolved when the son, recognizing that he cannot compete with father for mother's attention and affection, identifies with the father on the assumption that if he cannot have mother but becomes like father, he will get somebody like mother. That identification makes for the "chip off the old block" phenomenon.

However, the identification process is not always as smooth as the ideal. Sometimes the rivalry is perpetuated, either because the son believes that mother indeed prefers him to father or that he can still win the battle. That unresolved rivalry becomes unconscious. It is usually reflected in intense, angry competitiveness, with the father and subsequently others, which then leads the son to create his own business and, in effect, marry it. His business becomes symbolically his spouse, his child, his instrument for attaining personal and social power, and his device for mastery. Entrepreneurship is predominantly a male phenomenon, for though many women have started businesses, few have built them to significant size.

The rivalry phenomenon also reflects itself in a low self-image because, symbolically, the son is competing from an infantile position and must become all-powerful to defeat the surrogate enemy. The perpetual anger results from the repression of the unresolved conflict. It is that anger that fuels the intense drive to achieve, the dogged persistence to stick with the project against all odds, the unrelenting competitiveness, the need to overcontrol, and the inability to give up when it is time to yield the reins. Entrepreneurs are angry, determined men.

Though an entrepreneur may build an organization to even massive proportions, it is characterized by one dominant feature: There is great difficulty in establishing succession. The entrepreneur can tolerate no rivals and promptly slaps them down or ejects them when they become threatening to him. Henry Ford II, for all practical purposes an entrepreneur because he rebuilt the Ford company, fired Lee Iacocca when Iacocca came too close to the throne.

Characteristically, the entrepreneur is also paternalistic. He usually seeks to obtain the loyalty of his followers by being a "good father," by being beneficent and caring. Their affection enhances his self-image. However, his underlying motto is, "Look how good I am to you. Why don't you do what I tell you to do?" He wants the loyalty and fealty of all who work for him and he wants them all to serve him and his purpose, that purpose usually being to fulfill his own ego-ideal aspirations. Thus he manufactures guilt and makes detachment difficult.

All this is magnified in the family business. The father wants the sons, particularly, to serve him and to allow him to remain the head of the business as long as he possibly can. In my experience, only a very few fathers have stepped aside before they were compelled to do so. The father often communicates to the sons that he is building the business for them, that it is going to be theirs, that they should not be demanding of either appropriate salary or appropriate power because they are going to get it all anyway in due time. Nor should they leave the father and the business, because it is self-evident that he has been good to them and is going to give them so much. Thus they are manipulated into a continuously ambivalent position of wanting to become their own persons with mature adult independence on the one hand, and the wish to take advantage of what they are being offered on the other. If they leave, seemingly they will be ungrateful. If they threaten to depose the father or demand to share his power, then they will indeed destroy him. If they don't do as he says, then they are disloyal and unappreciative sons.

This problem is further complicated by the fact that not all of the sons are equally competent (and sometimes this applies to other relatives, too). Yet there must be a place in the business for each of them and each must be treated not on the basis of competence, but on the basis of position as a relative in the family. Those who are less competent are not subject to adequate supervision by the more competent—because, after all, they are presumably equal relatives—nor can they be fired, because family is family and blood is thicker than water. The family is never free of the business; all conversation and relationships seem to be built around it. Nor is the business ever free of the family. Neither can escape the other.

WHAT THEY DO BEFORE THE CONSULTANT COMES

There are only two conditions under which these issues can be resolved, and both have to do with the degree of pain felt by the eldest or dominant son in the relationship with the father. Usually because of the issues of guilt described above, the son is caught in a double bind. If he leaves, his guilt is exacerbated. If he doesn't, he runs the risk of being stamped out and losing his own momentum. Usually, in such cases, if the pain is severe enough for that son, he will seek clinical help and resolve the conflict. If the pain is not severe enough, then he will continue to rock back and forth in the perennial bind, feeling guilt no matter which way he turns and unable to move anything or take any action. In some instances, psychotherapy relieves the guilt sufficiently so that the son can indeed take over the business in which the father, usually because of age, has had to move into an advisory role. In such a case, the son must disregard the repetitive attacks of the father. Usually he is strong enough to do so only for having had outside psychotherapeutic help. He then must go about running the business as it should be run, rather than as his father thinks it ought to be.

One such father brought along an assistant with an array of charts to the consulting session to demonstrate the ways in which his son was causing the business to function ineffectively. Asked simply to talk about his feelings concerning his son and the business, the father could not do so—he could only attack in the way he was attacking. Actually, the son was handling the situation quite well by keeping his father at arm's length, appeasing him, cajoling him, and having him close by so that he could see that the business wasn't falling apart; nevertheless, it was a continuous battle until the father died.

Double Bind

Sometimes the situation is painfully threatening and tragic, as in the case of a man and wife who had built a profitable business and asked their son and his wife to take it over. The son, a business school graduate, had been employed by another company—but he responded to his father's entreaties and returned. However, the father and mother retained the controlling stock.

The father became increasingly senile and unable to respond to the needs and decisions of the business—yet he kept forestalling the son's wish and need to control. He would not put his stock in a trust or in any other way make it possible for appropriate decisions to be reached. Complicating matters, he was being pursued by a predatory potential buyer whose efforts threatened the son's position. Yet the father would not hear the problems or advice of the son, because he felt that the son was trying to take his company away from him. The mother, always loyal to her husband, would not vote her stock against the father.

The son was faced with a choice between (1) leaving and (2) staying with the business and continuing to build it, while continually running a risk that it might be swept from under him. There was nothing he could do to cope effectively with the situation. To leave would be to let his father down; to stay would be not only to run great risk, but also to dissipate the years— which, if devoted to his own or another business, would have enabled him to attain much greater success. The guilt feelings were too powerful. He stayed.

Frequently in entrepreneurial situations involving two or more sons the eldest brother is beaten down by a dominating father. As a result, he is not in a position to take over by the principle of primogeniture. The next younger son then takes over when the father dies or becomes unable to function. However, that younger son cannot have the support of the older son, nor can he fire him. The younger son must nevertheless direct the older son or assume responsibilities that the older son cannot assume. Even so, the older son demands his just due of income and position. He is unwilling to be in a secondary role, yet simultaneously is unwilling or unable to assume the leadership role.

If there are other sons, usually they have positioned themselves to have perquisites and powers of various kinds, having been assigned to managerial roles regardless of their competence. None wants to give up his perks or position. Sometimes each is also maintaining a foothold in order that his sons may come into the business on an equal footing with the sons of all of his brothers. Furthermore, none wants to be bought out; few have other occupational options open to them, and certainly not at incomes they draw from the business. Their position in the community, their stature, their role of power in the organization all hinge on their staying in the jobs that they have maintained for themselves. There is then an internal equilibrium that is difficult to disrupt despite the discomfort that it causes for some of the family members.

Water: Sometimes Thicker Than Blood

Usually, a consultant is sought by one of the younger sons to help alleviate the chronic pain of such a situation. But the consultant confronts the fact that no one wants to yield; no one sees enough of a problem to require interference by an outsider except the person who called the consultant; and no one wants any of the others to become more powerful, more adequate than he. Each has at least a negative vote that keeps the whole system from functioning as well as it might, though each cannot do what is required to enable it to function at maximum effectiveness. If, under such circumstances, the business must be sold for estate reasons, the antagonism of the respective brothers is translated into the behavior that would have taken place before had not the business held them together. They become separated from each other and lose touch with each other. Blood is not thicker than water except as a cliché with which to inhibit action.

This example illustrates another phenomenon. The most difficult problem in family business consultation is the fact that the key figure in that system does not have sufficient pain to want to change. Usually, the consultation is sought by a person of lesser power in the system—one who is experiencing pain and seeking a way to reach the entrepreneurial power or the person of greatest authority. (In the illustrative case above the younger son called for help.) The authoritative person ordinarily sees no problem or feels that he can manage it, or resents the intrusion of the outsider and the brashness of the family member who invited the consultant in.

Sons and Brothers

The power problem among sons is compounded if the elder son, as is typical of elder sons when they haven't been beaten down, is the more orderly, compulsive, aggressive, and intellectual. Usually, this eldest son wants to maintain tight control and high standards. The second son, who more often wants to be liked, thinks the former is being too controlling. The elder son thinks the younger is too easy-going and not a sharp enough businessman. If there is a third son, frequently he is dragging along behind unless he has a unique talent or ability that enables him to assure the success of the older ones.

When brothers who have maintained and even expanded an effective family business leave their business to their respective sons, in turn, because of death, frequently the brothers' rivalry is displaced onto the sons and they in turn jockey for position for their own sons. This problem becomes more acute if one son is dominant either because of competence or because of primogeniture. In a case of the competent son, the less competent ones may then begin to act out against the values of family and organization. This acting out may range from becoming playboys to carrying on various other irresponsible escapades that reflect on the company and the family reputation.

If the family succession is a matter of primogeniture, and particularly held in place by the senior brother of the two or more elder ones, there tends to be a seething rebellion underneath. The respective cousins are held in place by the force of their fathers, but underneath each is waiting to over-throw that senior person held in place by his dominant father. Each is wait-ing to go his or her own way when free of this kind of pressure. Most have already lost interest in the business, if they had any to start with, and seek only their portion of the inheritance. That means that the commitment to the organization is significantly limited to the dying brothers and those few people closer to the top who are jockeying for power. In such situations, again, the organization usually is ultimately sold because the power issues cannot be resolved.

In situations like this, the consultant faces the fact that people com-pelled to be together by their stake in the business really don't want to be, and the intensity of their anger with each other and their disappointment in each other, which has usually been going on for years, makes it difficult for him or her to find appropriate leverage. As in the case of the senile parent, it is not unusual for problems to be of clinical proportions.

In one instance, for example, the elder of two brothers had started the business and had scrounged under the most difficult of circumstances not only to build the business, but also to send his younger brother through col-lege. The younger brother's professional training contributed significantly to the growth and development of the business, but the fact that he had had such training and, in effect, had had an opportunity created by the older brother, left the older brother feeling that the younger was insufficiently grate-ful and that he, despite his lack of college education, knew more about how to operate the business than the younger. The younger with great patience tried to recognize the elder's efforts and express appreciation for the opportu-nities the elder had given him. However, he could not bring to bear what he had learned professionally without incurring the elder's wrath. The hassle between them produced severe chronic conflict that carried over into their family relationships.

Finally, the wife of the younger brother asked for consultation. The two brothers appeared for consultation for three successive sessions. When it be-came clear to the elder that he was the problem in the sense that he had become more paranoid and hostile as he had grown older, he withdrew from the consultation. The younger brother could not leave the elder, who had done so much for him, nor could he do so for fear that the business would collapse without his technical input. Yet the cost of staying was high and he would not himself seek individual therapy to enable him either to stay or to decide to leave.

One factor that may compound such problems occurs when one brother or another has a woman friend on the side. Sometimes these are long-stand-ing situations with implied or expressed promises of divorce and marriage. Such situations ultimately blow up and make for great family conflict within the family of that brother. That conflict, in turn, reflects on the others, who begin to take sides and become angry about the reflection on the family. If

sons of the couple having difficulty are in the family business, they too become split and that further upsets the equilibrium.

A Danger for the Family

The kind of consultant called in may pose a danger for the family. In
one case, for example, two brothers were battling vigorously and had been
battling for many years—yet they declined to follow advice that they seek
professional psychotherapeutic help with some of their problems. Instead,
they found a consultant with some background in group dynamics who offered himself as a trainer. That consultant quickly exacerbated the guilt of
both brothers and encouraged them to bring their wives to their meetings,
which they did. As the conflict he stimulated between the brothers mounted
in intensity, their respective wives applauded the consultant—because he
encouraged them to go at each other publicly, and each had been waiting for
a long time for her husband to attack the other. To make a long story short,
the consultant became the Rasputin of that organization; ultimately, no decision was made in it without consulting him. He developed a following of
sycophants and a list of enemies; the latter were gradually eliminated from
the organization. But when the business turned out to be less profitable than
before, the brothers were compelled to bring in a professional manager who
promptly threw the consultant out.

Daughters and Widows

In some situations, the sons are pushed aside for the daughter. Given
their psychological history, fathers rarely have rivalry problems with daughters. One way for a father to deal with this situation is to define the sons as
incompetent and to push them aside. That puts the daughter, who is usually
younger anyway, in the position of supervising her brothers and, in effect,
taking charge of them. For brothers who are probably already emasculated,
this increases the intensity of their feelings of dependency, rivalry, and helplessness. Unlikely to succeed in the organization, they become a continuous
burden.

That kind of problem usually will not be solved by consultation because
both the father and the daughter want things to be as they are and the sons
are too powerless to do anything about them. Sometimes the daughter is able
to marry a person who in turn takes over the managerial responsibilities of
the business. This usually happens when the sons have chosen to leave the
business and pursue their careers in other directions, usually more successful
ones than those represented in the business.

Situations in which one of an association of brothers dies, his wife takes
over his role, and his son is in the business can become very disruptive. Usually the widow has inherited the husband's share and automatically sides

with her son in business discussions. She will hear nothing of his inefficiencies or ineffectiveness and takes a fixed position reinforcing his. That creates severe managerial problems, particularly if a group of brothers (and perhaps others) are still involved, one among them being the senior or managing partner. In such situations the wiser course is for the family group to become a formal stock-owning partnership, then evolve a board of directors to manage the business and hire professional management.

If the family manages to stick together through three generations, usually the proliferation of family members by the third generation is such that few have specific interest in the business other than for income purposes. It is difficult to mobilize them to come to some agreement for appropriate decision making and, when professional managers have taken over, they usually have great difficulty maintaining coalitions of family members to accomplish their tasks. If the family members remain actively involved, their relationships are frequently contaminated by the pressures of spouses, each jockeying for position and particularly for advantages for their children.

Three Options

In most instances family members have three options. In some businesses each family member can have his or her own operation. In the Newhouse newspaper chain, for example, the family has bought a new newspaper or radio station or TV station for each eligible member. Given their independent activity, they are able to accept the counsel of senior members. Another version of this is a chain of independently owned department stores in the Midwest. Family members do their buying together, but each manages his own operation. That business has been eminently successful for all of them.

Failing such an arrangement, either family members have to leave the organization or the organization must be sold. Usually, the history of conflict has been so long and so severe by the time a consultant is called in that the problem is refractory to consultation.

INTERVENTION

These examples illustrate the fact that only rarely, perhaps in one incident out of each ten approaches, is a consultation process in a family business consummated. It is extremely difficult to get people in a family business to buckle down to the work of resolving the conflicts and problems in that business. The problems for which consultation is sought are rarely amenable to successful consultative effort. Careful diagnostic assessment is required lest the consultant find himself or herself entangled in a complex network of alliances and hostilities.

If a family is willing to accept a consultant and if therefore a consultant has entered into a family business, it probably will be wiser for that person to interview each of the people separately and at some length to get a sense of the family dynamics, the business problems, and the fears and anxieties of each of the participants. In the process, the consultant ideally will be establishing a degree of trust and rapport with each participant individually. When the consultant has established enough information and enough trust, he or she is then in a position to bring the respective family members together in a group, then ideally to summarize his or her findings anonymously and ask what they want to do about the problem.

In such circumstances, the consultant becomes the trusted "other" who enables the family to mobilize itself to deal with its problems. Ideally, each trusts the consultant (to varying degrees), though the family members may not trust each other. That continued trust is the basis for getting family members to agree on at least some of the major steps they must take. Those who do not like each other do not have to learn to do so; indeed, in most cases they will not. Nevertheless, they do have to learn to work together in their common interest.

The consultant who enters into consultation with a family business must recognize that he or she is entering an old battleground. What is to be learned and dealt with is not merely a matter of contemporary differences. Many of them are unconscious and go back for an almost literal lifetime. Understanding this, however, the consultant who maintains a focus on the contemporary problem-solving efforts of the organization, particularly around issues that threaten the livelihood or succession of the younger family members, may be able to sustain the working relationship long enough to help solve the problems.

SUMMARY

In summary, consultants should be wary of consultation with family businesses. Here's some other advice for consultants, with implicit interest of course to family members and others who work with them.

1. Expect contact by people who have pain but no power, and expect only one out of ten of those contacts to turn into a more formal consultation activity.
2. Recognize the deep complexities of the family business, the multiple rivalries, the difficulties of family secrets, and the displacements of hostilities from generation to generation; be especially careful about establishing individual trusting ties before trying to bring the family together, as in a family therapy model.

3. Recognize that many of the people caught up in the conflict have only minimal commitment to each other, to the family, and to the organization; they are held together by some expected gain for their own children or because they can't give up an advantage they already have. This makes it difficult to establish a sense of common purpose, except in the narrowest sense.

4. Weigh family ties carefully. A sufficiently intense wish on the part of the family to remain together as a family with a strong sense of family pride is an optimum condition for inviting them to consider how to go about resolving some of their differences. Where commitments are weak, it may be wiser to appeal to methods that should loosen the painful ties that bind the family members together and allow them to go their respective ways free of those burdens.

5. The Gordian knot in such situations is usually the pain of the single dominant son, who most often can resolve that pain only with psychotherapeutic help. With that, it may be possible also to bring son and father—or sons and father—together to resolve some of their other differences, but as long as one or more of the sons is in a double-bind situation, movement is unlikely.

6. Don't be overoptimistic about your chances for success. It is easier for the family members to split and run than to sit together to resolve their problems. In most instances there are many outside distractions and not enough centripetal force to hold them together for problem-solving efforts. Issues of intense rivalry over years cannot be surmounted unless somehow the consultant finds leverage that makes it most important for all involved to resolve the problems at hand.

7. Don't be disappointed if you fail.

11

WHAT MOTIVATES DIRECTORS?

HARRY LEVINSON

Board members aspire to significant organizational contributions. They serve, to perpetuate the organization; to sustain its momentum; to act in keeping with their, and its, values. To do so they must understand the organization's history and foster an alliance among themselves and the chief executive. They especially must appreciate the significance of change and organizational depression.

A chief executive officer of a corporation that owned several companies told me that his dominant motivation was to make a lot of money. I was a guest in his impressive home, in a fine residential area, which certainly was evidence of his wish. But that wasn't the whole story. On the walls of his family room were stuffed animal trophies and a collection of pictures that bore witness to his interest in hunting. Also prominent in that room was a picture of his father. My host played tennis regularly on his own tennis courts, as well as at the local country club. He was modest in his recounting of his achievements and a good listener to others. He was a partner in the ownership of several of the best restaurants in his community, and he enjoyed entertaining friends with their gourmet fare. Yet, he could enjoy, with even

From *Directorship*, 4(1), 3–11. Copyright 1996 by Directorship, Inc. Reprinted with permission.

greater pleasure, more modest meals at the homes of friends. He liked high-quality action movies. He was well read. His business interests ranged widely across the globe, and he traveled frequently to be in touch with them, often accompanied by his wife. They also took vacation breaks on some of those trips, which included the pleasures of Hawaiian beaches. Suffice it to say he also was a well-educated, professional man who still found time, occasionally, to practice his profession.

Although this man had said his dominant wish was to make money, clearly the range of his characteristic activities demonstrated that he enacted other aspirations as well. The fact that he was a hunter and frequent tennis player, as well as a fan of action movies, suggests a propensity and preference for an aggressive orientation. That propensity was tempered by a capacity for self-control that enabled him to listen and to consider thoughtfully what others had to say. It was further modified by his aesthetic appreciation of food and his interest in reading, both of which suggest delay of impulsive behavior. And there were still others that had to do with his role as a father and his several other family obligations, as well as his religious values. Like most of us, he was a multi-faceted person. Like most of us, he also took his other aspirations for granted, as being relatively unimportant. He would come to recognize their importance only when he could no longer pursue them.

As a member of a board of directors, what would motivate this man? Although he doesn't need the money, he would be paid as a board member, nevertheless. To be paid what other board members of nationally prominent corporations are paid would be symbolic evidence of his worth. Now that some companies are cutting back on directors' perks and asking them to take a significant stock position and to be paid in stock, remuneration in fixed dollars becomes less important (Auerbach & Lublin, 1995). To be chosen to be on such a board would be public recognition of his status in the business world, and his importance in the eyes of the chief executive of that corporation, and in the judgment of the personnel committee of the board. He would value the interaction with executive peers and the opportunity to bring, to board deliberations, insights and experiences from his global purview. As an avid learner, he would also profit from his association with others in similar roles, whose varied experiences would enrich his own.

EGO IDEAL AND SELF-IMAGE

To understand this man's motivation, one would have to encapsulate his multiple aspirations, including those of which he was only dimly aware, and perhaps some of which he was not at all aware. For example, although he could describe his father to the visitor who asked about the picture on the wall, it was not clear to this man that various aspects of his behavior, especially his personal values, were a direct product of his heritage. It was as if, from his place on the wall, his father, figuratively, was looking over his shoulder.

We can infer from this behavioral information that he would have little patience with obsessive deliberation or managerial inaction, but would give serious attention to other board members and the chief executive. The chief executive would find him non-defensive and straightforward, an easy person to talk to and one on whom he could depend.

Taken together, these enacted wishes and those that had to be inferred from his behavior comprise, what in professional jargon is called, an ego ideal. An ego ideal is a picture of oneself as ideally he or she would like to be if only he or she could be that good. All of us are always striving to reach our ego ideals, although often they are not altogether clear to us because, as in the case of this example, some of their origins lie in the earliest, often distorted, thinking of small children.

Also, we all have a self-image, a picture of ourselves as we think we are at any given time, which may be more or less accurate. That self-image is necessarily a long way from our ego ideals. No matter how much we achieve, we are never as good as we would like to be, and when we come close to our ego ideals, we raise our level of aspiration.

Thus, one is always in pursuit of a never-to-be-attained target of which he is only partially aware. When we feel we are moving toward our ego ideals, then we feel good about ourselves. When we feel we are not doing that, or indeed are moving away from our ego ideals, then we become angry with ourselves, push ourselves with greater effort to move toward those ego ideals, attack others when our anger spills over our controls, or become depressed when we define our disappointments as failures. Repetitive, unrelenting frustration, in the pursuit of our ego ideals, results in what we speak of as burnout, that degree of depression that leads us to withdraw from that particular competitive scene.

One can never fully know one's ego ideal because much of it is unconscious. However, one can tap into it by observing some of its origins and continuities. For example, think of the first thing you did that pleased your mother. As a mature adult, that may seem irrelevant to you. But if you recall that early experience, chances are that whatever the activity was became a constant in your life. Next, what were your father's values? What did your parents want you to be? Who were your subsequent models—teachers, preachers, relatives, historical figures, important older friends? When you first chose subjects, perhaps in junior high school, which did you choose over which others? And then, if you chose a college, which over which others? Who were your subsequent mentors, models, and exemplars? Looking back on all this should give you a sense of the continuity of the important activities in your own life. Then, when you identify those few peak experiences among those activities, and recall what you were doing at those times, you'll gain an insight into your own ego ideal. Note that the emphasis here is on the activities, not necessarily the goals. The continuity of the activities represents the psychological tracks of our unfolding pursuit of our ego ideal. These all lead ultimately to what we want to be remembered for.

If, as a chief executive, one is concerned about motivating his or her directors, then the fundamental question to ask is, "What will it take to enable this person to like himself or herself?" In the case of our example, one can infer from his self-created environment—the pictures and trophies on the wall, the oft-used tennis courts in the backyard, the association with peers, pursuit of profit in successful businesses—his ego-ideal pursuits, and, beneath all those, the parental value system elaborated by subsequent models and mentors.

WHY BECOME A DIRECTOR?

People become directors for many different reasons. Some want to protect their investments, some want the prestige, some wish to please a CEO friend. Whatever the specific reason, all want to be identified with a successful organization, or at least one that is trying hard to attain success. Few of us want to be identified with losers. Most, in my experience, are attracted to a board by the promise of association with the chief executive, and secondarily, with other directors that one regards as peers. Except for those chosen by special interests to act on behalf of those interests, members of a board are likely to be chosen by a chief executive or by a personnel committee that is significantly influenced by a chief executive. Therefore, they are likely to share the values of the chief executive and most of the other members of the board. By definition, they want to be good business persons. To the extent to which their ego ideals overlap, they share a collective ego ideal. Sometimes, significant aspects of that ideal are reflected in a statement of the organization's aspirations, by which it tells its employees and the public at large what it stands for, what it is striving toward, and the criteria by which it offers itself to be judged. The company's statement of purpose or mission sets forth the organization's ego ideal. In its formulation of policies and practices in keeping with that statement, the board assures the organization's movement toward its ego ideal.

Other aspects of an organization's ego ideal are reflected in the consensus among employees about what an organization stands for. When asked, employees can readily compare their company to others in the same industry or in the same community. They can describe its level of vitality, its competitiveness, its merits as a place to work, its reputation, and many of its other features, including the degree to which it effectively pursues its stated objectives.

The board is, simultaneously, the policy-making body of an organization and the agent of its future. In their decision-making, board members pursue those aspects of their own ego ideals that relate to the organization, and seek to assure the organization's movement toward the ego ideal they share for it. Since a fundamental indicator of a business organization's success is its profitability, and since the jobs of employees and the returns to stockholders depend on that profitability, successful pursuit of profitability is at the core of the shared aspirations of the board.

"Vision," the imagined future of the organization, is part of the ego ideal. In addition to the process of "getting there," how an organization does so is very much a part of its ego ideal. For example, for many years IBM limited its purchases from a given vendor and the size of its plants in a given community, so neither any vendor nor any community would become too dependent on IBM. That practice reflected an aspect of organizational values that is part of the organizational ego ideal.

When the organization is moving toward its ego ideal, then employees in it, as well as the board, feel very good about themselves. When it is not moving in that direction, people in the organization, including the board, are disappointed in, and angry with, themselves. Think of what must have been the feelings of members of the boards of General Motors, IBM, Eastman Kodak, and Sears when those organizations were losing out competitively.

PURPOSE: PERPETUATION

All business organizations are created to make money. Some, like many contemporary entrepreneurial high-tech firms, are deliberately created to become candidates for acquisition. Others intend to merge themselves into larger combinations. However, most established companies seek to perpetuate themselves. There are two basic reasons: no bank is likely to lend a corporation money unless it believes that organization will be able to pay it back; and, a company's guarantee has no value unless it remains in business. Furthermore, a recent Stanford study comparing companies that have been in business for many years concludes that those that concentrated on developing themselves for the long pull were six times as profitable as the comparable organizations that did not create the same conditions for themselves, and 15 times as profitable as the general market averages (Collins & Porras, 1994). According to the authors of the pioneering study, a core ideology, "a set of basic precepts that plant a fixed stake in the ground," in short, a corporate ego ideal, was central to that achievement. The continuity of that ego ideal over many years, through many changes in board members, and many other changes in chief executives, as well as the necessary changes in organization direction to remain competitive, give added weight to the relevance of both the organization's ego ideal and the necessary support of the successive boards that sustain the organization's momentum toward that aspiration.

When, a number of years ago, I wrote an article, "Criteria for Choosing Chief Executives" (Levinson, 1980), a board member of a company with which I was consulting laughed, "Nobody gives that much attention to selecting a CEO." That was a sad commentary. Probably no single act of a board is more important than the choice of a chief executive officer. That person must not only give the organization direction, but must also create the conditions for others in the organization to identify with him or her. Unless people want to emulate the leadership style of the chief executive, unless they can accept and be guided by his or her values, unless the goals he or she enunciates make sense to them, the CEO will not have the enthusiastic commitment of followers. His or her leadership style sets the behavioral example for all others in the organization. If people in the organization cannot identify with their leadership, then they cannot identify with each other, making it difficult to work together with common purpose and the momentum that can arise from cohesive effort.

Theoretically, the personnel committee of the board is continually evaluating corporate officers and high-potential executives as possible chief executive candidates. In doing so (unless the organization needs to be drastically reorganized, a situation for which John F. Welch of the General Electric Company is a prototype), they will certainly take into account the degree to which those candidates are likely to sustain, or regain, the momentum of the company toward its shared ego ideal. However, says *The New York Times* (Dobryznski, 1995), "In theory boards have always been responsible for hiring, monitoring and firing chief executives. In reality they rarely fired them, hardly monitored them and usually left the job of naming a chief executive to his predecessor." But, to the extent that was true, it is changing. In the same article, Thomas J. Neff, president of Spencer Stuart, a prominent search firm, is quoted as saying, "When the CEO is still there, five years ago the CEO was the client in 80 to 90 percent of cases. Now the board's search committee is the primary client in 80 to 90 percent of the cases . . . (reflecting) the growing independence of boards from CEOs, and acceptance by boards that they have this responsibility which is not to be delegated."

Another aspect of an individual's ego ideal is his or her integrity. Trust is a fundamental of human relationships. Similarly, the audit committee of the board monitors the company's financial integrity, another facet of the organization's ego ideal. Still another facet of the organization's ego ideal are those policies and practices that hold out and support an ethical position. Most people, in most organizations, want to respect themselves as individuals, and also want to respect the organizations that employ them and to have those organizations be respected by the community at large. Think, for example, how the other employees of Drexel, Burnham must have felt when Michael Milken was convicted of financial improprieties. Similarly, high standards of product or service are the source of great pride. The opposite is likely to be accompanied by low morale.

THE NEED FOR DIAGNOSIS

There is much criticism of companies for undertaking various managerial fads, for losing organizational memory in downsizing, and for diversifying into businesses that are not consistent with their basic competence. Intelligent judgment about organizational decisions requires a comprehensive understanding of the organization's history, tracing the development of the organization from its founder. The founder's conception determines the initial structure of the organization, the kinds of people who are recruited, and the personnel policies and practices instituted. Once established, these aspects of the organization are likely to be continued. AT&T, for example, was organized according to engineering principles: Theodore N. Vail called for describing every job and evaluating job performance statistically. That practice still continues at AT&T, although managerial behavior itself necessarily includes many issues that are not quantifiable. By way of contrast, when Julius Rosenwald structured Sears with three levels, he did so with the express intent of keeping middle managers from interfering with the independence and flexibility of store managers. That practice was lost. Ultimately, the subsequent multi-level structure was symbolized by the many floors of the Sears Tower, the world's tallest building.

A detailed corporate history will disclose the economic ups and downs, technical and product changes, the success or failure of various management initiatives, the impact of mergers and acquisitions, as well as downsizing, changes among competitors and in the marketplace, variants in leadership style, and personnel practices. When such a history is reconstructed, either by an outside consultant or someone in the organization, and inferences are drawn from that experience about the continuities of the organization's strength and direction, the result constitutes an organizational diagnosis (Levinson, 1972). Such information may not be common knowledge among executives and managers who are increasingly transient and, therefore, more vulnerable to seizing fads to solve organization problems. A board that knows its organization's own history is, therefore, in a position to be in better charge of the organization. It is more likely to question costly managerial actions that are inconsistent with the organization's character. A board that feels itself to be in charge is more likely to be motivated than one that is more lackadaisical.

What happened with electric power companies is a good example. Privately owned electric power companies started out as trolley car lines. They came into being when there was surplus electricity after the evening's homeward rush. The power plants and utility poles had been erected by laborers. After the Insull empire was dismembered by the federal government in 1933, public utilities had to concentrate on service, because their rates were regulated by state regulatory bodies. That made it impossible for them to compete with unregulated companies for managerial talent. In turn, they developed psychological contracts with the more psychologically dependent employees who gave up the possibility of rapid promotion in exchange for the implicit promise of long-term employment. Depending on the regulatory bodies for rates and the approval of their local communities for franchises, those companies encouraged their employees to invest themselves in their communities.

Such employees also had to have demanding consciences that required them to voluntarily leave their warm beds to restore service when blizzards and other catastrophes destroyed the lines. That shift in the required modal personality of utility employees (from transient labor to committed conscientiousness) led to a significant change in company character. The dependency of conscientious, long-term employees became a problem when subsequent deregulation required them to become increasingly competitive. Utility companies not only could not continue to guarantee long-term employment, but also had to demand that those highly dependent employees, whose competitive ardor had previously been eschewed, now compete aggressively for their organizational roles, and for their company's position in the marketplace.

Many public utility companies exhorted their employees to become more aggressive. In the words of the British historian, Trevor-Roper, that is like asking a jellyfish to stand on its hind legs and grit its teeth. Florida Power & Light Company's pursuit of total quality management resulted in its winning the coveted Deming Award. The overinvolvement of its management in that activity ultimately had to be deemphasized by new leadership because that preoccupation with TQM, however useful it might have been, was at the expense of managing the business.

The growing literature on the failures of costly fads (Shapiro, 1995) tells board members, as it tells everyone else, that it is not easy to make such drastic transitions in organizational character. Given their responsibility to sustain organizational character, to contain costs, and to maintain profitability of the organization, most board members will feel guilty when such fiascoes occur on their watch. They will feel even more guilty when poorly thought-through reorganization results in drastic "bloodletting." It is not unusual for consultants' recommendations, often merely the application of the consultants' preferred managerial systems or packaged solutions that do not take into account the organization's character and history, to result in unnecessary turmoil and human cost. When public outcry arises following such actions and government actions are threatened, directors are likely to be even more chagrined. The resulting individual and collective self-images are not attractive prospects for board members.

In my experience, when the board understands the momentum of the organization and the history of its characteristic way of coping with its problems, as well as its dominant style of behavior, then the board will be more likely to demand a logic for change, rather than support or endorse fads, or allow itself to be victimized by less knowledgeable managers.

There are times when aspects of the organization's ego ideal must be changed. I pointed out the changes in the economics and psychology of the public utility industry caused by external regulatory and economic forces. Others may be caused by values and practices, once highly admired, that constrain an organization's adaptability. The paternalism of IBM and General Motors contributed to the corporate narcissism (Levinson, 1993) that led to significant loss of market share, and to criticism for alleged executive paralysis. Those aspects of the organizational ideal, appropriate to an earlier era, favored organization stability. They also led to overvaluing the organization itself, at the expense of taking competitors and market information seriously. Such constraints simply had to yield to reality. The directors of IBM, General Electric, Eastman Kodak, and other companies that did not respond, in a timely way, to the criticism of the business press and major stockholders must have felt embarrassed by the public criticism of their inadequacy. The avoidance of such embarrassment is devoutly to be wished by all directors.

ASKING INTELLIGENT QUESTIONS

Intelligent directors want to act intelligently. With a careful diagnosis in hand, to serve as a frame of reference, they are in a position to ask of major managerial proposals, "Is this the appropriate action to solve this problem, in this company, at this time, given its history and characteristic mode of adaptation?" Such a question recognizes that there are no packaged solutions that fit all companies, that it's easy for managements to propose actions "because other companies are doing it," and for some to become enamored of clichés with little substance offered by charismatic speakers.

Directors like to think of themselves not only as intelligent, but also, implicitly, as wise. After all, they are operating at the highest levels of institutional responsibility in our society. Their decisions affect the lives and livelihoods of most of us. Their judgment is put to the test with mergers and acquisitions. Unfortunately, many of the former fail, and many of the latter do not realize their promise.

The board member who takes pride in a coup that enables his company to become the dominant competitor in an industry, may well feel himself to be a fool when that acquisition turns out to be a dud. Think of how the board of Eastman Kodak felt when, already under fire for not having moved quickly enough to choose a new chief executive, directors then had to divest the Sterling Drug Company, which had never become what the Kodak board had anticipated.

CULTURAL DIFFERENCES

At one time or another, most of us regret a decision we have made. Hindsight is much more perfect than foresight. Boards, with many more resources to evaluate business situations and much more experience in doing so, could reasonably be expected to be aware of differences in organizational cultures and the problems in bridging them. In addition, if mergers, acquisitions, or joint ventures are to bring together executive groups from different nationalities, the clash of those cultures should be self-evident. If board members are not to be merely "patsies" with respect to such decisions, then they will want to become knowledgeable about both the need to integrate people from diverse cultures and how that must be done.

When a board does not take cultural issues seriously into account, it risks repetitive failure and the repetitive question from the business press and Wall Street, usually formulated in more polite language, "How could you be so stupid?" For example, AT&T has repeatedly failed to gain the desired momentum for its computer operations because, its critics allege, of its "telephone culture." Such a phrase may describe a situation, but doesn't explain it, or suggest a remedy for change. I suspect members of the AT&T board are hard put to explain to their fellow country club members why their heavy investment in that competition has not paid off.

Boards of large retailing organizations have encountered embarrassed surprise when confronted by information about contractors who, unpoliced, have allegedly used Chinese prison labor or illegally indentured Thais. These allegations not only constitute operational problems for the executives of those companies, but also significant policy problems for directors. Formulating policy will not be enough to avoid future embarrassment. Motivated by their need for their own self-respect, boards must become more deeply knowledgeable about such issues.

An unrecognized function of most boards is that of absorbing hostility. Sometimes, incurring anger is a product of having to take a stand with respect to labor relations, or sometimes because of differences within the board with respect to a major policy decision. Inevitably, when downsizing occurs, employees feel intense rage toward directors, communities revile them, and the remaining frightened employees wonder why, when the organization is still profitable, such actions are necessary and what might happen to them. While corporate officers usually take most of the heat in such circumstances, to be able to live with their own consciences, members of the board must be a visible support of the chief executive officer. When the board is not visibly defending policy or practice, the chief executive, as happened with Union Carbide's Bhopal catastrophe, alone bears the antagonism.

AFFINITY OF "ELDERS"

In their role as the "wise elders" of an organization, a major task of the board is its need to continuously scan the horizon of the future. The motivation to do so arises largely from the self-image of the director, as a responsible independent thinker. The future is notoriously difficult to predict. Even the commitment to open a new plant of modest size requires the anticipation of the marketplace at least ten years hence. Despite the ambiguity and rapid changes of the contemporary business environment, long-term commitments are required for many projects. Newspapers, these days, must decide where to make major investments in telecommunications. Companies that process commodities must expand to meet market demands, incurring costs that may not be amortized for 20 years. Boards of directors usually lean heavily on corporate staffs to gather basic information on which to make such decisions. Nevertheless, they themselves will have to discern and interpret trends and directions, for they make the final decisions about where to place the financial bets. Therefore, they have to be able to conceptualize multiple factors and integrate those data or they must depend heavily, and perhaps uncritically, on the projections of corporate executives. The president of a component of a pharmaceutical corporation may recommend the acquisition of a complementary company, but the board will have to decide, in the light of the broader contemporary pharmaceutical and business scene, whether it wishes to follow through with such a commitment. The board must weigh many factors that the president of the division cannot consider. The research director of a pharmaceutical corporation may recommend allocation of research monies toward a given area, but the board will have to decide, in the light of the broader, contemporary pharmaceutical and business scene, whether to allocate those resources to the discovery and manufacture of the prospective drug. The board must weigh many factors that the director of research need not consider.

Here is the point at which the affinity of directors for one another, and for the chief executive officer, becomes most important. As they consider the many factors that must enter into a decision, and the related risks given the limits of their information, directors necessarily fall back on their relationships with one another. When they can talk with colleagues they trust, and arrive at mutually agreed-upon solutions, they are much more comfortable with those decisions than if they merely vote on them. The wish to work closely, in a mutually supportive relationship with peers, is a powerful motivation for directors. Although there may be differences among them, they are allied on behalf of the organization they serve.

That same alliance should be particularly helpful to the chief executive. The corporate employee members of the board, presumably, are already his allies. Among the non-employee board members, one or two should be the CEO's confidants. He or she cannot discuss some important issues, such as promotions, with the employee members. He should be able to discuss those and other confidential matters with the non-employee members. He or she should be able to confide concerns about the future of the business that might frighten employee board members. Such issues as symptoms of illness, assuming an important community responsibility, or prospective changes in his own family life that cannot yet be shared with all members, nevertheless might advantageously be discussed with selected individuals. For many board members, to be a valued confidant is an indication of the esteem and regard the chief executive officer has for his or her confidants and therefore should be a rewarding recognition of that esteem. Most of us cherish the esteem of our peers, and especially of those in any situation who have greater power in that context than we do. By definition, chief executives have greater power in their organizations than their board members.

THE NEED FOR FEEDBACK

Another important part of that alliance is the need of the chief executive officer for continuing feedback on his or her performance. Some companies, like the Dayton-Hudson Corporation, have formal performance appraisal of the chief executive by his or her board. Appraising performance is the least comfortable activity in management. Most executives avoid it, particularly at high levels. Nevertheless, if board members are to be trusted in their alliance with the chief executive, they must give him or her information about his behavior that will enable him to function effectively. Their motivation to do this will be helped by their discussion with each other and the collective conclusions they reach.

One problem of rising in a corporation is that of successively fewer controls over one's behavior. As a result, a chief executive's narcissism can easily lead to irrational actions. A common problem is the impulse to over-expand. One chief executive of a large corporation acquired a construction firm, a trucking firm, and a management consulting firm, all of which later had to be sold off at considerable loss. His board did not challenge him sufficiently, although he was the kind of person who would have listened. The non-employee members of the board had not been associated with him long enough to be his friends and allies.

Another frequent problem, arising from fewer constraints, is overcontrol that may result in turnover of key executives. Changes in chief executive behavior may reflect physical or psychological illness. Limitation of his or her ability to handle complexity reflects itself in the chief executive's sense of being swamped or his or her failure to innovate imaginatively. The non-employee members of the board, in preparation for their formal feedback, and out of their alliance with the CEO, should discuss such issues and call their collective observation to the chief executive's attention. To do so is not easy. A board member usually has a degree of ambivalence about a chief executive who is more powerful (in his own situation) than a given board member. The board member wants to respect and emulate that person on the one hand (or he or she would not be a board member). But on the other hand, the director doesn't want to be in a dependent position, which, to some degree, as a board member, is inevitable. The mutual support of the board members and their collective concern for the chief executive as a person and as their friend can serve as an important motivation for frank but supportive communication.

Drastic shifts in the behavior required of a chief executive are not new. For example, when Reginald Jones was CEO of the General Electric Company and Thomas J. Watson, Jr., CEO of IBM, both spoke of having to overcome their discomfort about speaking in public (Levinson & Rosenthal, 1984); neither became fully comfortable doing so. Others are not comfortable with the growing need to deal face-to-face with political officials or the public. My impression from consultation with them is that those shifts in required behavior are happening with increasing frequency, especially the pressure to take a global view of their marketplaces. Too often boards allow chief executives in such positions to flounder, rather than confront them early on, help them mobilize a plan of action if they can do so, and support them in the process of carrying it out.

In another situation, where drastic downsizing was called for in an organization the CEO had built over 25 years, the chairman of the board had some question about whether the chief executive could carry it out. (The two were different roles.) The chairman, who had worked with the chief executive for many years and thought well of him, simply took him aside to point out the inevitable difficulties he would encounter. The chairman then asked the CEO whether he thought he could manage the pain of contracting the organization. If not, how might he withdraw gracefully? The CEO chose to try to manage the organization's downsizing, knowing that he had the chairman's support and that together they could devise a graceful withdrawal if he could not do so. CEOs can motivate their boards to give them unpleasant information if they repetitively set aside board time for just such discussions.

Sometimes chief executives themselves take the initiative to communicate their problems to their boards, so that directors are not in the uncomfortable, perhaps embarrassing, situation of confronting the chief executive. Admirable examples of CEOs taking the initiative in this respect are Drew Lewis, CEO of Union Pacific Holdings, Inc., who announced that he would enter a clinic to combat his alcoholism, and the late James K. Batten, former CEO of Knight-Ridder, Inc. When Batten blacked out while driving and hit a utility pole, he gave his directors permission to talk to his physicians in detail, so that they could decide when, and if, he should step aside. When the previously undetectable brain tumor became manifest, he repeated his offer, and then himself retired, when it became apparent to him that he could no longer carry on.

Opera singers and other entertainers are frequently reminded by critics when it is past time to retire. Tennis players get their feedback from defeat. Baseball and football players get it from coaches. Chief executives and board members usually don't get such direct information unless the company is failing. But even when the company is doing well, sometimes chief executives and board members recognize that when the role becomes boring, when there are no longer challenges, when one finds oneself repetitively making the same kinds of decisions (or the same kinds of mistakes), or when the task is no longer fun, then it is time to do something else.

Sometimes board members may be physically present at board meetings, but not be present psychologically. They may be less involved in the discussions, less interested in the problems, and find themselves increasingly peripheral. Sometimes their growing detachment becomes evident in the number of board meetings they miss, or the fact that they fall asleep in board meetings. Non-employee members of the board, out of their concern for each other, and the recognition that they too may someday need the same information, and out of their respect for that person, can gently point out the implications of their colleague's behavior, and the fact that it's preferable for him to leave with his head up.

It is never easy to suggest to a board member that he or she leave. Yet, at times, the CEO must. A CEO might well point out that a board member is saying less at board meetings, reflecting loss of interest. He could point out, if that is the case, a decline in camaraderie with the other board members and himself. That suggests a loss of pleasure in taking part. The CEO could point to the growing distance between himself and the board member as a reflection of the diverging interest on the board member's part, or even a decline in congeniality between them: "We don't seem to share discussions as we used to."

It is easier for board members to give feedback on contemporary business issues because these must be immediately debated and discussed. In their self-image as businessmen, they are likely to continuously reassess the corporation's business. A technology shift may well mean that, whatever its business yesterday, that business no longer will be the dominant thrust tomorrow. The use of abandoned natural gas pipelines to carry fiber optic lines is a case in point. Natural gas transmission companies are now in a business they had never previously dreamed of, and no one knows what the future implications will be.

WHEN TO LEAVE

Anticipating the need for a new direction, when a board is not getting adequate response from the management, the pain of that experience gives rise to thoughts about whether a board member should leave the board or the board should get rid of the chief executive. For the board member who takes his or her role seriously, and recognizes the inescapable limits of the CEO, he or she is likely to want to oust the CEO. If they come to feel that participation and board activity is an exercise in futility, then they may well ask themselves the question, "What for?" A board member, strongly identified with a company and, therefore, unwilling to let it be diminished or destroyed by repetitively rancorous board meetings, may well continue to fight it out. If he or she no longer feels part of an alliance or pride in being a member of the board, or that he is making a useful contribution, then he is more likely to leave. If the board member has no significant attachment to the organization, or if the attachment is no longer important to him or her, it is time to leave. When value conflicts are unresolved, particularly when they result in loss of public respect for the company and its leadership, and other members of the board refuse to act in keeping with the organization's professed aspirations, board members who have powerful ego ideals are likely to leave.

As one matures, it is easy to lose touch with young people's thinking and behavior, with technology, and with the marketplace. Think of George Bush awkwardly hoisting a beer in a working-class Boston bar in a vain effort to demonstrate that he understood the problems of the blue-collar working man. The illustration may be somewhat far-fetched, but few members of corporate boards are empathetically in touch with the feelings and attitudes of line employees (or even of youthful customers). Therefore, they can unwittingly lend themselves to formulating policies and practices that undermine the necessary commitment of those very people. A wise CEO helps his board members learn firsthand the realities of his employees' work lives. Some CEOs take their board members on tours of their various facilities. One CEO took his board members deep into a coal mine his company owned.

But how many board members of airlines, for example, know how much aggravation airline counter clerks must cope with, especially when there are storm-caused delays, what effect such stresses have on them, and therefore what provisions should be made to alleviate and ameliorate such problems. While ostensibly this is a management problem, as differentiated from a board problem, there might well be spillover into other labor problems, as anger from one situation is offloaded onto another. In some cases, corporate officers lunch with employees to stay in touch with such issues. Board members should be included.

All board members are old enough to have suffered the death of a loved one. Most have seen friends move away or have themselves moved from one community to another. Many have experienced divorce. Many, too, as employees, have moved from one company to another. All, therefore, have experienced powerful attachments to other people and other places. And all have experienced the pain of severing such attachments. Societies and religions have mechanisms through which people may mourn the loss of significant attachments. There is an important implication of this common human experience: all change is loss, and all loss must be mourned. The effect of mourning practices is to enable the mourner to accept the fact of loss, and to detach oneself from those people and places once affectionately held dear.

Since organizations are composed of people, and organizations are necessarily forever changing, managements must incorporate in those change activities, opportunities for people to mourn the losses.

Sometimes, losses will be of role, sometimes of dominant skill, sometimes of community attachment, and sometimes of relationships to, and with, each other. These losses precipitate depressions. The depressions, in turn, become drags on organizational adaptation. Too few organizations understand the concept of depression or take appropriate steps to combat it. Board members, taking to heart their own life experiences, must understand this phenomenon in order to ask appropriate questions about how executives are managing, the impact on the organization and the communities in which the firm operates, and what ameliorative and remedial steps are being taken to assuage the pain.

The collective aspiration of board members is their never-to-be-achieved goal—the illusion of what the organization ideally could be—whose yardsticks are the qualitative and quantitative goals that are surpassed along the way. Their ultimate gratification is that they have a significant effect on something that is larger than each of them individually, and all of them collectively, whose success is a product of their acumen and their wish for success.

SUMMARY

Board members are the responsibility "elders" of a corporation. To be effective, they must understand that individuals and organizations pursue ego ideals—aspirations for achievement. Collective ego ideals of board members are the propellant of organizational direction and the source of organizational values. Direction and values are products of the organization's evolution. A diagnostic history of the organization is a frame of reference for board decisions. The alliance of board members with each other and with the chief executive, built on trusted communications, is fundamental to board cohesion and organizational momentum.

REFERENCES

Auerbach, J. and Lublin J.S. (1995). "ITT Corp. Shaves Annual Pensions and Perks for Outside Directors," *The Wall Street Journal*, September 25, p. B4.

Collins, J.C. and Porras, J.I. (1994). *Built to Last*. New York: Harper Business.

Dobrynski, J.H. (1995). "The Right Choice for the Job?" *The New York Times*, September 7, p. D1.

Levinson, H. (1993). "Why the Behemoths Fell," *American Psychologist*, 49:5, 428–436.

Levinson, H. (1980). "Criteria for Choosing Chief Executives," *Harvard Business Review*, July–August, 58:4, 113–120.

Levinson, H. (1972). *Organizational Diagnosis*. Cambridge, MA: Harvard University Press.

Levinson, H. and Rosenthal, S. (1984). CEO: *Corporate Leadership in Action*. NY: Basic Books.

Shapiro, E. (1995). *Fad Surfing in the Board Room*. Reading, MA: Addison-Wesley.

12

HOW ORGANIZATIONAL CONSULTATION DIFFERS FROM COUNSELING

HARRY LEVINSON

Organizational consultation involves the consultant in a much broader and more complex set of phenomena than individual counseling. The organization consultant has to take into account economic, financial, sociological, social psychological, psychodynamic, and anthropological conceptions, as well as organization theory and the policies and practices of any given organization. He or she must try to understand the interrelationships among these ways of viewing organizational phenomena to arrive at an appropriate diagnosis and a logical intervention. The consultant must see himself or herself as a psychological anthropologist who must be familiar with the culture, behavioral norms, and the psychological foundations of policies and practices in order to intervene successfully.

Not only does the consultant have to deal with greater complexity, but also in organizations the consultant must deal with the already established

Reprinted from "What is Consultation? That's an Interesting Question!" by T. Backer et al., 1992, *Consulting Psychology Journal: Practice and Research, 44,* pp. 21–22. Copyright 1992 by the Educational Publishing Foundation and the Division of Consulting Psychology.

organizational momentum, often a product of many years of evolution through several generations of leadership. That evolution has also led to the entrenchment of policies and practices that themselves are difficult to uproot and change. They become even more difficult to deal with when the consultant also has to deal with the multiple individual motivations, and differences in group and component cultures. Among the components of a given organization there may well be vastly different norms, cultures, and required behaviors, especially if those components are regional or national.

In contemporary business organization, there is frequently rapid and continuous change, fluctuating direction, transient leadership, and foci which range from the hazy to those that are repetitively reformulated. All this changes organizational relationships and the sources of affection, support, and ego ideal gratifications that are significant elements in both motivation and adaptation. Repetitive change requires coping with the repetitive decomposition and reconstitution of work groups in a context of changing conceptions of appropriate leadership styles. Thus, there is repetitive stress and the exacerbation of feelings of helplessness and paranoia.

To cope with all this, the organizational consultant does not have the security of his or her own office as a frame of reference. Instead, he or she must be in the middle of the organization's turmoil where he or she must maintain a certain equanimity, stability, and self-confidence, while concomitantly maintaining appropriate psychological distance from the turmoil. Thus, one must deal with the turmoil, while being constantly immersed in it, as contrasted with dealing with a client's individual turmoil for an hour or so per session. Indeed, organizational consultation differs significantly from individual counseling.

13

GIVING PSYCHOLOGICAL MEANING TO CONSULTATION: CONSULTANT AS STORYTELLER

HARRY LEVINSON

Much psychological testing fails to yield predictions about behavior and requires supplementary interviews for integration and prediction. Data alone are of little help in consultation because they require integration and interpretation. Storytelling is basic to all science. It is no less basic to consultation. In short, the good consultant must be a good storyteller.

In their study of executive selection practices, Yeager and Brenner (1994, p. 6) concluded that "The old-fashioned pencil-and-paper way merely gives a generalized label without a meaningful answer about what is really going on." They complained that there has been an overemphasis on statistical versus experimental orientations in executive selection. The result of this effort to be "objective," they asserted, is a melange of different tests that tap disparate variables that cannot be integrated because these variables largely describe self-identified behavior but do not explain why the behavior occurs or the causes of whatever behavior is being reported. They pointed out that

This article was originally presented as an invited address at the annual meeting of Division 13 of the American Psychological Association, August 12, 1995, New York. Reprinted from the *Consulting Psychology Journal: Practice and Research*, 48, 3–11. Copyright 1996 by the Educational Publishing Foundation and the Division of Consulting Psychology.

correlation is not causality. Without an underlying integrative theory, psychologists have difficulty tying together the results of different tests. As a result, according to their study of 68 psychologists who reported on their selection work with high-level executives in major corporations, "the interview was the one test all agreed to be indispensable in the assessment process" (p. 1). Furthermore, "a subliminal strategy among assessors appears to be responsible for their continued success" (p. 3). Assessors build a story out of words; they communicate their findings by means of still more words.

This very important finding raises serious questions about so-called objectivity in psychological testing and the psychologically blind, heavy reliance on numbers. If this finding is drawn from work with the top management of major corporations, how relevant is it likely to be for efforts to select lower level people in organizations in which there is much more psychological testing, for career guidance in academic and doctoral choices, for outplacement activity, and for career transitions?

Furthermore, their finding provokes serious questions about how data from tests and other instruments that rely heavily on numbers may be "dumped" on clients without adequate interpretation, a reasonable sense of timing, or an appreciation of the client's readiness to receive the information. It is not unusual to hear from former advisees, now college graduates, that they had been told by counselors on the basis of psychological test profiles that they should not go to college. Nor is it unusual for managers with serious behavioral problems to be told by computerized psychological test reports consisting of packaged paragraphs that theirs were simple adjustment problems. In one mode of practice, consultants gather reams of data about malfunctioning individual executive clients and then simply dump those data on their overwhelmed clients to the clients' angry dismay. In a publicized instance of psychological testing for career guidance, an investigative newspaper reporter was told that she was in the wrong occupation because she was somewhat aloof, distant, and suspicious. She pointed out in public rebuttal that those very features enabled her to treat her sources more objectively, to dig into information rather than accept it at face value, and to maintain her professional integrity.

Thus, operating by the numbers in pursuit of objectivity, many psychologists have buried their heads in the psychological sand. When a consultant confuses statistics with objectivity and objectivity with numbers and equates numbers with science, that frequently leads to inadequate, if not destructive, psychological consultation.

SCIENCE AS STORYTELLING

As Schrank (1990) pointed out, we can understand intelligence better by examining people's behavior in their everyday lives than by giving them trivial test problems. He argued that to understand intelligence, we need to understand stories: their structure, their acquisition, their retelling.

As a matter of fact, all scientists tell stories to explain their findings, just as Yeager and Brenner's participants did. Psychology as a science leans heavily on metaphor (Shimko, 1994), so telling stories is a natural extension. Much that is not yet testable is necessarily the subject matter of hypothesis and, often, of speculation. Einstein's theory of relativity, for example, was decades ahead of empirical validation. Physicists are still searching for quarks and astronomers for black holes. The proclivities and effects of various pharmaceuticals must be interpreted. Economists, long the dismal scientists, increasingly have come to recognize the need for understanding and hypothesizing about that which they cannot yet put into statistical terms and models (M. Levinson, 1995).

As Gould (1994, p. 26) has said with respect to paleontology,

> The subject of modern human origins is particularly hard for a variety of reasons: scientists must work with distinctions on a very fine scale during slices of geological time so short that resulting key questions become difficult; many of these issues depend crucially upon inferences about the very aspects of human life (particularly behavior and language) that cannot be directly observed in the fossil records; finally, explanations can rarely be validated by the conventional scientific style of prediction and deduction from known laws of nature but must be formulated in the *narrative* (emphasis added) more as contingent sequences of events, each crucially dependent on the full range of antecedent states.

This narrative mode is not intrinsically more difficult or less secure than others, provided that the historical evidence be so rich and full that the antecedent sequences may be verified:

> We are storytelling creatures who should have been named *Homo Narrator* (or perhaps *Homo Mendax* to acknowledge the misleading side of tale telling) rather than the often inappropriate *Homo Sapiens*. The narrative mode comes naturally to us as a style for organizing thoughts and ideas . . . the tales themselves, like all fruitful theories, have served as marvelous devices for suggesting questions and avenues of future research. Good theories are, above all, useful . . . [and illustrate] the centrality of narrative style in any human discourse (though scientists like to deny the importance of such rhetorical devices—while using them all the time—and prefer to believe that persuasion depends on logic and fact alone). (Gould, 1994, p. 28)

> We are more frequently with a plethora of information than left clutching a few facts to form the basis of speculation. Narrative style, therefore, becomes central, primarily as a vehicle for making so much information comprehensible. (Gould, 1994, p. 28)

There are many variants of storytelling in psychology. Of course, the classical is psychoanalytic practice, in which the client unfolds his or her story, the analyst offers interpretations to help clarify that story, and the client and analyst together examine the relationship between them (issues of transference) to elaborate the story. "There seems to be no doubt," Spence (1982, p. 21) wrote, "that a well constructed story possesses a kind of narrative truth that is real and immediate and carries an important significance for the process of therapeutic change." "From the beginning, psychoanalysis and the telling of stories have been linked" (Edelson, 1992, p. 99).

Edelson (1993) stated, "I find it of great interest to note how much the major discoveries and ideas of psychoanalysis can be discussed, without loss, in language about telling and enacting stories" (p. 294). He reported about his patients that "their plight is that they are trapped in such scenarios (trapped is the operative word here). Their symptoms may be regarded as signs that they are caught in such a scenario, that they are compelled to participate in the scenario from time without end, and that they struggle to escape from the world of that scenario" (p. 295). How similar is this description of the individual caught in a psychological web to people in organizations who voice the same sense of hopeless desperation about their organizational traps? And, just as "a patient tells a story at a particular time for a particular time for a particular reason" (p. 296), so an interviewee in a corporation tells us about his particular situation, often recognizing his limited perspective by adding, "Maybe others don't see it the same way." The same caution extends to understanding what one hears: "Interpretation of the set of stories (depends) not only on picking up repeated themes, but on careful observation across units of sequences" (p. 308). Finally, "If a psychotherapist, making use of particulars imparted to him by a patient, told a good story, the patient was likely to feel listened to and take in and use what the psychotherapist had said" (p. 315). The same is true for a consultation report.

Now a new form of storytelling has arrived—narrative therapy (Cowley & Springer, 1995). The theory, akin to Edelson's thesis, is that if our dominant stories center on problems, they can become spiritual prisons. The narrative therapist helps people spot omissions in their stories to help them recover forgotten strengths that are overshadowed by those problem-dominant stories. Thus, the therapist helps the client externalize the problem and to identify those "sparkling moments" when the client has not been dominated by the problem, thereby recognizing his or her own strengths.

Weick and Roberts (1993, p. 357) spoke of the collective mind of people working together "as a pattern of heedful interrelations of actions in a social system. Agents in the system construct their actions (contributions) understanding that the system consists of interconnected actions between themselves and others (representation), and interrelate their actions within the system (subordination)." In other words, they create a story of and for themselves as they join together to accomplish a complex task. Furthermore, they added,

Narrative skills . . . are important for collective mind because stories organize know-how, tacit knowledge, nuance, sequence, multiple causation, means–end relations, and consequences into a memorable plot. The ease with which a single story integrates diverse themes of heed in action foreshadows the capability of individuals to do the same. A coherent story of heed is mind writ small and a repertoire of war stories, which grows larger, through the memorable exercise of heed in novel settings, is mind writ large. (p. 368)

Projective techniques require the participant to create stories. Murray's (1938) Thematic Apperception Test requires the participant to tell stories about vague pictures, from which motives may be inferred and then interpreted. McClelland, Koestner, and Weinberger (1989), building on Murray's work, gave closer attention to the achievement, power, and affiliation motives. Comparing the interpreted stories of his participants with conclusions formulated from inferences drawn from paper-and-pencil test results, he found that the interpreted stories predicted people's subsequent behavior more accurately than did their responses to the interpretations from inventories.

Morgan (1993, p. xvii) observed, "Ideas about organization are always based on implicit images or metaphors that persuade us to see, understand, and manage situations in a particular way." He asked his clients to describe themselves, their bosses, their subordinates, and their roles, in the form of images. Once he had elicited the various images from a group of respondents, he asked them to explore the differences in their imagery as a basis for finding issues of conflict or misunderstanding. He noted, "Clarity in telling a story creates a strong sense of shared understanding and getting to the heart of many issues" (p. xvii). Then he asked his clients to create a new story to develop the personal and organizational competencies required to make their story of the future a reality.

TACIT COMMUNICATIONS AND SHORT STORIES

In many forms of organizational consultation, questionnaires, whether morale studies, attitude surveys, performance feedback, or other data-gathering information, are commonplace. They often embody the same problems as paper-and-pencil psychological testing. For example, attitude surveys and morale studies invariably report deficiencies in communication. Too often management takes these results at face value and increases media communications to little avail. Psychologists who do not consider the tacit communications behind the manifest responses fail to understand that the issue of inadequate communications for most employees is not the need for more words, but rather the unsatisfactory nature of the relationship between any employee and the person to whom she or he is accountable. When people respond that communication is inadequate, what they usually are saying is that they want closer and more frequent relationships with their superiors. They not only want to hear words directly from the mouths of those persons, but also want to be able to read their faces.

Similarly, much of performance appraisal is an exercise in futility (H. Levinson, 1976). There is a heavy reliance on numbers, and almost invariably the ratings pile up at the high end of the scale. This problem is refractory to changes in the form or to attempts to make the appraisal process more effective by use of other modes of arriving at judgments like behaviorally anchored illustrations. The failure of performance appraisal efforts is due significantly to two factors: (a) the absence of specific information about behavior in role, and (b) the unconscious guilt that makes it extremely difficult for the appraiser to be honest and direct. To cope with this repetitive failure, psychologists have asked people to appraise themselves, to seek 360-degree feedback, or both. Self-appraisal usually results in appraisees steering a middle course between self-inflation and self-criticism. Three-hundred-sixty-degree feedback suffers from multiple difficulties, especially inadequate interpretation of the feedback that threatens one's self-image or that fails to recognize characterological behavior that is refractory to change. In addition, both techniques enable the manager to evade his or her responsibility for giving the appraisee accurate behavioral information that both identifies achievements and inadequacies in the process of meeting the previously defined demands of accountability.

Historically, efforts to establish objectivity in job descriptions and to base salary levels on that "objectivity" flounder on the inability to compare various roles adequately, to equate pay for performance, and to resist the manipulation of such descriptions and the salary levels on which they are based. Little attention is given to the underlying unconscious psychological assumptions about compensation, let alone the underlying cognitive structure of managerial roles and the cognitive trajectories of individuals (Jaques & Cason, 1994).

Much organizational consultation in the form of ad hoc techniques that address only limited problems in organizations are akin to short stories. They fail to take into account the complexities of the organizations to whom they apply such techniques, and frequently their efforts fail.

Although timing of feedback and the readiness of the client to receive it are important considerations for some consultants (Schein, 1969), others (Argyris, 1993) are more direct. Beckhard and Harris (1977) reported creating and using a case similar to the problems of their consultee organization as a basis for developing discussion about its problems.

CORE IDEOLOGY AND MASTER STORIES

There are a number of implications of these experiences. The most profitable and enduring organizations have a core ideology (Collins & Porras,

1994). This ideology becomes the organization's "master story" (Steinfels, 1995), a basic story that defines how they see their business worlds, where they stand in terms of their competitiveness, and the assumptions and psychological contracts (H. Levinson, Price, Munden, Mandl, & Solley, 1962) that are the basis for their behavior.

Therefore, to have integrity, all organizational consultation must tell a comprehensive story about the organization, taking into account the origins and history of a given organization and the vicissitudes of its experience, as well as its values and characteristic modes of coping with its problems. To varying degrees, those problems must be seen as a product of the organization's momentum and the variations of that organizational behavior in different eras and environments. It must recognize that many forces have combined to create the way the organization is and the focal problems it faces. The task of the consultant is to gather information or to help those in the organization gather it, identify problems, put names on them, and open avenues for attacking them. The consultant's logic must proceed from facts to inferences to interpretations. Thus, the consultant is always dealing with assumptions and theory, whether tacit or explicit, and must recognize that he or she is always dealing with hypotheses. Those hypotheses are tested by means of organization participants' critical evaluation of the findings and their recommended avenues for change. Such responses enable the consultant to revise his or her diagnostic hypotheses and maintain a psychologically sound scientific effort. Thus, only by telling stories can one be truly scientific.

Useful storytelling in consultation occurs when complex situations must be elucidated without becoming oversimplified to be understood. For example, consider this way of storytelling, excerpted from the diagnosis of a public school administration:

> There are many complex critical relationships in [the school system]. These relationships are difficult to separate and clearly identify, since they are dynamic and continually changing.
>
> The most important of these relationships seem to be among town government, the residents of the town, and the school system. Finding it difficult to describe the key interactions succinctly, we have resorted to the use of an analogy with which nearly everyone can identify: the family. In this metaphorical family, there are four identifiable persons: two authority figures (parents or elders) and two dependents (children).

There are two authority figures in the family, each with a distinct personality. Their personalities might be characterized as follows:

1. An older, conservative, honest person; knowledgeable about business and finance; well educated, but many years ago; affluent; a long-term resident of the town; and possessor of the type of wisdom which comes from experience. A believer in

the work ethic, this figure is friendly but shrewd, and reflects the traditional Yankee virtues of thrift and "value received for money spent." A good provider and well liked by his or her neighbors, this person enjoys a fine reputation state-wide and is well represented in the town government.

2. The second authority figure is younger than the first person, well educated (but fairly recently), affluent, aggressive, intelligent, and more highly mobile. Unpredictable about stands on issues, this person is consistently vocal and articulate. Because of his relative transience, he is not well represented in town elected and official positions.

3. The third person in this metaphorical family is a school system. It is dependent on the two authority figures as are the other town departments, the fourth person in the family. As an individual, the school system may be characterized as bright, well-educated and cosmopolitan, creative and socially aware. It is expected to conduct its affairs in concert with the interest and values of the two authority figures, despite variations inherent in their philosophies. This individual has an excellent reputation among its peers (other school systems), but some rivalry and resentment exists between it and the second dependent (other town departments). The school system is virtually guaranteed its budget each year, due to fiscal autonomy legislation. Although it has never used this legal protection and each year presents its request to the authority figures for approval, its favorite status (or perceived favorite status) has caused some resentment from the less favored dependents of the family (other town departments).

In an examination of the interaction occurring within this family, three issues continually surfaced and are individually discussed below: trust and mistrust; leadership; and internal issues having to do with the day-to-day activities of the schools.

Such a story, elaborating on the interactive behavior stemming from these characteristics, gave dramatic quality to the consultation report which, in turn, made it more easily understandable to the respective parties involved. Then, in effect, those participants had to rework their failed efforts.

To help the superintendent understand the bind in which he found himself (and the reason for asking for the consultation), the consultant told this story:

When the current superintendent was hired, the school board was perceived to have a strong collective personality and took on the role of leader of the school system. The role of the new superintendent was established as clearly subordinate to that board. The board took the initiative in making policy and setting goals and the superintendent implemented that initiative on their behalf.

Over time, however, the membership of the school board changed and there was a gradual shift away from this pattern of leadership. Later boards began to require more leadership from the superintendent as they began to assume a more "trustee" role as overseers of the public interest, rather than as operating manager of the school system itself. Simultaneously, certain town boards became more involved with the operations of the schools (advisory board, building committees), and some personnel functions were contracted out, so that the leadership function became more fragmented. Inevitably, with the superintendent tending to remain in his original subordinate role, the school board assuming a trusteeship role, and others involved with school business having greater input into the decision-making process, a leaderless quality developed which has continually appeared in our data.

Recounting this story for the superintendent made it clear to him that the changed environment required a style of behavior considerably different from his own. Thus, not only was he able to retire from the scene without loss of face, but also the other members of the community family could recognize their contribution to the problems that the school system faced and how they could begin to correct their collective failure.

Think of the impact of this summary on the desperate top management of a company that has been struggling to regain its momentum:

> I asked each interviewee to think of the company as if it were a person and to describe that person to me. Almost invariably the imagery was the same. Almost everybody described that person as a big man, sometimes overweight, sometimes fat, trying to be lighter and healthier, sometimes very strong, sometimes a boxer or a wrestler, sometimes robust, hyperactive, even a giant pushing against a wall. He was described variably as arrogant, proud, overbearing, despotic, impulsive, insensitive, castrating, and suppressive. He was further described as having a confusion of values, as not using his brains, as considering himself as elite, and more concerned with what others say than operating the business, as saying one thing and then another, as being disorganized and not in control of what he does, as being cyclothymic, unstable, and working hard.

> On the positive side, there was an occasional comment that at heart he is good, faithful to those he can trust, but feels vulnerable. He is worried lest he fall into a vacuum any minute. There were only two exceptions to this imagery. One interviewee described the image as that of a middle-aged woman who was going to a surgeon who doesn't know which part of her body to cut out first. Another described his image as that of a strong, healthy person going through adolescence. The last was the only optimistic image in all 55 interviews.

Consider this summary that tells the story, faults the leadership, and simultaneously adds momentum to the leadership effort to change:

The Pioneer Laboratory is comprised of a wide range of people. Some come from other parts of the company where there are different cultures. Some come from academia, some from government, some are long-term, and some are new hires. These widely disparate people would not be readily integrated and certainly not quickly under any circumstances, let alone in two years. The difficulties of integration have been compounded by the financial and economic problems people have experienced in moving from other parts of the country. Because of budget restrictions, top management neglected the developmental and supportive issues in favor of sustaining and increasing the momentum of basic research. Adopting that course resulted in a relative lack of resources devoted to supporting people's needs and resulted also in creating internal conflict. The leadership obviously made mistakes in the beginning by choosing this course of action. By undertaking the consultation reported here, the leadership is now trying to determine what those mistakes have been and to try to make sure that they do not occur again.

CONCLUSION

In summary, people are always telling stories: to organize experience, to try to understand and solve problems, to offer examples and metaphors to enhance argument or logic, to explain, to teach oneself and others, to protest or to act against their oppressors, to advance science, to enrich literature, to amuse and entertain, to unify generations, to discharge anxiety and rage, to regret and mourn. Stories constitute the psychological grist of life. Necessarily, therefore, they have an important place in consultation, and all good consultants who would also be good scientists should become good storytellers.

REFERENCES

Argyris, C. (1993). *Knowledge for action*. San Francisco: Jossey-Bass.

Beckhard, R., & Harris, R. (1977). *Organizational transitions: Managing complex change*. Reading, MA: Addison-Wesley.

Collins, J. C, & Porras, J. I. (1994). *Built to last*. New York: Harper Business.

Cowley, G., & Springer, K. (1995, April 17). Rewriting life stories. *Newsweek*, pp. 70–71.

Edelson, M. (1992). Telling and enacting stories in psychoanalysis. In J. W. Barron, M. N. Eagle, & D. L. Wolitsky (Eds.), *Interface of psychology and psychoanalysis* (pp. 99–124). Washington, DC: American Psychological Association.

Edelson, M. (1993). Telling and enacting stories in psychoanalysis and psychotherapy. In A. J. Solnit, P. B. Neubauer, S. Abrams, & A. S. Dowling (Eds.), *Psychoanalytic study of the child* (Vol. 48, pp. 294–318). New Haven, CT: Yale University Press.

Gould, S. J. (1994, October 20). So near and yet so far. *New York Review of Books*, pp. 24–28.

Jacques, E., & Cason, K. (1994). *Human capability*. Falls Church, VA: Cason Hall.

Levinson, H. (1976, July–August). Appraisal of *what* performance? *Harvard Business Review*, pp. 30–46.

Levinson, H., Price, C. P., Munden, K. J., Mandl, H. J., & Solley, C. M. (1962). *Men, management, and mental health*. Cambridge, MA: Harvard University Press.

Levinson, M. (1995, April 10). Dismal science grabs a couch. *Newsweek*, pp. 41–42.

McClelland, D. C., Koestner, R., & Weinberger, J. (1989). How do self-attributed and implicit motives differ? *Psychological Review*, 96, 690–702.

Morgan, G. (1993). *Imaginization*. Newbury Park, CA: Sage.

Murray, H. A. (1938). *Explorations in personality*. New York: Oxford University Press.

Schein, E. H. (1969). *Process consultation*. Reading, MA: Addison-Wesley.

Schrank, R. C. (1990). *Tell me a story*. New York: Scribner.

Shimko, K. L. (1994). Metaphors and foreign policy decision making. *Political Psychology*, 15, 655–671.

Spence, D. P. (1982). *Narrative truth and historical truth*. New York: Norton.

Steinfels, P. (1995, April 15). Beliefs. *New York Times*, p. A25.

Weick, K. E., & Roberts, K. H. (1993). Collective mind in organizations: Heedful interrelating on flight decks. *Administrative Science Quarterly*, 38, 357–381.

Yeager, J., & Brenner, J. (1994). The assessment interview: Metalinguistic strategies in management assessment practices. *Consulting Psychology Journal*, 46, 1061–1087.

14

THE CLINICAL PSYCHOLOGIST AS ORGANIZATIONAL DIAGNOSTICIAN

HARRY LEVINSON

In recent years there has been considerable concern with organizational change and organizational development. Much of this concern has stemmed from the group dynamics movement, and those who have practiced organizational development have been largely social psychologists, sociologists, and others in a variety of disciplines who have applied variations of group dynamics techniques. A number of clinical psychologists have also been involved in this new direction.

Like nondirective therapy, organizational development practices concentrate largely on having people express themselves to each other about their mutual working interests and problems, on working together on the resolution of common problems, and on having people weigh out loud and with each other their organizational aspirations and goals. Often problem-specific and frequently intuitive, these efforts are largely atheoretical. It is presumed that the same general methods will apply to all organizations.

This article is taken from material prepared for presentation as part of the symposium, "Clinical Psychology in Industry: A Needed Revolution," at the meeting of the American Psychological Association, September 1972. Reprinted from *Professional Psychology: Research and Practice*, 3, 34–40. Copyright 1972 by the American Psychological Association.

The field is presently in a fluid state, marked primarily by ad hoc problem-solving efforts and by a heavy emphasis on expedient techniques, ranging from games to confrontation, whose rationale frequently is poorly thought through and whose sometimes untoward consequences are either unrecognized or denied. However, as any skilled clinician knows, not all patients will prosper equally well with the same therapy, and there are severe limitations to that kind of clinical intervention which merely enables people to clarify their conscious feelings and to work on problems consciously perceived. For dealing with more complex problems at deeper levels, the clinician requires a comprehensive theory of personality and a range of therapies of choice.

SCIENTIFIC VIEW

Little of what is presently called organizational development involves anything like formal diagnosis. That is, while it is traditional for a responsible clinical psychologist to evaluate his client or patient both from the point of view of that person's problems and the capacity he has for dealing with them—and most psychologists would find it irresponsible to work with clients or patients otherwise—such processes are not within the purview of most people involved in organizational development. A psychologist cannot act responsibly in consultation, whether individual or organizational, unless he maintains a scientific point of view about what he does. This means that he must formulate a diagnosis which is essentially a working hypothesis about what he is dealing with, and then he must formulate methods (whether they be treatment, intervention, training experiences, or other devices) which will be effective tests of the hypothesis he proposes or which will compel him to revise his hypothesis and change his methods accordingly.

A diagnosis, whether of an individual or an organization, requires a comprehensive examination of the client's system. That examination of the individual client will frequently involve measures of intelligence and intellective or cognitive functions, defensive and coping structures, modes of managing emotions, pinpointing focal conflicts, and understanding personal history as the context for character formation and styles of adaptation. The examination will frequently involve psychological testing and often consultation with a neurologist, pediatrician, or a psychiatrist. Indeed, some psychologists specialize in diagnosis alone, a process so helpful that in many of the best kinds of psychological and psychiatric clinics such diagnostic formulations guide the therapy regardless of who conducts it. Thus, a comprehensive examination, leading to a sensitive and sophisticated diagnostic statement, becomes the basis for predicting the best kind of therapeutic process, its likely course and outcome, and possible danger points. That process also permits the professional to review what goes on in his relationship with his client, to modify his behavior and activity in keeping with changes in his diagnostic hypotheses, and ultimately to compare his examinational findings at different points in time to measure progress.

It is quite unfortunate that this process seems not to be an intrinsic part of contemporary organizational development. There are a number of reasons why this is so. There is no systematic body of professional knowledge about organizational development. Most books on the subject are piecemeal, made up of unintegrated papers. Most techniques are ad hoc, with limited rationale. Many, if not most, people who work with organization development have had limited training, some no more than having been in T-groups or, at best, having had T-group internship. Most have had no training in depth to understand the dynamics of individual personality, even those who have degrees in social psychology or sociology, let alone any sophisticated understanding of group processes. Many lean heavily on psychological cliches like "self-actualization" or "9-9, 5-5" or similar slogans derived from rubrics used in psychological research without refining these rubrics into syndromes or formulations that create the conditions for intervention. Finally, much of OD seems to hinge on one device, T-group or confrontation, which, because it is the single technique for all problems, necessarily becomes merely a gimmick. With respect to organizational development, we are at that point in time comparable to the use of leeches in medicine. Just as they served the purpose of drawing bad blood, so the single technique in OD seems to be justified in terms of serving the purpose of drawing out bad feelings or emotions.

FAILURE TO DIAGNOSE

This state of affairs inevitably leads to certain kinds of failures, disillusionments, destructive consequences, and other negative outcomes which ultimately cause the public—in this case, the companies or other institutions—to withdraw, as many have, from group dynamics and encounter techniques. Here are some examples where the failure to diagnose led to untoward consequences.

1. A rigid, authoritarian company president, who built his organization into international prominence, was disappointed that he could not seem to retain a corps of young managers who had top management executive potential. While he hired many, they left after two or three years with the organization, usually moving up into higher level roles in other companies. He himself attributed this loss to an inadequate management development program and sought the help of a social scientist well-versed in the concept of confrontation. Certain that

the problem was the executive himself, and equally certain that the executive would profit by attack by his subordinates, the social scientist arranged an organizational development program whose first steps included just that kind of confrontation. In the course of the experience, the president became livid with frustrated rage, angry that his paternalism was unappreciated, and abandoned his efforts to develop the company further. In impulsive anger, he sold it, a fact which ultimately cost him dearly and enmeshed his management in the adaptive problems of a merger which made them merely an appendage of a larger organization.

2. A major division of a large corporation undertook, with the help of a prominent and responsible consultant, an OD program intended to "open things up" to foster group cooperation. Shortly after this developmental effort, the division head was removed from his position when it was discovered that he had manipulated and exploited his subordinates, that he had sponsored orgies at sales meetings in violation of company ethics, and in various other psychopathic ways had acted irresponsibly and manipulatively. The consultant, however well-qualified in working with groups, knew nothing about individual psychology and, as a result, his efforts to "open people up" served only to make people potentially more vulnerable to exploitation. Under such circumstances that group of managers would have been much better off to have learned ways of becoming more highly guarded and protected.

3. A major consulting organization undertook to advise on the drastic reorganization of a client firm. The consequence of this drastic reorganization was that many people who had previously held power were successfully deprived of their power, although they retained their positions. The firm traditionally had insisted on and rewarded compliance so these men did not openly complain, but there was widespread depression and anger among them for which the consulting firm assumed no responsibility. In fact, it is doubtful whether their developmental efforts included any recognition of the psychological consequences of what they did.

4. As part of a developmental effort in a company, thought to be a wise course to "open people up," a trainer undertook encounter experiences which involved having the executives touch each other and engage in activities which brought them physically closer to each other. Two executives, whose latent homosexual impulses (unconscious and well-controlled) could

not tolerate such closeness, had psychotic breaks and had to be hospitalized.

These are examples of destructive consequences of organizational consultation without diagnosis. I could offer many more examples, but these will suffice.

FORMAL DIAGNOSIS

In order for a consultant to avoid these kinds of consequences, he must have a systematic knowledge of individual motivation as well as organizational motivation and small group theory and be able to evolve modes of intervention based on diagnoses which include that multiple level understanding. Now, by way of contrast, let me indicate what a formal diagnostic process should provide.

As is now known, the U.S. State Department has been subject to widespread criticism, several outside commissions, sensitivity training, and a variety of other interventions, to little or no avail. The problems of its bureaucracy remained and still had to be dealt with. Diagnosis of that system indicated that an organizational structure was unlikely to be changed by pressure from the outside alone, pressure from the inside alone, or pressure from leadership alone. It could not significantly be altered by T-group methods, as had already been demonstrated, or by leadership. If the basic problems were structural, that is, bureaucratic, then change could occur only by altering the whole structure and by evolving mechanisms for keeping it open. This conception led to the establishment of 13 simultaneously operating task forces of 20 some people each. Thus, some 250 people were turned loose in a self-critical appraisal of their own structure. They produced from this a 600-page volume and have since had a series of follow-up outcome statements on their recommendations. There was minimal work by the consultant, which consisted largely in his instructing the task force leaders, supporting organizational leadership, and helping the task force leaders and the organizational leadership anticipate the kinds of hostility they were going to encounter.

A president with a good managerial history was brought in to head a scientific company whose keymen neither understood nor wanted to be subject to professional management. When they threatened to resign, and some did, urgent consultation was requested. Diagnosis of this situation took into account organizational history and scientific values, desertion by the company's founders, exploitation by a previous president, cohesion of the ingroup, and the need to retain adaptive profitability. On the basis of a comprehensive assessment, it was decided to hear the men out in individual interviews, then summarize those interviews and present them to the interviewees and the president together. This procedure offered them problems and issues to deal with, but without subjecting the group to the possible exploitation of the president, which they feared, and not running the risk of their destroying him under confrontation attack. The consultant became, in effect, an intermediary. On the one hand, his job was to help the president understand the nature of the complaints and the kinds of people he was dealing with, as well as certain basic psychological principles; on the other, his task was to help the group recognize their need for a professional manager and to offer them more constructive ways of giving him support and guidance. After the initial contacts of three three-day sessions, the consultant maintained a distance from the group so that he would not be seen as "running the company." Many of the key managers individually took part in executive seminars to learn more about the psychology of management, and he was available to all of them as individuals by phone or occasional personal contact. This enabled the president and his key figures to develop a working relationship in which all could count on the distant but supportive influence of the consultant and the new and consistent pattern of leadership the president established.

Once general comfort was attained with this relationship, and the men could come to trust the president, in part because the consultant drew off some of their hostility toward himself, they then decided that it would be wise to get together as a whole group at monthly intervals to open up avenues of communication which they knew needed opening but which would have been destructively explosive had they been opened before. The group continues to function effectively together now more closely than ever. However, this process of carefully differentiated steps has taken a three-year period.

Following the devastating effect of the reorganization of the company mentioned above, and a subsequent year of turmoil, a consultant was asked to undo the situation. Initial interviews with the executives indicated the severity of the depression each was experiencing and provided information on the turmoil in the rest of the organization. Building upon a clinical understanding of depression following the experience of loss, an appreciation of the sense of responsibility the managers in the organization felt, the sensitivity of the new leadership, and important changes in external forces which the organization now confronted, the consultant recommended that the 100 top management people be brought together for a meeting of several days. In this meeting, he recommended, the chief executive officer should present the history of the organization, its achievements, its present state, and its future potential, and indicate clearly what was happening in the outside environment and what drastic changes had to be made. Such a statement was then followed by opportunity for the 100 men in small groups to discuss and analyze what they had heard and to mourn the loss as well as to confront reality. While regretting the past, they could begin to see clearly what the future held and what kinds of adaptive efforts might have to be made.

They were than reconvened to hear presentations about future trends in their field, as well as in society at large, to set in context what they were up against. They then had the opportunity to discuss and digest their impressions and to see how such forces related to them. On the basis of those discussions in small groups, they established priorities for action, coalesced them in large plenary sessions, and evolved a charter for their functional operations. Thus, they began to turn their aggressions outward on real problems which they faced together, while working through their sense of loss and depression.

These examples are cited not to illustrate in detail a diagnostic process but only to indicate that one was in motion which required different interventions for different organizations and with different people under varying circumstances. Whether the diagnoses made were correct ones is not the point. Since they were made consciously, they could exist as testable hypotheses, always subject to change. The consultant could then make interventions of choice. In effect, he exercised control over what was happening, testing his choices rather than assuming that one method worked equally well in all circumstances.

PSYCHOLOGICAL POLLUTION

There is a devastating trend of psychological pollution in contemporary organizational circles. Destructive influences arise out of merger, reorganization, individual and organizational obsolescence, and change. These forces are going to continue for the foreseeable future. That kind of pollution can be dealt with through the medium of organizational intervention, providing the consultant has sufficient understanding of diagnostic and therapeutic conceptions to discern the phenomena he is dealing with and to be able to act on them. We cannot afford the continued blundering by untrained people, which is destructive to organizations as well as to individuals, but we do have resources to deal with the problem. The clinical psychologist, trained as he is in individual diagnosis and therapy, has a basic frame of reference for looking at organizational problems the same way. He can extend his knowledge and subsequently his efforts to include organizations as systems as well as individuals or families as systems. This requires a formal diagnostic process built on his clinical skills but expanding his point of view to see the organization as the client system and to include group and organizational processes within his purview.

This can be done (as I have recently done it in a book called *Organizational Diagnosis* to be published by Harvard University Press) by following a five-step procedure. This procedure should include (a) a detailed organizational history which will delineate both the forces impinging on the organization over time and its characteristic adaptive pattern as well as its modes for coping with crisis; (b) a description of the organization which would include its organizational structure, physical facilities, people, finances, practices and procedures, policies, values, technology, and context in which the organization operates; (c) an interpretation of observations, interviews, questionnaires, and other information about the organization's characteristic ways of receiving, processing, and acting upon information, as well as the personality characteristics of the dominant organizational figures and the style of organizational personality; (d) a summary and interpretation of all these findings with a diagnostic formulation; and (e) a feedback report to the organization to establish a basis for organizational action toward solving its problems.

Such a process is extended from and based on the clinical case study method. It views the organization as an open system with a range of semiautonomous interacting subsystems. Both the subsystems and the organization as a total system can be evaluated in terms of how effectively they adapt to the environments in which they operate, where organizational and subsystem strengths and weaknesses lie, and what kinds of steps can be delineated to utilize the assets to cope with the weaknesses.

In undertaking this kind of organizational diagnostic process, the clinician must give careful attention to the psychology of the individual people involved as well as the collective psychology of groups, since many people working in the same organization share common elements of personality. Similarly, the nonclinician familiar with group and organizational processes, but unfamiliar with personality theory and clinical diagnostic practice, can expand his learning to include both. The ultimate practice of organizational development might better be called applied clinical sociology.

This usually means careful attention to leadership and continued work with the leadership, feedback of the diagnosis to the client system to become the basis for formulating common action, and dealing with resistances and transference problems to the consultant. In the last analysis such a consultation is the management of a relationship between the consultant and the organizational system—thus a problem of clinical management for therapeutic purposes.

The need for such a diagnostic process is imperative because of disillusionment not only with organizational development but with many aspects of community psychology. Despite much talk, community psychology has not had significant impact on social systems, like churches, schools, and similar community agencies. No amount of ad hoc expedience, no amount of talking about "growth," and no amount of depreciating the old as being "in the medical model" will substitute for solid knowledge systematically organized, interpretations based on a comprehensive conceptual system, and diagnostic hypotheses amenable to continuous testing and alterations. Only with a solid clinical base can one come to community and organizational development with a prospect of long-term gain. Inevitably, if he is to have a community impact, the clinical psychologist must become an organizational diagnostician.

III

STRESS

15

A PSYCHOANALYTIC VIEW OF OCCUPATIONAL STRESS

HARRY LEVINSON

Although much has been written about occupational stress and the meaning of work, there is as yet no comprehensive overview which could serve as a basis for organizing the multiplicity of studies and conceptions as well as a framework for continued research. In this paper I propose to advance such a framework.

Much of the work in both the study of occupations and occupational stress has been empirical, inductive and limited to first order psychological abstractions. Often the variables have been idiosyncratically defined by experimenters or theorists, independent of any comprehensive theory of personality or without significant relationships to other already developed empirical or theoretical work. The consequence is that the field of industrial psychology and derivative fields like contemporary organizational development, are burdened with studies which repetitively yield small correlations among poorly defined variables. However significant these correlations may

Presented at the Occupational Stress Conference of the Center for Occupational Mental Health, September 23, 1972. From *Occupational Mental Health*, 3, 2–13. Copyright 1973 by Harry Levinson. Reprinted with permission.

be statistically, they account for only a small part of the statistical variance. To illustrate, many studies on morale, productivity, selection and so on result in low correlations between those factors and whatever else respective authors propose as influencing them. Furthermore, these multiple low correlations seem to be incapable of being integrated into more significant configurations related to such matters. Thus, for example, progress towards determining what combination of factors has a heavy influence on productivity in which organizations under what conditions has been severely limited. This repetitive futility has resulted in a discouraging loss of interest in the Division of Organizational and Industrial Psychology of the American Psychological Association and much internal complaint among its members. It has also resulted in a rush into activities broadly called Organizational Development, which involves variations of T-groups, confrontation and discussion of organizational issues and similar activities directed to building teams of people in changing organizations. These OD efforts usually are not dealt with in experimental fashion, also because the variables are too complex to lend themselves to simple research models.

For the same reason, namely inadequate development of variables with interrelating concepts which offer potential for integration from the clinical side, studies on occupational stress have been limited in scope. They have been frequently oversimplified in design, often unrelated to the general body of clinical knowledge, and inadequate as a basis for intervention.

Even when there have been important correlations, there has remained the difficult problem of bridging from one variable to another. For example, if there is a correlation between, let us say, role ambiguity or role conflict and the appearance of certain physiological or psychological symptoms, what psychological factors underlie that correlation? Why should that relationship exist? What are the intervening processes and variables and how do we come to understand them? When applied to studies of mental health and mental illness, traditional empirical psychology and sociology, tend to beg the explanatory question and to be content with merely describing relationships with the hope that ultimately by the sheer weight of evidence one might arrive inductively at explanations. This is an extremely time-consuming, hit-and-miss mode of developing knowledge. Certainly it is faster and much more comprehensive to develop a broad theory which, by being tested at certain points, gives validity to a whole conceptual structure and thereby provides scientific conceptual tools with which to understand, predict, and in some cases, control phenomena.

PSYCHOANALYTIC FRAME OF REFERENCE

Psychoanalytic theory offers an avenue for attempting to cope with both of these problems. To review the main elements of the theory briefly, psychoanalytic theory approaches personality functioning from five points of view.

The first point of view has to do with psychological energy. This is called an economic point of view and calls our attention to the issue of cost/efficiency ratios in the distribution of energy. The theory makes the assumption that since there are two continuously operating biochemical forces—anabolism and catabolism—in all living matter, and since these have to do with growth and death, such forces must have some effect on a personality. The theory posits that these forces are the basis of two fundamental drives, sexual and aggressive, both of which are necessary for the survival of the species. These drives in turn are reflected in feelings of love and hate, with some qualifications which we need not discuss here. The drives constitute the motive power of the personality and, together with the feelings, wishes, impulses and fantasies derived from them, must be managed in such a way that the sexual or constructive forces of the personality—those related to growth and love—are fused with the destructive forces and by their dominance make the combined energy of both available for adaptation.

This dual drive theory, heavily routed in biochemical and physiological processes, makes it possible to deal with the interaction of emotions and physical symptoms as well as to examine the expression of drives and their direction in the work situation. Since drives can be expressed in only four ways—in the performance of tasks; in displacements onto substitute targets; by being over-controlled and therefore internalized; and finally by being turned against the self as in depression and accidents—we have a ready gauge for estimating the adequate functioning or malfunctioning of drive expression. For example, one can see sabotage, theft, absenteeism, some strikes and similar phenomena as displacements or as self-destructive.

The second point of view is a conceptual structure for the personality. The personality is viewed as a total system which is arbitrarily divided conceptually into three sub-systems. This is an attempt to understand and conceptualize the multiple major interacting forces within the person. The words ego, id, and superego are concepts which describe these multiple functions. The ego is conceived of as the executive part of the personality to which is attributed the sensing, processing, and acting components of the personality. The ego is viewed as the mediating structure between the id and the superego which has the responsibility also of continually testing reality, The superego represents what colloquially is known as the conscience which is that component of personality that includes values, rules, aspirations and the capacity for creating acceptable cognitive maps for governing the expressing of feelings, thoughts and behavior. These are the essential governing functions of the personality. The id is conceptualized as that component of the personality which includes memories of which the person is no longer aware, and subliminal psychological postures and attitudes derived from those memories, as well as the drives themselves and the basic feelings derived from them.

These three sub-systems or components of the personality are conceived to be continually in conflict and psychoanalytic theory is therefore a conflict psychology. All behavior is viewed as the result of compromises among these three structures and the interaction of the whole with reality.

The third point of view is the topographic conceptualization, which refers to levels of consciousness. This conceptualization accounts for the fact that people are aware of some aspects of their feelings, thoughts and behavior which are referred to as being conscious. Some other aspects of their feelings and thoughts can readily be recalled or made conscious while still others cannot be recalled and are therefore unconscious.

The fourth point of view is a conception of the development of the personality. This point of view refers to the course of physiological, specifically neurological, development of the person and the psychological reactions which flow from the interaction of person and environment as a consequence of this developmental sequence. The developmental point of view includes Freud's conception of stages in psychosexual development and Erik Erikson's complementary conception of psychosocial development. There are other non-psychoanalytic but parallel developmental conceptions such as those of Piaget on conceptual development, Kohlberg on moral development and Chomsky on linguistic development, which give added weight to the concept of innate developmental sequences.

Finally there is the adaptive point of view. This concept includes the equilibrium-maintaining aspect of the personality as the ego seeks to mediate the forces of the id and superego and effect the adaptation of the person to his environment.

In its early development, psychoanalytic theory was an id psychology. That is, much of the attention of psychoanalysts was devoted to understanding unconscious memories and their expression in behavior. It was then also primarily a drive psychology. In more recent years, much more attention has been given to ego psychology or the adaptive aspects of the personality.

EGO PSYCHOLOGY

Since work, and therefore occupation, is a major mode of adaptation, much of the work on occupational stress may fruitfully be viewed from the viewpoint of ego psychology. That is, our concern will largely have to do with the manner in which people maintain an equilibrium among all of these forces in the context of their relationship to each other at work and their work environment. When we speak about psychological stress on the job or related to the job, one way or another we are speaking of the disruption of the psychological equilibrium which then produces certain kinds of less adaptive or maladaptive efforts to restore the equilibrium. From a psychoanalytic point of view all symptoms are efforts to maintain or restore the equilibrium of the personality. By extension, conflict and malfunctioning in organizations may similarly be viewed as a consequence of equilibrium disruption for numbers of people.

The fulcrum for disequilibrium is the internalized alarm system of the personality. This alarm system, described in its physiological mode by Selye and others who have followed him, has three psychological components which in turn relate to the ego, superego and id. The first of these is fear, which is self-explanatory. However, unless fear (not phobia) is chronic or life-threatening, usually it is not seriously disruptive to the equilibrium of the personality. The reason is simply that people usually know what they are afraid of and can take action with respect to it. Avenues for action provide the ego with methods of maintaining its equilibrium. The second alarm reaction—that stemming from the superego—is guilt. Guilt is a more difficult phenomenon to deal with, partly because so much of it is unconscious and people therefore do not know what they are dealing with or why they feel guilty. The third alarm mechanism is anxiety. While anxiety is a common word which covers everything from "nervousness" to "breakdown," in this conceptual frame of reference it refers to the threat, as the individual experiences it, that he will lose control over himself and particularly of the expression of drives, feelings and thoughts. It refers to that kind of dread, disquiet or uneasiness that one experiences without quite knowing why. It is the most difficult of all alarms to deal with, simply because one cannot understand what is happening to him.

Of all of the alarm signals, the major one with which we are most likely to be concerned with respect to occupational stress is guilt, for reasons which I will discuss later.

POINTS OF VULNERABILITY

Drives

Malfunction or dysfunction occurs with respect to the drives when the two become defused, when the constructive energies of the personality derived from the sexual drive no longer adequately temper the aggressive drive. The aggression is thereupon diverted from most effective utilization in problem-solving activities. Such defusion may occur in response to external stimuli which provoke anger. It may also occur in people who are chronically angry and who therefore vent their anger onto others. Thus we may see scapegoating, sadistic behavior, over-controlling behavior, absenteeism, accidents, sabotage, resistance, and internal strife.

It is difficult for many people to express affection, support and approval; sometimes because of their own personalities and sometimes because organizational norms do not encourage such behavior or organizational pressures militate against it. This deprives their subordinates of the infusion they need to sustain the dominance of their own constructive energy. Anger in one form or another then erupts. Frequently one encounters persons in authoritative roles who say, "I'm not going to hold people's hands," or, "It's not my job to listen to their problems," or "They come to work and they go home, and that's all there is to it. They get their big kicks and that's what work is for." Thus anger may be provoked by executives, managers, and supervisors who are unwilling or unable to provide adequate support and direction to others or to help subordinates resolve organizational and interpersonal problems.

Defusion occurs also when people are unable to adequately control their impulses, either because these impulses are too powerful and therefore overwhelm them or because organizational pressures precipitate outbursts. Unrelenting pressure for productivity, inability or unwillingness to solve frustrating problems or simple inefficiency are typical precipitants. Inadequate or incorrect information which leads to feelings of unworthiness or threat is another.

Dysfunction occurs also when there are inadequate or inappropriate channels for the constructive expression of aggression, that is, when people can't get at—let alone resolve—problems inherent in the work situation. This is seen in extreme cases when people attack each other, as in intraorganizational struggles or destroy their own property as in race riots.

Some organizations have established methods for handling intergroup conflicts which threaten the whole. A typical way is to transfer people. In South American republics, those who lose in the power struggle may be made ambassadors. In a monastery, the losing faction in an election may be dispersed into outlying missions.

To recapitulate, dysfunction may occur when the aggressive drive gets out of hand in an individual or groups of individuals, either because of character structure or because of external stimulation, or because of inadequate or inappropriate channels for the constructive expression of aggression. While there are similar problems in the expression of the sexual drive, which takes the form of difficulties in managing the wish to love and be loved, these are less frequently a problem in organizations.

Superego Conflict

Turning to the structural aspect of personality, one sees in organizations frequent and intense conflict between ego and superego. This may occur when people are asked to behave in ways which violate their own internal standards as, for example, in producing shoddy products or misrepresenting goods and services or to carry out company policies and practices inimical to others. The guilt which results is readily evident. We have seen examples of guilt-induced behavior with respect to the leaks of government information.

There are many other more commonplace examples in criticisms of the advertising industry and of high pressure tactics in the sale of retirement homes.

Less evident but no less pressing is the guilt which arises when the gap increases between the ego ideal—that component of the superego which represents the image of oneself as one ideally would like to be—and the self-image, how one sees himself as he presently is. The greater the gap between these two, the lower self-esteem and the greater the self-directed aggression in the form of guilt. The gap can be increased as a result of organizational practices on the one hand and personal change on the other.

The self-image, and therefore self-esteem, is lowered when people feel manipulated by forces beyond their control, when they feel themselves to be demeaned or their work role is demeaning, when they are pitted against each other and are compelled to identify themselves as losers, when they are victimized by organizational policies and practices, and when they view themselves as manipulators or exploiters of others. Arbitrary managerial decisions, much of the current vogue of management by objectives, most organization practices related to promotion and compensation and many of the job demands created by mechanistic systems of industrial engineering and accounting all contribute to such feelings. In particular, the inability to view themselves as valued members of organizations contributing significantly to the resolution of problems which confront the organization is a major source of lowered self-esteem in contemporary organizations of all kinds.

Guilt is further engendered when people are asked to evaluate or appraise others and experience those practices as being destructive of others because unconsciously to be critical of someone else is the same as to destroy the other. Similar feelings are engendered by intense rivalry, particularly in triumphing over older and more experienced persons in the organization and in having to discharge others. Similarly, guilt is experienced when people have to maneuver around organizational policies and channels in order to accomplish their tasks.

On a more personal level, the gap between ego ideal and self-image increases when people age and no longer feel themselves to have the same adaptive skills they had before. This is especially true in a context of intense competitive rivalry.

Obsolescence

The aging process and occupational obsolescence both contribute to the decreased capacity of the ego to adapt. When people have become too specialized or are no longer technically up to date, they feel themselves to be less adequate and therefore more readily threatened. If in the course of aging or moving from place to place they lose contact with valued friends and associates, or are unable to use favored modes of behavior, or are deprived of environmental support or of leaders whom they had trusted, they commonly experience loss which is followed by anger with self and others and frequently depression. Merger, retirement, transfer, promotion, all carry with them the seeds of such losses despite whatever gains may result.

Change

The ego is also beleaguered when new demands are made on it. For example, when historically highly controlled organizations must become more decentralized, when previously authoritarian managers are asked to become more democratic, when dependent employees are required to become more aggressive, the simultaneous experience of loss and new demand creates heavy burdens for the ego. Characteristically, people at first try to deny the reality of change. They then attempt to define the reality of the change. Upon discovering it they tend to panic and to feel first overwhelmed and then incompetent. They then begin to mourn the loss, to feel adrift and demoralized.

The ego may have difficulty in adapting because the person does not get adequate information from peers. Without that information the person may not know what to do or how to do it or what is coming next. Rumors replace facts. Reality is ambiguous. Organizational structures may be inchoate or unstable. Key figures may no longer be present; panic ensues.

Contractual Violation

Another threat to the ego, because it lowers self-image and increases anxiety, is the loss of the context for the ego's equilibrium-maintaining activities. People unconsciously select organizations and kinds of work largely on the basis of an unconscious psychological contract. That is, people choose organizations and work which fit their unconscious needs for managing their drives, the demands of the superegos, including the ego ideal, the use of their skills and capacities, and for dealing with reality. There is a configurational pattern of feelings, thoughts and behavior which we call personality which the person either fits to a matching configurational pattern in an organization or adapts part of that organization to match his pattern. There is, for example, a different personality configuration among people who seek managerial roles in AT&T as contrasted with their counterparts in IBM. Both in turn differ significantly from those who are managers for Sears, Roebuck. These differences are readily recognizable by anyone who has contact with all three groups or other similar groups. Each company has its characteristic way of doing business and its characteristic organization structure. People who remain in those organizations are likely to do so because they are comfortable with both. Employees frequently unconsciously view their employing organization as being maternal or paternal. Seeking an organization into which one can fit means not only using one's skills but also finding a congenial situation for the practice of one's values, or the expression of his preferred modes of handling drives and of relating to people. Organizations, therefore, become supportive contexts through which work becomes a medium for maintaining the psychological equilibrium by fulfilling the unconscious psychological contract.

When that contract is violated by organizational practices or organizational change then people experience loss, alienation, and mounting anger.

Organic Change

Physiological impairment is another way in which the ego's adaptive ability is weakened. In some organizations this poses a difficult and dangerous problem. For example, some years ago the medical director of a well-known railroad was concerned about screening engineers who might be accident-prone, following a series of train accidents. Questioning disclosed that most men did not become engineers until they were at least 55 years old at which time there were beginning to be organic brain changes in some. Many in their 70's were still operating trains. These men were examined annually by their own physicians. None was required to have a neurological examination. As it turned out, some would operate their engines at 70 miles per hour in a 35 mile per hour zone, no longer able to see or react to the speed limit signs quickly enough, and accidents would result.

Ego Development

The ego's adaptive processes can also be inhibited by inadequate developmental experiences. This is one of the problems now facing organizations as they employ increasing numbers of people who have been educationally, culturally and perhaps psychologically disadvantaged.

Still another aspect of adaptation which is only now beginning to be touched upon is that of age-appropriate activities. Adult life, according to Erikson's conceptualization, is divided into three stages. The first stage, that of intimacy, is also the period when a person establishes himself in his career, acquires the skills of that career and is most vigorous in his potentially novel attack on the problems of that career period. This is followed by the stage of generativity or middle age, where there is heavy concentration on the development of others, while simultaneously renewing one's own goals and values, and finally by the period beyond 55, the stage of completion which meets the demands of his ego ideal. There is as yet no adequate differentiation in organizations among people of these respective age groups with respect to the kinds of work which are most suitable for one or another stage. However, we are beginning to see better use of people who retire early from active executive roles in the form of their involvement in long range planning where they can integrate their understanding and knowledge of the organization, together with the wisdom they have acquired, with a concern for future trends and problems. It is irrational to expect most middle aged people to approach a task with the same kind of innovative flair as younger people, yet frequently that is what is expected when competition is placed on a simplistic plane. The psychological inability to meet the requirements of a given task because of one's life stage is a source of great stress as the ego is expected to meet demands with which it can no longer cope or are unrelated to its stage of development.

Role Conflict and Ambiguity

A primary problem for the ego in its adaptation in an organizational structure, or even with respect to independent professional activity, is its inability to meet the demands of the ego ideal. Most of the issues which are to be found in the literature of occupational mental health have to do with this phenomenon. For example, if one asks why role ambiguity or role conflict should create difficulty psychologically and therefore physiologically, he is called upon to define an intermediate variable between role ambiguity and the symptoms. Role ambiguity reduces the ability of people to act competently. Given the severity of most people's superegos, and the consequent tendency to be hypercritical of themselves, in the absence of information to the contrary, people quickly jump to self-criticism which in turn leads to the lowered self-image that in turn leads to forms of defensive behavior which frequently are counter-productive. Furthermore, they run the risk of external criticism of their performance which in turn will lower the self-image. It is a commonplace that when most people in organizations are asked, "How do you know where you stand?" they respond, "By the squawk index." This means that most people perennially operate from a defensive position, ready to be criticized and threatened with lowered self-image. They see themselves as always vulnerable to loss of self-esteem and potentially unable to meet the internalized ego ideal which involves considerations of being good, doing well, and demonstrating competence.

Given the harshness of the superego—and the more competent people are, the more self-demanding they are, and therefore the more prone to be self-critical—the superior–subordinate relationships become particularly important. I have often asked executive groups the question, "How do you know where you stand?" In response they will usually delineate the statistics of performance, feedback from peers, subordinates, appraisals, and other criteria. I then ask, "Suppose that you know by your own internal standards that you've done a good job and your boss doesn't say anything, what do you do?" For a moment the executives deny that the boss' reaction has much meaning. But then typically, they delineate a sequence of behavior that would be likely to follow. They would first try to call his attention to what they have done. If he did not respond, then they would begin to doubt their performance and their standards. Then they would work harder to try to prove themselves. If the boss still did not respond, they would try to talk with him. If he were still noncommittal in conversation, then their anger would mount. They would then very likely take an extra drink and displace some of their hostility onto their children or their subordinates. Then they would begin to withdraw from their work, getting by with minimal effort. Finally, they would ultimately quit.

The point is that despite all of the presumed objective criteria of performance, the crucial variable which recurs repetitively is the need for confirmation (approval) from superiors. In the studies of role stress, the crucial role senders are the superiors. In a more recent study of role ambiguity the same crucial experience of superior–subordinate relationship arises. Given the power of the parents over their children and given the concept of transference—the attitude toward superiors which are unconsciously derived from previous attitudes towards the parents—the superior–subordinate relationship takes on even more significant proportions than we had previously assumed.

Relationship to Research

The point is that we can understand both the studies and their relationship to symptoms only if we have an intervening variable like the ego ideal. Thus we can see this aspect of occupational stress as being directly related to the whole of psychoanalytic personality theory on the one hand and physiological as well as behavioral outcomes on the other. Such a conception makes it possible to open new avenues of research by measuring people's self-judgments against internalized ideals and to relate this gap between them to both physiological and psychological symptoms of stress.

Organization Structure and Practice

There are similar possibilities with respect to the relationship of organizational structure and organizational practices to the self-image and the ego ideal. Although much is said about organizations as instruments of achievement for individuals, and their motivational practices as being more rewarding than punishing, the fact of the matter is that bureaucratic organizations essentially are geared for defeat. That is, for each person who is promoted a number are left behind. Given an organizational value system which emphasizes managerial achievement, such a practice leaves behind many "career people" who are angry with themselves and their organizations because they have been passed over. In essence they are told, "You are nothing, you have had it, you are a defeated one." The consequence is considerable chronic repressed anger in many organizations. Lawrence Peter has made a universal joke out of the "Peter Principle," the notion that people rise to their level of incompetence. I am sure that many people become incompetent because they are made incompetent by the underlying depression which paralyzes their activities after they had been defined as defeated and failures. This phenomenon is made even worse by the intense pressure toward early retirement, which is essentially a castration of mature people who have had little opportunity and less support to adapt to rapidly changing economic circumstances. As a consequence they see themselves as utter failures. Executives in such a position frequently ask the question uncomprehendingly, "What did I do wrong?"

There are many ways of relating physiological, sociological and socio-psychological phenomena by means of these psychoanalytic intervening constructs. But why should one do so? Correlational studies are just that. They report the correlations of one variable with another. But they offer no insight as to the "Why's" of the relationships. Without such insight the studies yield no direction for ameliorative action. Studies of occupational stress are of little value unless they help to point to a direction for the prevention or alleviation of stress. The simple experience of piling empirical fact upon fact upon fact will not get us there.

Object Attachments

There is still another way in which the ego finds it difficult to adapt and that is when it cannot meet the pressures of the id to which I referred earlier. When the ego loses avenues for discharge of drives or feelings derived from them it experiences difficulty. When it loses objects of affection and thereby sources for the return of affection the ego experiences deprivation, loss and helplessness. Disappointment and anger follow. When sources of support and affection are gone, when people's networks of relationships by which they have accomplished their work are disrupted by management-by-objective conceptions which tend to pit people against each other at the expense of being able to work together, then depressions result. When there is no time for managers to support people or when the span of control is so wide that people who need support no longer have it, then, again, depression follows. All of these losses are captured in the characteristic failure story in management. The repetitive example managers use is the good salesman who is promoted to become a poor sales manager. A good salesman characteristically devotes himself to pleasing his customers. From serving them and in continuous contact with them, even to the point of joking and drinking and entertaining them, he receives signals of approval, he is held in esteem, he is continually patted. When such a person is made sales manager, he shuffles papers. He loses the avenues for support and affection which previously were so important to him and in turn he is unable to support the salesmen who report to him because he needs so much affection himself. Such problems occur in many different forms at almost all levels in organizations.

Overstimulation

There are also difficulties in adaptation when there is increased stimulation of the drives beyond which people can handle. Psychologists and psychiatrists who served in the military forces know of the sexual stimulation brought about merely by proximity to others which frequently results in homosexual panic. Such panic reactions have also occurred in encounter groups and similar training activities frequently undertaken by naive managements. It occurs also when there is invasion of already well-defined uni-sexual groups, as, for example when young and pretty telephone operators are introduced into a group of maiden lady operators. Such problems are likely to escape the notice of characteristic sociological and socio-psychological studies unless there is a thorough understanding of personality variables.

There are, then, such stimulations which can make for adaptive difficulties on the part of the ego, when it is unable to meet the pressures of the id.

Neurotic Conflict

In addition, there are focal problems for the ego which stem from id conflicts. These are seen in classical failures like the man who, promoted to a vice-presidency, jumps from an 18th story window on the first day of his tenure. Frequently one sees an executive who has done very well in his upward climb until he achieves success beyond his father's level. When it becomes clear to him, however unconsciously, that he has exceeded (in his mind that equals defeated) his father, he fails. Neither he nor those around him know why a man who has been highly successful suddenly fails. I have seen the governor of a state do just that exactly under those circumstances. In recent years we have seen the same phenomenon in major political figures who could not move into adequate managerial roles because of the psychological significance to them of being in those roles. And incidentally we have also seen some of the problems of major political figures who could not accept and manage their own aggressive impulses, for to express aggression in the form of taking on the leadership role in which one had to give direction to others, to manipulate political forces and to act on (as contrasted with talking about) what one believes, presented them with a conflict which they could resolve only by rejecting the leadership role.

This same phenomenon, the inability to accept and utilize one's own impulses, particularly aggressive ones, plagues certain kinds of organizations such as hospitals, church institutions, educational institutions and the like. People who choose work which takes them into such institutions usually do so in part out of the need to deny more open expression of aggression in the form of competitive effort. For example, if one asks students in a graduate school of business why they are there they will speak quite freely of their wish for power and achievement, money and position. They have few problems in identifying themselves as aggressive-competitive people. However, when one asks the same question of people in schools of hospital, educational or public administration, the response will usually be in terms of contribution to the public good, which frequently masks and rationalizes the unconscious wish for power. As a result, the underlying aggression, unacceptable in consciousness, will tend to be managed in a more clandestine fashion in the form of manipulation behind the scenes. Consequently, it is much more difficult in such institutions to know what is going on and there is frequent complaint of dirty politics. These issues frequently pass for role conflict.

So much for the adaptive problems of the ego with respect to the superego, the id and the environment and the ways in which one might begin to explore these issues and their relationship to occupational stress.

Let us turn now to the third perspective on personality, namely the topographic. Between the lines of the discussion up to this point we have referred to conscious and unconscious phenomena, but at this time I see little possibility of fruitful avenues of research on occupational mental health through the path of the topographic point of view although it is a crucial avenue for study of creativity.

Developmental Issues

However, we can begin to look at some of the difficulties which arise from that stress which is either a consequence of fixation at a given level of development or produces a regression to a given level of development. Some of the difficulties which arise from developmental issues have to do with the misplacement of people in roles which are more adequate to persons in another developmental life stage. We have already referred to placing middle age men in competitive tasks more appropriate to younger men. We might also view the same issue from the obverse point of view: frequently young men are asked to merely wait in line for their managerial places and promised the opportunity to act in their later years, a time more conducive to reflection than to action. Increasingly we are confronting opportunities and wishes for multiple careers, mid-career changes, middle age crises and the trauma associated with retirement. In addition, certain occupations are specifically related to life stages and are marked by transitional difficulties. Professional athletes notoriously must deal with this problem. Scientists, creative artists, aircraft controllers and many others frequently find themselves in occupational stress situations related to the specific life stages.

Fixation and Regression

People whose occupational choice appears to be significantly related to a stage of personality development are likely to have symptoms indicative of a regression to more primitive forms of that stage of development under oc-cupational stress. It is not without reason that the major symptom among people in the newspaper business is alcoholism. Those in advertising, acting, editing and other occupational roles which have an important oral compo-nent seem to have greater difficulty in managerial roles which require them to take charge of a situation and to act aggressively in a manner which is more comfortable for people whose occupational choices are more firmly rooted derivatives of the anal or phallic stages of development, which lead to greater comfort in controlling and self-assertion.

Conversely, a person whose occupational choice is more firmly anchored in the anal stage of development and who is a tightly organized, compulsive person is more likely to have greater difficulty when, for example, as an ex-ecutive vice president of a consumer goods company he must deal with me-dia people on advertising, promotion, creative art and other more oral ac-tivities requiring greater flexibility and looseness. Such a person has great difficulty tolerating the fantasy life of more creative people, their difficulty in maintaining schedules and their inability to respond to tight organiza-tional control. Similarly a man in his mid-fifties whose forte is managerial control is likely to have great difficulty coping with rapidly changing styles which are the stock in trade of a department store and supervising younger people in their early 20's who are in touch with the moods of that age period and who themselves exhibit some of the sensitivity to flair and buying and selling which are the essence of profitability in such a business. The older man has difficulty being in touch with the thinking of younger people, with impulsive irregularity of such a business and with his inability to control it to make it profitable by his systems.

One of the major tasks of managers and executives is to train their re-placements, and an important concern in business organizations therefore is management development. It is difficult to get people from 21 to 35 to be concerned about developing other people. They are at that stage in their own lives where they are necessarily preoccupied with their own careers. That pe-riod is, therefore, a self-centered one, and one intimately bound up with devel-oping the network of adult relationships and in the generation of new families to allow sufficient psychological energy for the development of others, let alone to contribute to the development of potential rivals. On the other hand, it is equally irrational to expect a man of 54 to operate at the same level of intensity as a man of 25 in the same occupation. Such a person who already has estab-lished himself might do far better in the development of others where he can bring to bear his wisdom and experience, integrated with his need to maintain a contributing but less competitive role than he had before. Finally, the tasks of reorganizing, of integrating the prospective future with the momentum of the past are the tasks of older people, those of 55 and beyond.

These issues will become even more complex as more women enter the workforce and find their ways into managerial and executive roles. There is much research to be done on differentiating tasks psychologically with respect to ages and stages of development and to delineating the developmental periods in adult life so that a better fit can be evolved for people and jobs. By so doing we can prevent much occupational stress. By the same token we will know better how to relieve stress arising from such psychological binds.

Rivalry

There are special stresses of occupation related to development which have gone largely unrecognized. Among them are the classical problems of intense rivalry with a parent, which stem from the Oedipal period. This is seen most vividly among entrepreneurs. Characteristically entrepreneurs have had great unresolved Oedipal struggles with their fathers and as a result cannot accept supervision from other men. Given this kind of conflict, characteristically they cannot tolerate rivalry. As a result they exploit their organizations. They tend to "marry the organization" and to use the organization as if it were a mistress while simultaneously also their means of identification and their "baby." They tend to engage in internecine warfare with up and coming people in their own organizations and immediately cut down anyone who seeks to rise to a position of power in their organization, thereby threatening to take it away from them. As a result, such organizations have great difficulty in adapting as their progenitors age and are unable to change with changes in the environment. The organizations become obsolete. People in them run great job risk and many are suppressed by such positions. When such a leader either retires or leaves his organization, he usually leaves behind a highly dependent group of people who now suffer from the loss of a charismatic leader and are left with a maladaptive organization. This is a source of great stress to many people and the stress becomes even more severe when, following his demise, there is exacerbated rivalry for a position of power, or the organization is merged with another or simply falls apart. Ultimately, since organizations are such an important component of society, we will probably see the day when organizations abused in this way by their founders will be taken from them just as children are rescued by agencies of society when they are abused by their parents.

A subset of this problem is the intensity of conflict in family businesses. There are some 15,000 family businesses in the United States. They are more common in other countries. The intensity of rivalry and the exacerbation of conflict and guilt in such businesses is more severe than in non-family businesses. This is a source of stress about which there is as yet little information and even fewer ways of helping people to cope.

Middle Age

I referred earlier to the problems of middle age and to middle age crises. The 35–55 age range encompasses that time when men (we do not yet know about women) begin to measure where they have come against whatever their ego ideals have held out for them. They begin to reassess their values as it becomes apparent to them that they are growing older and have lost their youth. This is a time when depression manifests itself more frequently, sometimes masked by increased physical symptoms, drinking and efforts to regain their lost youth. Sometimes those efforts include a flight into a mid-career change. While there are many good reasons for seeking mid-career changes—the need for additional stimulation, gratification, growth and things of that kind—one must be aware of the readiness to flee into change and to be aware of the pain of the developmental experience in this stage.

Character Problems

Between the lines of our discussion so far, we have also talked about adaptation. We have viewed occupation as a mode of coping with the equilibrium-maintaining activities of the personality and stresses as dysfunctions or malfunctions in the capacity to maintain an effective adaptation level. However, there are some forms of maladaptive behavior which are best seen through the adaptational perspective. Many of the characteristic problems with which clinicians deal—unresolved conflicts and character problems—might usefully be viewed through the adaptational perspective. There is, for example, the rigidity of certain kinds of people, which, though useful up to a certain point in time or certain stage in their occupational development, becomes dysfunctional. Characteristically dependent or rigid people who may do well in highly formalized, controlled organizations begin to lose out when they move into higher level responsibilities requiring greater initiative and more flexibility, or when such organizations are required to become more flexible as the result of increasingly differentiated market circumstances. This has happened in recent years in banks, petroleum companies, insurance companies, large retail organizations and even in many manufacturing organizations. The adaptational problems of such people become very severe. There are few guidelines for organizational leadership to evolve transitions with minimal trauma.

Similarly, some men seek executive positions as a reaction formation to an unconscious feeling of helplessness. This compensatory effort to acquire power leads such people into overcontrol which stimulates rebellion, intensifies rivalry, and paralyzes initiative. Such men can be successful to a certain point and then are called upon to develop others or allow for greater initiative. If they cannot do so, they are forced into premature retirement or out of their positions of responsibility with consequent stress. They may, meanwhile, sabotage efforts to make their organizations more flexible and to involve others more directly in organizational decision-making. They frequently demoralize their organizations, exploiting and manipulating people in them for their own psychological needs.

There are the problems of the mediator–leader who cannot make decisions, of the narcissistic character and the manipulative character disorder as well as those of the paranoid leader, all of which have devastating effects on the people who must work under them. Such problems have long been known clinically but they have not been examined from the point of view of understanding them better in an organizational context in order to prevent destructiveness to people and organizations, and to alleviate the potential stress.

Threats to Adaptation

Another dimension of adaptive effort has to do with the psychological contract. As I noted earlier, people seek occupations and organizations which fit their psychological needs and support their equilibrium-maintaining efforts. There is, therefore, an unconscious psychological contract between the person and the organization, usually recognized only in the breach when people are disappointed at what has happened to them. As a consequence we will increasingly see pressures toward unionization and other modes of compelling management to make up in money and in rigidity of both security and tenure provisions for having failed to recognize and respond to, or for having violated, the psychological contracts of employees. People who have worked hard, who have done what is expected of them, who have been loyal to the organization and who suddenly find themselves out of a job or who are manipulated and exploited in a merger or required to shift to psychological directions which are uncongenial to their equilibrium-maintaining efforts, feel they have been done an injustice, no matter how much the economic decisions may seem to support that action. When enough people experience injustice they will react collectively in response to that feeling. Thus the major task of research in occupational stress will be to help managements rise to more abstract conceptual understanding of what they are doing, to yield mechanistic practices in favor of sophisticated psychological practices, to evolve ways of understanding that there is a difference between effectiveness and efficiency and that in the long term interests of the organization they must work differently with those who are part of it. This must be done in an age which leans ever more heavily on computers. Though computers may process great amounts of information, decentralized decisions are required at ever more fractionated and diverse marketplaces. Those who make decisions will have to do so at higher conceptual levels taking into account a wider array of forces. For people who have viewed themselves as expedient operators who "flew by the seat of their pants," this pressure toward higher level conceptualization of what they do will in turn be an increasing occupational stress for they will be required to handle inputs of data far beyond what was required of them before. We do not know much about helping people rise to higher conceptual levels, particularly when some of those same people fled into work requiring only concrete numbers to avoid thinking conceptually.

The adaptive task for people in managerial ranks at least, involves increasing intensity of demand on those people for performance, particularly in organizations whose heads are preoccupied with running them for quarterly reports to security analysts. Such a focus inevitably means that people are moved up and down an organizational hierarchy like yo-yos with increasing pressure to make the results look good. That phenomenon now pervades all organizations—the need to look good by the numbers. Organizations, like competitive children, must look good to those whose approval they require and that approval in turn requires straight A's on every report card.

That pressure in turn leads to putting people in occupational roles which they experience as overwhelming because they simply do not have the capacity to adapt to them. Sometimes this is done because a person who has been successful in one role is idealized. Then on the basis of that idealization he is moved to another where he fails.

Adaptation involves coping with one's own character defenses in the face of tasks which are age-specific, stage-specific, and congenial to one's equilibrium-maintaining efforts. Adaptation involves managing the drives, managing the distance between the ego ideal and the self-image and managing one's focal conflicts in the face of institutional requirements which may magnify or intensify them, or conversely make them incongruous in a given situation. The leadership of organizations, still relatively unsophisticated psychologically and characteristically less sensitive to feelings of individuals, now must take such issues into account, which intensifies the stress on leadership. These are dimensions of occupational stress which require our careful attention.

SUMMARY

In summary, the five perspectives on personality functioning which constitute the core of psychoanalytic theory provide multiple views of functioning of the person and groups which make it possible to relate external pressures in organizations to the feelings of individuals and in turn to symptoms and difficulties which appear both in individuals and in organizations. These conceptions can help us bridge the gap between environmental pressures and physiological sequelae. We are now at the point where we must begin to differentiate among different needs, different groups of people, and the difficult multiple role functions of different groups in different cultures. We have tended to treat people en masse in our socio-psychological investigations. We have tended to generalize from one population to another, often to our discomfort and dismay. In our psychophysiological studies we have tended to correlate activities with symptoms without recognizing the need for intervening variables. Both of these modes of research leave us with undifferentiated generalizations which in turn are adequate bases for the application of preventive or ameliorative measures. Increasingly we must be thinking in terms of psychological man, in terms of configurations of needs and drives and defenses as well as adaptive patterns. We must learn how to quantify configurations of organization and task. Either we move in that direction or we are left perpetually to additive summaries of odds and ends of this variable and that which can neither be summed nor integrated.

Some of the central issues which are thrown open to investigation by consideration of the psychoanalytic perspective on personality are to be found around the gap between the ego ideal and the self-image. Western society is heavily superego oriented. Achievements and obligations, good and evil, love and hate comprise its polar struggles. As a result it is a society characterized by a pervasive feeling of inadequacy and guilt stemming from the ego ideal–self-image gap.

These pervasive feelings of inadequacy and guilt are exacerbated by the typical bureaucratic hierarchical organizational structure, by increasingly intense competition within such structures, by artificially manipulated management-by-objectives processes, by appraisal processes which are guaranteed to intensify the pressure on people within such a system to defeat each other. These activities are undertaken on the basis of motivational assumptions derived from manipulating rats in mazes, dogs in harnesses and the handicapped or deviant incarcerated in institutions. The result of such pressure based on psychological assumptions invalid for human beings who have greater freedom than animals in mazes is characteristically destructive to the individual and to organizations alike.

Among the consequences of the need to continuously evolve more competitive economic institutions is the loss of self-esteem as people are put aside and are no longer able to use their skills; are merged into organizations where they feel like stepchildren (and frequently treated as such); where promises of rapid advancement or job tenure may be undermined by ineffective management. Some people, despite constructively creative and competitive efforts on their part, are displaced for economic reasons beyond their control and have no place to use the adaptive skills they have often painfully acquired. The fate of engineers in the defense industry from 1969 to 1971 is a case in point.

In the face of such forces, the adaptive ego is frequently at a loss and suffers from a pervasive sense of helplessness. To feel oneself to be helpless while a mature adult in stern society is only to suffer increased guilt as the harsh self-judgment both indicts and convicts the individual for failing.

Thus the most pressing mental health issues with respect to organizational stress have to do with the fear–guilt–anxiety dimensions, particularly guilt dimensions related to the ego ideal, and the pervasive feelings of inadequacy in the face of both rising levels of self-expectation and those which are held out by school and society. We must evolve avenues for action, for helping people learn to adapt, for changing organizations so people can fit into them and be masters of them rather than be mastered by them.

16

BETWEEN CEO AND COO

HARRY LEVINSON

The CEO and COO are engaged in a partnership that differs from other managerial relationships, because its implications for succession involve not merely succession in role, but also passing the baton on leadership. It is important to understand the complex feelings involved in that relationship and the problems that frequently result. Important lessons can be learned from the failures of this relationship and what both parties can do to help make it successful.

The relationship between the chief executive officer and the chief operating officer in any organization is fraught with many psychological complexities. Perhaps it is the most difficult of all organizational working relationships because more than any others, it is a balancing act on the threshold of power.

At the top management level, chief executive officers usually seek to manage more collegially than is customary at the lower levels, even in these days of participative management, teams, empowerment, and the development of consensus. Top management discussions are necessarily the precursor of decision making in complex organizations.

From *Academy of Management Executive*, 7(2), 71–83. Copyright 1993 by the Academy of Management. Reprinted with permission.

Nevertheless, there is a power differential around which both parties tread carefully. The word "boss" is no longer fashionable (even discount department store clerks are called "associates"). It is even less so at such a lofty executive altitude. However, except in unusual circumstances, by definition, the CEO has greater power than the COO. Usually, the CEO is contributing to the further development of the COO as his or her likely successor. In such instances, the COO is an understudy standing in the wings.

There are excellent examples of highly successful CEO–COO relationships: Roberto Goizueta, CEO, Coca-Cola Company, and Donald Keough, COO; Michael Eisner, CEO, Walt Disney Company, and Frank Wells, president; Thomas Murphy, CEO, Capital Cities/ABC, Inc., and Dan Burke, COO/president.[1] Burke became CEO in 1990; Murphy is still chairman. These relationships have long, congenial histories where there is both clear division of labor and agreement on decisions.

Unfortunately, however, there are many instances where the relationship is troubled or burdened with disappointment or disillusionment, and where it ultimately fails. There are, of course, varied reasons for the rocky roads. In this article, I shall delineate some of the more frequent sources of friction. Then I shall suggest what might be done to avoid, temper, or ameliorate them.

THE GENERIC HAZARDS

Thy wish was father, Harry, to that thought:
I stay too long by thee, I weary thee.
Dost thou so hunger for mine empty chair
That thou will needs invest thee with mine honours
Before thy hour be ripe?

Henry IV, Part II, IV, V, 91–95
William Shakespeare, 1564–1616

The built-in, and therefore endemic, hazards to the CEO–COO relationship are primarily exacerbated rivalry and corresponding defensiveness. The fact that his or her prospective successor may be taking over usually arouses feelings of rivalry and competition in a CEO that often are denied. No one wants to be displaced, let alone from such a powerful position. In addition, any successor will be assuming responsibility for what the predecessor had built during his or her tenure. Whatever changes a successor may make are implied critiques of what had gone before: if something had to be changed, obviously it is no longer good enough. In effect, if the COO does succeed, such changes become an implicit indictment of his or her erstwhile boss, unless the former CEO is still on the board and shares in those decisions. Anticipating such changes, a CEO may become possessive of his or her innovations and defensively resistant to changing them.

Unconscious feelings of rivalry may be intensified if the CEO is threatened by the growing competence of his or her likely successor. They may be even more difficult to tolerate if the COO's capacity to handle complexity grows beyond that of the CEO, enabling the former to envision aspects of the business and its competitive world the CEO cannot grasp.

For his or her part, the putative successor usually finds it difficult to await his turn. Psychologists speak of this strain as the goal gradient hypothesis: the closer one gets to the goal, the greater the tension. It's an old story that those who try to escape from prison do so more often close to the end of their sentences. They are less and less able to tolerate the tension aroused by the prospect of their freedom. The same is likely to happen frequently with prospective successors. The closer they get to the time of succession, the more difficult it is for some to tolerate the wait.

Of course, sometimes the CEO can't wait for her successor to take over to do what she knew had to be done but perhaps couldn't do herself as well. John F. Welch, Jr., of the General Electric Co., is a case in point. His predecessor, Reginald H. Jones, a quiet, gentle, unpretentious, financial executive, retired early at 62. Jones recognized what had to be done, but also knew he was not the type of person who could easily "burn and slash" as Welch had to do for an abrupt turnaround for which he earned the sobriquet "Neutron Jack."

To avoid or resolve some of the differences that arise between CEO and COO, it may be useful to review some of the failures in that relationship. The reasons for the failures can be classified into repetitive scenarios, among them, these:

- inadequate selection of either party
- specific personality features, usually reflected in aberrant behavior
- misconception about the role on the part of either party
- guilt that precludes timely decisions
- changes in the direction of a business

INADEQUATE SELECTION

Few boards of directors give the intensive, careful, psychological consideration to the selection of chief executive officers that those roles deserve. Concerning an article on that topic,[2] a board member of a major corporation told me, "Nobody gives that kind of attention to selecting a CEO." In too many instances in my experience, he is right. Here is an example of the negative consequences:

When Ian K. MacGregor was CEO of AMAX, he counted on his long-term protégé, Pierre Gousseland, to follow the path that he had laid out.

Specifically, he had planned that Standard Oil of California (SOCAL) would buy the remaining eighty percent of AMAX stock that it did not already own. But Gousseland wanted to be his own man, and, despite their long years together, would not go along. Critics said that, in choosing Gousseland as his COO, MacGregor had picked a low-profile successor who would not challenge him, but who, once on his own, would not be able to follow the same strategy. "It's almost enough to make me cry," said MacGregor of what he regarded as the SOCAL fiasco.

It has been said that one should not choose one's own successor by himself because he is almost guaranteed to choose one who is likely to fail, partly because of a CEO's unconscious rivalry, partly because he is likely to choose somebody in his own self-image, and partly because he is likely to choose a successor that he wants to carry on single-mindedly what he has created.[3]

A major problem occurs when the CEO, having been instrumental in elevating a subordinate as her potential successor, becomes disappointed. That becomes a difficult situation because then she must admit the mistake to her board and perhaps publicly, if the company is publicly held. She then must face the difficult task of terminating the COO, a task that might become even more complicated if that person already has a constituency within the organization and a following outside it in the form of public members of the board or key financial people who have established regard and respect for her. This is an example:

> As a result of the CEO's intercurrent illness, the board of a large conglomerate naturally turned to the financial vice president who the CEO had indicated was to be his COO. He had no other internal candidates and there was no time to go outside. The vice president became the COO. The subordinates of the new COO identified with him and his management style. He incorporated them and their thinking in the form of meetings and discussions. Unaccustomed to that style of management, the CEO complained that the COO had too many meetings.
>
> The CEO was highly respected for his significant contributions to the community and his community leadership. His works were legendary. The COO had few such identifications. He didn't share the CEO's community service social values and obligations, a fact that dismayed the CEO. Furthermore, the CEO was a man of considerable kindness, but also considerable guilt. As a result, when, on occasion, employees were transferred or fired because they couldn't perform, often they turned to him. He would take up their cause with lower level managers and even rehire some in unnecessary positions. When the CEO could no longer function in that role, the COO succeeded to the CEO role because of the board's dependence on his financial acumen. The new CEO wouldn't interfere with the judgments of his subordinates; the wounded ones still came to the now-retired CEO. Their complaints exacerbated his guilt. He was enraged that his successor, in effect, would destroy the organization's reputation for

community leadership and for being considerate of employees. That rage translated into repetitive complaints to his successor and embarrassing public complaint to anyone who would listen.

The "office of the chief executive" is a managerial abomination because nobody knows to whom he or she really should go, or who will hold one accountable for what, or who will give specific guidance and direction. Usually, such a structure is created when the CEO doesn't quite know what to do, or for political reasons seeks to evade making a choice among candidates. Fortunately, such arrangements don't last long, but, while they do, they create turmoil.

Apart from the confusion about who's in charge, turmoil arises because in such a situation rivalry is exacerbated among the incumbents who rarely want to be thrown together in what can become a corporate goldfish bowl or to be held responsible for actions for which they are not accountable. Furthermore, what do subordinate vice presidents do when they get conflicting directions?

> Those were some of the issues when, rather than cope with the selection of a COO, a CEO included three executive vice presidents into an office of the chief executive, in effect, making each a COO. In this case, each was reluctant to assume initiative lest he be seen by the others as too competitive. Each had his own following, executives who turned to him because of earlier experiences or relationships. For all practical purposes, a paralysis of top management resulted until, tired of their untenable positions, two retired early.

When a CEO tries to remedy a selection error by a continuing effort to change the character of a COO, the result is chronic disappointment of the CEO and chronic COO resentment. Under such circumstances, the COO has a hard time maintaining his self-confidence.

> A Brahmin CEO of high community status recruited a bright, but relatively unpolished COO. The COO was somewhat rough in manner, having come from a working-class family and schooled in a professional school in a public university. The CEO was a man of considerable stature in his own community, with an Ivy League education, and a conservative New England tradition. He had chosen the COO from another company because of his demonstrated technical knowledge.
>
> The CEO sought to polish his subordinate by criticism and managerial training, and by offering himself as a model. The predictable result was that the COO repeatedly struggled with the impulse to leave. At times both he and the CEO were at the point of parting, but neither could make the break. With psychological help, they patched up their relationship. In time, the COO did indeed acquire enough polish to be acceptable. Their relationship had gone on long enough and profitably enough that the erstwhile COO became CEO, but he never gained the community stature that his progenitor had.

Often an entrepreneurial CEO has one or more successors who usually serve the purpose of victim. One of the things he demonstrates, as was exemplified by the late Armand Hammer, CEO of Occidental Petroleum Co., is that nobody can succeed to his role. Hammer fired each recently recruited potential successor in turn. The only executive who managed to make it was Ray Irani who was still in the COO position when Hammer died. Irani promptly had to divest parts of Occidental that previously had served more to appease Armand Hammer's vanity than to earn profits.

BEHAVIORAL PROBLEMS

These include the COOs who can't hear, who can't leave, who can't grow, and who cannot control themselves. They include also the CEOs who can't act, can't confront, can't relax controls, and can't allow the COO to be visible. Sometimes, COOs act impulsively, thereby undermining themselves. At other times, their tension leads to minor faux pas that, nevertheless, have the same effect as making a deliberate error. They result in the CEO no longer trusting the COO, who then must leave.

> The CEO of a freight brokerage firm, who devoted most of his attention to customers and industry matters with considerable success and public recognition, led his COO to believe that he would retire early to devote himself to public activities. The COO, in his mid-fifties, felt that if the CEO waited until his early retirement age of 62, he himself would be too old to be chosen the successor. He urged the CEO to declare himself early on and to shift soon to his prospective new role. When the CEO, reluctant to give up his corporate role that was the source of his public image, failed to move in that direction, the COO became increasingly agitated. With continuing counsel from a consultant and others in the organization, he restrained his impatience. The more certain he became that the CEO would not yield, however, the greater his aggravation. His impatience became agitation. When there was no one around to help him maintain his self-control or restrain him, he could hold on no longer. In an impulsive confrontation, he forced his own termination.

Under a pressure that makes him defensive, a COO risks losing his cool and undermining his relationship with the CEO. All too often, only one such incident is enough to sour a relationship and vitiate the COO's chances of succeeding his CEO.

> In one situation, both CEO and COO were thoughtful and deliberate men. The CEO delicately expressed his concern about the behavior of the COO's spouse in the course of her professional activities. She was a prominent, outspoken attorney who not only was often in the news, but also was given to public statements that reflected poor judgment.

She was identified in the press frequently as the wife of the COO, leading inevitably to reflections on the COO and, in turn, the company. When the CEO broached this problem with his COO, the latter reacted in hostile, paranoid fashion. He could not understand why the CEO should be concerned, and further, what his wife did was none of the CEO's business. His defensive inability to recognize the CEO's sensitivity, and together to consider their options, put an end to their working relationship.

Overcontrol is an occupational hazard among CEOs. Developing a balance between necessary controls and allowing sufficient flexibility for subordinates is a delicate task. It becomes even more difficult in down times when the need to control costs becomes more imperative. Some CEOs respond to their own insecurity by dominating their subordinates into a state of submission.

A CEO of a large printing firm was catapulted into that role because of the dismal failure of the previous incumbent. A former financial vice president, his task was to stanch the losses. He himself was an overcontrolling workaholic. He saw no reason why the vice president he chose for his COO shouldn't sacrifice his family obligations to his new leadership role. The COO, however, saw no reason why he could not continue to lead a more balanced life, nor did he want to make such sacrifices for what he saw to be some of the unnecessary busy work in which the CEO became involved. According to interviews with the CEO's other subordinates, the CEO could not see the forest for the trees. Neither the COO nor the vice presidents could get the CEO to think strategically, nor could the consultant he had brought in to help him cope with their discontent. Outside board members, seeing the same problem, resigned. The CEO could not relent and decided that the COO wasn't sufficiently motivated. He fired the COO and within the year was himself terminated.

Some CEOs can't face the reality of their situation and yield their positions gracefully. Some continue to intrude into the business of the organization after they retire by maintaining contacts with their former subordinates, the subject of their luncheon invitations being company business. Others react to their loss in more blatant ways.

The reluctant CEO of a medical instrument manufacturing company simply couldn't accept the fact of his compulsory retirement. When his COO took over the CEO role, the CEO remained in his same large, well-appointed office until his successor, despairing of the futility of repeated hints, confronted him directly and insisted that he had to move to another location. He did, but still feels his unfair and inconsiderate successor betrayed him. One can imagine what had transpired between them before.

Of all the personal qualities that interfere with effective executive performance, none seems to occur more frequently than rigidity. Rigidity precludes sensitivity. Rigidity makes it difficult to hear, to sense how the other feels, to entertain different points of view, to respond and react flexibly. The vividly descriptive images aroused by such phrases as "iron assed" and "hard nosed" capture that behavior.

> A highly sophisticated, successful entrepreneur built a multi-billion dollar organization. Its growth had been facilitated by a COO who was instrumental in developing its structure. The COO had a reputation for having an open door through which many subordinates passed. He listened to them considerably. They usually felt they indeed had been heard. However, the COO already had defined his positions for himself on the various issues people raised. The CEO repeatedly pointed out this flaw. But, try as he might, the CEO could not get the COO to overcome his resistance to his subordinates' views. Although the COO tried desperately to grasp what the CEO observed and to follow his suggestions, he simply couldn't understand what the CEO was talking about. He did indeed listen to people, did he not? His personal rigidity precluded his understanding. He did not become CEO.

Some CEOs try to cope with what, for them, are difficult interpersonal situations by avoiding them. When avoidance is accompanied by an inability to sense one's own feelings and to tolerate one's own anger, the result is loss of initiative.

> Having observed how a predecessor stumbled with key figures on the board, a CEO sought to placate them. In his character, though highly intelligent and analytic, he was not a man of action. Although he was sensitive enough to the pain of his employees to comfort them when tragedy occurred, he could not attune himself to their more subtle feelings and concerns. He did not make decisions. He did not like differences, let alone conflict. Hence, he never had group meetings of his top management team, but met one-on-one with his direct reports. In short, he didn't lead. His direct reports chafed at his passivity, shrouded in verbalized expectations of distant, unpredictable success.
>
> Two successive COOs dealt with this man in different ways. The first bolted to become CEO of another company in the same industry. There he was able to grow that organization, something he could not do in his previous COO role. His successor, in the same non-action context and in the face of declining profitability, went over the head of the CEO to the board. Already on tenterhooks because of the organization's poor performance, the board asked for the resignation of the CEO. The CEO had many rationalizations about why the board took such hostile action. He failed to see the fact that he could not tolerate his own aggressive impulses made it impossible for him to act on the problems that he and the board confronted.

MISCONCEPTIONS

When either party operates on the basis of unverified assumptions and unclarified expectations about the reasons why the COO is chosen, predictably problems result.

> When, being recruited to that role in a family business, a COO misconceives both the role and the power, he gets into trouble. That's what happened with Semon E. "Bunky" Knudsen and the late Henry Ford II. Ford ostensibly wanted a COO, so he appointed Knudsen president. Knudsen served in that role from 1968–1969. Some said, however that Ford wanted a COO who would control Lee Iacocca. Knudsen, trying to reverse his father's experience of failure at General Motors, and to establish himself as a dominant figure in the automobile business, thought he was supposed to take over the Ford organization. Henry Ford II brought him to an abrupt halt, reminding him that the name over the door was Ford. A contributing factor to his difficulties as COO, some alleged, was that Lee Iacocca and those loyal to him refused to accept Knudsen as their leader.

Misconceptions often are a product of someone's best intentions. Frequently, a CEO recognizes the need to resolve a succession problem and undertakes a rational effort to do so, only to run afoul of an agenda he has hidden from himself. This is especially a problem in family businesses.

> Relationships in family businesses are extremely complicated. Often a family-head CEO, recognizing the need for a non-family professional manager, recruits such a person with the promise of the CEO role to come. All too frequently he fails to deliver, even on an explicit promise. Usually, there are also many cross-current family rivalries, in addition to those that are inherent among other managers in the organization. Sometimes, unlikely events intrude to undermine the promise. In one instance, the prospective CEO was undone when the divorced incumbent married a trophy wife, a woman nearly half his age who didn't like the wife of the prospective successor.

Not all succession plans are objectively rational, nor do such subjective actions always result in disaster. To illustrate:

> Sometimes the CEO–COO rotation is an amusing dance, an illusion for the COO and the public. When a famous CEO appointed a less than optimum successor who desperately wanted to succeed him, other executives and Wall Street thought the CEO was deluded. How could the CEO make such an appointment? Even retired, the former CEO, still chairman of the board's executive committee, remained the dominant figure in the company. He could afford to gratify the fantasy of his lieutenant. The latter, having been CEO for a short time, could say he had been in the role. He soon was succeeded by an executive of greater stat-

ure. The CEO had had his fun, the COO his illusion. Fortunately, the organization did not suffer.

GUILT

Probably no feeling inhibits or cripples rational decision making in management more than guilt. The feeling of guilt usually results in procrastination, or worse yet, reparation. One of the most painful CEO guilt problems occurs when a long-term loyal subordinate has helped build a large organization that, in the process, has outgrown him or her. Frequently, the pair has played a white hat–black hat game, the CEO enacting the good-guy role and the COO being the nay-sayer. In such circumstances, the hostility that had been building for years among their subordinates erupts in resistance to the prospect of the COO becoming CEO, thus undermining both COO and CEO. Usually when that happens, the friction has become too heated and continued too long to be attenuated. Sometimes such loyal servants are shunted into some kind of plateau role, such as vice chairman.

> A COO had been harshly overcontrolling the organization for years. He made sure that variances from budget were instantly remedied—in no uncertain, often impolite terms. His nay-saying about resources and capital appropriations was notorious. His CEO had depended heavily on him over their nearly two decades together. As the organization grew, the COO didn't have the conceptual capacity to handle the increased complexity. He was therefore less able to be on top of his role. He tried to cope with his mounting anxiety by becoming even more overcontrolling. Although the CEO knew the COO was by now in over his head, a perception urged on him by the board and the increasingly loud protests of the vice presidents, the CEO was reluctant to terminate him. With the support of consultation, he confronted his subordinate, worked out a golden handshake, and bade him good-bye with thanks. Having been confronted with the hostility he had engendered, and forced to face up to his inadequacy, the contrite COO was relieved to escape the situation.

Misconception of a different kind penalizes a prospective CEO, namely the view of an incumbent CEO that he perpetuates his organization best by assuming a charismatic posture. The CEO-rescuer role is a case in point. If the rescuer doesn't leave a revived organization within three to five years, he risks destroying it by overshadowing his successor.

> Lee Iacocca's recent reign is illustrative. Robert J. Eaton succeeded Iacocca, but it is highly unlikely that Eaton has the same spectacular exhibitionistic orientation. That kind of public posture not only keeps the COO obscure, but also presents him with footprints bigger than life to step into. He will have to tolerate both being in the shadow and being

viewed as less competent than his predecessor. It will take a long time for Chrysler employees to accept Eaton as a legitimate leader. Certainly Eaton also will have to earn his reputation in the public arena if he is to match the public acceptance of Iacocca.

CHANGING ENVIRONMENT

It is not unusual for a putative CEO to be chosen to fit the requirements of one business environment, only to have it change before his very eyes. The demand for marketing-oriented leadership in a technical company, Apple Computer, Inc., is an example. The contemporary recruitment of executives who can control costs even forces out predecessors who had other competences, as is illustrated by the case of Lawrence Bossidy, CEO of Allied-Signal, Inc.

> In some situations, the CEO had inadvertently left a miserably difficult task for the COO successor who was chosen because he had another strength. John S. Reed became CEO of Citicorp because of his competence in retail banking on which Citicorp increasingly would depend. His close working relationship with predecessor Walter B. Wriston arose out of Reed's rescue of Citicorp's back office fiasco by applying Ford factory management techniques, and his push to develop automatic teller machines. However, Reed is still trying to cope with the residual morass of those large, Wriston-era, non-performing foreign loans that additionally burden his efforts to deal with the anchor-dragging effects on non-performing real estate loans.

What does one do about these kinds of problems?

1. The CEO should have a considerable, frequent consultation with trusted members of his board and also wisely with somebody who can help him or her understand his own behavior and that of the subordinate. Usually that is somebody with psychological sophistication. Under these circumstances, a CEO cannot afford to be counterdependent or to assume omniscience, to deny that he has a problem and that he needs help.
2. The CEO needs to give specific direction and guidance to the COO. This calls for a highly detailed behavioral job description formulated with the help of the board and the agreement of the COO. Then, the CEO and COO need to talk consistently and continuously about the managerial issues between them, especially how they are going to share responsibilities and carry out different functions.
3. They need to talk also about their individual wishes and aspirations and about what's going on psychologically between

them. With a helpful outsider, they can look at the vicissitudes of their respective feelings and the ways in which they offend each other's sensitivities. Often an outsider, sensitive to the subtleties of human feelings, can be particularly helpful with such discussions.

4. They need to talk about what they want to have happen in the future, the CEO about what's going to happen to what he built and the COO about what steps should be taken to enhance the company's competitive position. Ideally, both should agree on a course of action, as a result of which there is a smooth flow from one to the other.

5. Ideally also, the CEO must pass on a tradition, even if it began only with him or her. There should be consistency of values as a product of having defined organizational purpose. Those values should permeate the organization, reinforced by a performance appraisal system that is trustworthy, accurate, and detailed with specific behavioral incidents.[4]

6. Although executives at these top management levels don't much favor appraisal of their performance, a CEO and a COO both need feedback. The CEO ideally should be getting it from the board, as is the practice at the Dayton-Hudson Corp., and the COO should be getting direct feedback from the CEO. Both need to be guided by information that they can trust.

7. They must not allow differences to simmer. When differences are papered over, they will more likely erupt in explosions of one kind or another or resentment that becomes increasingly difficult to conceal. Those suppressed frictions ultimately will sour their relationship. If there is significant disappointment, then this should be discussed straightforwardly early on so that the COO can make alternative plans.

8. The CEO should work diligently and consistently to bring the COO out of the shadows. John W. Hanley, then CEO of Monsanto Company, paved the way for the acceptance of his successor, Richard J. Mahoney, as president and COO by showcasing Mahoney at golf and dinner parties, in community leadership activities, and in conspicuous major roles with directors and employees. No doubt many other CEOs do the same.

9. A CEO should not depend on a single potential successor. In addition to a COO, or in the case of some large international or multi-national corporations, several presidents or executive vice presidents who are, in effect, COOs of respective divisions, the CEO should have a range of potential candidates to meet different organizational and environmental conditions. A person in the COO role ideally should have a sig-

nificant constituency of executives behind him or her. The CEO should know those people well enough and work frequently enough with them to be able to assess their capacity for handling complexity and the degree of fit between their strengths and those required by the corporation at any given point in time.

10. The COO should recognize, as must all people who are about to assume new responsibilities, that the scenario may change, that the business direction therefore may have to change and she may no longer be the optimum candidate. One can't have a role because one has earned it or one deserves it, but only because one fits the task to be done. Failing that, succession won't work. Better that the COO goes where he can be successful than figuratively to beat his head against a wall in a situation that he doesn't fit.

ENDNOTES

1. John Huey, "Secrets of Great Second Bananas," *Fortune*, May 6, 1991, 64–76.

2. Harry Levinson, "Criteria for Choosing Chief Executives," *Harvard Business Review*, July–August 1980.

3. Harry Levinson, "Don't Choose Your Own Successor," *Harvard Business Review*, November–December 1974.

4. See, for example, Andrew S. Grove, *High Output Management* (New York: Random House, 1983), Ch. 13; Andrew O. Manzini and John D. Gridley, *Integrating Human Resources and Strategic Business Planning* (New York: AMACOM, 1987), 187–188; David L. DeVries, Ann M. Morrison, Sandra L. Shullman, and Michael L. Gerlach, *Performance Appraisal on the Line* (New York: Wiley, 1981); Allan M. Mohrman, Jr., Susan M. Resnick-West, Edward E. Lawler III, *Designing Performance Appraisal Systems* (San Francisco: Jossey-Bass, 1989); Michael Nash, *Managing Organizational Performance* (San Francisco: Jossey-Bass, 1983); Harry Levinson, "Appraisal of *What* Performance?" *Harvard Business Review*, July–August 1976.

17

APPROACHING RETIREMENT
AS THE FLEXIBILITY PHASE

HARRY LEVINSON AND JERRY C. WOFFORD

When Victor L. Lund, the chief executive of the American Stores Company, was told by his predecessor, Lennie Sam Skaggs, over a plate of eggs in 1992 that Mr. Skaggs had personally chosen him to take the helm of the then troubled supermarket company, Mr. Lund knew he was taking on a big challenge. What he did not know was that one of the biggest problems he would face would be Mr. Skaggs himself.

—The New York Times[1]

Managers and executives approaching retirement are often reluctant to quit. Frequently, they do not know what to do next. Retiring executives can be more innovative if they consider their retirement as entering the flexibility phase of their lives, a time of continued contribution and potential gratification. The flexibility phase is the retirement stage in which managers experience more freedoms of time, location, activities, and opportunities. For a successful transition into retirement, managers need to examine and talk over their feelings and options. Their successors need to understand both the predecessors' conflicts and their own. Together they can make a mutually satisfying transition.

Conflicts between managers and their successors are not uncommon when the predecessor will not let go and interferes with the successor's dealings. There can be a variety of causes; an outgoing manager like Skaggs may have too much time on his hands; or maybe he's trying to tweak management to move faster on getting its stock price up (it was $25.375 in January 1996; $40.875 on August 27, 1997). In the view of one analyst, "This seems

From *Academy of Management Executive*, 14(2), 84–95. Copyright 2000 by the Academy of Management. Reprinted with permission.

to be just Sam rattling the cages and having a little fun." Skaggs had hired Goldman Sachs to advise him on what to do with his 18.3 percent stake in the company and filed documents with the Securities and Exchange Commission stating his intent to explore "alternatives" for the company's future. Continued the same analyst, "But smart investors can see there is a turn-around here, and so there seems to be a degree of irrationality at work." Indeed! Personal conflicts of the later work years can result in irrationality.

We refer to the executive's retirement years as the flexibility phase because of the many crucial options one must face. Freedoms of time, location, activities, and opportunities provide a flexibility that can enrich life. They can also add to the anxieties, stresses, and conflicts that often accompany uncertainties and choices. Our purpose is to understand the underlying stresses and emotions inherent in the flexibility phase, to explore steps in transitioning into retirement, and to share some insights into ways of smoothing the path into this phase of life. We draw on psychoanalytic theory, as well as on case studies of managers accumulated during many years of experience in consulting practice and interactions with managers.

SPECIAL ISSUES FOR MANAGERS NEARING RETIREMENT

How can we begin to understand such conflicts and what might be done to avoid or alleviate them? In order to answer that question we must begin with trying to grasp the complex situation of the senior executive and other managers. There are likely to be a growing number of such conflicts as life expectancy for males continues to rise. No doubt there will be similar problems for managerial women as their numbers increase.

As illustrated above, explanations for these conflicts may be speculative or cliches about generational conflict. Such explanations may describe, but they do not explain. Some facts are clear: Life expectancy for American males in 1900 was 47 years; in 1993, it was 76. Those who are now 65, on average, can expect to live until they are 81, and those turning 65 in the year 2040, until they are 85.[2] As Peter Drucker has observed, health for a person at 65 is as good today as it was at 55 in the 1920s. The average is likely to improve. In an information- and knowledge-based economy, many people will be able to continue to work into their later years. The legal age at which a person may be required to retire has been raised to 70, and even this limit is often not upheld by the courts. Given these figures, there is likely to be pressure to raise the limit even higher, especially since increasing numbers of prospective retirees indicate that they want to continue to work beyond 65 and larger numbers already do so. Even in high-level managerial ranks there are legendary examples like Armand Hammer of Occidental Petroleum Corporation and Royal Little of Textron Corporation, both of whom headed their respective companies until they died, Hammer at 91 and Little at 87. Peter

Drucker, still widely respected as an innovative management thinker, was born in 1909. The retirement age chosen by managerial personnel in most companies continues to be near 65. Some companies, like IBM, have provisions for managers to choose earlier retirement. Yet the age at which most board members retire is 70.

Taken together, these factors suggest that men and women will be staying in managerial roles much longer. Corporate boards already lift the retirement boundaries when a CEO is still in the process of building an organization or, as in a family firm, where the CEO controls the board. We could even be approaching the Japanese practice of valuing age in chief executives for the purported wisdom it brings. We might even start asking, as a Japanese executive did at a seminar conducted by the first author: "How do you get rid of a CEO?"

The aging manager needs to guard against potential losses in several areas of functioning: diminished conceptual ability, obsolescence, rigidity, and dependency. People differ in the trajectories of their conceptual ability, or their capacity to deal with the complexity of the information they must process.[3] This is evident in the fact that some promising managerial candidates plateau (sometimes also because of poor interpersonal relations or lack of the knowledge needed for high-level roles), and that some highly successful corporate division presidents fail when they are promoted to head groups of such divisions. Although intelligence, as measured by intelligence tests, declines with age for most people up to 60, and tends to level off until age 69, it does not decline as rapidly among bright people.[4] However, subtle organic brain changes that impair judgment can begin in the mid-fifties.[5] Drucker did not have tongue in cheek when he said that senility in high places is one of the most degenerative diseases of an organization. Therefore, it probably would not be a good idea to raise the mandatory retirement age.

Aging carries with it the threat of obsolescence. Most people lose contact with various features of the environment as they age, simply because they narrow their social and occupational purviews. If they are in high-level managerial positions, they may lose touch with what goes on at lower levels in their organizations. Some tend not to keep in touch with the continuous shift in the way things are done, and complain about what appears to them as the strange vocabulary, outlandish dress, and atrocious manners of the young. These managers are concerned that cherished values are being lost. Worse still, they risk being out of touch with their competitive environments.[6]

People who lose touch with their changing social environments as they age tend to become more conservative, including those in managerial ranks. Evidence for this is provided by faculty members of advanced management programs, who note that some of the more senior middle managers who come to such programs seem not to want to learn anything new. Their conviction that they already know the program's content, and their refractoriness to the learning opportunity for which their companies are paying significant sums, reflects the narcissism of aging that protects people from the sense of potential helplessness that can accompany growing older.

In general, men become more dependent as they age, while women become more assertive. Thus, men, who are typically reluctant to lean on other men, want to lean more on their spouses, at a time when their wives want to become more active on their own. The concomitant declines in energy and mental sharpness can lead to a greater inward orientation, including reduced involvement with one's family and others.[7] This inward orientation may occur even by the mid-forties, well before the social losses of aging and the decline of social interaction are more common.

STRESSES AND EMOTIONAL RESPONSES BROUGHT BY THE LOSSES OF AGING

Losses associated with aging may take place gradually, like tiny pin pricks in a large balloon, gradually deflating one's ego and possibly leading to a deep-seated fear of retirement. Some successful managers try to cope by denying the prospect of retirement, especially those who have Type A personalities. For such intensely driven people, the unrelenting pursuit of success can be an enraged effort to cope with unconscious feelings of helpless dependency. To retire, to be out of action, is to lose that coping mechanism. Lee Iacocca says he has failed at retirement and misses the sense of challenge of his action-oriented career.

The fear of retirement has many facets of which prospective retirees should be aware. One is the fear of dropping out of sight, of no longer being where the action is, of not being in the game. Another is the loss of heroic posture, the sense of being somebody in an official position whose title defines one's place in society. A third facet is losing contact with the business or professional world about which one was knowledgeable, a fundamental context of one's life. Fourth is the concern about one's legacy and the perpetuation of organizational values to which one had dedicated oneself. Managers approaching retirement may experience some or all of these fears.

Other less obvious losses may be even more painful. The curmudgeonly literary critic, H. L. Mencken, remarked that people work in order to escape the depressing agony of contemplating life. Put more scientifically, our brains function continuously whether we are engaged in deliberate thought or not. As a result, we all experience a continuous flow of memory images or fantasies that, at more relaxed moments, we recognize as daydreams.[8] Many images refer repetitively to still unresolved emotional problems stemming from early childhood, with which we are still struggling mentally and which we try to keep out of our awareness. Concentrating our attention on something else, like work, is a common method for keeping these images at bay. That is why some people say they would go crazy if they did not work. That same heavy concentration can interfere with family life and inhibit social relationships, a problem that many young people who work long hours complain about. Some managers cherish the long hours because the intense involvement keeps them from having to supervise, direct, evaluate, and otherwise interact more closely with people outside work.

A decline in sexual potency, a withdrawal of libido, can result in the diminution of feelings of affection that temper the expression of feelings of aggression. This loss may result in greater irritability toward others and ambivalence toward those who are emotionally close. If we overcontrol anger to avoid offending others, we may turn it onto ourselves, resulting in feelings of depression. The depressive feelings are reflected in the recurrent complaint that the younger person does not care enough about the senior, nor about the corporation's external obligations or its employees. A former CEO of a service company complained bitterly to the first author that his successor failed to continue the charitable contributions and community leadership that had earned him and his company many plaudits, and that his successor was inconsiderate of longtime employees. When the successor wanted to shed these employees as superfluous or inadequate, the former CEO tried to have them rehired. In another instance, the head of an office supply company complained to the senior author about subordinates who were not as committed to the values and success of the organization as he was.

RIVALRY WITH THE SUCCESSOR AS RETIREMENT NEARS

The losses of aging may become more threatening when rivalry between the executive and the heir apparent intensifies as the time for retirement nears. Even in relatively flat organizations, managers have more power than those who report to them. Rivalry for power is inevitable. In cases where the retiring executives have built the business or a significant part of it, they may feel that their self-sacrificing effort is inadequately appreciated. This lack of appreciation can be manifested in the inattention from their recognized successors and others who no longer wish to inform them or consult them about important matters. These feelings can exacerbate the elders' normal envy of younger individuals who have not only their futures before them, but also continuing influence within the organization, thus stimulating feelings of jealousy, rivalry, and resentment.[9] Such feelings may be coupled with a fear and envy of the young people, who intimidate with their knowledge and self-confidence. They have not yet had salt in their wounds, as one senior executive put it.

All this may occur against an anomalous social context. In the course of human development, we grow from one psychological stage into another, each holding out the promise of continued evolution to more sophisticated behavior.[10] However, there is no social definition of that period beyond retirement, and no well-defined, characteristic set of behaviors outlining the transition into it. The transition out of it, which most people dread, is only too vividly clear. Some retirees find that to be aged is to be part of an unwanted generation. Betty Friedan contends that the mystique of age is much more deadly than what she called "the feminine mystique."[11] Although many welcome it, for most people who have no clear idea what to do, retirement can be the most difficult transition of life.

Just as children become disappointed when they discover their parents' imperfections, so lower-level managers must cope with similar feelings about those seniors whom they have held in esteem, from whom they have learned, and whose achievements they hope to emulate and exceed. If seniors are reluctant to yield their roles, juniors may feel that they are angry, rivalrous old fossils who should have passed on the batons a long time ago, but who just cannot let go. This is particularly likely for seniors who have built the organizations, especially if they have undertaken reorganizations or if the executives attempt to thwart prospective successors. The late Dr. Karl A. Menninger, a mentor of the first author, would eliminate a staff member's position or change the organization structure whenever the staff member rose in the esteem of the other staff to the point where they expected him to succeed the boss. Dr. Menninger wanted to keep the organization under family leadership.

Younger executives are often impatient to make their own marks. To differentiate themselves from their predecessors, they must make changes, whether necessary or not. Sometimes drastic changes are indeed necessary because of rapidly changing competitive circumstances, even though the successor executive undertakes them with trepidation. This was the case when John F. Welch succeeded Reginald H. Jones at the General Electric Company. It was Welch who pointed out from his own experience: "When you're running an institution like this you're always scared at first. You're afraid you'll break it. People don't think about leaders this way, but it's true. Everyone who's running something goes home at night and wrestles with the same fear: 'Am I going to be the one who blows this place up?'"[12] That trepidation lies behind the facade of self-confidence of every successor. Wise executives anticipate the high cost of rivalry by mentoring the upward movement of their likely successors. When John W. Hanley was CEO of Monsanto, he paved the way for his successor, Richard J. Mahoney, by inviting him to high-level social affairs at his home and country club and by pushing him into community leadership roles.[13]

KEY STEPS TO SUCCESSFUL TRANSITION INTO THE FLEXIBILITY PHASE

Recognize the Complexities of the Transition

For a successful transition, both the executive and the successor must recognize that the process of retiring can be a painful and difficult phase of life. Therefore, the first step in dealing with the transition is for both parties to recognize the complexities discussed above. This is best done by talking with each other, preferably with the help of a psychologically trained consultant, who can help avoid the psychological shoals on which they might shatter their relationship, and who can help them temper their differences. It is frequently helpful for managers to learn that much of what they are struggling with is typical and not blameworthy. In one such situation, the first author counseled an executive over a five-year period about candidates to succeed him, and the candidate who was ultimately chosen later undertook his own separate consultation to better manage the transition with his predecessor. Both were pleased with the highly successful outcome.

Choose New Work and Life Activities

Seniors need to accept the fact that they must not retire from active work and life. As the late comedian George Burns asked: "Why should I retire? I'm doing the same things now that I've been doing all my life and I love it. The only time you should retire is if you find something you enjoy doing more than what you are doing now." Burns enunciated the two fundamental principles that apply to retirement: Continue what you enjoy doing and develop a parallel activity that can become even more enjoyable. There are many ways for managers to continue what they enjoyed in their work—becoming a consultant, helping embryonic organizations get started, moving into a government role, heading a smaller company in difficult straits, or joining a venture capital group.

When Harold Moore retired as managing director of the North Texas Contractors Association, he became active in arbitration and mediation work, which he was still enjoying at age 72. When one consultant lost his constituency because younger managers who did not know him were taking over in his client companies, the first author suggested that he and some of his retired peers might form a firm that would invest in small businesses. These investments would enable them to continue their relationships with the business world and be directly helpful to others. They accepted the suggestion and found the experience highly rewarding. Some managers have found that the Peace Corps, the Service Corps of Retired Executives, and the International Executive Service Program provide opportunities for continued contributions and travel that they could enjoy with their spouses. Others have found such activities to be devices to continue avoiding their spouses.

Often, however, managers whose work has been paramount do not have another consuming interest and do not know how to go about developing one. It is easier to do so if one has a cause. One high level executive of a high-tech company, a loyal engineer alumnus of his university, became intensely committed to raising money for its engineering school. Another executive, dedicated to finding a cure for muscular dystrophy, became highly knowledgeable about that illness and became involved with the leading research-ers in neurobiology. Others have invested themselves in community activi-ties where their business knowledge enables them to strengthen museums, orchestras, schools, and similar local services that perennially need manage-ment help as well as financial resources. Those who do not have a com-mitment must create one. For example, like the executive of the high-tech company mentioned above, some people could find it stimulating to become knowledgeable about and supportive of their universities, departments, and professors who have areas of interest close to theirs. That may require an invitation from the university president or an academic dean. Prospective retirees cannot sit by and wait for others to create their opportunities for them. Carl Sloane, who headed a highly successful consulting firm, created such an opportunity for himself when he became a Harvard Business School professor.

Recognize and Deal With Loss

All change involves loss. No matter how desirable or advantageous the change, one loses familiar faces, characteristic patterns of daily routine and behavior, the support of colleagues and friends, and other sources of gratifi-cation. Anyone who has ever been promoted or transferred to a new site knows the sweet and sour nature of that experience. The less welcome the change, the more painful the losses.

Human beings are anchored in social networks. We have ties to friends, relatives, and others. We are anchored in intellectual networks—ideas, memo-ries, values, religious beliefs—and in our characteristic stance toward the world around us. We see the world in certain idiosyncratic ways and act on the basis of these perceptions. We are anchored in physical networks: home, neighborhood, office, plant, community.

Change often uproots us from this psychologically nourishing and sup-portive soil; therefore, we may experience loss. In some cases, this loss results in feelings of sadness and depression.[14] Psychologically, we cry inside our-selves for what we have lost. But crying inside ourselves does not help much. In an effort to keep our feelings from showing, we may deny them even to ourselves. "It doesn't bother me," we say. "I should be able to manage my problems without becoming emotional," we may add. We keep a stiff upper lip. But fundamentally, we humans are emotional. Our limbic brainstems, the sources of sexual and aggressive drives, are the primitive powerhouses of behavior. When we overcontrol our emotions, we merely try to keep them buried. They do not disappear. This means we have to continue to overcon-trol them, because as long as they are inside us, we remain afraid they will erupt. Therefore, we must devote energy to the controlling process, and such overcontrol inhibits spontaneity. The more effort we devote to controlling ourselves, the more stiff and cold we appear to others.

Not only can there be loss in separating from an organization, but also from giving up the activities and people with whom we have worked for many years, as well as the perquisites and supports. Frequently, there are multiple additional losses, such as the death of a friend. "It is natural that, as the years pass, we should increasingly consider our twilight," Pope John Paul wrote to his "elderly brothers and sisters."[15] He continued: "If nothing else, we are reminded of it by the very fact that the ranks of our family members, friends, and acquaintances grow ever thinner."

So we need to express anger at our losses and disgorge the feelings of sadness. In short, we need to mourn. If we cannot mourn, then we are less able to adapt effectively to new situations, for we continue to live with underlying feelings of depression and anger. We still remain preoccupied with the past. Besides, chronic depression threatens physical health. Moving successfully from one stage of life to another requires a mechanism for mourning— someone to talk to early on about the prospective losses and concerns about the future. Doing the necessary grief work ideally involves time spent talking with one's spouse, with colleagues in the same situation, or with a professional counselor.

If there are colleagues in the same situation, it can be helpful to have a talking group, especially the year before retirement. For high-level executives, this may be done better in sessions away from their companies, with similar level executives in other companies. Alternatively, it may be done with one of a growing number of executive coaches. One needs ways of examining prospective plans out loud, of looking carefully at issues that one might not have seen clearly, and of examining options critically.

The executive group sessions should include spouses because the changes brought by retirement will have significance for them as well. They too must share the discussions and the planning, and have the opportunity to deal with their feelings, as well as those of the prospective retiree. They too must adapt. Sometimes, there will be special problems to be dealt with, like elderly parents or chronically ill children, and perhaps the impact of the choices of one partner on the work role of the other. If spouses are left in isolation, additional problems may occur. For example, the effects of isolation appear to be evidenced by reports of a growing number of homebound alcoholics. Some firms that do appliance maintenance in condominium communities report that their servicemen are sometimes called to repair appliances that are not broken. It may be that, for the price of an appliance repairman's time, a lonesome wife has someone to talk to while her husband is following his own interests.

Wives particularly welcome the opportunity to get their husbands to talk. Talking serves the purpose of mourning and is the stimulus to begin restitution activities. But some men have great difficulty talking about situations that precipitate intense feelings, even severe feelings of loss. For example, when an executive friend of the first author lost his wife in an airplane crash, the author called him and suggested that he talk with a professional colleague of his. "No," the executive said, "I'm a Stoic. I'm a stubborn old Dutchman." "That's what I am afraid of," Levinson replied. "We know from studies in England that there is a disproportionate death rate among widowers age 54 and older in the first six months after their spouses' deaths."

Fortunately, more of today's managers have learned to exercise, to watch what they eat, to temper their drinking, and to use consultants and facilitators. Increasingly, they are giving themselves permission to talk.

The transition process has an additional hazard: the ambivalence of close relationships. The closer we are to someone else, the more dependent we become on that person, and the more vulnerable we are to that person's behavior. The closer we are, the more easily we become angry and frustrated by the behavior of another whom we may not like or who rubs us the wrong way. In good marriages the partners learn to accept their differences and feelings of conflict. However, in transitional times, in moving from one phase of life to another, from one major activity to another, ambivalence is heightened because the usual boundaries of family and organization have been loosened. The prospective retiree should anticipate increased ambivalence and allow plenty of time to talk differences out.

Expecting that they will lose old friends and associates, people entering the flexibility phase should work at establishing new friends, counteracting the tendency toward constricting their social circles, and rebuilding sources of personal companionship. Helping others who are having difficulty turns the associations into a mutual support system.

Engage in Self-Assessment

In our mind's eye, we all have a picture of ourselves as we would like to be. This is our ego ideal.[16] This ideal view of self has many sources, but we are aware of only a few of them. Some of them we were never clear about, and others have become obscured by time. We do not have a fixed picture of that ideal, but can see its outlines if we look back on our life experiences and view them as an unfolding process, a pattern of our striving. We can get a sense of our direction, our values, those experiences that were highly gratifying, and those that were not. We can get another view of our ego ideal by the exercise of writing our own obituaries. What we want to have accomplished and the image that we want to present to others is what we are striving toward but never fully attain.

We also have a self-image, a picture of ourselves as we think we are now. The self-image may be more or less accurate. Since our ego ideals tend to be perfectionistic, there is always a gap between the ego ideal and the self-image. That gap leaves us feeling highly self-critical for not being as good as we think we should be. We are our own harshest critics.

To the degree that we are self-critical or angry with ourselves, we become depressed. Conversely, the closer we come to our ego ideals, the more elated we become. That gap, therefore, is the source of our ambition. The motivation for our striving is to narrow that gap. There is no motivation as powerful as the wish to like ourselves, and this occurs when we feel that we are moving toward our ego ideals.

In the retirement process, three problems arise from the ego ideal–self-image phenomenon. The first is that the ego ideal has a significantly irrational component. Not only do we strive for perfection, but our dreams and aspirations range far more widely than our ability to achieve them. We simply do not have the time or the resources to do all that we once thought possible. So we always have to make choices, to give up something. Coming into the retirement period means unequivocally that we must give up some wishes that have been important to us. Active people often say, as they regretfully settle for less than they had hoped for, "There was so much more I wanted to do." One academic colleague heaved a deep sigh as he discarded all the material he had been saving for a book that he now knew he would never write.

The second troublesome aspect of the ego ideal has to do with dependency. We are all born helpless in cognitive and physical abilities. We are all mortal. As we age, we can overcome our helplessness and mortality by acquiring skills and competencies, by achieving, and by having others depend on us. Managers who deny that they have strong dependency needs should consider the popularity of, indeed the demand for, executive employment contracts that afford protection against those on whom we are dependent. In our culture, to be independent and self-sufficient is the highest virtue. Yet aging means that, to varying degrees, we are likely to become more dependent, more helpless. Thus we must cope with the lowered self-image that aging can bring. We must also cope with our anger toward ourselves for being less adequate and less competent in some ways than we once were and still want to be.

The third negative aspect of the ego ideal phenomenon has to do with the rupture of the relationship with the organization where one has worked. Frequently, with that rupture comes significant loss of one's social status, power, income, use of certain skills and knowledge, perquisites, and one's place in an organizational structure. For all of their previous efforts and achievements, most people are less likely to be recognized for what they have done as the years pass. Newcomers do not know them. If they have been heroic, those who knew of their heroism are now likely to be gone or to be preoccupied with pursuing their own ego ideals. In his retirement, Fritz Roethlisberger, the late grand old man of human relations in the Harvard Business School, passed many students each day as he went to lunch in the faculty club. Yet few knew he was among them. We must come to terms with the fact that we may become less valued by those to whom we have given so much.

Recognize the Significant Psychological Meaning of This Stage

The psychoanalyst Erik H. Erikson described three major stages of adult life.[17] The last of these, the period from approximately age 55 on, he spoke of as the stage of integrity. At that time, he pointed out, people begin to draw their life experiences to a close and into an integrated whole. In doing so, they review the past and take leave of it. Looking back on their life experiences, they inevitably judge how well they have used their lives. If they are far from where they had hoped to be, they are likely to become depressed, even though such expectations might have been unrealistic. This is the psychological basis for the depression of old age or what technically is called involutional melancholia.

In the flexibility stage, we must come to terms with having already lived a large portion of our one and only life and accept the fruits of our efforts. Ideally, we should have acquired wisdom. We should have contributed something to society through the medium of our work and our families, and we should have left our mark in the lives of other people. Presumably, in the later years of our work, we have brought to bear our acquired wisdom and passed on that knowledge and experience to younger persons.[18]

HANDLING THE TRANSITIONS

A person moving into the retirement period must deal with the experience of loss, with lowered self-image, with the feelings of growing helplessness, and with the issues of the integrity stage. He or she must handle the transitional disruptions, as well as the realities of that period of life. The person who does this well maintains a flexibility that enables the pursuit of a wide variety of pleasurable activities of his or her own choosing and pace. How does one go about doing that? We offer the following four rules of conduct that can guide a person through the process of moving into the retirement period.

Anticipate Change

Anticipation leads us to buy life insurance. It should also lead us to acquire psychological insurances. In the flexibility phase, most of us have a range of choices and anticipations about what we can do about our lot in life. We have already referred to the need to talk about our constricting life experience, about our sense of falling behind, about our increasing dependence, about the loss of friends and colleagues, about leaving our life's work and its environment, about growing impatience and irritability, about the sense of being passed by and being unwanted, about extending our present working horizons and developing new commitments, and about how to enjoy our grandchildren. In short, we need to talk about the need to mourn, to renew hope, to find pleasure, to give back, and to leave some indelible mark.

Expect Ambiguity

Before we leave our organizations and, perhaps, our communities, preparation and the expression of feelings that go with it counteract some of the potential feelings of anxiety and depression, of anger and frustration. These feelings can arise as we move from a situation that has been highly structured and in which we are well experienced, to a situation of considerable ambiguity and possibly unanticipated threat. Talking with friends or counselors may help us in examining our plans and in looking at dimensions and options that we may not have considered carefully. One manager, for example, wanted to start immediately on a book he had long promised himself he would write. He was brought up short when it was pointed out that he needed to supplement his retirement funding to meet his continuing financial obligations.

Take a Formal Leave

Knowing that we will lose our ties to the work organization, it is important to think of a formal goodbye or leave-taking process. Sometimes that is done by gradually cutting back on the time we work, sometimes by taking longer vacations, or by taking on more external responsibilities. Some executives depart abruptly to avoid the pain of parting or to elude the discomfort of emotional expressions of appreciation of their contributions. One petroleum company executive did just that: Rather than following advice to take his leave openly so as not to deprive his colleagues and subordinates of the need to say their goodbyes, he bolted to an around-the-world cruise. Even when one is glad to leave, smooth detachment is better than ripping up relationships. Besides, when one runs or hides, others are denied their right to mourn and to regret the departure. It is better to detach gradually and to mourn each detachment.

Let Go

Of course, it is natural to be reluctant to leave.[19] Executives who try to hang on make it difficult for others who are no longer certain of these executives' roles and what their formal relationships to them should be. Under such circumstances parting is not sweet sorrow. Reluctance to say goodbye may be a mask for the wish to stay, to deny that one is really leaving. One board chairman who refused to take his leave was signaling exactly that and continued to try to run the company through his successor. The successor quit. Another executive found it increasingly difficult to find CEO lunch partners, though still a member of the board. He also suffered from the loss of old friends who were dying off. When he busied himself with luncheon appointments with the managers who used to report to him, it did not sit too well with his successor.

Anticipating the flexibility phase as another in the life cycle, one can concentrate on the psychological work of adjustment the period may require. The tasks involve supporting one's self-image, meeting those unfulfilled demands of the ego ideal that can be fulfilled, and maintaining one's mastery of self and environment as long as possible. One must recognize that one is going through a crisis of normal development. Crisis means shock, surprise, dismay, anger, fear, threat. People who weather crises best not only anticipate them, but also have close relationships with other caring people. The highest suicide rate is among elderly single men.[20] Clearly, it is crucial that the laws of transition be applied effectively.

ACTION STEPS FOR RETIRING MANAGERS

What, in addition to developing new commitments and talking, are the action steps that a retiring executive should take? Since a fundamental issue is the need for a support system, that is a place to begin.

Recognize That the Environment is Fundamental for Your Support System

A person must decide where to live in this new flexibility phase. One decision about this issue is whether to stay where the family is presently living or to retire to another community. Perhaps one prefers a change of climates. There may be certain kinds of activities to pursue. Being near friends or children may be important. Whatever the case, the location should provide maximum opportunity for flexibility in choosing activities and developing interests.

The prospective retiree and spouse should examine this situation together, preferably beginning in middle age. Simply put, some communities are not, by themselves, hospitable. To be accepted in them, people must create their own psychological settings. The newcomer must take the initiative. By the time they have reached retirement, couples who intend to retire to a new community should have already begun to establish roots there. Some do this by repeatedly going to the prospective new community on vacations, by establishing local contacts, by becoming involved in local political, social, and business activities, and by beginning to develop work possibilities. Some do so by buying vacation homes, others by making trial moves. By establishing ties and supports in this new community, one has provided for oneself a place to hold on to when he or she must leave old relationships behind.

Develop Activities That Gratify Support Needs

Loneliness can be the curse of the aged. It is especially a problem for those executives whose careers have been the basis of their social relationships and activities. Almost everyone needs to be able to talk to others. However, once separated from old friends and relatives either by their moving, aging, or death, or one's own move, there is a great tendency not to replace those ties. It is more difficult to do so when one is a stranger in a new situation. To move into a new context where there are social mechanisms and devices for doing this makes life considerably easier, particularly when one is socially congenial. Some people do this by going to retirement communities, but many, especially those who want to maintain contact with people of all ages, feel that going to such a community is a withdrawal from reality, involving an acceptance of age segregation. Others develop a new context by being in settings where the nature of their work allows them to interact with others of various ages, and still others through churches, synagogues, mosques, temples, fraternal lodges, and various kinds of service organizations and community activities. There is a growing movement toward life-long learning programs, some developed by local colleges and some in which retirees teach each other, as at the Eckerd College in Florida. Retirees may also use their knowledge to enrich the cultures of their communities. A physician with a love for opera organized several operatic series in communities near his retirement home. A new community can provide the opportunity for one to continue to make use of one's skills and further one's interests. It should provide the stimulus for sampling and developing new skills and interests.

When one has not done the preliminary work on community location, then it must be done at the time of retirement. A person may lose several retirement years in searching for a new residence if the preliminary work was not done before retirement. This simply adds more burdens to a time of stress and ambiguity.

Contribute to the Development of Young People

For the prospective retiree who does not have children or grandchildren, or whose children are grown and gone, it may be important to help young people. Perhaps that may take the form of teaching skills, or finding a substitute grandson or granddaughter with whom one can maintain a continuing relationship or interest. This could be a gratifying way to have a stake in the development of a young person. Some retired physicians have helped undergraduate students with their papers on health care.

Do the Things You Always Wanted to Do

This may be anything from a long desired vacation trip, to undertaking a special task or project, to supporting a favored cause, or to championing a political issue. One should have the freedom to pick up some dream that was left behind and to follow up on it. One executive who had spent a professional lifetime in a staff function had always wanted to demonstrate to himself that he would have been a good line executive. He retired early and bought a small business which he ran with great pleasure.

A special interest or hobby can be an important medium for developing and sustaining ties to others. Some people do so with flowers or Japanese prints. One group of former managers built and flew an airplane. It is astonishing to see the range and quality of artistic and craft skills that become visible in exhibitions of retirees' talents, many of which were developed after they retired.

Consider a Consulting Role

There are many advantages to being in a consulting role. Younger managers are more likely to employ an older consultant whom they do not see as competing for their jobs. Older managers may value retired executives as peers, perhaps also reluctant to trust younger people with less experience. Still others may value the continuity and stability they represent without having them tied to the organization permanently. When one executive in the plastics molding industry had built his company from a small struggling business to a large, highly profitable one, he retired from the company and began consulting. For one of his major clients, he evaluates four or five companies a year for their potential for acquisition.

For the retirees' part, many have great flexibility to come and go as they wish and to work at whatever they choose in whatever parts of the world they find themselves. The competencies retired executives carry with them constitute their portable skill bank. There are never enough people in any organization to solve all of the problems that have to be solved. The trick is to define a role for one's self, to define the problems that one is expert at solving, and to let prospective clients know of one's availability.

The flexibility phase requires a change in orientation in which we accept separation from our organizations. Retired executives must accept the reality that they now stand on their own independent feet, make their own choices, and follow their own directions outside the corporate world. They should fully accept the idea that they are dealing with their own lives, their own choices, and their own activities.

HOW ORGANIZATIONS CAN FACILITATE A SUCCESSOR'S ADAPTATION TO A MANAGER'S RETIREMENT

A fundamental task for every manager is to provide for his or her own succession.[21] The crucial factor in the adaptive process for the successor is patience. In psychology, the goal gradient hypothesis refers to the fact that the closer one gets to a goal, the greater the tension resulting from the urgency to attain the goal and the greater the extra effort required to control the impulse to act prematurely. Those who cannot control such an impulse risk losing their opportunity. One president of an insurance company became a former president when, with too much passion and vigor, he urged his chairman to leave. Another executive became inappropriately defensive about a delicate suggestion from his boss that his lawyer wife not attend a meeting that included spouses. The wife was a partner in a firm in litigation with a subsidiary of the corporation and company plans were to be discussed at the meeting. It takes years to build a trusting relationship, but often it takes only a trivial act or a slip of tongue to destroy it. It is a reasonable guess that candidates have undermined their chances when they are heard to speak of losing out because of politics, a plot, or nefarious motives. True, there are the proverbial incidences of the CEO's spouse who does not like the potential successor's spouse, but those influences are far fewer with increasing numbers of outside board members who usually make up the personnel committees.

If, however, a senior person does not give a junior colleague adequate and timely information about the latter's prospects, then the junior person is likely wiser to go elsewhere. Lower-level executives, too, must manage their own careers and should have their own counselors with whom to examine their options. These counselors may also help them to realize the degree to which their rivalrous feelings may get in the way. The opportunity to examine options and feelings should enable junior managers to maintain appropriate perspectives and to inhibit impulsive actions.

The continuing relationship with a retired predecessor requires careful attention. For all of the reasons above, retirement is a psychological bruise for many managers. No matter how much it may have been desired, separation can precipitate feelings of depression. Recovery from loss is made easier when others show that they care. In management relationships, this is advantageously done when junior executives continue to use retired seniors as mentors by occasional consultations. Sometimes the successors must take such radically different directions that the predecessors do not have much guidance to offer. In those circumstances, the successors can at least explain what is being done differently and why. Although predecessors may disagree with their successors' courses of action, their sensitivity has been considered.[22] It is easy for predecessors to experience changes as indictments of their regimes, especially if the changes have been announced with great public fanfare. Successors may also disdain or ignore their predecessors. One high-tech company CEO who did so found himself displaced when he learned, too late, that his predecessor still had significant influence on the corporate board. Taking a different perspective, one CEO makes sure his board members and those who report to him keep in touch with his predecessor so they can benefit from the senior's knowledge and wisdom.[23]

Many companies make excellent use of retirees who represent organizational memory and still have skills to contribute. Former executives can be helpful in representing the organization to some of its publics, chairing its charitable giving, and boosting internal morale with ambassadorial visits to work sites. Like all others who are accountable to the organization, they can function best and avoid misunderstanding when the successor gives them a well-defined task with clear focus, boundaries, and time limits. Where their relationship is close enough to do so, the successor may encourage the predecessor to talk about some of the feelings associated with retirement, in effect giving him or her psychological permission to do so. The shared feelings may help the successor to better prepare for future retirement.

With retirement comes flexibility: The freedom to make choices about new life endeavors, reordering of priorities, giving time to long-ignored interests, and acquiring new pursuits. Success in making the retirement transition begins with recognizing the complexities and opportunities that this phase of life affords. Social and emotional adjustments are important for dealing with the changes of this transition phase. These adjustments are augmented by social support of family, friends, and colleagues, and by interesting and valuable contributions to companies, the community, and individuals. These contributions may involve the investment of the retired executive's time, expertise, council, or financial resources. Opportunities for retired managers can be exciting and rewarding, but to be successfully taken advantage of, they require preparation and action.

ENDNOTES

1. *New York Times.* 1996. It's a clashing of the guard (old vs. new) at American Stores. Aug. 28, D1.

2. U.S. Senate, Select Committee on Aging, 1987–1988.

3. Jaques, E., & Cason, K. 1994. *Human capability: A study of individual potential and its application.* Falls Church, VA: Cason Hall & Company.

4. Schaie, K. W. 1979. The primary mental abilities in adulthood: An exploration in the development of psychometric intelligence. In P. B. Baltes & O. G. Brim, Jr. (Eds.) *Life-span development behavior.* Vol. 2. New York: Academic Press. Horn, J. L. 1982. The theory of fluid and crystallized intelligence in relation to the concepts of cognitive psychology and aging in adulthood. In F. I. M. Craik & S. Trehub (Eds.), *Aging and cognitive processes.* New York: Plenum.

5. Perlmutter, M., & Hall, E. 1992. *Adult development and aging* (2nd Ed.) New York: John Wiley, 112.

6. Tichy, N. M., & Cohen, E. 1997. *The leadership engine.* New York: Harper Business, 16.

7. Neugarten, B. 1964. *Personality in middle and later life.* New York: Atherton Press.

8. Vaillant, G. E. 1993. *The wisdom of the ego*. Cambridge: Harvard University Press. 338.

9. Kets de Vries, M. 1988. The dark side of CEO succession. *Harvard Business Review*, 88, 56–60.

10. Erikson, E. H. 1963. *Childhood and society*, 2nd Ed. New York: W. W. Norton. Erikson, E. H., & Erikson, J. M. 1981. On generativity and identity: From a conversation with Erik and Joan Erickson. *Harvard Educational Review*, 51, 249–269; Erikson, E. H., & Hall, E. 1987. Erikson: The father of the identity crisis. In E. Hall (Ed.), *Growing and changing*. New York: Random House. Levinson, D. J., Darrow, C. N., Klein, E. B., Levinson, M. H., & McKee, B. 1978. *The seasons of a man's life*. New York: Knopf.

11. Friedan, B., 1984. *The feminine mystique*. New York: Dell Publishing Company. Friedan, B., 1993. *The fountain of age*. New York: Simon and Schuster.

12. Tichy, N. M., & Sherman, S. 1993. *Control your destiny or someone else will*. New York: Doubleday/Currency, 1993.

13. Levinson, H., & Rosenthal, S. 1984. *CEO: Corporate leadership in action*. New York: Basic Books.

14. Lieberman, M. A. 1983. Social contexts of depression. In L. D. Breslau and M. R. Haug (Eds.), *Depression and aging*. New York: Springer. Holahan, C. K., & Holahan, C. J. 1987. Self-efficacy, social support, and depression in aging: A longitudinal analysis. *Journal of Gerontology*, 42, 65–68.

15. *New York Times*, 1999. Pope describes his feelings in unusual letter to the aged. October 27, A5.

16. Chasseguet-Smirgel, J., *The ego ideal*. W. W. Norton & Company, 1985.

17. Erikson, op. cit.; Erikson & Erikson, op. cit.; Erikson & Hall, op. cit.

18. Wills, G. 1992. Enabling managerial growth and ownership succession. *Management Decision*, 30, 10–26.

19. U.S. Bureau of the Census. 1990. *Statistical abstract of the United States*, 110th ed. Washington DC: U.S. Government Printing Office.

20. Vancil, R. F., 1987. *Passing the baton*. Boston: Harvard Business School.

21. Ciampa, D., & Watkins, M. 1999. The successor's dilemma. *Harvard Business Review*, 77:6, 160–168. Levinson, H., 1974. Don't choose your own successor. *Harvard Business Review*, 52:6, 53–62.

22. Lamb, R. B., 1987. *Running American business: Top CEOs rethink their major decisions*. New York: Basic Books, 247–273. Sonnenfeld, J. 1986. Heroes in collision: Chief executive retirement and the parade of future leaders. *Human Resource Management*, 25, 305–333.

23. Vancil, op. cit.

IV

LEADERSHIP

18

YOU WON'T RECOGNIZE ME: PREDICTIONS ABOUT CHANGES IN TOP-MANAGEMENT CHARACTERISTICS

HARRY LEVINSON

Everyone in today's business world is familiar with the pressures that result in reorganization, restructuring, decentralization, and attention to the near term. Recently, we have seen the fall of Richard J. Ferris, CEO of Allegis, allegedly because he attempted to build his organization for the long term. Psychological catastrophes that accompany these pressures are no longer news.[1] In addition, the concentration on cutting costs and attacking competitors frequently results in abandoning research and product development. The heavy emphasis on paying for the bottom line has all too often led to loss of innovation and depreciation of those qualitative features of an organization representing the core of its character.

Yet the majority of CEOs remain heavily focused on the numbers, a pressure exacerbated by the threat of possible takeovers and the increasing

From *Academy of Management Executive*, 2(2), 119–125. Copyright 1988 by the Academy of Management. Reprinted with permission.

demand of large stockholders, such as pension fund managers, for high returns in the short run. Search consultants report they continue to be asked to find prospective CEOs who will tightly control organizations for short-term results.

Although these results often bolster stock prices, making the firm more attractive to institutional buyers, they start a spiral of escalating demands for "lean and mean" cultures. The phrase "lean and mean," taken from the world of professional sports, is now widely used. The implication in that phrase is that one should be willing to incapacitate the opponent whenever possible,[2] and highlights the struggle for so many executives between being hard and soft, between being nonemotional and emotional, between being hard-nosed and a "bleeding heart."

The fact of the matter is most business management has always been hard, in the sense of emphasis on measurement by the numbers and relative insensitivity to and inadequate understanding of psychological issues. So, the new model says, "Become harder in the face of stress. Tighten up." It is exactly that mode of defense which, when practiced by an individual under stress, can lead to ultimate burnout and breakdown.

I have reservations about what is promising to become the "uptight" organization. The tighter the organization, the greater its rigidity and the harder for it to adapt flexibly to change. A tight organization implies significant control by its leadership and correspondingly less input from others, threatening the flow of information from those closest to the customer. An uptight organization is likely to be a driven organization. It is difficult to sustain the morale and commitment of people who are under unrelenting pressure. Physical and emotional exhaustion are likely to follow, with high turnover and loss of key personnel. Driven by bottom-line pressures, more managers are likely to take only marginal risks with respect to environmental, legal, and financial regulations. These can have financial costs and reflect on the reputations of those organizations.

There is considerable criticism of established hard-nosed leadership. Roger B. Smith, chairman of General Motors, has such a difficult time with the critics that he has developed a psychosomatic skin rash.[3] Thomas G. Wyman, who tried to bring better business management to CBS, seemed unable to deal with the mix of personalities in his organization. Harold Geneen of ITT, James Dutt of Beatrice Foods, and the late Charles Bludhorn of Gulf + Western have been criticized for their insensitivity to the feelings of employees and customers alike. That insensitivity is characteristic of all hard-nosed management.

When costs have been cut to the bone and controls tightened into rigidity, the resulting insensitivity and lack of flexibility will inhibit competitive adaptation. That likely outcome leads me to predict that there will have to be a significant change in the personality characteristics of chief executives if their organizations are to be successful. That prospective requirement, however, will increase the sense of helplessness on the part of many top managers. In this article I will discuss both of those issues, the likely change, and the increase in the sense of helplessness.

PREDICTED CHANGE IN EXECUTIVE PERSONALITY

Other forces are operating that will alter the type of personality required for top management. There is a significant change in the psychology of middle managers as larger numbers of organizations press their managers to be more participative and afford subordinates greater involvement in decisions affecting them. In many cases, these efforts have resulted in the improvement of quality and profitability, which has happened at Celanese, Ford, and other companies.

Many organizations are now breaking themselves down into smaller, more flexible units, and the hard-nosed manager is finding the adaptation difficult. I recall with some dismay meetings I had with four candidates for the presidency of a major corporate division. I asked about management styles and each spoke about participation. But participation meant different things to each of them. One candidate decided what ought to be done, asked his subordinates what they thought, and then tried to persuade them to his point of view. The others were less blatantly manipulative, but they were manipulative nonetheless. When these forms of manipulation fail—as they must— hard-nosed executives will yield to another type of person. What will the new executive look like? One clue comes from what is happening to political candidates.

Contenders for the presidency of the United States are softening their images.[4] They are showing emotions, talking about their feelings, and revealing intimate details of their past histories. That is a significant change from 1974, when Edmund S. Muskie lost his chance for the Democratic nomination after he broke down and cried. Now, according to the *New York Times*, the candidates are in a race to show who has a soul, a heart, competence, and passion. Vice-President George Bush has talked about the loss of a three-year-old child. Senator Robert Dole discussed the wartime injury to his arm and hand. Former candidate Senator Joseph Biden was open about the accident that killed his wife and daughter and the plagiarism that occurred while he was in law school. There is an enhanced societal emphasis on people knowing themselves, on honesty and self-examination and character, with which Gary Hart has had to deal.

According to Geoffrey Garin, a Democratic polltaker quoted in the *Times* article, there is a growing feeling that compassion should be an important element of government and that there is a rebellion against the impersonal technology that has been central to politics. The same theme is echoed by historian and biographer Doris Kearns Goodwin:

> Character is becoming increasingly important. The deeper part of it has to do with a recognition that between the Vietnam War and Watergate, and now the whole contra affair, that perhaps the most important thing to understand about a president is the general temperament, values, and ways of operating he brings to office, particularly since stances on issues and policies are not often what guide him when he gets into office.[5]

The reason, according to political analyst Richard Sennett, is that

> The American people seek out purity and innocence in their leaders . . . to attract votes the candidates must find a path to our soul. To do so, they must bare theirs. . . . A political discourse grounded in openness and directness allows individuals who otherwise share little in common to believe themselves bound together. We have nothing to hide. Examination and confession are the discourse of national unity.[6]

I predict that we will soon find the same trend with executives. This will be in part a product of the generation of the 60s and 70s, with its emphasis on psychological knowledge, experiential learning, the teaching of organizational behavior, and participative management. It will also be in part a product of the need to understand customers and employees better.[7] The growing number of women in management, and the complexities of dual careers and family obligations, have already brought new psychological considerations to many in the executive ranks. Downsizing, outplacement, and better employee selection have made today's organizations more responsive to psychological issues as well. Looking back over the past 34 years of my activity in this field, there has been a radical change of late in executives' willingness to accept referrals to psychologists and psychiatrists. The growing emphasis on dealing with stress, drugs, and alcoholism in the workplace makes psychological issues an everyday topic for executives.

Another contributing factor in the potential evolution of the top manager is the accumulation of organizational tension, a final product of the pressures operating in today's business world leading to the "uptight," nonadaptive corporation. Many organizations are blundering through change processes involving downsizing, reorganization, merger, and acquisition. Early retirements have left others bereft of organizational memory. There is much reinventing of the wheel. Once loyal employees who are waiting for the other shoe to drop will never regain the enthusiastic commitment they began with. Delegating responsibilities to division heads for a good bottom line, with fewer organizational staff controls on how it is achieved, gives some executives license to whip those organizations into shape. The ethics of the utilitarian sometimes override the ethics of moral rights and justice. The ends are used to justify the means. Unfortunately, the short-term results will become difficult to sustain.

In the present climate, when many managers are afraid of losing their jobs, they merely murmur fears and criticisms. However, there will soon be shortages of good managers, predicted even now by the difficulty of recruiting college students for traditional collegiate service jobs. In addition, and most significantly, there will be the pervasive need for participation. The ethos demands it. Innovation, product quality, and cost control require it. Corporations like Monsanto are creating innovative subsidiaries from within their organizations rather than buying up entrepreneurial companies. They are creating companies to pursue scientific and technological leads into manufacturing and marketing. These relatively independent entities, turned loose to make their own way, are built significantly around team concepts. Digital Equipment Corporation has pioneered entrepreneurial productivity to great success.[8] Other large companies are forming start-up joint ventures to merge technologies. What does this mean for leadership?

A summary of the literature on leadership in isolated military missions concludes:

> On short-term space missions and submarines, the leadership structure is clearly established because of military tradition. . . . In sociometric studies aboard the Sealab submersible, it was found that the most desired leaders were rated as being more task-oriented and aloof as compared with leaders who were social and interactive with the crew. In contrast, on longer Antarctic missions, status leveling occurred over time, with the most valued leaders being characterized as having a democratic style and showing concern for the well-being and emotional state of their men.[9]

Managers and executives will necessarily have to be more closely involved with their subordinates over the longer period of time required to establish and maintain commitment. The implication for me is that they will have to become more psychologically minded; that is, they will have to understand the personalities of their subordinates better, particularly the unconscious factors in motivation. They will also need a better understanding of what goes on in groups, how to develop and sustain appropriate authority–subordinate relationships under conditions of less rigid external controls, and how to deal with significant personality differences while resolving conflicts and developing subordinates.[10]

Despite the problems inherent in more open communication,[11] executives will have to become more like today's presidential candidates. I am not predicting a millennial change in executive character; rather, I am predicting a trend in that direction. Recall the earlier comment by Richard Sennett that ". . . discourse grounded in openness and directness allows individuals who otherwise share little in common to believe themselves bound together." For reasons I shall discuss below, different levels of an organization do indeed share little in common.

INCREASED SENSE OF EXECUTIVE HELPLESSNESS

The second set of issues arises from the feelings of increased helplessness on the part of many people in high-level management. In 1987, 70% of U.S. firms have foreign competitors, a rise of 50% during the last two decades. Competing on a worldwide basis with less governmental protection and support is intimidating to many executives. Today's executive must understand a range of marketplaces, varied needs of disparate customers, and more intense competition. Some months ago while waiting for a plane in Boston, I met an old colleague who had been dean of a business school and was now in the international consulting business. He was en route, once again, to the Far East. He told me with some anxiety his fear that the United States was going to lose out competitively with the Japanese, predicting dire consequences. Only shortly before, articles in the business press had alerted us to the growing danger of Japanese dominance of the microchip industry. Other articles, however, stated that there was no danger; that the chips the Japanese were making were elementary compared with those being made by IBM, AT&T, and TI.

Similarly, we are given conflicting advice that we should fear the massive foreign exchange debt and that we have nothing to fear as far as the debt is concerned. Some say we should be wary of predatory takeovers, while others contend that financial manipulation is good for shaking out stodgy management. In short, one can find an opinion for almost anything one wants to believe. This is very confusing for managers who are striving to make sense out of all this. Sense making becomes critical if managers are rewarded solely on the basis of short-term quarterly reports.

Part of the resulting feeling of helplessness among managers arises from the fact that there are many people in high-level management whose cognitive capacity, to use Elliott Jaques' term,[12] is simply not adequate to grasp all the data with which they now must deal. This is particularly a problem when they face issues of corporate strategy and global competition. That problem—the inability to conceptualize greater complexity—is complicated by the fact of aging CEOs and superannuated boards. For example, I met with some senior executives of a major corporation that competes in high-tech areas. The chief executive is close to retirement; his potential successor is already 55. The same week we talked, *Business Week* had a cover picture of William Gates III, a 31-year-old high-tech prodigy and CEO of Microsoft. High tech is a young person's game. In its present form with its present policies, that older organization will not be able to compete effectively. I recommended that significant numbers of younger, technically knowledgeable people be included among the potential successors and the board. No one in that organization has moved to do so. Faced with such a problem when he was CEO of Citicorp, Walter B. Wriston deliberately set about bringing highly intelligent younger people into the organization.[13] He assumed that if they were bright and ambitious, they would make work for themselves, and indeed they did. This caused tremendous conflict in Citicorp, but Wriston followed through, even to the point of naming a young successor.

Furthermore, it has become harder for those who speak as the loyal opposition in an organization to hold their places with such threatened managements.[14] I have recently seen two instances in which forthright managers who stood for the best in the organization's values and ethics were scapegoated and blamed for the very problems they detected, reported, and tried to resolve. I have had reports from others about top managements who didn't want to hear about malfeasance in their organization and punished the messengers.

Corporate problems such as these lead to selection errors. Naturally, executives who are limited in their conceptual capacity are likely to choose others who are equally limited. That, in turn, makes it difficult for the organization to compete. It also sets off repetitive reorganization and restructuring in an effort to regain competitive advantage, demoralizing employees and making the organization uptight out of fear and ambiguity. When individuals are subject to repetitive instability and threatened by loss of role and function, they lose a sense of direction. Their efforts then become random and repetitive; they become preoccupied with self-preservation. Anxiety paralyzes all initiative.

IMPLICATIONS

The psychologically knowledgeable executive must have a mental model of what an organization is, what it must do, what it takes to hold it together and, ultimately, what it must do to advance.

There is indeed such a model, one that has been used through the ages to justify major changes in social structure, even revolutions. That is the model of the biblical Exodus. Michael Walzer has analyzed and detailed the process implications of the Exodus with careful sensitivity.[15] You will recall that Moses, the Stranger, led the Israelites out of Egypt. The Israelites were a people weighed down by oppression, crushed, and made subservient. Some were eager to return to bondage under the Pharaoh, where they knew their place and had the security of familiar structure, however painful. Many murmured against Moses and Aaron, who had brought them out of bondage and opened the sea for them, destroyed the Pharaoh's army, and sustained them in the Wilderness. That should have been enough, but it wasn't.

How familiar that phenomenon is as executives work with people in organizations who don't want to change, who would rather go back to the familiar and the comfortable, even when they are turned loose to be more free and to use skills and competences more adequately. Moses found in the Israelites what all senior executives find in their organizations; namely, that there are individuals of broad conceptual ability who take the strategic perspective and recognize the tactical sacrifices that must be undertaken to realize that perspective, and that there are people of limited conceptual ability who, instead, seek immediate gratification. All significant change processes in organizations, therefore, must simultaneously deal with these two sets of values built on differing conceptual capacities and limitations. In addition, they must also deal with a third set of values; namely, the values of those who operate between the bottom and the top—middle management.

Executives must differentiate their work, perhaps in Jaques' terms, grouping what he calls Strata I and II; III, IV, and V; and VI, VII, and VIII. In Jaques' conception of the development of intellectual capability, called Stratified Systems Theory, Stratum I work involves shaping or taking an action once the path and goal is laid out by others: bricklaying, typing, etc. Stratum II involves reflection on the activities involved in Stratum I, e.g., compiling a social service history and planning a service program. Stratum III is the level of a plant manager; Stratum IV, the level required to manage several plants with different processes; and Stratum V, the management of a whole division or other unit competing in a worldwide context. Strata VI, VII, and VIII are corporate-level roles with worldwide competitive activity on many fronts. That is why I said earlier that different levels in an organization share little in common.

Larry Lemasters developed such three-level groups at American Transtech and Bell Laboratories.[16] The first was a "core group" of people from the four top levels of management, the second a "family group" made up of supervisors, and the third a "community group." The first group dealt with policy and mission, the second with operations, the third was the scene of "state of the business" meetings. The groups dealt not only with hard business facts but also with people's feelings, particularly about change.

The Israelites who left Egypt were motley groups of tribesmen, yet it was necessary for them to become a nation. They did so by taking on a new bondage. This time, however, the new bondage was voluntary and psychological, involving law, obligation, and response—namely, the new standards of behavior Moses brought down from Sinai. These standards were oppressive because they required that people behave in keeping with them. However, they also offered vision and hope, a code for living, and a relationship to the unknown. The transition was difficult, difficult for the people and difficult for Moses. As the 12th century Hebrew philosopher, Maimonides, said, "For a sudden transition from one to another is impossible . . . it is not in the nature of man that, after having been brought up in slavish service . . . he should suddenly wash off from his hands the dirt [of slavery]." How aptly that quotation fits contemporary large organizations undergoing strategic change in turbulent environments.

In the contemporary business world, the structure and direction John Sculley imposed on Apple Computer was resented and resisted by many in that company after the formless freedom that they had previously enjoyed.[17] Nevertheless, in doing so he gave Apple a new competitive posture that assured its survival.

Moses offered us the first example of what today would be regarded as the ideal model of participative management. He was, in Walzer's terms, a pedagogue of the people and their defender before God. In contrast to his predecessors, Moses did not rule like a prince. In the Exodus story, he is depicted repeatedly as arguing with the people, much as he argues with God—and in neither case does he always get his way. Walzer notes that Moses was rather more successful with God than with the people.

With respect to interaction with followers, Stuart Rosenthal and I report in our book *CEO* how Walter B. Wriston's subordinates decided to manufacture a terminal for Citibank's unique credit card, despite Wriston's wish that they not do so. Ian K. MacGregor, when he was a recently appointed head of AMAX, said he had never given an order in his life, and Reginald H. Jones said much the same thing as he revamped the General Electric of those years. John W. Hanley came into Monsanto with a heavy hand, but soon found himself engaged with his own people in more informal discussion that tempered his behavior. From the first computer onward, Thomas J. Watson, Jr. involved his people in the task forces that ultimately put IBM at the head of the computer pack. And Arthur O. Sulzberger still tours the halls and bowels of the *New York Times* building to stay in touch with his people.

To return to the Exodus, the transition took a long time. The Israelites wandered in the wilderness for 40 years, which Walzer argues was not by chance. The life span at the time was threescore years, except for Moses, who was allowed twice as much. That meant that all of the Israelites who were 20 years or older at the time of the departure from Egypt would die natural deaths before reaching the Promised Land. Therefore, the people who arrived at the Jordan were not the same ones who had left Egypt. It was this new generation of Israelites to whom Moses taught the laws and rituals of Israel's new religion and, even more important, to be teachers themselves in their turn. And it was this new generation, unfamiliar with oppression, who were now ready to fight their own battles as a political society committed to one another and to the covenant that bound them together. Moses freed himself for this top management or leadership task by accepting Jethro's advice to leave the daily management to others. He remained the guide, the translator, the master teacher.

The new executives, I project, will be more sensitive and more aware of their own feelings. They will be uptight, not about their feelings, but about their commitment to the quality of what they do. They will be concerned with creating cohesion and identification among their followers to perpetuate their organizations.

What CEOs must formulate is not a mission—not merely goals and objectives—but a sense of transcendent purpose. They must put forth a dream to be shared by all organizational participants, one that constitutes the underlying ego-ideal standard with which all can identify and toward which they all can strive. Pascale and Athos speak of superordinate goals,[18] but my concept implies a deeper meaning. Purpose can never be achieved; it is always an aspiration. Only from transcendent purpose can there be an organizational character. Only with such a transcendent sense can goals and objectives be derived and be internally consistent. Only when purpose is defined at three different conceptual levels with corresponding goals and objectives can both longer- and shorter-term needs be met.

However, there are three steps to be taken once transcendent purpose is defined.

The first step is to evolve appropriate structure. To my knowledge, only Elliott Jaques has created a logical structural theory firmly rooted in cognitive psychology. Jaques defines work as the exercise of discretion within specified time boundaries at designated quality levels. The time span of discretion reflects the level of conceptual capacity required to carry out a given task. He delineates eight strata or levels of conceptual capacity required to carry out organizational requirements, which I outlined briefly above. These are translated into levels of organizational structure, providing an underlying psychological basis for that structure. Only with such a conceptual structure can people be placed according to their ability to handle complexity.

The second step is to examine how reward–punishment conceptions of motivation undermine and even inhibit the very commitment and identification that leaders must establish. Almost all organizational compensation systems are based on what I have called The Great Jackass Fallacy.[19] The assumption underlying the design of these systems is that employees are jackasses to be motivated by carrots and sticks, and that the upper-level managers have the right to manipulate those below with these carrots and sticks. It is far wiser to work toward a concept of return on investment that is nonmanipulable when based on adequate performance appraisal.

The third step is to evolve behavioral job descriptions—highly detailed maps explaining to employees what behavior is really expected of them in the multiple facets of their roles. Such behavioral job descriptions should also include accountability for developing subordinates by recording significant incidents and reporting them as immediate feedback to subordinates.[20] By doing so managers become teachers, and as teachers instruments of organizational perpetuation as well as subordinate growth.

We cannot reasonably expect managers to maintain the same continuous relationships in organizations that were possible in a previous era. Nevertheless, when workers identify with a leadership style that offers conceptual strength, firm direction, and sensitivity to their feelings they, in turn, operate in and become teachers of that style.

Although scattered, oppressed, and persecuted throughout their history and even to the present day, the Jewish people sustained a commitment to each other and to their religion as they spread throughout the world. That commitment kept them adaptive and, subsequently, became the source of a tremendous creativity.

The participative movement, with its penchant for making everyone equal, tends to confuse being authoritative with being authoritarian. When executives confuse the two, they have difficulty taking charge and they fail both as leaders and teachers. Henry Rosofsky, former dean of Harvard's Faculty of Arts and Sciences, points out that

> ... [academic] chairmen, deans, provosts, and similar levels are appointed, not elected, and they can be dismissed. This is crucial because academic elections tend to result in weak leadership. What professors in their right minds would vote for a dean who advocated cuts in their departments? ... We have a system of governance that permits non-consensual and unpopular decisions to be made when necessary. We have learned that not everything is improved by making it more democratic.[21]

Executives must maintain appropriately authoritative positions.

Top executives must see themselves as leaders, as teachers. They must learn to endure the murmuring, the doubt, the anxiety, the hostile interaction with their own followers as they guide, direct, cajole, persuade—and are rebuffed and frustrated. They must understand that organizations cannot be changed rapidly despite the apparent illusion that some organizations have. Employees need to identify with their organizations and with their leadership. They need the mutual support of their work groups and they need the training to master themselves and their tasks. And they need guidance and someone to steer their ship.

No, our corporate image is not to be lean and mean. It must be closer to what John Sculley has to say about leadership, which he sees as somewhat like sailing: "One has to make a lot of navigational decisions and then continually trim sails and do lots of things to adjust to currents and winds." What a beautifully simple model for leadership.

ENDNOTES

1. For a summary of the effects of acquisition and reorganization on employees, see David M. Schweiger, John M. Ivancevich, and Frank R. Power's "Executive Actions for Managing Human Resources Before and After Acquisition," *Academy of Management Executive*, May 1987, pp. 127–138.

2. B. J. Bredemeier and D. L. Shields note the radical differences between the behavior of athletic team competitors on the playing field and their behavior in ordinary social relations in "Values and Violence in Sports Today," *Psychology Today*, October 1985, pp. 23–32.

3. Alex Taylor III reports on that pressure in "It's No Fun Running No. 1 When You're Taking Heat," *Fortune*, August 3, 1987, pp. 26–27.

4. Maureen Dowd reports these and other findings from her interviews with political consultants and her observations of candidates in "With Tears and Revelations, '88 Contenders Soften Their Images," *New York Times*, April 26, 1987, p. 1.

5. Doris Kearns Goodwin, whose biography of Lyndon Johnson (*Lyndon Johnson and the American Dream*, New York: NAL Penguin, 1977), established her as an authority on presidential matters, has become even more authoritative following the publication of her more recent book on the Kennedys, *The Fitzgeralds and the Kennedys* (New York: Simon & Schuster, 1987). Charles Kenny summarizes her views in "Trying Presidential 'Character' on for Size," *Boston Sunday Globe*, July 5, 1987, p. A17.

6. Richard Sennett, "A Republic of Souls," *Harper's*, July 1987, p. 41.

7. John W. Slocum, Jr. of the Edwin L. Cox School of Business at Southern Methodist University, reminds me that this is Erich Fromm's central thesis in his books *Escape From Freedom* (New York: Avon, 1971) and The *Nature of Man* (with Ramon Xirau; New York: Macmillan, 1968). To paraphrase: As man pursues his quest to return to nature, he is further alienated from society. I am also indebted to Professor Slocum for other suggestions and comments on this article.

8. Kenneth H. Olsen talked about his philosophy of management, which encourages criticism from within the organization, at the 1987 MIT commencement. His speech was reported under the headline "The Education of an Entrepreneur," *New York Times*, July 19, 1987, p. F2. Olsen and Digital are also described in "America's Most Successful Entrepreneur," *Fortune*, October 27, 1987, pp. 24–32.

9. The U.S. Navy has for years studied what happens to undersea crews on long voyages and difficult assignments. Those studies that refer to leadership under such circumstances are summarized by Nick Kanas in "Psychological and Interpersonal Issues in Space," *American Journal of Psychiatry*, June 1987, 144(6), pp. 703–709.

10. Richard E. Byrd succinctly summarizes the forces compelling psychological-mindedness and integrates the contemporary discussions of leadership response to them in "Corporate Leadership Styles: A New Synthesis," *Organizational Dynamics*, Summer 1987, pp. 34–43.

11. Opening up communications in organizations often creates as many problems as it resolves, as Eric M. Eisenberg and Marsha G. Whitten report in "Reconsidering Openness in Organizational Communication," *Academy of Management Review*, 1987, 12(3), pp. 418–426.

12. Elliott Jaques has developed the most comprehensive and sophisticated contemporary conception of levels of conceptual thinking applied to organizational structure and leadership selection. His work, based on more than 30 years of consultation, thinking, and research is, in my judgment, 25–50 years ahead of its time. See Jaques' book *A General Theory of Bureaucracy*, New York: Halsted Press, 1976. He is updating that work in another volume to be published this year.

13. Stuart Rosenthal and I interviewed six major CEOs who had effected sweeping changes in their organizations: Reginald H. Jones of General Electric; Walter B. Wriston of Citicorp; Ian K. MacGregor of AMAX. Inc.; John W. Hanley of Monsanto Company; Thomas J. Watson, Jr. of IBM; and Arthur O. Sulzberger of the New York Times Company, and six colleagues of each CEO who had the opportunity to observe him. We described their practices to stimulate vitality and innovation in *CEO: Corporate Leadership in Action*, New York: Basic Books, 1984.

14. The importance of a loyal internal opposition in organizations is brilliantly examined from an economist's point of view by Albert O. Hirschman in *Exit, Voice, and Loyalty*, Cambridge, MA: Harvard University Press, 1970.

15. In *Exodus and Revolution* (New York: Basic Books, 1984), Michael Walzer traces many situations in which the Exodus has been used as a model. His lucid explanations of the psychological implications of the Exodus for leadership should be "must" reading for all leaders and would-be leaders.

16. Report in *HRM Perspectives*, June 1987, p. 2.

17. John Sculley (with John A. Byrne), *Odyssey*, New York: Harper & Row, 1987.

18. Richard T. Pascale and Anthony G. Athos, *The Art of Japanese Management*, New York: Simon & Schuster, 1981.

19. I have explained this conception in greater detail in *The Great Jackass Fallacy*, Cambridge, MA: Harvard University Press, 1973.

20. In "Appraisal of What Performance?" (*Harvard Business Review*, July–August 1976, pp. 30–37), I elaborated on the concept of significant incidents and behavioral job descriptions.

21. Henry Rosofsky, "Highest Education," *The New Republic*, July 13 and 20, 1987, p. 13.

ABOUT HARRY LEVINSON

Harry Levinson, PhD, is Chairman Emeritus of The Levinson Institute and Clinical Professor of Psychology Emeritus in the Department of Psychiatry at Harvard Medical School and the former head of the section on organizational mental health of the Massachusetts Mental Health Center.

Born in Port Jervis, New York, Dr. Levinson received his BS and MS degrees from Emporia State University in Emporia, Kansas. He took his training in clinical psychology to the Veterans Administration–Menninger Foundation–University of Kansas program, which led to his PhD from the University of Kansas in 1952. He is certified by the American Board of Professional Psychology.

While coordinator of professional education at Topeka State Hospital from 1950 to 1953, Dr. Levinson played a key role in the dramatic and widely acclaimed reformation of the Kansas state hospital system. In 1954, Dr. Levinson created, and for the next 14 years directed, the Division of Industrial Mental Health of The Menninger Foundation. In 1968 he moved to the Harvard Graduate School of Business and privately established The Levinson Institute, which he ran until he retired in 1992. He has lectured and consulted widely to business, academic, and governmental organizations in the United States and abroad.

During the 1961–1962 academic year, Dr. Levinson was a visiting professor in the Sloan School of Management at the Massachusetts Institute of Technology. In 1967 he taught in the School of Business at the University of Kansas. From 1968 to 1972, Dr. Levinson was Thomas Henry Carroll-Ford Foundation Distinguished Visiting Professor in the Harvard Graduate School of Business Administration. From 1972 to 1992, he was Clinical Professor of Psychology in the Department of Psychiatry in the Harvard Medical School. He has been an adjunct professor in the Boston University School of Business Administration and in the Pace University Graduate School. Dr.

Levinson was a Ford Foundation visiting professor at the H. C. Mathur Institute of Public Administration in Jaipur, India, in the summer of 1974. He was a visiting centennial professor at Texas A&M in April 1976, and in September 1979, he conducted the international course on occupational social psychiatry for the Finnish Government Institute of Occupational Health, under the sponsorship of the Nordic Council of Ministers. In the 1995–1996 academic year, he was a visiting professor at Florida Atlantic University.

Dr. Levinson received the Perry L. Rohrer Consulting Psychology Practice Award for outstanding achievement in psychological consultation in 1984; the Massachusetts Psychological Association's Career Award and the first award of The Society of Psychologists in Management in 1985; the Organizational Development Professional Practice Award for Excellence from the American Society for Training and Development in 1988; and the I. Arthur Marshall Distinguished Alumnus Award of The Menninger Alumni Association in 1990; he was named corecipient of the American Psychological Association (APA) Award for Distinguished Professional Contributions to Knowledge in 1992. In 2000 Dr. Levinson received the APA Gold Medal for Life Achievement in the Application of Psychology. The Massachusetts School of Professional Psychology presented him with an honorary degree, Doctor of Humane Letters, in 2004. In the same year, APA's Division 13 (Society of Consulting Psychology) recognized him with its Distinguished Service Award.

Dr. Levinson is past president of the American Board of Professional Psychology, past president of the Kansas Psychological Association, and former chairman of the Kansas Advisory Committee to the United States Civil Rights Commission. He has authored 18 books and numerous articles in professional, management, and popular publications. A list of his publications is provided in the section that follows.[1]

PUBLICATIONS

(1943). *P-L-S journalism test* (with G. S. Phillips & H. E. Schrammel). Emporia, KS: Bureau of Educational Measurements.

(1948). Mathematics aptitude. In O. J. Kaplan (Ed.), *Encyclopedia of vocational guidance* (Vol. II). New York: Philosophical Library.

(1948). *A study in neglect* (with V. L. Norris & H. Moore). Topeka: Kansas State Board of Health.

(1949, October). The contribution of social workers to the interviewing skills of psychologists (with J. T. Dickson, I. Stamm, & A. Leader). *Journal of Social Work, 30,* 318–324.

---

[1]Please refer to PsycINFO (http://www.apa.org/psycinfo) for further information on secondary sources in which these works have been excerpted or reprinted.

(1950). *Behind these walls*. Topeka, KS: Shawnee County Association for Mental Health.

(1952). *Doors are to open*. Topeka, KS: Topeka State Hospital.

(1952). *The relation of after image duration to certain aspects of personality*. Unpublished doctoral thesis, University of Kansas, Lawrence.

(1953, Winter–Spring). State hospitals are different now. *Menninger Quarterly, VII*(2), 7–12.

(1954, Winter). When is it sick to be sad? *Menninger Quarterly, VIII*(2), 16–20.

(1954, Summer). The machine that made pop. *Menninger Quarterly, VIII*(3), 20–26.

(1954, Fall). Industrial mental health: Some observations and trends (with W. C. Menninger). *Menninger Quarterly, VIII*(4), 1–31.

(1955, Winter). Consultation clinic for alcoholism. *Menninger Quarterly, IX*(1), 7–13.

(1955, Spring). What can a psychiatrist do in industry? *Menninger Quarterly, IX*(2), 19–21.

(1955, June). Of gifts and givers. *The Campfire Girl, 34*(3).

(1956). (Ed.). *Toward understanding men*. Topeka, KS: The Menninger Foundation.

(1956, January–February). Why work? *Personnel Service*, 1–7.

(1956, March). Employee counseling in industry. *Bulletin of The Menninger Clinic, XX*(2), 76–84.

(1956, June). Experimental seminars in industrial mental health. *Menninger Quarterly, X*(2), 21–23.

(1956, September). A significant decade. *Menninger Quarterly, X*(3), 6–8.

(1956, November). Seminars for executives and industrial physicians. *American Journal of Psychiatry, CXIII*(5), 451–454.

(1956, December). We are the learners. *Menninger Quarterly, X*(4), 11–14.

(1957, March). The illogical logic of accident prevention. *Menninger Quarterly, XI*(1), 19–26.

(1957, June). The next step. *Menninger Quarterly, XI*(2), 22–24.

(1957, June). Review: Industrial mental health. *Menninger Quarterly, XI*(2), 17–21.

(1957, July). Social action for mental health. *Mental Hygiene, XXXXI*(3), 353–360.

(1957, September). Emotional first aid on the job. *Menninger Quarterly, XI*(3), 6–15.

(1957). Alcoholism in industry. *Menninger Quarterly, XI*(4, Suppl.).

(1957). *Human understanding in industry* (with W. C. Menninger). Chicago: Science Research Associates.

(1958). The nature and genesis of prejudice. In G. Noar (Ed.), *Proceedings of plain states conference on human relations education* (pp. 6–10). University of Omaha, Omaha, Nebraska.

(1958). What makes us work safely? [President's Conference on Occupational Safety, Washington, DC]. *U.S. Department of Labor Bulletin, 196*, 71–73.

(1958, June). What you can do about stress (with H. C. Modlin). *Nation's Business*, 46(6), 34–35, 90–95.

(1958, September). Know yourself. *Supervisory Management*, 3(9), 32–39.

(1959). Executive awareness and health. In *Readings in management planning and principles*. New York: Corn Products.

(1959, March 15). New way to fight tension. *New York Herald Tribune*, pp. 21, 23.

(1959, July). Open letter to my son. *National Jewish Monthly*, 73(6), 26.

(1959, September–October). The psychologist in industry. *Harvard Business Review*, 37(5), 93–99.

(1960, May). Dilemmas of the occupational physician in mental health programming: Part II. *Journal of Occupational Medicine*, 2, 205–208.

(1960, September). First aid for worried workers. *Nation's Business*, 48(9), 54–55, 58, 60, 61.

(1961). Industrial mental health: Progress and prospects. *Personnel*, 38(3), 35–42.

(1961). *Interdisciplinary research on work and mental health: A point of view and a method* (with others). Topeka, KS: The Menninger Foundation.

(1961, April). Cause and cure of personality clashes. *Nation's Business*, 49(4), 84–86, 88–89.

(1962). *Men, management, and mental health* (with H. J. Mandl, C. M. Solley, K. J. Munden, & C. R. Price). Cambridge, MA: Harvard University Press.

(1962, January). Seminars for executives and occupational physicians. *Bulletin of the Menninger Clinic*, XXVI(1), 18–29.

(1962, July–August). The executive's anxious age. *Think*, 28(7), 22–25.

(1962, September–October). A psychologist looks at executive development. *Harvard Business Review*, 40(5), 69–75.

(1963). Work and mental health. In *Encyclopedia of mental health* (pp. 2027–2048). New York: Franklin Watts.

(1963, January–February). What killed Bob Lyons. *Harvard Business Review*, 41(1), 127–144.

(1963, Spring). Men, management, and mental health. *Menninger Quarterly*, 17(1), 19–25.

(1963, May–June). The executive and his teenage children. *Think*, 29(5), 26–30.

(1964). *Emotional health in the world of work*. New York: Harper & Row.

(1964). *Human needs in housing: Report on a round table conference* [Occasional Paper No. 4]. Chicago: U.S. Savings & Loan League.

(1964). Management by guilt. In Manfred F. R. Kets de Vries (Ed.), *The irrational executive: Psychoanalytic explorations in management* (pp. 132–151). New York: International Universities Press.

(1964). Work and mental health (with C. Price). In A. B. Shostak & W. Gomberg (Eds.), *Blue collar world: Studies of the American worker* (pp. 397–405). Englewood Cliffs: Prentice-Hall.

(1964, January–February).What work means to a man. *Think, 30*(1), 7–12.

(1964, March–April). Anger, guilt and executive action. *Think, 30*(2), 10–14.

(1964, May). Turn anger into an asset. *Nation's Business, 52*(5), 82–86.

(1964, June). The changing meaning of the organization. In T. Heim & W. Fenton (Eds.), *Fifth annual personnel officers seminar: A report* [Special Report No. 128; pp. 27–35]. Lawrence: Governmental Research Center, University of Kansas.

(1964, October 27). [Review of the book *The act of creation*]. *National Observer*.

(1964, November–December). Why women work. *Think, 30*(6), 2.

(1965). Foreword. In C. A. Ferguson et al., *The legacy of neglect: An appraisal of the implications of emotional disturbances in the business environment* (pp. vii–viii). Fort Worth, TX: Industrial Mental Health Associates.

(1965, January–February). The problems of promotion. *Think, 31*(1), 7–10.

(1965, March). Reciprocation: The relationship between man and organization. *Administrative Science Quarterly, 9*(4), 370–390.

(1965, March–April). Stress at the bargaining table. *Personnel, 42*(2), 17–23.

(1965, March–April). What is mental health. *Think, 31*(2), 24–28,.

(1965, April). The future of health in industry. *Industrial Medicine & Surgery, 34*, 321–334.

(1965, April). How to get out of a dead-end job. *Popular Science Monthly, 186*(4), 104–105, 194.

(1965, May– June). Do you look for culprits—or causes? *Think, 31*(3), 14–18.

(1965, June). [Review of the book *Organizational stress*]. *Administrative Science Quarterly, 10*(1), 125–129.

(1965, September–October). What an executive should know about scientists. *Think, 31*(5), 6–10.

(1965, November– December). Who is to blame for maladaptive managers? *Harvard Business Review, 43*(6), 143–158.

(1966). *Are you nobody?* (with P. Tournier, V. E. Frankl, H. Thielicke, P. Lehmann, & S. H. Miller). Richmond: John Knox Press.

(1966). The changing meaning of the organization. In T. O. Wedel & R. P. Scherer (Eds.), *The church and its manpower management*. New York: Department of Ministry Vocation and Pastoral Services, National Council of Churches of Christ in the USA.

(1966, January–February). What ever happened to loyalty? *Think, 32*(1), 8–12.

(1966, July–August). How to undermine an organization. *Think, 32*(4), 15–19.

(1966, September–October). The high return on enlightened giving. *Think, 32*(5), 21–24.

(1966, October). [Review of the book *The executive in crisis*]. *Administrative Science Quarterly, 11*(2), 297–299.

(1966, November). Service is management's responsibility. *Cooking for Profit*.

(1967). George R. R. Pflaum. In R. L. Roahen (Ed.), *Qualities of greatness II* (pp. 53–55). Emporia, KS: The Kansas State Teachers College Press.

(1967). [Review of the article "The anarchist movement and the T-groups: Some possible lessons for organizational development"]. *The Journal of Applied Behavioral Science, 3,* 232–233.

(1967, January–February). Problems that walk in your door. *Think, 33*(1), 13–16.

(1967, Spring). Mentally ill puzzle industry. *Menninger Quarterly, 21*(1), 7–13.

(1967, May). [Review of the book *Mental health with limited resource*].*Archives of Environmental Health, 14,* 783.

(1967, May). [Review of the book *Psychological and theological relationships in the multiple staff ministry*]. *Bulletin of the Menninger Clinic, 31*(3), 187–188.

(1967, May–June). Turning tame ones into tigers. *Think, 33*(3), 24–28.

(1967, July). [Review of the book *Mental health in a changing community*]. *Archives of Environmental Health, 15*(1), 134.

(1968). *The exceptional executive.* Cambridge, MA: Harvard University Press.

(1968). Psychiatric consultation in industry. In Mendel and Solomon (Eds.), *The psychiatric consultation* (pp. 159–180). New York: Grune & Stratton.

(1968). Some responses from outside the company: The exceptional executive. In *Managing organizational stress: Proceedings of the Executive Study Conference: November 29–30, 1967* (pp. 135–178). Princeton, NJ: Educational Testing Service.

(1968, January–February). Is there an obsolescent executive in your company—Or in your chair? *Think, 34*(1), 26–30.

(1968, February). [Review of the book *The job hunt: Job-seeking behavior of unemployed workers in a local economy*]. *Archives of Environmental Health, 16*(2), 296–297.

(1968, February). [Review of the book *A psychiatrist for a troubled world: Selected papers of William C. Menninger, M.D.*]. *Archives of Environmental Health, 16*(2), 296–297.

(1968, March–April). What an executive should know about his boss. *Think, 34*(2), 30–33.

(1968, April). The Menninger Foundation Division of Industrial Mental Health. *Industrial & Labor Relations Review, 21*(3), 470.

(1968, June). The trouble with sermons . . . . *The Journal of Pastoral Care, XXII*(2), 65–74.

(1969). The exceptional executive. In *Proceedings of a Symposium, The Exceptional Executive* (pp. 6–24). Ohio: Division of Research, College of Business Administration, Ohio University.

(1969). Seminars for executives and occupational physicians. In Ralph T. Collins (Ed.), *Occupational psychiatry: International psychiatry clinics* (Vol. 6, No. 4, pp. 141–158). Boston: Little, Brown.

(1969). When love of labor is lost. *Contemporary Psychology, 14*(7), 367–369.

(1969, January). [Review of the book *To work is human*]. *Industrial and Labor Relations Review*, 22(2), 303.

(1969, Spring). Technology: Human challenges. *The McKinsey Quarterly*, V(4), 41–52.

(1969, July). [Review of the book *Work and human behavior*]. *Contemporary Psychology*, XIV(7), 367–368.

(1969, July–August). On being a middle-aged manager. *Harvard Business Review*, 47(4), 51–60.

(1969, August). Emotional toxicology of the work environment. *Archives of Environmental Health*, 19(2), 239–243.

(1969, October). [Review of the book *Motivation through the work itself*]. *Monthly Labor Review*, 92(10), 68–69.

(1969–1970, Winter). Managing executive stress. *Panhandle Magazine*, 4(2), 16–19.

(1970). *Executive stress*. New York: Harper & Row.

(1970). The impact of organization on mental health (with L. Weinbaum). In A. A. McLean (Ed.), *Mental health and work organizations* (pp. 23–49). New York: Rand McNally.

(1970, March–April). A psychologist diagnoses merger failures. *Harvard Business Review*, 44(2), 139–147.

(1970, July–August). Management by whose objectives? *Harvard Business Review*, 44(4), 125–134.

(1971, March–April). Conflicts that plague family businesses. *Harvard Business Review*, 45(2), 90–98.

(1971, May). Various perspectives on managerial theory and practice on motivation in industry. *Archives of Environmental Health*, 22(5), 612–618.

(1971, October). Psychiatry in industry. *Psychiatric Annals*, 1(2), 60–71.

(1971, November). [Review of the book *Work, creativity and social justice*]. *Bulletin of the Menninger Clinic*, 35(6), 488–490.

(1971, December). The quiet revolution at Foggy Bottom (with C. Petrow & T. Stern). *Management Review*, 60(12), 4–14.

(1972). [Review of the book chapter "Motivation and management" in Joseph W. McGuire (Ed.), *Contemporary management: Issues and Viewpoints*, Englewood Cliffs, NJ: Prentice-Hall.]

(1972). *Organizational diagnosis* (with A. G. Spohn & J. Molinari). Cambridge, MA: Harvard University Press.

(1972). Problems that worry executives. In A. Marrow (Ed.), *The failure of success* (pp. 67–80). New York: American Management Association.

(1972, Winter). The clinical psychologist as organizational diagnostician. *Professional Psychology*, 3(1), 34–40.

(1972, Spring). An effort toward understanding man at work. *European Business*, 33, 19–29.

(1972, Spring). [Review of the article "What should you know about the working wife and mother?"]. *Occupational Mental Health*, 2(1), 8.

(1972, April). Management by objectives: A critique. *Training and Development Journal*, 26(4), 3–8.

(1972, September–October). Easing the pain of personal loss. *Harvard Business Review*, 50(5), 80–88.

(1973). *The great jackass fallacy*. Cambridge, MA: Harvard University Press, The Division of Research, Graduate School of Business Administration.

(1973, January–February). Asinine attitudes toward motivation. *Harvard Business Review*, 51(1), 70–76.

(1973, Summer). A psychoanalytic view of occupational stress. *Occupational Mental Health*, 3(2), 2–13.

(1974). The age of leadership. *Pegasus* (Mobil Services Co. Ltd.).

(1974). [Review of the book *Mental health in the world of work*]. *Administrative Science Quarterly*, 19(2), 260–262.

(1974). [Review of the book *Victims of success: Emotional problems of executives*]. *Contemporary Psychology*, XIX(5), 400–401.

(1974, April 19). *Dilemmas of top management: A second look*. Paper presented at the Alumni Board Quarterly Lecture, University of Minnesota College of Business Administration, Minneapolis, MN.

(1974, June). *Ages and stages in occupational choice*. Paper presented at the International Interdisciplinary Symposium on Society, Stress and Disease: Working Life, Stockholm, Sweden.

(1974, June). Models of motivation and their implication for behavioral stress. Paper presented at the International Interdisciplinary Symposium on Society, Stress and Disease: Working Life, Stockholm, Sweden.

(1974, November–December). Don't choose your own successor. *Harvard Business Review*, 52(6), 53–62.

(1975). The conceptual context for compensation. In E. L. Cass & F. G. Zimmer (Eds.), *Man and work in society* (pp. 150–173). New York: Van Nostrand Reinhold Company.

(1975). Motivating administrators and organizations for change. In H. M. Mathur (Ed.), *Development policy for change*. Jaipur, India: HCM State Institute of Public Administration.

(1975, July–August). On executive suicide. *Harvard Business Review*, 53(4), 118–122.

(1976). *Psychological man*. Cambridge, MA: The Levinson Institute.

(1976, Winter). The changing role of the hospital administrator. *Health Care Management Review*, 1(1), 78–89.

(1976, July–August). Appraisal of what performance? *Harvard Business Review*, 54(4), 30–46.

(1977, May). How adult growth stages affect management development. *Training*, 14(5), 42–47.

(1977, May). [Review of the book *Knowledge in action*]. *Bulletin of the Menninger Clinic*, 41(3), 291–292.

(1977, June). Managing psychological man. *Management Review*, 66(6), 27–28, 37–40.

(1977, June). [Review of the book *Systems of organization: Management of the human resource*]. *Administrative Science Quarterly*, 22(2), 362–365.

(1977, Fall). [Review of the book *A general theory of bureaucracy*]. *The Columbia Journal of World Business*, 12(3), 132–136.

(1977, September). Dealing with personal problems of top management in a changing world. [In official proceedings of the Food Marketing Institute's International Management Conference; pp. 21–29].

(1977, December). Oedipus in the board room. *Psychology Today*, 11(7), 45–46.

(1978). Being good isn't good enough. *Bell Telephone Magazine*, 57(1), 25–26.

(1978). The mid-life crisis—And how to make the best of it. *New Jersey Bell Magazine*, 2.

(1978). Organizational diagnosis in mental health consultation. In T. E. Backer & E. M. Glaser (Eds.), *Proceedings of the Advanced Workshop on Program Consultation in Mental Health Services* (pp. 23–50). Los Angeles: Human Interaction Institute.

(1978). In search of a mentor. *MGR*, 4.

(1978, March 27). Office politics—A path to success [Interview with Harry Levinson]. *U.S. News and World Report*, 75–76.

(1978, May). The abrasive personality at the office. *Psychology Today*, 56(3), 86–94.

(1978, May–June). The abrasive personality. *Harvard Business Review*, 56(3), 86–94.

(1978, October). Is HRD a hoax or a necessity: Answers from an organizational psychologist and a no-nonsense executive. *Training*, 52–54.

(1978, October 25). *Managing the stress of reorganization* [AT&T Management Forum Series].

(1979). Picking up the pieces. *Manager*, 1, 10–13.

(1979). Portrait V [Interview with Harry Levinson]. In T. E. Backer & E. M. Glaser (Eds.), *Portraits of 17 outstanding organizational consultants* (pp. 79–105). Los Angeles: Human Interaction Research Institute.

(1979). [Review of the books *Consulting with human service systems* and *The consultation process in action*]. *The Journal of Applied Behavioral Science*, 15(2), 239–243.

(1979, January). [Review of the article "Sexual dysfunction in the 'two-career' family." *Medical Aspects of Human Sexuality*, 13(1), 16–17.]

(1979, March). At their own hands. *Executive*, 5(2), 30–33.

(1980). Motivational issues and compensation: An integrative overview. In D. J. McLaughlin (Ed.), *Executive compensation in the 1980s*. San Francisco: Pentacle Press.

(1980). An overview of stress and satisfaction: The contract with self. In L. A. Bond & James C. Rosen (Eds.), *Competence and coping during adulthood* (pp. 224–239). Hanover, NH: University Press of New England, Vermont Conference on the Primary Prevention of Psychopathology.

(1980, June). Power, leadership, and the management of stress. *Professional Psychology, XI*(3), 497–508.

(1980, July–August). Criteria for choosing chief executives. *Harvard Business Review, 58*(4), 113–120.

(1981). *Executive: The guide to responsive management*. Cambridge, MA: Harvard University Press.

(1981, February). Deskbound managers on the way out. *InterNorth, 81, 2.*

(1981, May–June). When executives burn out. *Harvard Business Review, 59*(3), 73–81.

(1981, Fall). [Comments on the article "The failing company: In the long run, consultation doesn't help"]. *Consultation, 1*(1), 34–43.

(1981, Fall). Seminar on organizational diagnosis. *Consultation, 1*(1), 45–47.

(1982). *Casebook for* Psychological Man. Cambridge, MA: The Levinson Institute.

(1982). *Casebook for* Psychological Man: *Instructor's guide*. Cambridge, MA: The Levinson Institute.

(1982). Diagnosis and intervention in organizational settings. In H. C. Schulberg & M. Killilea (Eds.), *The modern practice of community mental health* (pp. 289–311). San Francisco: Jossey-Bass.

(1982). The need for comprehensive performance appraisal. In *Executive compensation and performance* (pp. 81–124). New York: Pentacle Press.

(1982). [Review of the books *The Stress Check* and *The work stress connection: How to cope with job burnout*]. *The Journal of Applied Behavioral Science, 18*(2), 239–245.

(1982, Spring). Professionalizing consultation. *Consultation, 1*(2), 38–41.

(1982, June). Interview with Harry Levinson, diagnostician and theorist [Interview by Marshall Sashkin]. *Group & Organization Studies, 7*(2), 135–162.

(1983). After the change. *Long Lines, 63*(1).

(1983). Clinical psychology in organizational practice. In J. S. J. Manuso (Ed.), *Occupational clinical psychology* (pp. 7–13). New York: Praeger.

(1983, Spring). Intuition vs. rationality in organizational diagnosis. *Consultation, 2*(2), 27–31.

(1983, May–June). A second career: The possible dream. *Harvard Business Review, 61*(3), 122–129.

(1983, Summer). Consulting with family businesses: What to look for, what to look out for. *Organizational Dynamics, 12*(1), 71–80.

(1983, June). Getting along with the boss. *Across the Board, 20*(6), 47–52.

(1984). *CEO: Corporate leadership in action* (with S. Rosenthal). New York: Basic Books.

(1984). Executive selection. In R. J. Corsini (Ed.), *Encyclopedia of psychology* (p. 460). New York: Wiley.

(1984). Organizational diagnosis. In R. J. Corsini (Ed.), *Encyclopedia of psychology* (p. 473). New York: Wiley.

(1984). *A psychologist looks at executive development* [Cassette tape]. The Consolidated Capital Foundation.

(1984). [Review of the book *The psychoanalysis of organizations*]. *Journal of the American Psychoanalytic Association, 32*(3), 704–706.

(1985). On business and medicine (with M. F. Shore). *New England Journal of Medicine, 313*(5), 319–321.

(1985, Summer). Invited commentary: Consultation by cliche. *Consultation, 4*(2), 165–170.

(1985, October). Acting out the family on the job [Interview by Sally Van Wagenen Keil]. *The Tarrytown Letter, 52,* 3–7.

(1985, Fall). Fate, fads, and the fickle fingers thereof. *Consulting Psychology Bulletin, 37*(3), 3–11.

(1985, December). Leading vs. Just Managing [Interview by Ron Nelson]. *GTD Manager, General Technology Division,* pp. 1–2.

(1986). Leadership: The critical difference in business management [Interview by Joseph D'Eramo].*The Consultant, 3*(2), 1–2.

(1986). *Ready, fire, aim: Avoiding management by impulse.* Cambridge, MA: The Levinson Institute.

(1986, July 15). "How to handle troublesome people [Interview with Harry Levinson]. *Boardroom Reports, 15*(14), 13.

(1986, July–August). The dark side of entrepreneurial personalities. *The President, 1.*

(1986, September–October). Healthcare leaders: Architects of transcendent purpose. *Healthcare Executive, 1*(6), 30–34.

(1987). Panel on organizational consultation. In J. Krantz (Ed.), *Irrationality in social and organizational life* (pp. 44–51). Washington, DC: A.K. Rice Institute.

(1987). Psychoanalytic theory in organizational behavior. In J. W. Lorsch (Ed.), *Handbook of organizational behavior* (Vol. 2, pp. 51–61). Englewood Cliffs, NJ: Prentice-Hall.

(1987, June). How they rate the boss. *Across the Board, 16*(6), 52–58.

(1987, August 11). *Trends in consulting practice.* Paper presented to the annual meeting of the Academy of Management, New Orleans, LA.

(1988). Organizational psychology. In G. Dixon (Ed.), *What works at work: Lessons from the masters* (pp. 278–287). Minneapolis, MN: Lakewood Books.

(1988). To thine own self be true: Coping with the dilemmas of integrity. In S. Syrivastva et al. (Eds.), *Executive integrity: The search for high human values in organizational life.* San Francisco: Jossey-Bass.

(1988, May). You won't recognize me: Predictions about changes in top management characteristics. *Academy of Management Executive, 2*(2), 119–125.

(1989). (Ed.). *Designing and managing your career.* Boston: Harvard Business School Press.

(1989, September). To see ourselves . . . . *Intrapreneur,* 17–19.

(1990). Freud as an entrepreneur: Implications for contemporary psychoanalytic institutes. In L. Lapierre (Ed.), *Clinical approaches to the study of managerial and organizational dynamics* (pp. 227–250). Montreal, Canada: Ecole des Hautes Etudes Commerciales.

(1990, January–February). The case of the perplexing promotion. *Harvard Business Review*, 68(1), 11–21.

(1990, August 13). *Can we develop leaders?* Paper presented to the annual meeting of the Academy of Management, San Francisco.

(1990, Fall). Leadership anyone? *Consulting Psychology Bulletin*, 42(3), 1–7.

(1991). Diagnosing organizations systematically. In M. Kets de Vries (Ed.), *Organizations on the couch* (pp. 45–68). San Francisco: Jossey-Bass.

(1991, Winter–Spring). Counseling with top management. *Consulting Psychology Bulletin*, 43(1), 10–15.

(1992). *Career mastery*. San Francisco: Berrett-Koehler.

(1992, Winter). Fads, fantasies, and psychological management. *Consulting Psychology Journal*, 44(1), 1–12.

(1992, Summer). How organizational consultation differs from counseling. In Backer et al., What is consultation? That's an interesting question! *Consulting Psychology Journal*, 44(2), 21–22.

(1992, June). Shadow excellence. *Vision/Action*, 11(2).

(1992, Fall). Bearding the lion that roared: A case study in organizational consultation (with J. Sabbath and J. Connor). *Consulting Psychology Journal*, 44(4), 2–16.

(1993). Between CEO and COO. *Academy of Management Executive*, 7(2), 71–83.

(1993). Looking ahead: Caplan's ideas and the future of organizational consultation. In W. P. Erchul (Ed.), *Consultation in community, school, and organizational practice* (pp. 193–204). Washington, DC: Taylor & Francis.

(1993). Teacher as leader. In A. G. Bedian (Ed.), *Management laureates: A collection of autobiographical essays* (Vol. 2, pp. 177–214). Greenwich, CT: JAI Press.

(1993, January–February). Talented or just temperamental? *Harvard Business Review*, 71(1), 142–143.

(1993, June). *Organizational diagnosis*. Paper presented at the Symposium of the International Society for Psychoanalytic Study of Organizations (pp. 2–24), New York.

(1994). The practitioner as diagnostic instrument. In A. Howard (Ed.), *Diagnosis for organizational change: Methods and models* (pp. 27–52). New York: Guilford Press.

(1994, Winter). Beyond the selection failures. *Consulting Psychology Journal*, 46(1), 3–8.

(1994, Spring). The changing psychoanalytic organization and its influence on the ego ideal of psychoanalysis. *Psychoanalytic Psychology*, 11(2), 233–249.

(1994, May). Why the behemoths fell: Psychological roots of corporate failure. *American Psychologist*, 49(5), 428–436.

(1996). Introduction. In L. Sperry, *Corporate therapy and consulting* (p. xi). New York: Brunner Mazel.

(1996). What motivates directors? *Directorship*, 4(1), 3–11.

(1996, January–February). The leader as analyst. *Harvard Business Review, 74*(1), 158.

(1996, Winter). Giving psychological meaning to consultation: Consultant as storyteller. *Consulting Psychology Journal, 48*(1), 3–11.

(1996, Spring). Executive coaching. *Consulting Psychology Journal, 48*(2), 115–123.

(1997, Fall). Organizational character. *Consulting Psychology Journal, 49*(4), 246–255.

(1999). A clinical approach to executive selection. In R. Jennerett & R. Silzer (Eds.), *Individual psychological assessment* (pp. 228–242). San Francisco: Jossey-Bass.

(1999). Diagnosis before investment. In L. E. Urson & R. A. Geist (Eds.), *The psychology of investing* (pp. 83–100). New York: Wiley.

(1999, September–October). A recipe to change. *HSM Management Magazine* [Brazil], *16*.

(2000). Approaching retirement as the flexibility phase (with J. C. Wofford). *Academy of Management Executive, 14*(2), 84–95.

(2000). On becoming an entrepreneur. *Psychologist-Manager Journal 4*(1), 91–95.

(2001). Executive selection. In W. E. Craighead & C. B. Nemeroff (Eds.), *The Corsini encyclopedia of psychology and behavioral science* (Vol. 2, 3rd ed., pp. 524–526). New York: Wiley.

(2002). Assessing organizations. In R. H. Lowman (Ed.), *The California School of Organizational Studies handbook of organizational consulting psychology: A comprehensive guide to theory, skills, and techniques* (pp. 315–343). San Francisco: Jossey-Bass.

(2002). Foreword. In L. Sperry, *The effective leadership* (ix–xi). New York: Brunner Mazel.

(2002). *Organizational assessment: A step-by-step guide to effective consulting.* Washington, DC: American Psychological Association.

(2002). Psychological consultation to organizations: Linking assessment and intervention. In R. H. Lowman (Ed.), *The California School of Organizational Studies handbook of organizational consulting psychology: A comprehensive guide to theory, skills, and techniques* (pp. 415–449). San Francisco: Jossey-Bass.

(2002). Understanding the personality of the executive (with L. Pratch). In R. F. Silzer (Ed.), *The 21st century executive: Innovative practices for building leadership at the top* (pp. 43–74). San Francisco: Jossey-Bass.

(2003). Organizational immersion and diagnosis: The work of Harry Levinson [Interview by Michael Diamond]. *Organisational and Social Dynamics, 3*(1), 1–18.

(2003, September). Putting psychology back into psychological contracts (with M. Meckler & B. H. Drake). *Journal of Management Inquiry, 12*(3), 217–228.

(2006). *Harry Levinson on the psychology of leadership.* Boston: Harvard Business School Press.

INDEX

Athos, Anthony G., 298
AT&T, 67–68, 70, 85, 197, 200
Attachment, 244
   and change, 23
   and corporate failure, 84–85
Attack devices, 149–150
Attitude surveys, 108
Authoritarian, 299
Authoritative positions, 168–169, 299
Avoidance, 86, 116
   and CEO–COO relationship, 260
   of CEO to be interviewed, 121
Awareness, levels of, 17

Bakke, W. Wight, 47
Batten, James K., 203
Beatrice Foods, 290
Behavioral job description, 23, 263, 298
Behavioral problems, with CEO–COO relationship, 258–260
Behavioristic psychology, 21
Behavior modes, 14–15
Bell Laboratories, 296
Bhopal catastrophe, 200
Biden, Joseph, 291
Birkenstock, Jim, 94
Blame, 86
Bludhorn, Charles, 290
Board members, 191–206
   assessment interviews with, 151
   and corporate cultural, 199–200
   ego ideal/self-image of, 192–194
   feedback to/from, 202–204
   intelligent questioning by, 199
   motivation of, 194–195
   and need for diagnosis, 197–199
   and perpetuation of organization, 195–196
   relationships of, 200–202
   severance of, 204–206
Board of directors
   CEO's performance appraisal by, 92–93
   feedback from, 264
   predecessors on, 86
   recommendations to, 74
Bonding, 83–84
Bossidy, Lawrence, 263
Brain changes, 241, 269
Brainstorming, 24
Brain tumor, 203
Brenner, J., 211
Brothers, 185–187
Bureau of the Census, 35

Burke, Dan, 254
Burns, George, 273
Bush, George, 89, 205, 291
Business Week, 294

Capital Cities/ABC, Inc., 254
Career guidance, 23
Career Mastery (H. Levinson), xvii
Career paths, 20
Career planning, 23
Casebook for Pschological Man (H. Levinson), xvii
Casebook for Psychological Man: *Instructor's Guide* (H. Levinson), xvii
Case study method, 142, 230
Catabolism, 235
Cause-finding, 141
Causes, worthwhile, 273–274
CBS, 290
CEO: Corporate Leadership in Action (H. Levinson and S. Rosenthal), xvii, 297
CEO–COO relationship, 253–265
   and behavioral problems, 258–260
   and changing environment, 263–265
   guilt in, 262–263
   misconceptions about, 261–262
   remedies for problems in, 263–265
   rivalry/competition in, 254–255
   and selection problems, 255–258
CEOs. *See* Chief executive officers
Change(s)
   anticipating, 278–279
   continuous, 81
   as indictment of predecessor, 86
   limits to characterological, 75
   and mourning process, 94
   with new successor, 272
   organic, 241
   over time, 107–108
   peak of success as time to think of, 85
   repetitive, 210
   resistance to, 295
   and stress, 240
Change management
   and corporate failure, 90
   and psychoanalytic theory, 23–24
Characterological behaviors, 5–7, 66–69
Character problems, 249–250, 292
Charcot, Jean-Martin, 15
Charisma, 262–263
Charismatic chief, 118
Chief executive officers (CEOs)

assessment interviews with, 151
board as confidants of, 201–202
board support of, 200
COO relationship with. *See* CEO–COO
    relationship
incapacitation of, 203
performance appraisals of, 202
in rescuer role, 262–263
selection of, 196
Chief operating officer (COO). *See* CEO–
    COO relationship
"Chimneys," 85
"Chip off the old block" phenomenon, 181
Chomsky, Noam, 236
Chrysler, 263
"Churning," 66
Citibank, 297
Citicorp, 155, 263, 294–295
Clarity, in storytelling, 215
Clinical psychology training, xiii–xiv
Clinical sociology, 230
Clinton, Bill, 89, 95
Coaches, executive, 275
Coca-Cola Company, 254
Cocaine, 15
Cognitive capacity
    and accountability hierarchy, 89–90
    and aging, 269
    and assessment interviews, 153, 158
    and coping with organizational prob-
        lems, 76
    of executives, 82
    increasing need for, 294–295
    levels of, 296, 298
    to manage complexity, 90–92
Cognitive domains, 158
Cognitive processes, of leaders, 157–159
Cognitive psychology, 20, 298
Cohesion, 71–72
Cold proposals, 143
Collective ego ideal, 194
Collective mind, 214–215
Commitment, 82, 186
Communication, 93, 159–161
Communist political systems, 149
"Community group," 296
Community involvement
    and CEO–COO relationship, 256–257
    commitment to, 82
    of traditional family businesses, 180
Community mental health center (case
    study), 124–126

Community psychology, 230
Company tour, 152
Compassion, 291
Compensation
    and organizational structure, 89–90
    and psychoanalytic theory, 24–25
Competence issues
    in CEO–COO relationship, 255
    with consultants, 140
    in entrepreneurial family businesses,
        182–183
    in family businesses, 185
Competitiveness, in CEO–COO relation-
    ship, 254–255
Competitive position, 71–72, 80
Completion stage, 241
Compliments, 50
Comprehensive personality theory, 130
Computers, 250
Conceptual development, 236, 250
Conceptualization, intuition vs., 57
Confidentiality, 143, 152, 153
Conflict, avoiding, 50
Conflict psychology, 19, 236
Conflictual family businesses, 180–181
Conformity, 86
Confrontation, 226
Confronting people, with realities, 73–74
Conscience, 86
Conscience, development of, 16
Conscious awareness, 17
Consciousness, levels of, 236
Consistency, 66
Constituencies, 95
Consultant(s)
    as diagnostic instrument, 145–147
    responsibilities of, 102–103
    retirees as, 282
    role of, 70–72, 100
    types of, 139–140
Consultation
    focus of, 138–139
    individual counseling vs., 209–210
    precipitating events for, 139
Contract, formal, 144
Contractual violations, 240–241
Control, fear of losing, 76
COO (chief operating officer). *See* CEO–
    COO relationship
"Core group," 296
Core ideology, 195, 216–220
Corporate culture, 80, 199–200

Dreams, 281–282
Drexel, Burnham, 196
Drive expression, 235
Drucker, Peter, 36, 44, 268–269
Dual-drive theory, 15–17, 22, 235
Dual-loyalty studies, 41
Dulles, John Foster, 109
Durant, William C., 82
Dutt, James, 290

Eastman, George, 82
Eastman Kodak, 68, 83, 90, 199
Eaton, Robert J., 262–263
Economic point of view, 235
Edelson, M., 214
Ego, 17
    change and burdens on, 240
    defined, 235
Ego development, 241–242
Ego ideal
    of board members, 192–194
    collective, 194
    corporate, 195
    of founder, 150
    of organization, 71
    and retirement, 276–277
Ego ideal–self-image gap, 16–17, 239, 252,
    276–277
Ego psychology, 236–237
Eisner, Michael, 254
Eldest son, 183–185
Electric power companies, 70, 197–198
Elementary schools, 154
Emotion, loss and, 274
Emotional atmosphere, 72
Emotional first-aid stations, xv
Emotional Health in the World of Work (H.
    Levinson), xv
Employee assistance programs, xv
Employees
    assessment interviews with, 153
    long-term, 51–52
    staying in touch with, 205
Emporia State Teachers College, xiii
Empowerment, 69
Encounter groups, 101, 226–227, 245
Enemy, 71
Engineers in defense industry, 252
Englehoff, Bill, 129
Enron, 156
Entitlement, sense of, 88

Entrepreneurial family businesses, 181–183,
    248
Entrepreneurs, 154
Environment, retirement support system and,
    280
Envy, 271
Epiphenomenon, 12
Erikson, Erik, 236, 241, 278
Ethnic discrimination, 126–129
The Exceptional Executive (H. Levinson), xvii
Excesses, of leadership, 155–156
Executive coaches, 275
Executive coaching, 100, 167–177
    case study of, 172–177
    method for, 168–172
    qualifications for, 167–168
Executive narcissism, 88–89, 156
Executive personality, 289–299
    Exodus as model of, 295–297
    factors affecting, 290–291
    helplessness in, 294–295
    and intellectual capability, 296
    predicted changes in, 291–293
    transcendent purpose of, 297–298
Executives
    behavior of, 13
    helplessness of, 73
    organizational affiliation of, 35
Executive Stress (H. Levinson), xv
*Executive: The Guide to Responsive
    Manatgement*, xvii
Exodus (Biblical story), 295–297
Expectations, 42
Experts, 175
Extended family, 33

Facts, 146
Fads, management, 198
Failure
    corporate. *See* Corporate failure
    fear of, 84
    of organizational diagnosis, 225–227
Family, extended, 33
Family business(es), 179–190
    cautions for consultants to, 189–190
    and CEO–COO relationship, 261
    conflictual, 180–181
    consultants as dangers to, 187
    daughters/widows in, 187–188
    double-bind situation in, 183–184
    entrepreneurial, 181–183
    interventions for, 188–189

relieving, 36
and stress, 252
and superego conflict, 238–239
Gulf + Western, 290

Hammer, Armand, 258, 268
Hanley, John W., 264, 272, 297
Harry Levinson on Psychology of Leadership (H. Levinson), xvii
Hart, Gary, 291
Harvard Business Review, xvi, xvii
Harvard Business School, xvi
Harvard Medical School, xvi
Harvard Psychological Clinic, 22
Hawthorne studies, 11, 99–100
Helplessness
and adaptive ego, 252
and attachment, 244
executive, 294–295
of top management, 73
Henry IV (W. Shakespeare), 254
Herman Miller Company, 87
Herzberg, Frederick, 45
Hierarchy(-ies)
and accountability, 89–90, 157
and organizational structure, 85
power, 149–150
History
corporate, 197
organizational. *See* Organizational history
psycho-, 24
Hobbies, 282
Homoerotic orientation, 83
Homosexual panic, 226–227, 245
Hospitals, 36–37
Hull, Webster, 129
Huxley, Aldous, 39

Iacocca, Lee, 182, 261–263, 270
IBM, 80–83, 85–89, 91, 92, 94–95, 108, 161, 195, 199, 203, 269, 297
Id, 16, 235
Idealization, 18
Identification, with organization, 150–151
Id psychology, 236
Immersion, 62–63
Impatience, 258, 272
Incompetence, level of, 243–244
Indictment, of predecessor, 86–87
Individual character, 66
Individual counseling, 209–210

Individual psychology, 12–13
Industrial Mental Health, xiv
Industrial–organizational (I-O) psychology, 99–100, 139–140
Industrial psychology, measurement in, 31–32
Industrial relations, 13
Infants
early rage of, 8
parent management by, 66
Inferences, 146
In-group narcissism, 81
Initial interview, 143
Initiative, and CEO–COO relationship, 260
Input communication, 159
Institutions
with characteristics of benevolence, 37–38
and transference, 37
Insull, 197
Integrity, 196
Integrity stage, 278
Intellectual capacity (IQ), 158
Intelligence, aging and, 269
Intermediary, consultant as, 228
Interpretation, 146, 230
Interpretive data, 144
Interventions, for family businesses, 188–189
Interviews
with employees/management, 153–154
initial, 143
Intimacy stage, 241
Intrinsic motivation, 20
Introjection, 18
Intuition, conceptualization vs., 57–59, 63
Involutional melancholia, 278
Inward orientation, 270
I-O psychology. *See* Industrial–organizational psychology
IQ (intellectual capacity), 158
Irani, Ray, 258
Irrationality, 50, 268, 277
Irritability, 271
Israelites, 295–299
ITT, 290

Japanese culture, 84, 269
Jaques, Elliott, xvii, 24, 25, 35, 89, 157–159, 294, 296, 298
Jewish people, 298–299
Job description, behavioral. *See* Behavioral job description
Job role, 23

and corporate failure, 85–86
and leadership, 157
and psychoanalytic theory, 24–25
and stress, 243–244
Organizational tension, 292
Organizations
long-term survival of, 40
policies/practices of, 13
Out-groups, 81
Outline, of organizational assessment, 147
"An Outline of General Systems Theory"
(L. von Bertalanffy), xvi
Output communication, 160
Outsiders' perspectives, 93–94
Overcontrol
and CEO–COO relationship, 259, 262
effects of, 149
and stress, 249
and turnover of key executives, 202
Overkindness, 53–55
Oversimplification, 217
Overstimulation, 245

Paleontology, 213
Parallel processing, 158
Paranoia, 155, 156
Paranoid anxiety, 35
Paranoid leaders, 250
Paranoid rage, 8
Parents, management of, 66
Participant-observation, 62–63
Participative management, 20, 291, 297, 299
Partisanship, 39
Part-problems, 141–142
Part theories, 14–15, 22
Pascale, Richard T., 298
Passive president (case study), 114–118
consulting in crisis, 115
problems in consultation, 117–118
results of diagnosis, 116–117
Paternalism
in entrepreneurial family businesses, 182
in "family" organizations, 82
in traditional family businesses, 180
Patience, 283
Pepsi-Cola, 91
Perception, 20
Performance appraisals
of CEOs, 92–93, 202
futility of, 216
and psychoanalytic theory, 24
in state agency, 112

Perpetuation, of organization, 195–196
Personality, and industrial psychology, 32
Personality development, 236, 246–248
Personality structure, 235–236
Personality theory, 12
Peter, Lawrence, 243
"Peter Principle," 243
Pharmaceutical research and development
group (case study), 126–129
concerns about leader, 126–128
consultant's concerns, 128–129
Physical illness, 94
Physician-patient model, 102–103
Physiological impairment, 92, 241
Piaget, Jean, 236
Picasso, Pablo, 24
Police departments, 75
Political appointees, 109, 112, 113
Political candidates, 291–292
Porcupine analogy, 3
Power, exercise of, 128–129
Power conflicts. in family businesses, 184–185
Power hierarchies, 149–150
Preconscious, 17
Preliminary exploratory proposal, 143–144
Presidential candidates, 291–292
Price, Charlton R., xv
Pride, 69
Primogeniture, 184, 185
Process data, 144
Processing communication, 159–160
Procrastination, 50
Profitability, 195
Projection, 18
Promotion
from within, 82–83
and succession issues, 155
Proposal, formal, 144
Protestant churches, 154
Prudential, 65–67, 69, 71–75
Psychoanalysis, storytelling in, 213–214
Psychoanalytic theory, 15–18
adaptive, 18
behaviorist, 21
cognitive, 20
contributions to, 18–19
developmental, 17–18
dual-drive, 15–17
in executive coaching, 168, 172
importance of, 26–28
and industrial psychology, 32

Vroom, V. H., 20

W. L. Gore and Associates, 87
Walt Disney Company, 254
Walzer, Michael, 295, 297
Watson, Thomas J., Jr., 82, 86–88, 94–95, 161, 203, 297
Watson, Thomas J., Sr., 82, 86
Weick, K. E., 214–215
Welch, John F., 84, 196, 255, 272
Wells, Frank, 254
Western society, 252
"We–they" phenomenon, 81, 83
White, William Allen, xiii
White hat–black hat game, 262
Whitmore, Kay R., 83, 90
Whyte, William F., 46
Widowers, death rate of, 276
Widows, in family businesses, 187–188
Wilmer, Harry A., 37

"Wise elders," 200
"Woman friend on the side," 186
Women
    growing assertiveness of, 270
    and occupational stress, 247–248
Women's movement, 83–84
Wood, Robert E., 68
Work
    Jaques' definition of, 298
    lost sources of gratification in, 33
Working long hours, 270–271
World Trade Center, 6, 152, 161
Wriston, Walter B., 263, 294–295, 297
Wyman, Thomas G., 290

Yeager, J., 211
Young people, development of, 281

Zaleznik, A., 22

ABOUT THE EDITORS

Arthur M. Freedman, MBA, PhD, is a principal in Freedman, Leonard & Marquardt Consultancy and chair of the research committee for the non-profit World Institute for Action Learning. He earned both his BS and his MBA at Boston University's College of Business Administration and his PhD in personality and clinical psychology at the University of Chicago. He has been a member of the NTL Institute since 1969.

Dr. Freedman is a visiting scholar at the University of Pennsylvania. He has consulted throughout North America as well as in Estonia, Latvia, Lithuania, Serbia, Sweden, Germany, Russia (and the former Soviet Union), Vietnam, Singapore, and Zimbabwe. He is a fellow of the American Psychological Association's (APA's) Divisions 13 (Society of Consulting Psychology) and 52 (International Psychology). He is a past president of the Society of Psychologists in Management. Dr. Freedman is a member of the Board of Advisors for the National Hispanic Institute and cofounder of the Nieto–Freedman Center for Organization and Community Development. He is a member of the editorial boards of both the *Journal of Applied Behavioral Science* and the *Consulting Psychology Journal.*

Dr. Freedman received the RHR International Award for Excellence in Consulting Psychology from APA's Division 13 in 1994. He received the Most Outstanding Article award from the editorial board of the *Consulting Psychology Journal* in 1998, for his article "Pathways and Crossroads to Institutional Leadership." In 2007, he received the Harry and Miriam Levinson Award for Exceptional Contributions to Consulting Organizational Psychology.

Kenneth H. Bradt, PhD, is an organizational psychologist whose interest in and efforts to help with the "people problems" faced by organizations derive from his training and experience in many areas. After receiving his PhD in general psychology from Northwestern University, he worked for the U.S.

Army, as a civilian and in uniform, as a specialist in both personnel and attitude–opinion research and as chief clinical psychologist in an Army hospital. After serving as chief psychologist with the U.S. Central Intelligence Agency, he focused on leadership training for managers, heading programs under the auspices of the Center for Creative Leadership in Greensboro, North Carolina, and others developed by Eckerd College in St. Petersburg, Florida. He is a founding member of the Society of Psychologists in Management, a fellow of the American Psychological Association (APA), and a past president of APA's Division 13 (Society of Consulting Psychology).